HEART

3

CHITOSE KAIDO

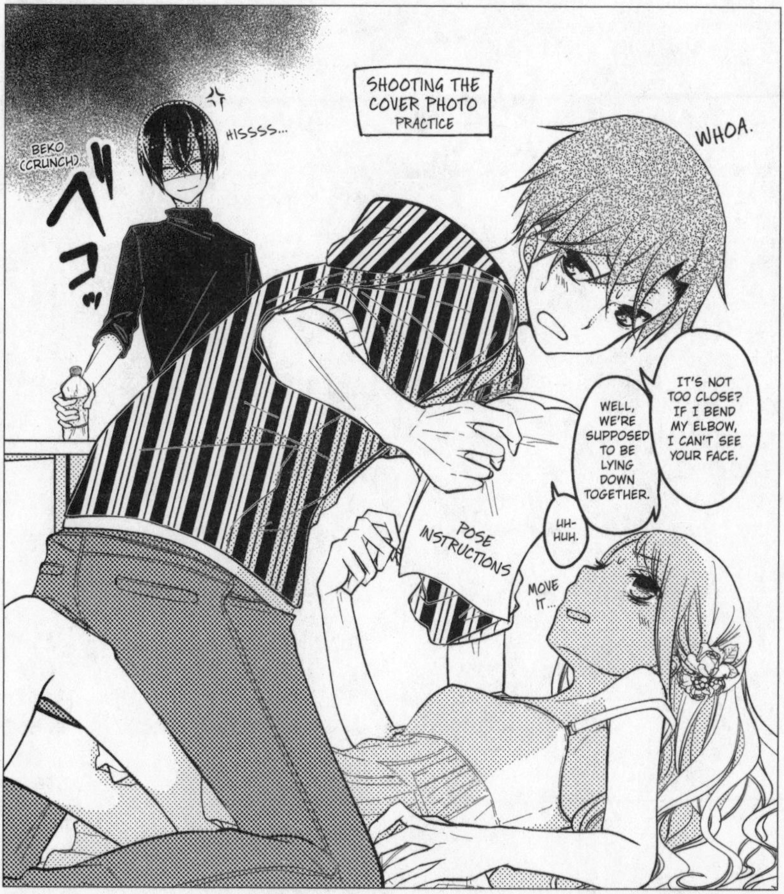
WHOA.
SHOOTING THE COVER PHOTO PRACTICE
HISSSS...
BEKO (CRUNCH)
ベコッ
IT'S NOT TOO CLOSE? IF I BEND MY ELBOW, I CAN'T SEE YOUR FACE.
WELL, WE'RE SUPPOSED TO BE LYING DOWN TOGETHER.
UH-HUH.
POSE INSTRUCTIONS
MOVE IT...

CONTENTS

LOVE AND HEART

#33

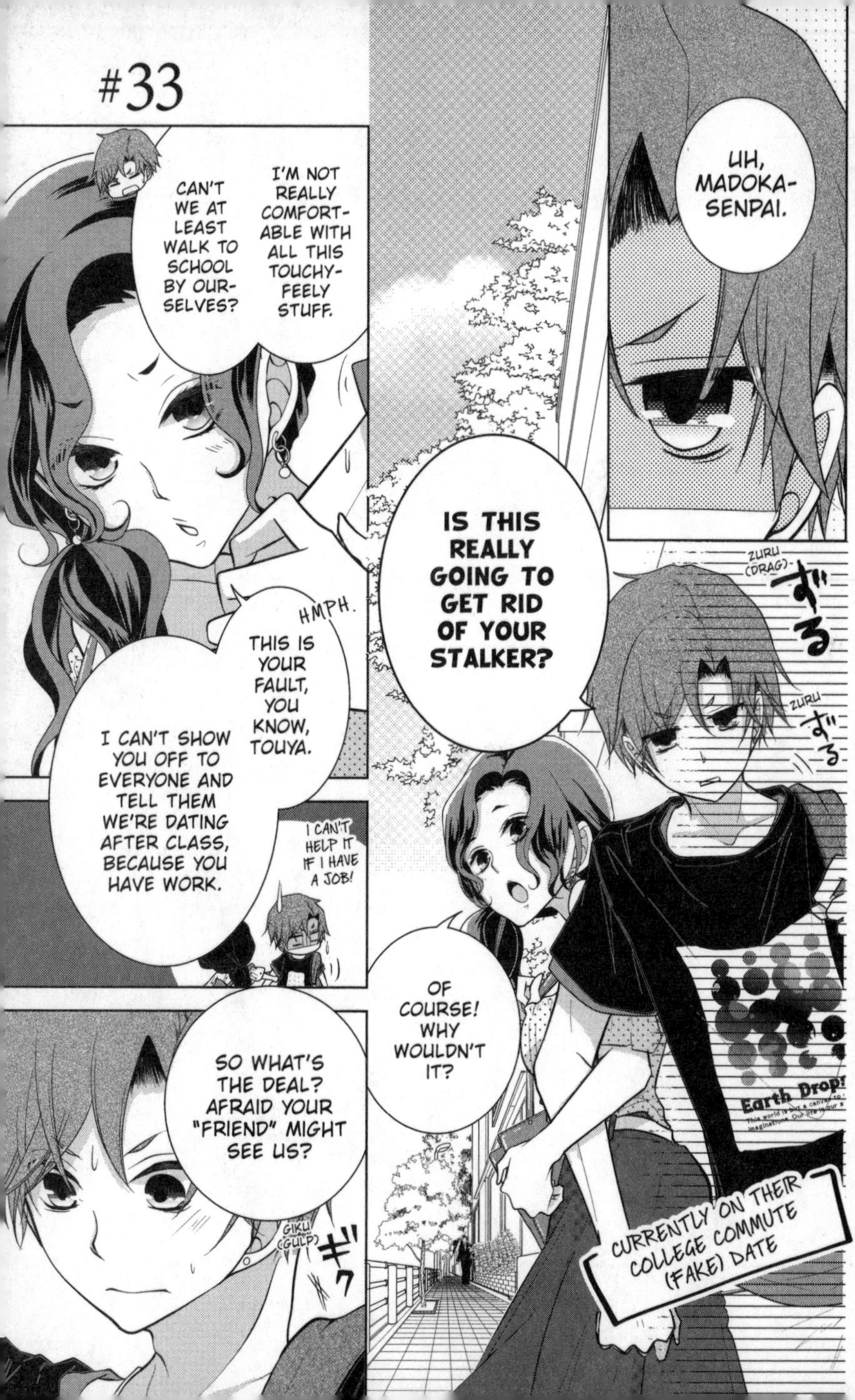
UH, MADOKA-SENPAI.
IS THIS REALLY GOING TO GET RID OF YOUR STALKER?
ZURU (DRAG)
ずる
ZURU
ずる
OF COURSE! WHY WOULDN'T IT?
Earth Drop!
CURRENTLY ON THEIR COLLEGE COMMUTE (FAKE) DATE
I'M NOT REALLY COMFORTABLE WITH ALL THIS TOUCHY-FEELY STUFF.
CAN'T WE AT LEAST WALK TO SCHOOL BY OURSELVES?
HMPH.
THIS IS YOUR FAULT, YOU KNOW, TOUYA.
I CAN'T SHOW YOU OFF TO EVERYONE AND TELL THEM WE'RE DATING AFTER CLASS, BECAUSE YOU HAVE WORK.
I CAN'T HELP IT IF I HAVE A JOB!
SO WHAT'S THE DEAL? AFRAID YOUR "FRIEND" MIGHT SEE US?
GIKU (GULP)
ギク

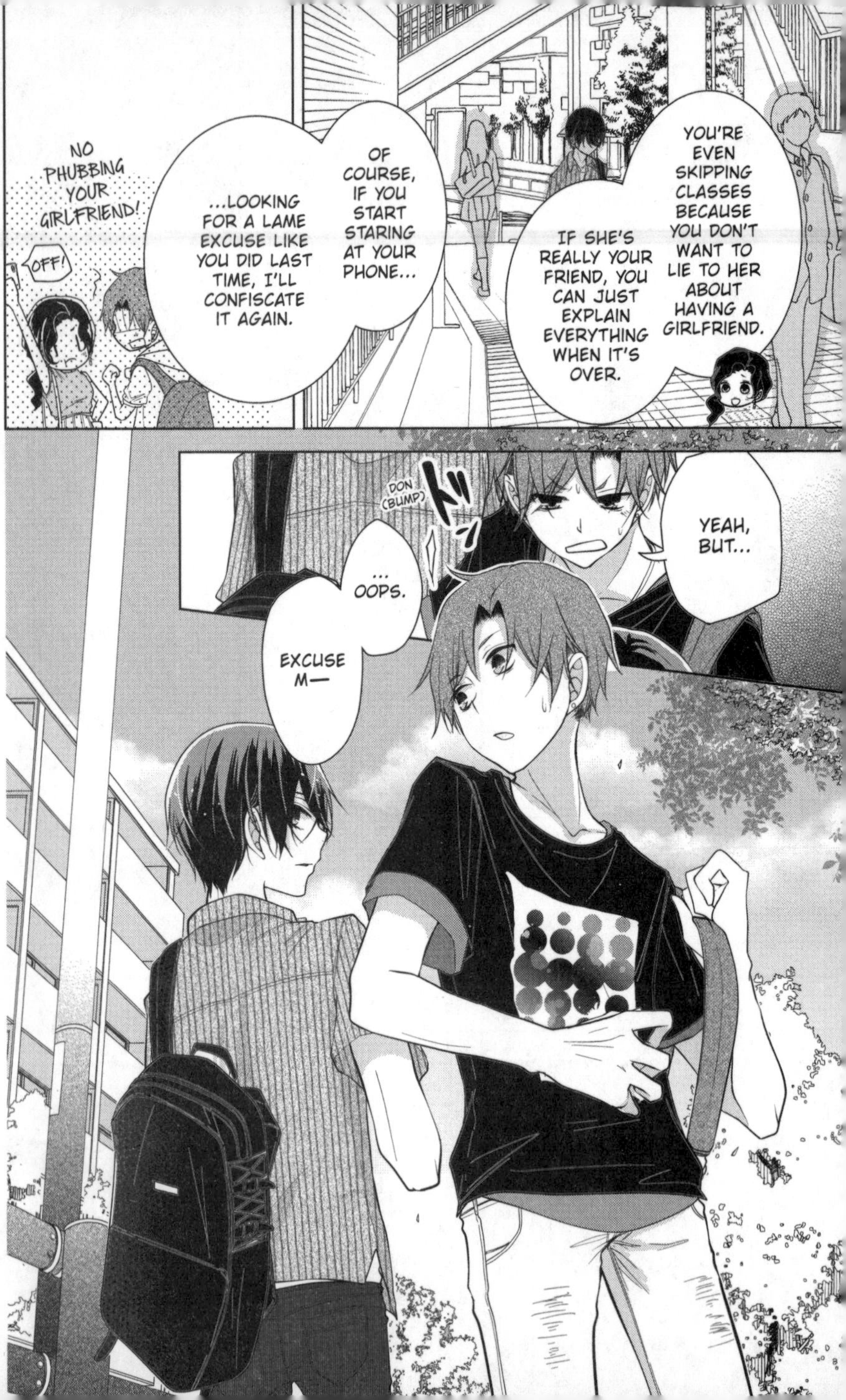
YOU'RE EVEN SKIPPING CLASSES BECAUSE YOU DON'T WANT TO LIE TO HER ABOUT HAVING A GIRLFRIEND.
IF SHE'S REALLY YOUR FRIEND, YOU CAN JUST EXPLAIN EVERYTHING WHEN IT'S OVER.
OF COURSE, IF YOU START STARING AT YOUR PHONE...
...LOOKING FOR A LAME EXCUSE LIKE YOU DID LAST TIME, I'LL CONFISCATE IT AGAIN.
NO PHUBBING YOUR GIRLFRIEND!
OFF!
YEAH, BUT...
DON (BUMP)
... OOPS.
EXCUSE M—

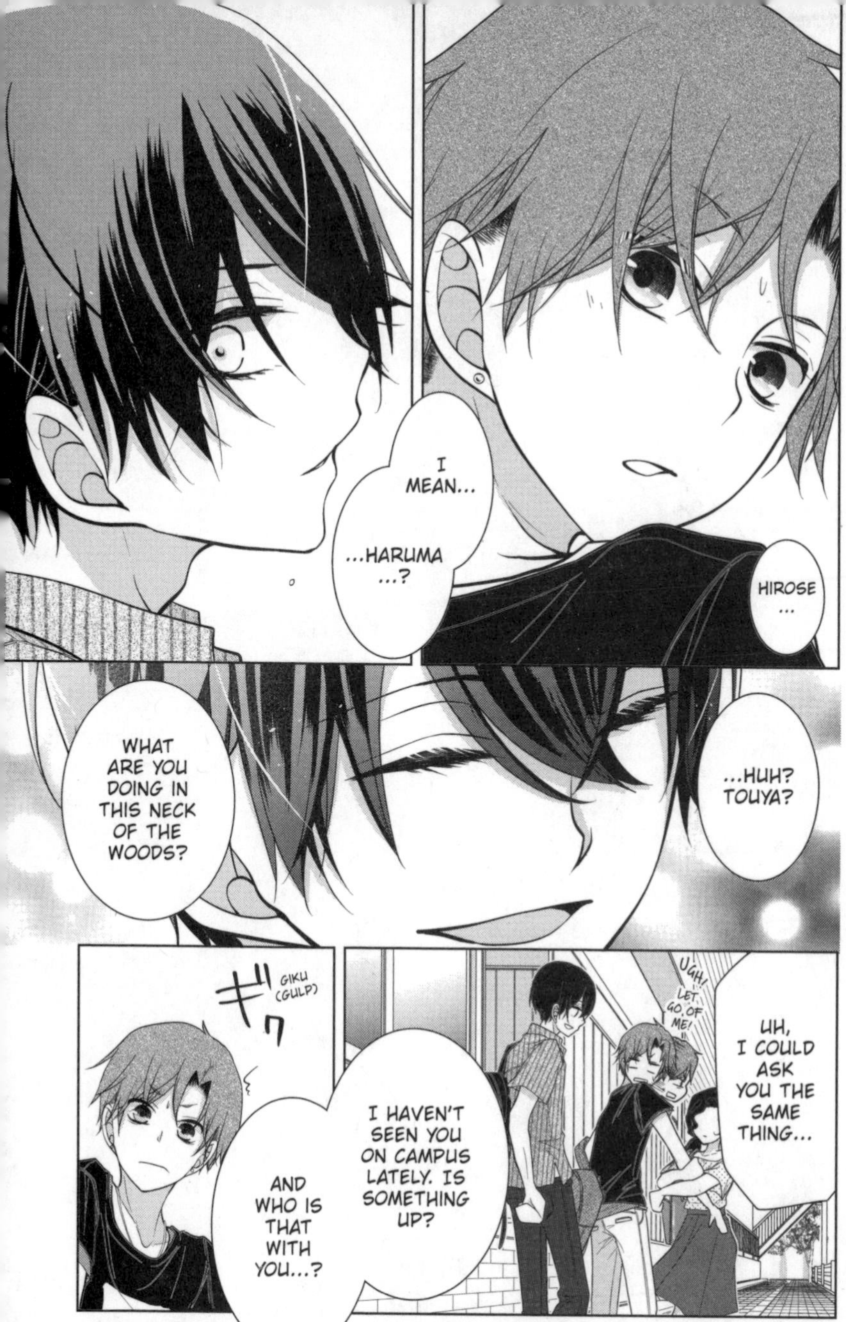
HIROSE ...
I MEAN...
...HARUMA ...?
...HUH? TOUYA?
WHAT ARE YOU DOING IN THIS NECK OF THE WOODS?
UGH! LET GO OF ME!
UH, I COULD ASK YOU THE SAME THING...
I HAVEN'T SEEN YOU ON CAMPUS LATELY. IS SOMETHING UP?
AND WHO IS THAT WITH YOU...?
ギクッ
GIKU (GULP)

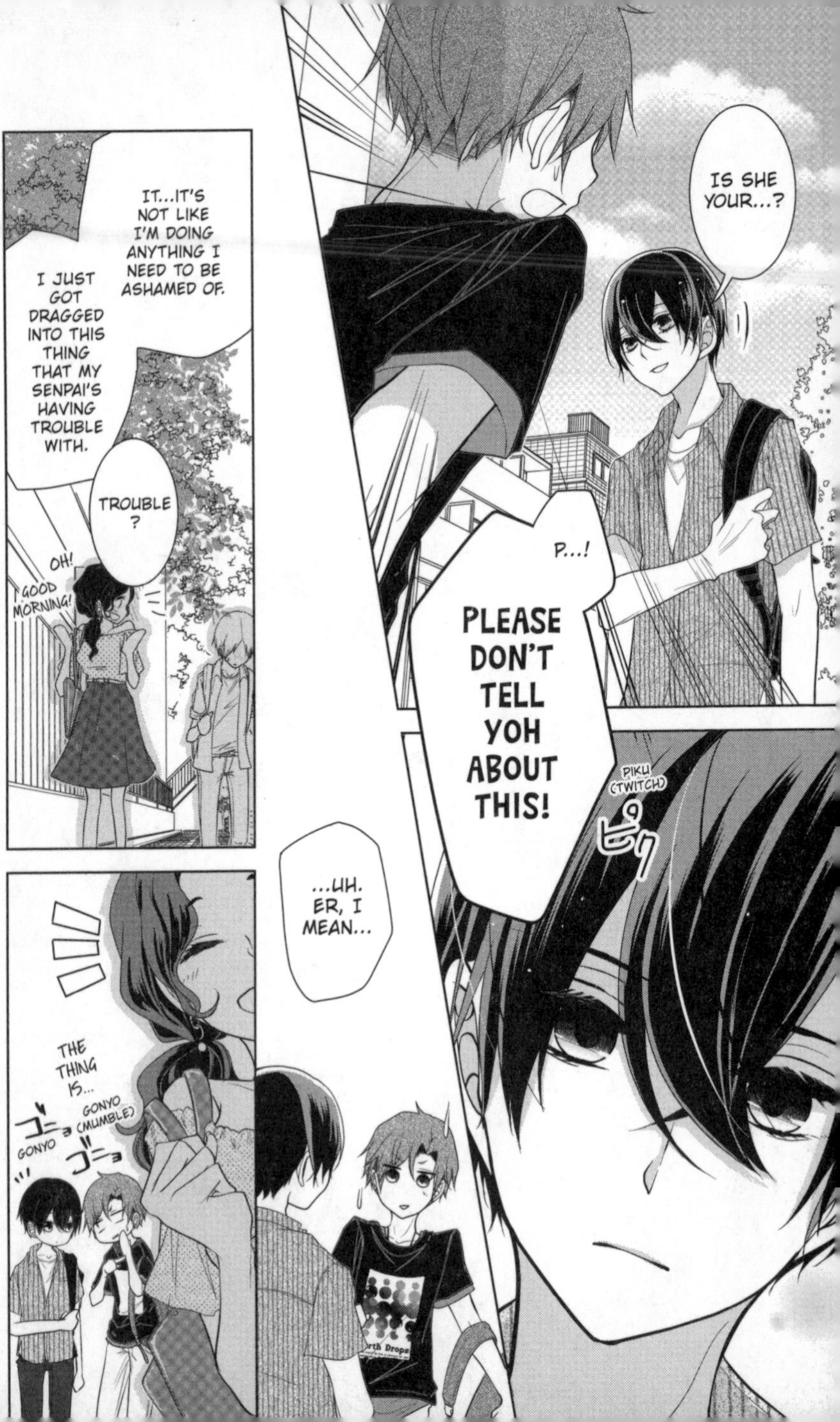
IS SHE YOUR...?
P...!
PLEASE DON'T TELL YOH ABOUT THIS!
PIKU (TWITCH)
ピク
...UH. ER, I MEAN...
IT...IT'S NOT LIKE I'M DOING ANYTHING I NEED TO BE ASHAMED OF.
I JUST GOT DRAGGED INTO THIS THING THAT MY SENPAI'S HAVING TROUBLE WITH.
TROUBLE?
OH!
GOOD MORNING!
THE THING IS...
ゴニョ
GONYO
ゴニョ
GONYO (MUMBLE)

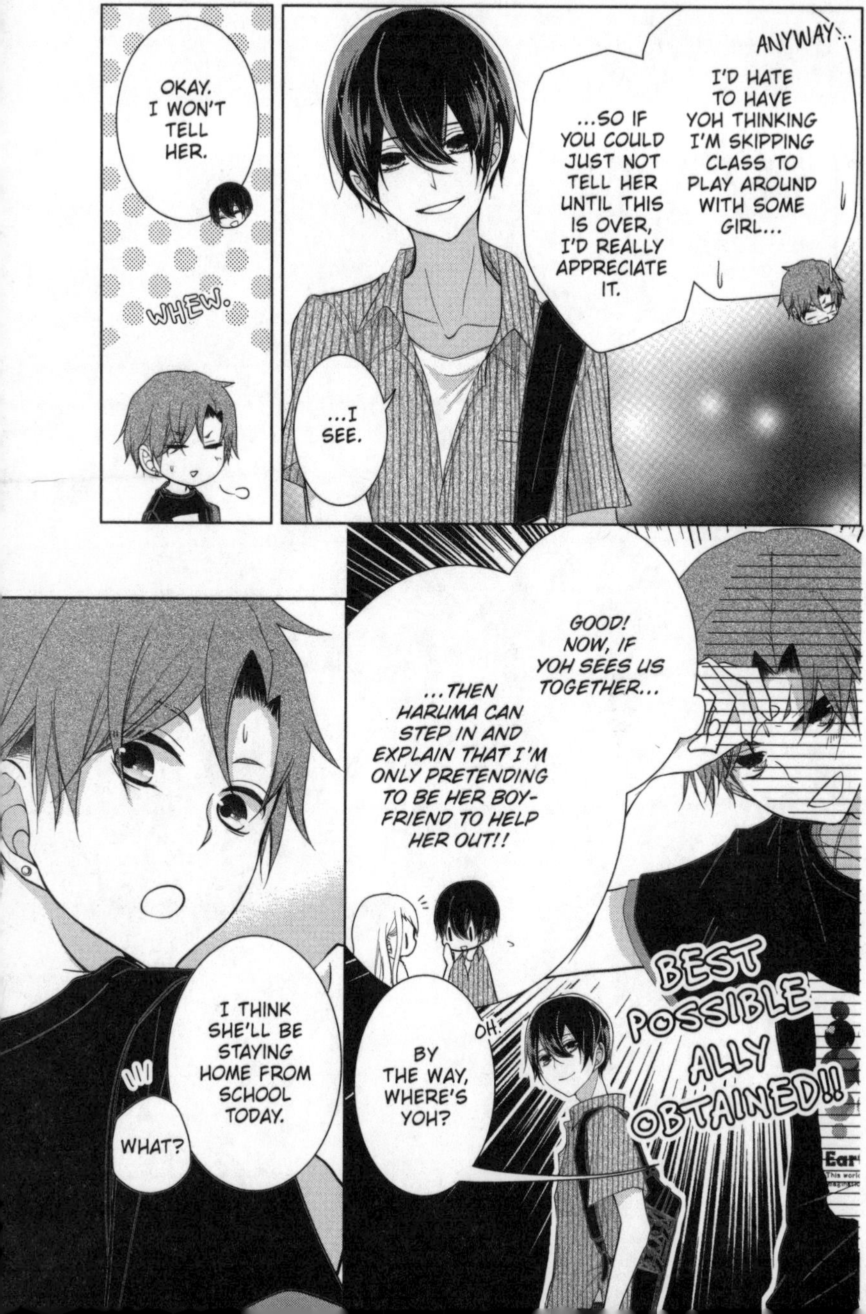
ANYWAY...
I'D HATE TO HAVE YOH THINKING I'M SKIPPING CLASS TO PLAY AROUND WITH SOME GIRL...
...SO IF YOU COULD JUST NOT TELL HER UNTIL THIS IS OVER, I'D REALLY APPRECIATE IT.
...I SEE.
OKAY. I WON'T TELL HER.
WHEW.
GOOD! NOW, IF YOH SEES US TOGETHER...
...THEN HARUMA CAN STEP IN AND EXPLAIN THAT I'M ONLY PRETENDING TO BE HER BOY-FRIEND TO HELP HER OUT!!
BEST POSSIBLE ALLY OBTAINED!!
OH!
BY THE WAY, WHERE'S YOH?
I THINK SHE'LL BE STAYING HOME FROM SCHOOL TODAY.
WHAT?

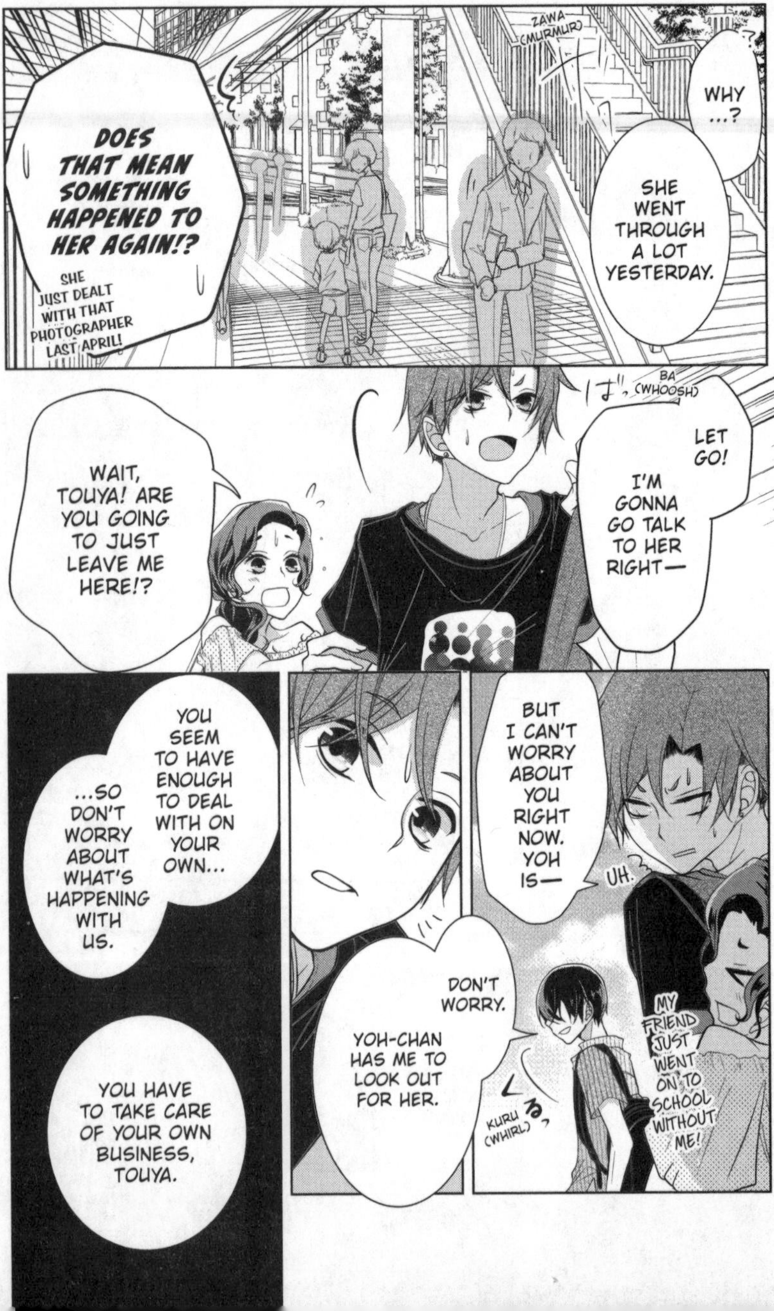
WHY ...?
SHE WENT THROUGH A LOT YESTERDAY.
ZAWA (MURMUR)
DOES THAT MEAN SOMETHING HAPPENED TO HER AGAIN!?
SHE JUST DEALT WITH THAT PHOTOGRAPHER LAST APRIL!
BA (WHOOSH)
LET GO!
I'M GONNA GO TALK TO HER RIGHT—
WAIT, TOUYA! ARE YOU GOING TO JUST LEAVE ME HERE!?
BUT I CAN'T WORRY ABOUT YOU RIGHT NOW. YOH IS—
UH.
MY FRIEND JUST WENT ON TO SCHOOL WITHOUT ME!
DON'T WORRY.
YOH-CHAN HAS ME TO LOOK OUT FOR HER.
KURU (WHIRL)
YOU SEEM TO HAVE ENOUGH TO DEAL WITH ON YOUR OWN...
...SO DON'T WORRY ABOUT WHAT'S HAPPENING WITH US.
YOU HAVE TO TAKE CARE OF YOUR OWN BUSINESS, TOUYA.

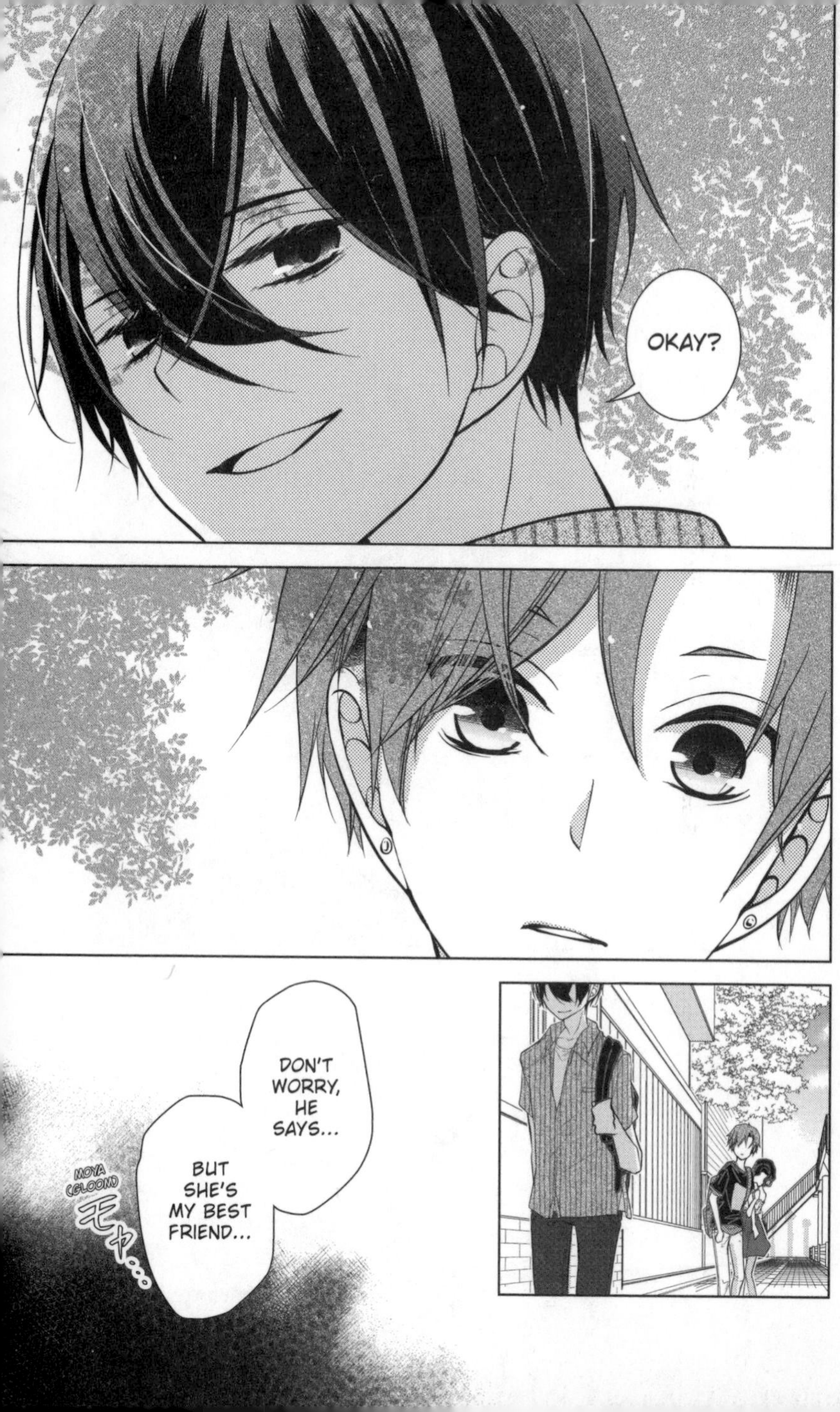
OKAY?
DON'T WORRY, HE SAYS...
BUT SHE'S MY BEST FRIEND...
MOYA (GLOOM)
モヤ...

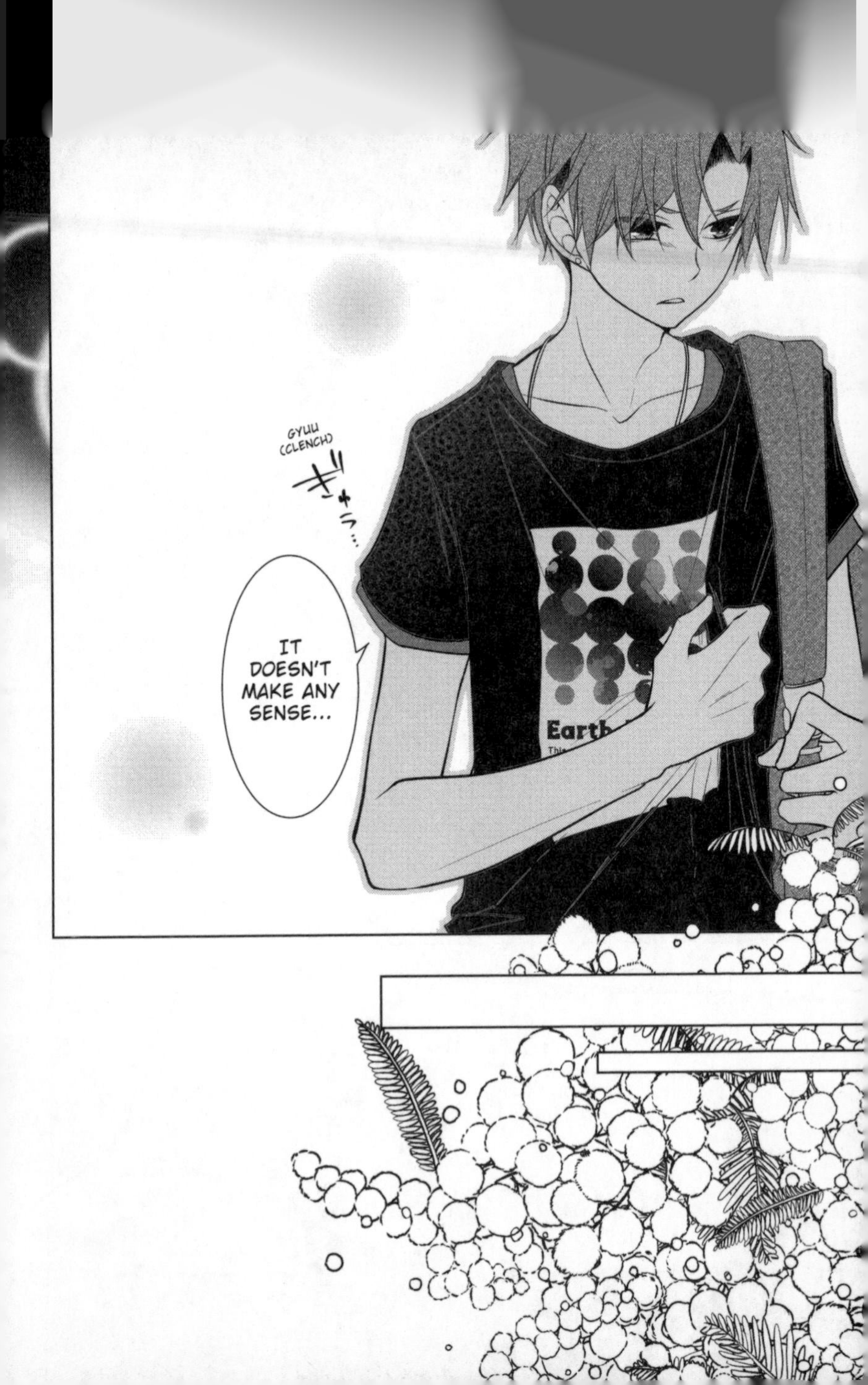
GYUU (CLENCH)
ギュ…
IT DOESN'T MAKE ANY SENSE...

#34

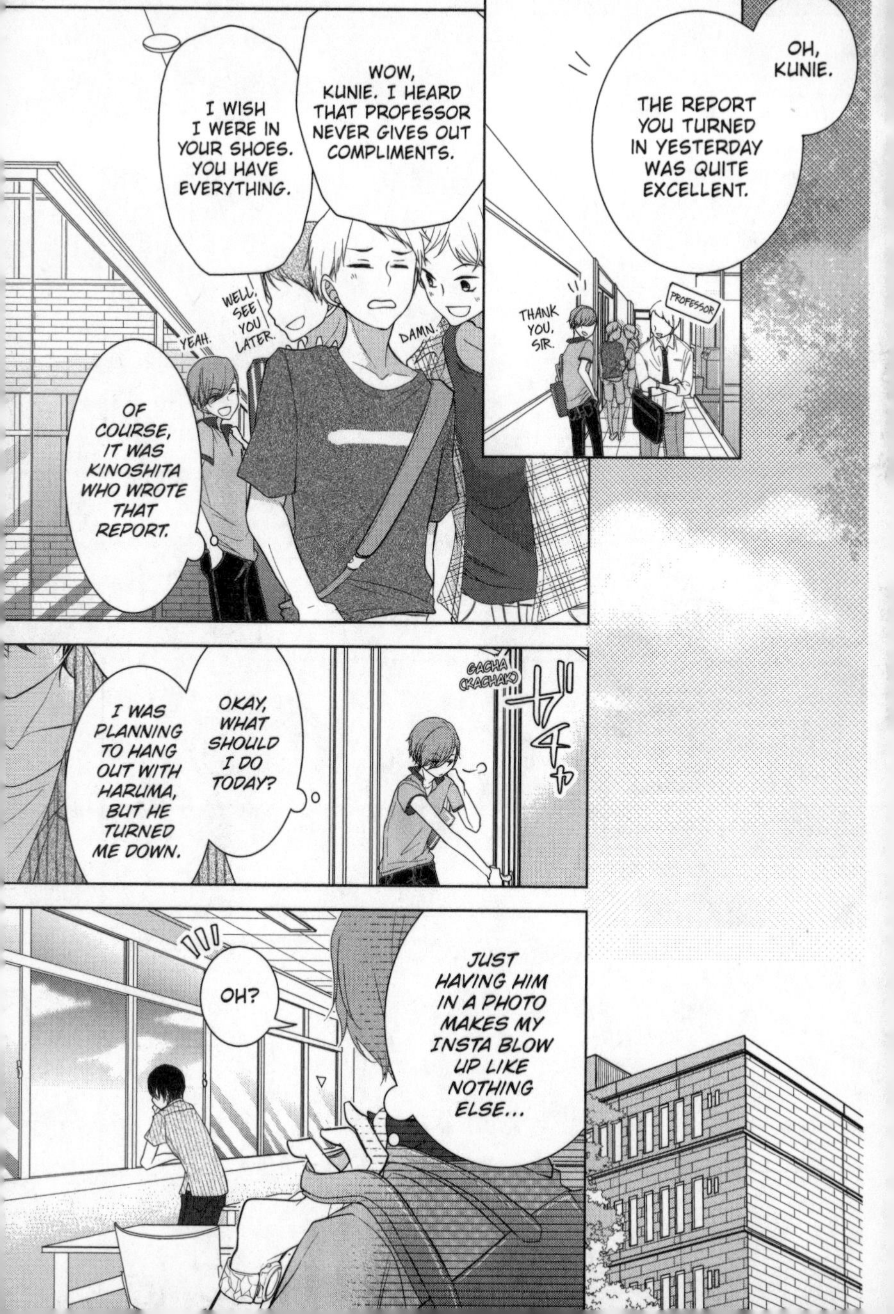
OH, KUNIE.
THE REPORT YOU TURNED IN YESTERDAY WAS QUITE EXCELLENT.
PROFESSOR
THANK YOU, SIR.
WOW, KUNIE. I HEARD THAT PROFESSOR NEVER GIVES OUT COMPLIMENTS.
I WISH I WERE IN YOUR SHOES. YOU HAVE EVERYTHING.
DAMN.
WELL, SEE YOU LATER.
YEAH.
OF COURSE, IT WAS KINOSHITA WHO WROTE THAT REPORT.
GACHA (KACHAK)
OKAY, WHAT SHOULD I DO TODAY?
I WAS PLANNING TO HANG OUT WITH HARUMA, BUT HE TURNED ME DOWN.
JUST HAVING HIM IN A PHOTO MAKES MY INSTA BLOW UP LIKE NOTHING ELSE...
OH?

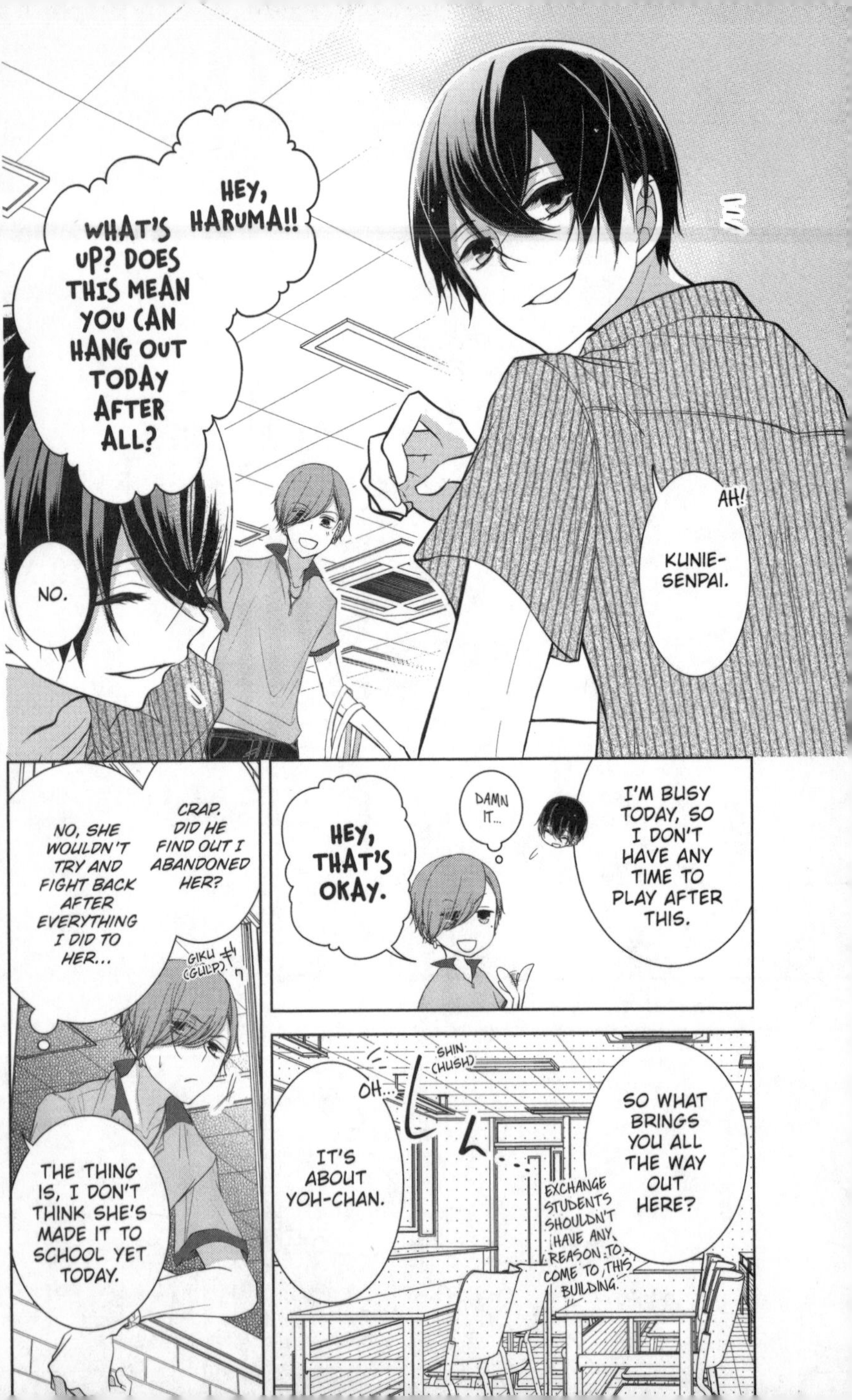
AH!
KUNIE-SENPAI.
HEY, HARUMA!!
WHAT'S UP? DOES THIS MEAN YOU CAN HANG OUT TODAY AFTER ALL?
NO.
I'M BUSY TODAY, SO I DON'T HAVE ANY TIME TO PLAY AFTER THIS.
DAMN IT...
HEY, THAT'S OKAY.
SO WHAT BRINGS YOU ALL THE WAY OUT HERE?
EXCHANGE STUDENTS SHOULDN'T HAVE ANY REASON TO COME TO THIS BUILDING.
SHIN (HUSH)
OH...
IT'S ABOUT YOH-CHAN.
CRAP. DID HE FIND OUT I ABANDONED HER?
NO, SHE WOULDN'T TRY AND FIGHT BACK AFTER EVERYTHING I DID TO HER...
GIKU (GULP)
THE THING IS, I DON'T THINK SHE'S MADE IT TO SCHOOL YET TODAY.

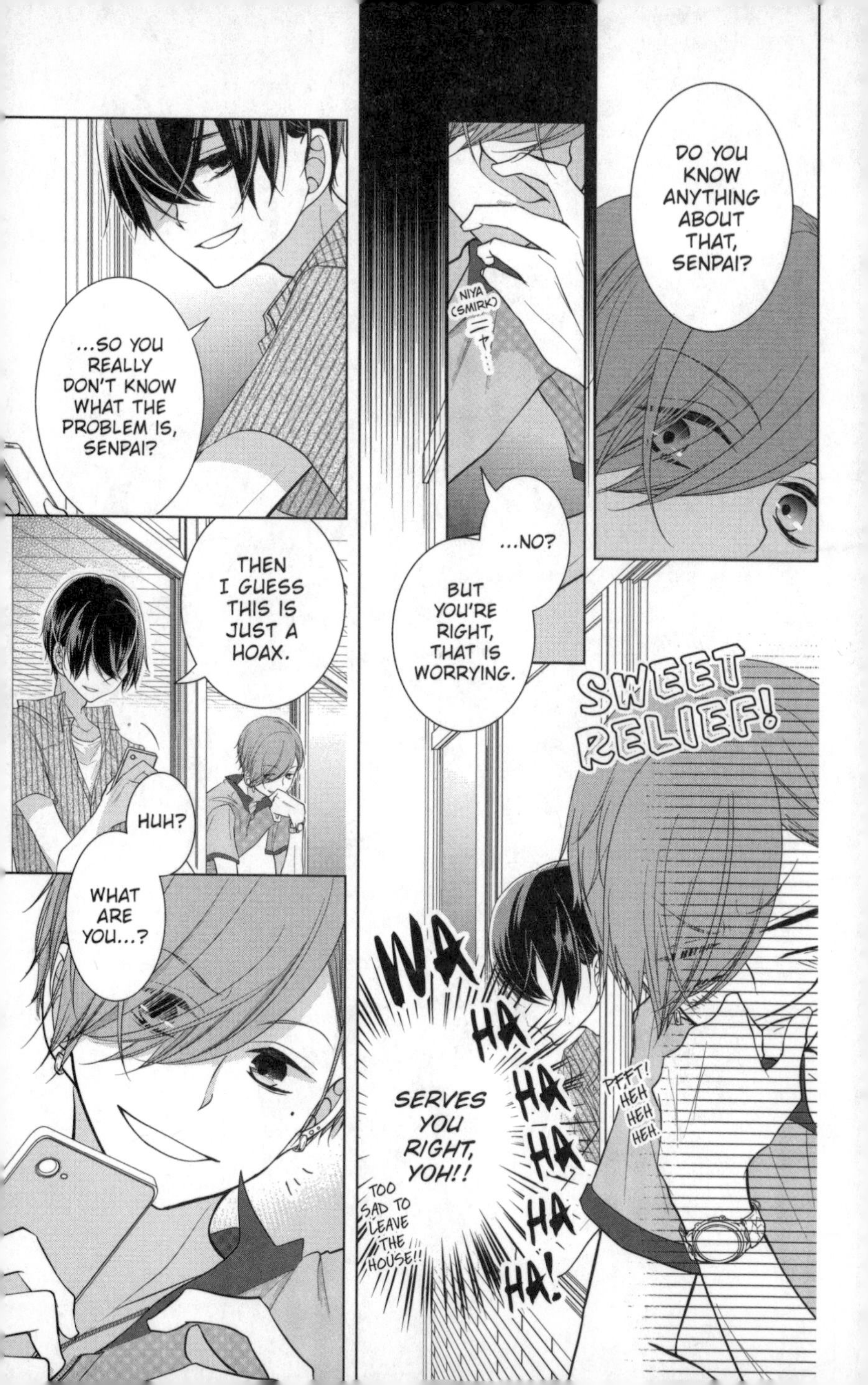
DO YOU KNOW ANYTHING ABOUT THAT, SENPAI?
NIYA (SMIRK)
ニヤ…
...NO?
BUT YOU'RE RIGHT, THAT IS WORRYING.
SWEET RELIEF!
PFFT! HEH HEH HEH.
WA HA HA HA HA HA HA!
SERVES YOU RIGHT, YOH!!
TOO SAD TO LEAVE THE HOUSE!!
...SO YOU REALLY DON'T KNOW WHAT THE PROBLEM IS, SENPAI?
THEN I GUESS THIS IS JUST A HOAX.
HUH?
WHAT ARE YOU...?

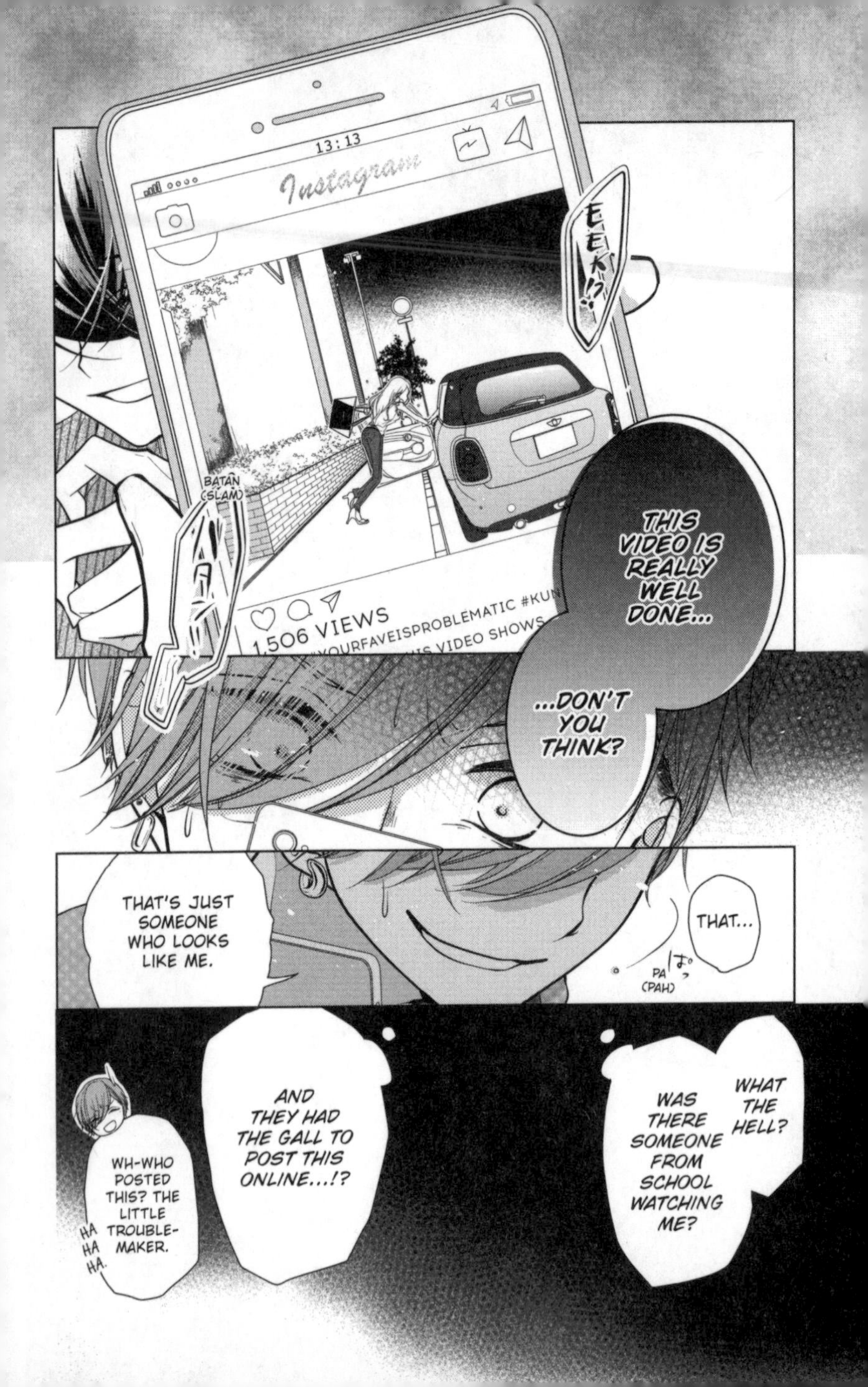
13:13
Instagram
1,506 VIEWS
#YOURFAVEISPROBLEMATIC #KUN
BATAN (SLAM)
THIS VIDEO IS REALLY WELL DONE...
...DON'T YOU THINK?
THAT...
PA (PAH)
THAT'S JUST SOMEONE WHO LOOKS LIKE ME.
WHAT THE HELL?
WAS THERE SOMEONE FROM SCHOOL WATCHING ME?
AND THEY HAD THE GALL TO POST THIS ONLINE...!?
WH-WHO POSTED THIS? THE LITTLE TROUBLE-MAKER.
HA HA HA.

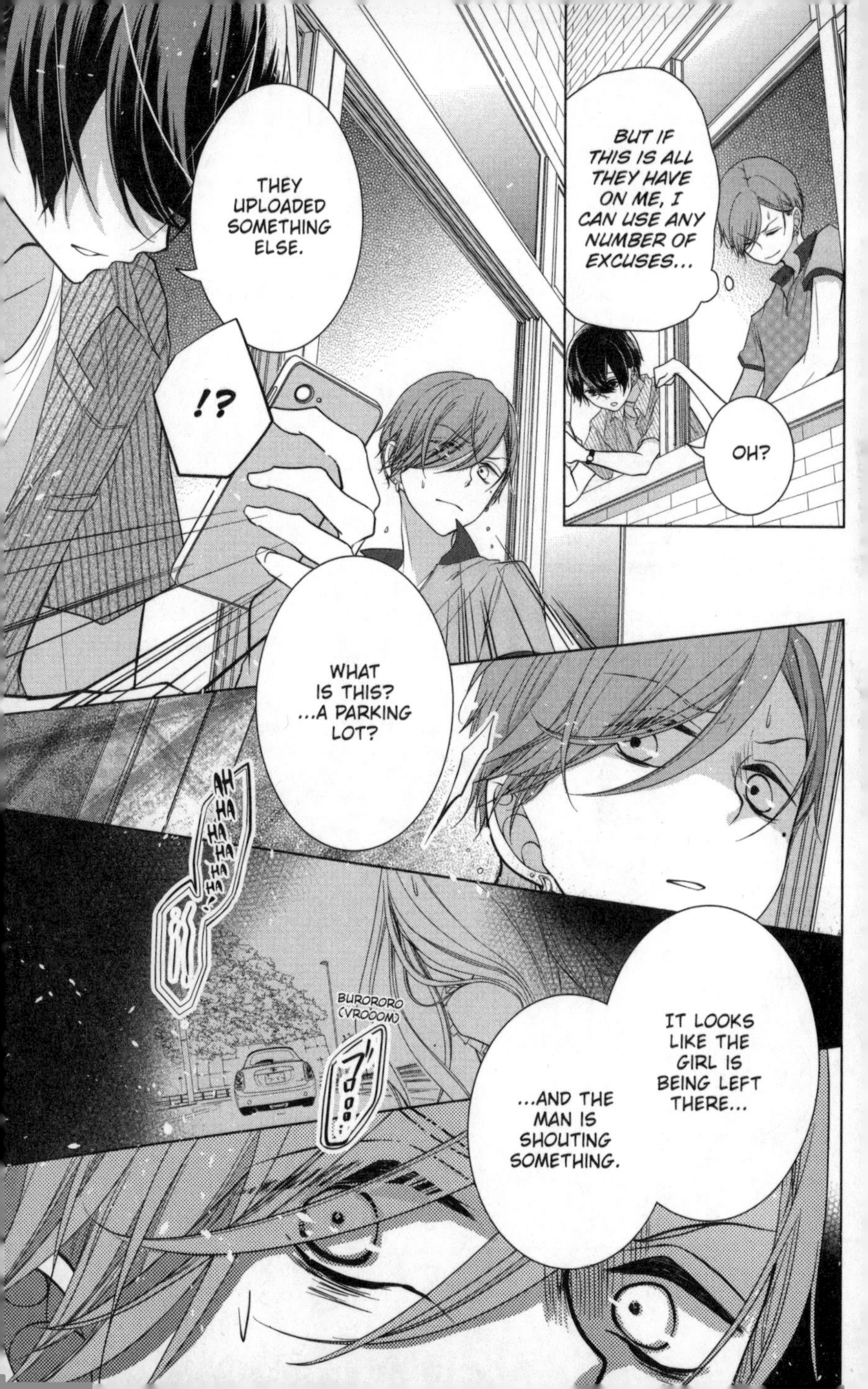
BUT IF THIS IS ALL THEY HAVE ON ME, I CAN USE ANY NUMBER OF EXCUSES...
OH?
THEY UPLOADED SOMETHING ELSE.
!?
WHAT IS THIS? ...A PARKING LOT?
AH HA HA HA HA HA
BURORORO (VROOOM)
IT LOOKS LIKE THE GIRL IS BEING LEFT THERE...
...AND THE MAN IS SHOUTING SOMETHING.

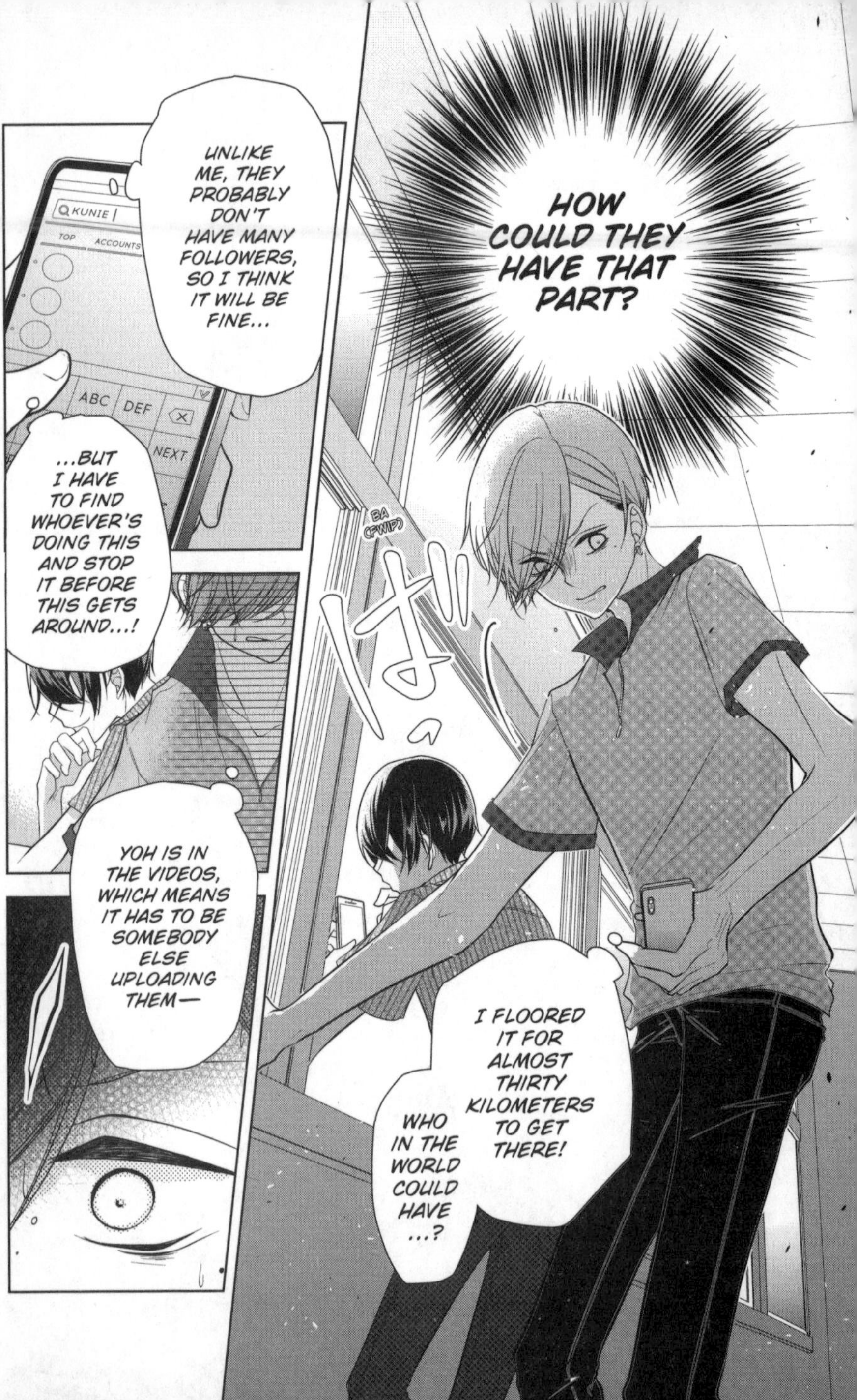
HOW COULD THEY HAVE THAT PART?
BA (FWIP)
I FLOORED IT FOR ALMOST THIRTY KILOMETERS TO GET THERE!
WHO IN THE WORLD COULD HAVE ...?
KUNIE
TOP
ACCOUNTS
ABC
DEF
NEXT
UNLIKE ME, THEY PROBABLY DON'T HAVE MANY FOLLOWERS, SO I THINK IT WILL BE FINE...
...BUT I HAVE TO FIND WHOEVER'S DOING THIS AND STOP IT BEFORE THIS GETS AROUND...!
YOH IS IN THE VIDEOS, WHICH MEANS IT HAS TO BE SOMEBODY ELSE UPLOADING THEM—

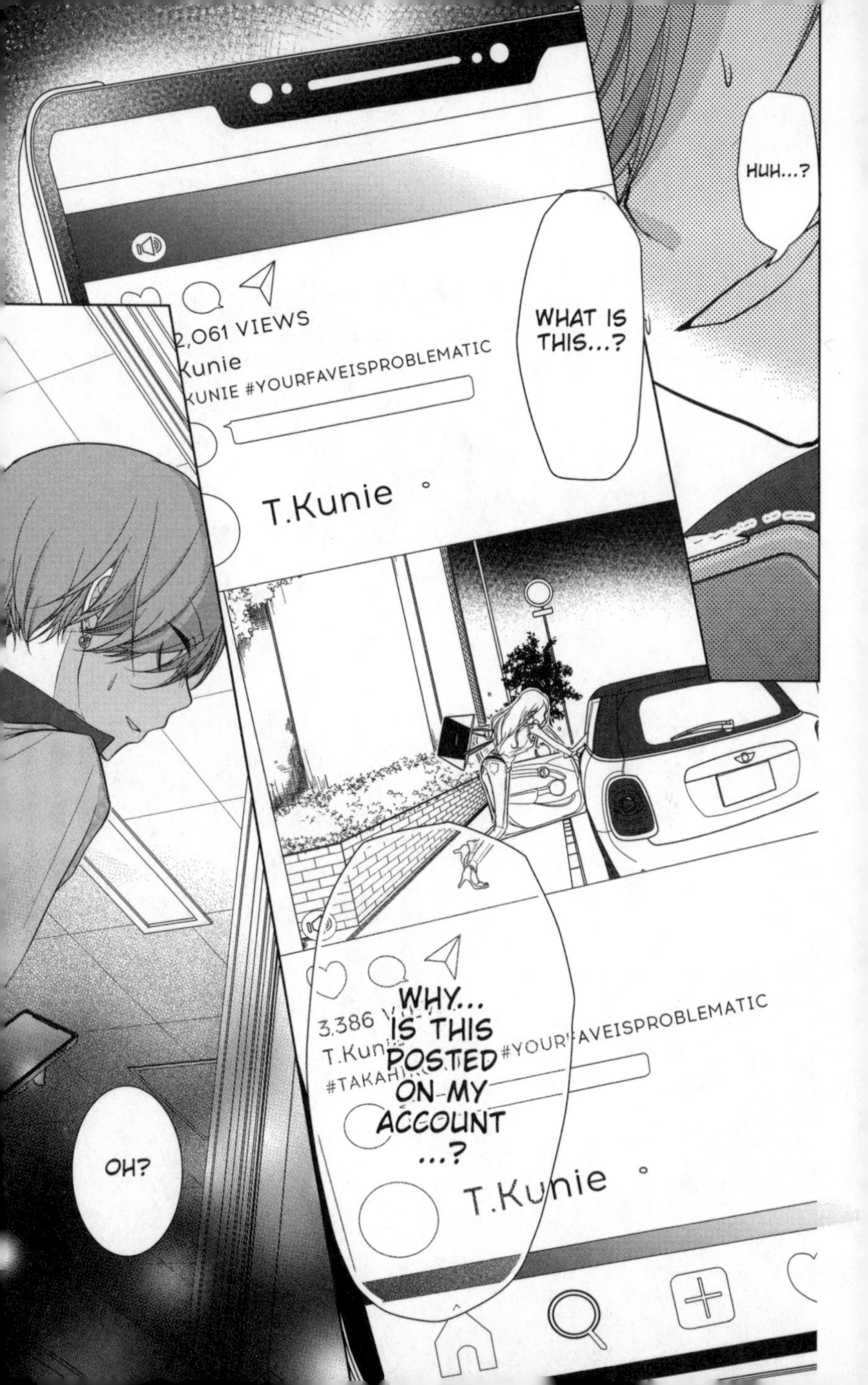

HUH...?
WHAT IS THIS...?
2,061 VIEWS
KUNIE #YOURFAVEISPROBLEMATIC
T.Kunie
WHY... IS THIS POSTED ON MY ACCOUNT ...?
#YOUR FAVEISPROBLEMATIC
T.Kunie
OH?

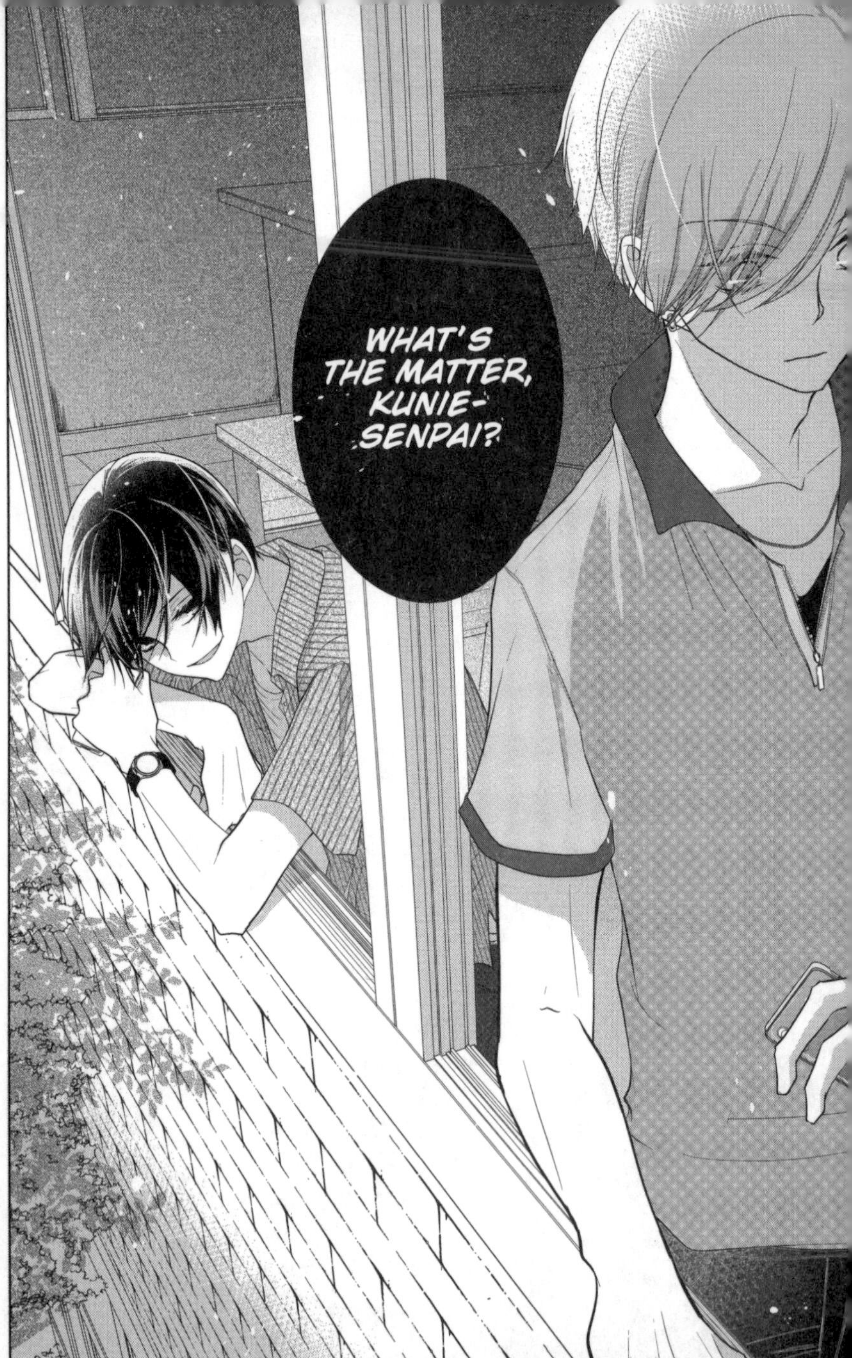
WHAT'S THE MATTER, KUNIE-SENPAI?

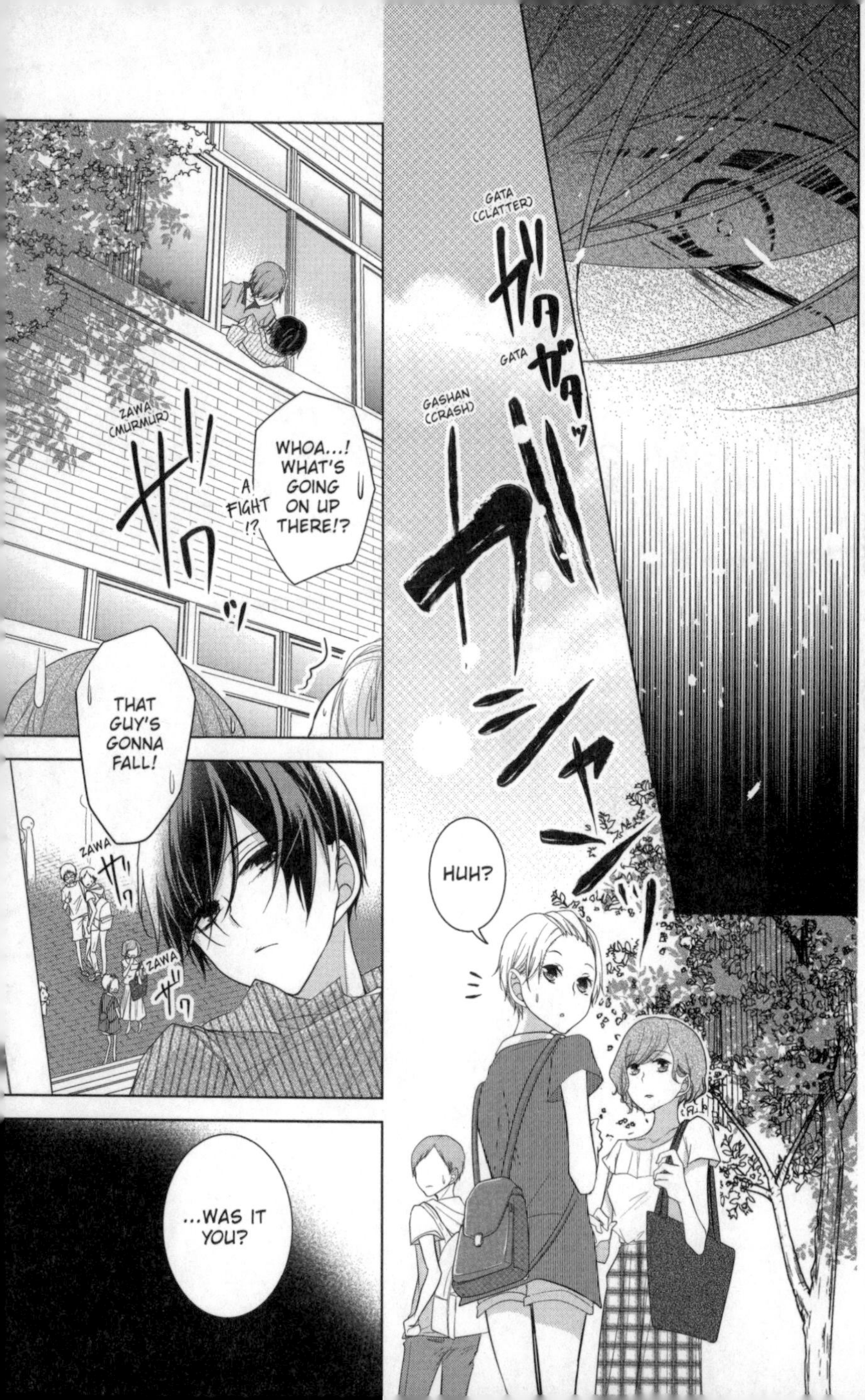
GATA (CLATTER)
GATA
GASHAN (CRASH)
HUH?
WHOA...! WHAT'S GOING ON UP THERE!?
A FIGHT !?
ZAWA (MURMUR)
THAT GUY'S GONNA FALL!
ZAWA
ZAWA
...WAS IT YOU?

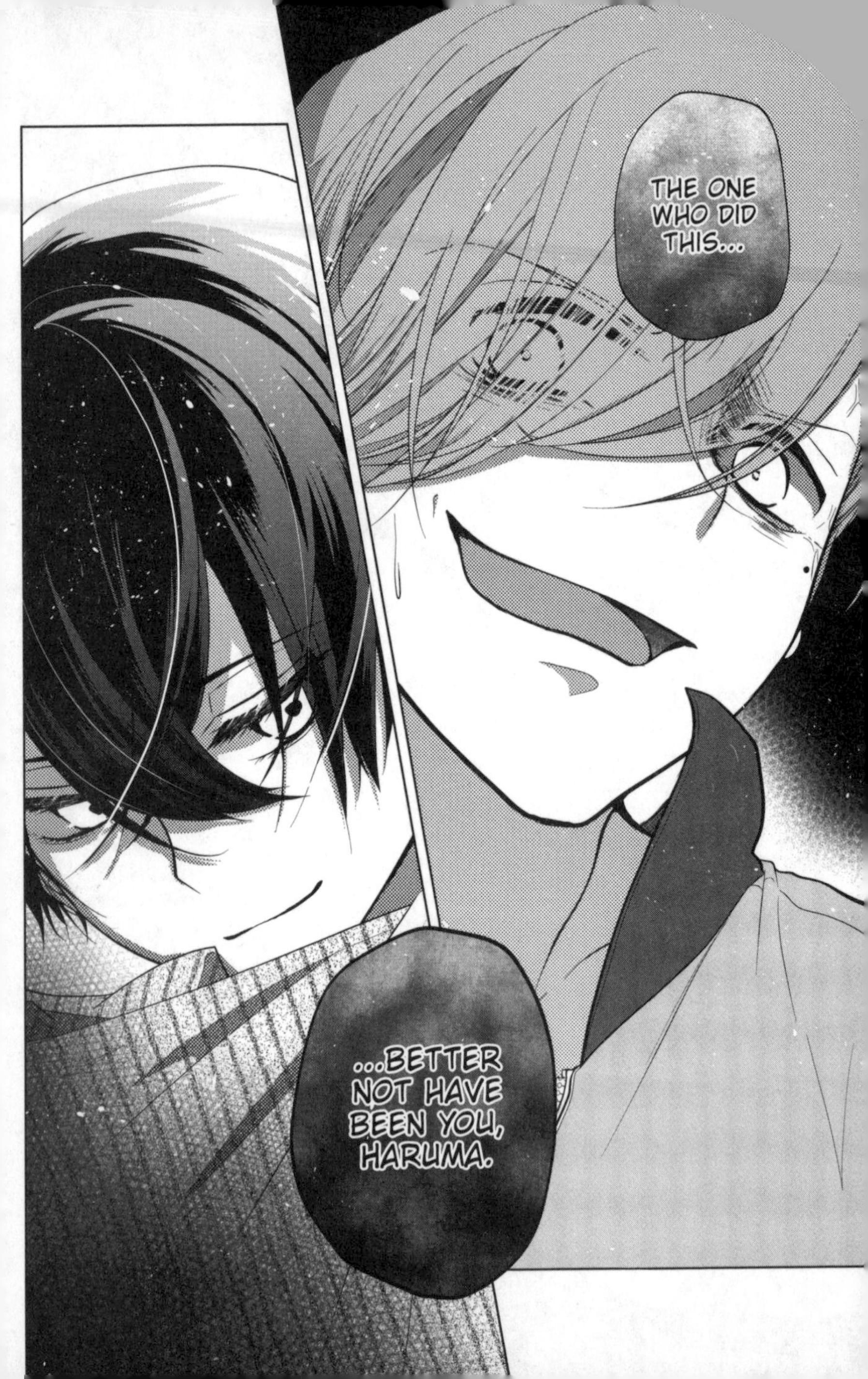
THE ONE WHO DID THIS...
...BETTER NOT HAVE BEEN YOU, HARUMA.

#35

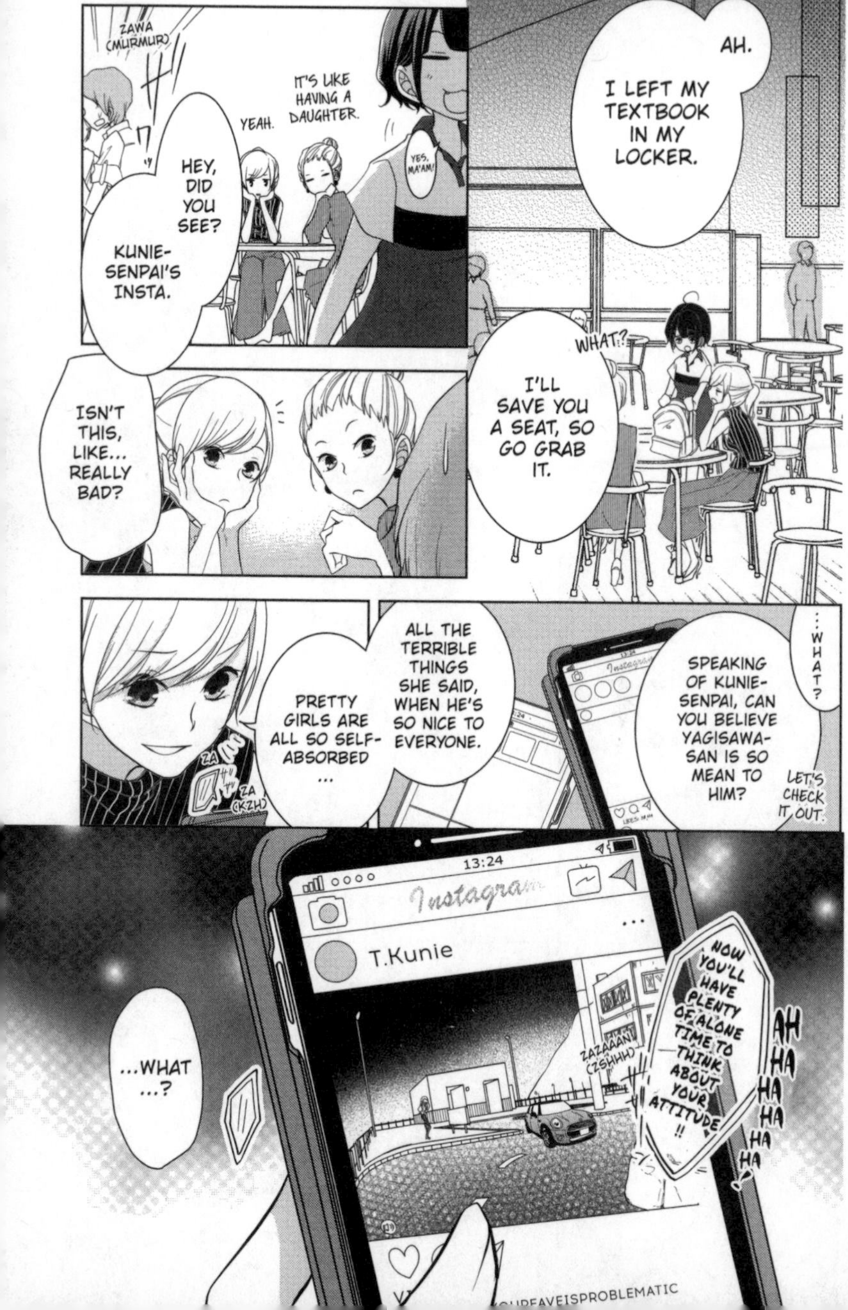
AH.
I LEFT MY TEXTBOOK IN MY LOCKER.
WHAT?!
I'LL SAVE YOU A SEAT, SO GO GRAB IT.
YES, MA'AM!
IT'S LIKE HAVING A DAUGHTER.
YEAH.
HEY, DID YOU SEE? KUNIE-SENPAI'S INSTA.
ZAWA (MURMUR)
ISN'T THIS, LIKE... REALLY BAD?
...WHAT?
SPEAKING OF KUNIE-SENPAI, CAN YOU BELIEVE YAGISAWA-SAN IS SO MEAN TO HIM?
LET'S CHECK IT OUT.
ALL THE TERRIBLE THINGS SHE SAID, WHEN HE'S SO NICE TO EVERYONE.
PRETTY GIRLS ARE ALL SO SELF-ABSORBED...
ZA ZA (KZH)
AH HA HA HA HA HA
NOW YOU'LL HAVE PLENTY OF ALONE TIME TO THINK ABOUT YOUR ATTITUDE!!
ZAZAAAN (ZSHHH)
13:24
Instagram
T.Kunie
...WHAT...?
OURFAVEISPROBLEMATIC

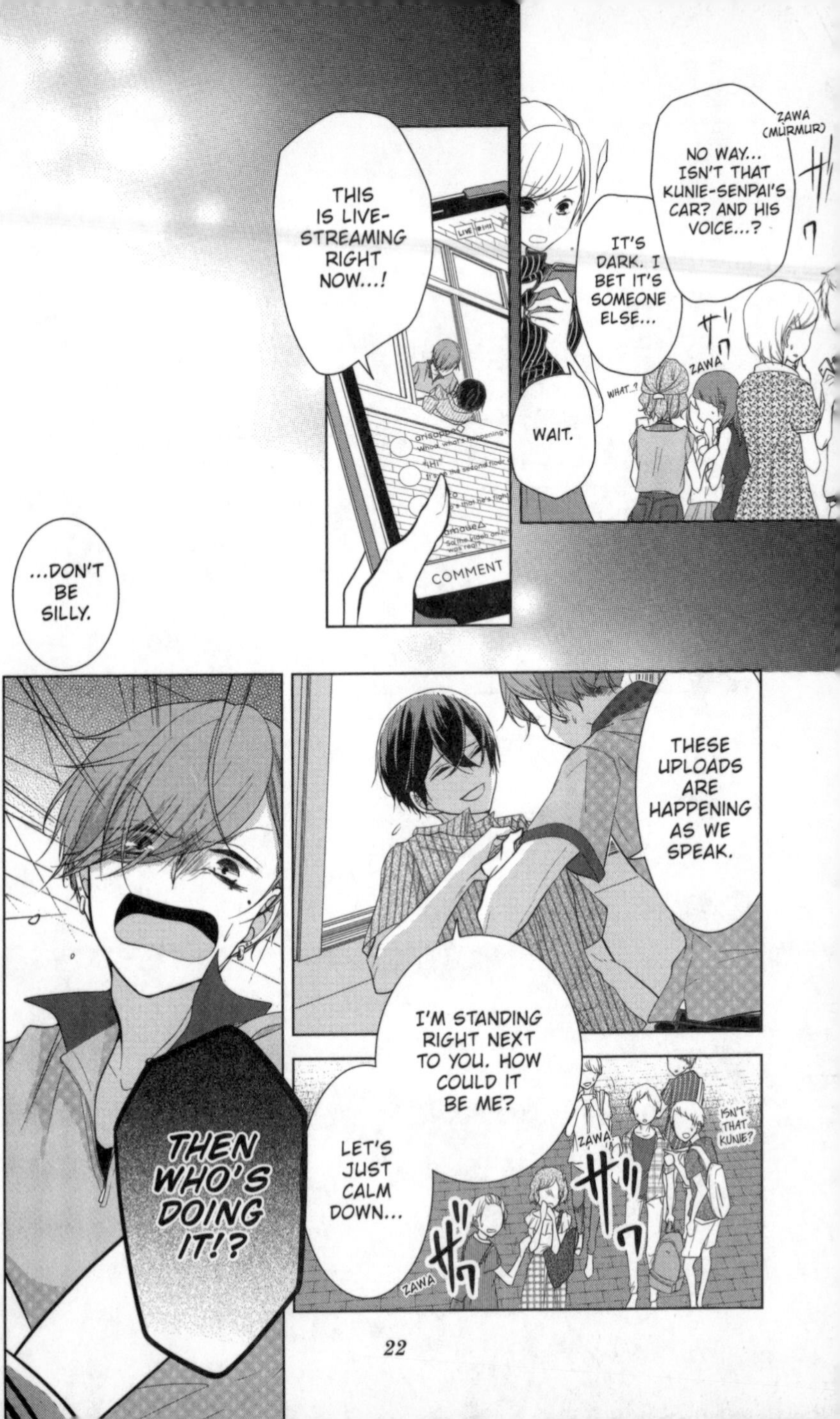
ZAWA (MURMUR)
NO WAY... ISN'T THAT KUNIE-SENPAI'S CAR? AND HIS VOICE...?
IT'S DARK. I BET IT'S SOMEONE ELSE...
ZAWA
WHAT...?
WAIT.
THIS IS LIVE-STREAMING RIGHT NOW...!
COMMENT
...DON'T BE SILLY.
THESE UPLOADS ARE HAPPENING AS WE SPEAK.
I'M STANDING RIGHT NEXT TO YOU. HOW COULD IT BE ME?
ISN'T THAT KUNIE?
ZAWA
LET'S JUST CALM DOWN...
ZAWA
THEN WHO'S DOING IT!?

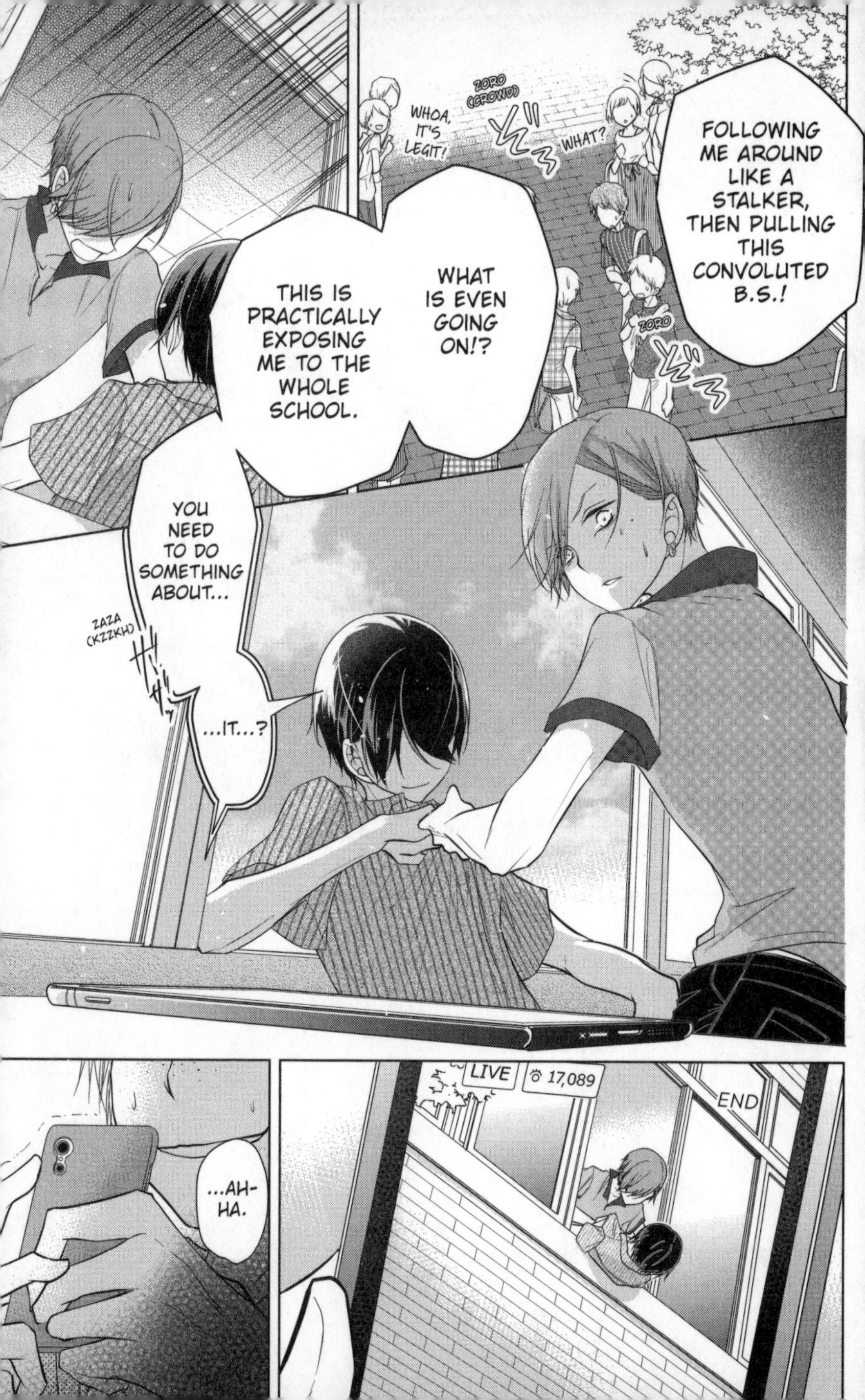
FOLLOWING ME AROUND LIKE A STALKER, THEN PULLING THIS CONVOLUTED B.S.!
WHAT?
ZORO (CROWD)
WHOA, IT'S LEGIT!
ZORO
WHAT IS EVEN GOING ON!?
THIS IS PRACTICALLY EXPOSING ME TO THE WHOLE SCHOOL.
YOU NEED TO DO SOMETHING ABOUT...
ZAZA (KZZKH)
...IT...?
LIVE
17,089
END
...AH-HA.

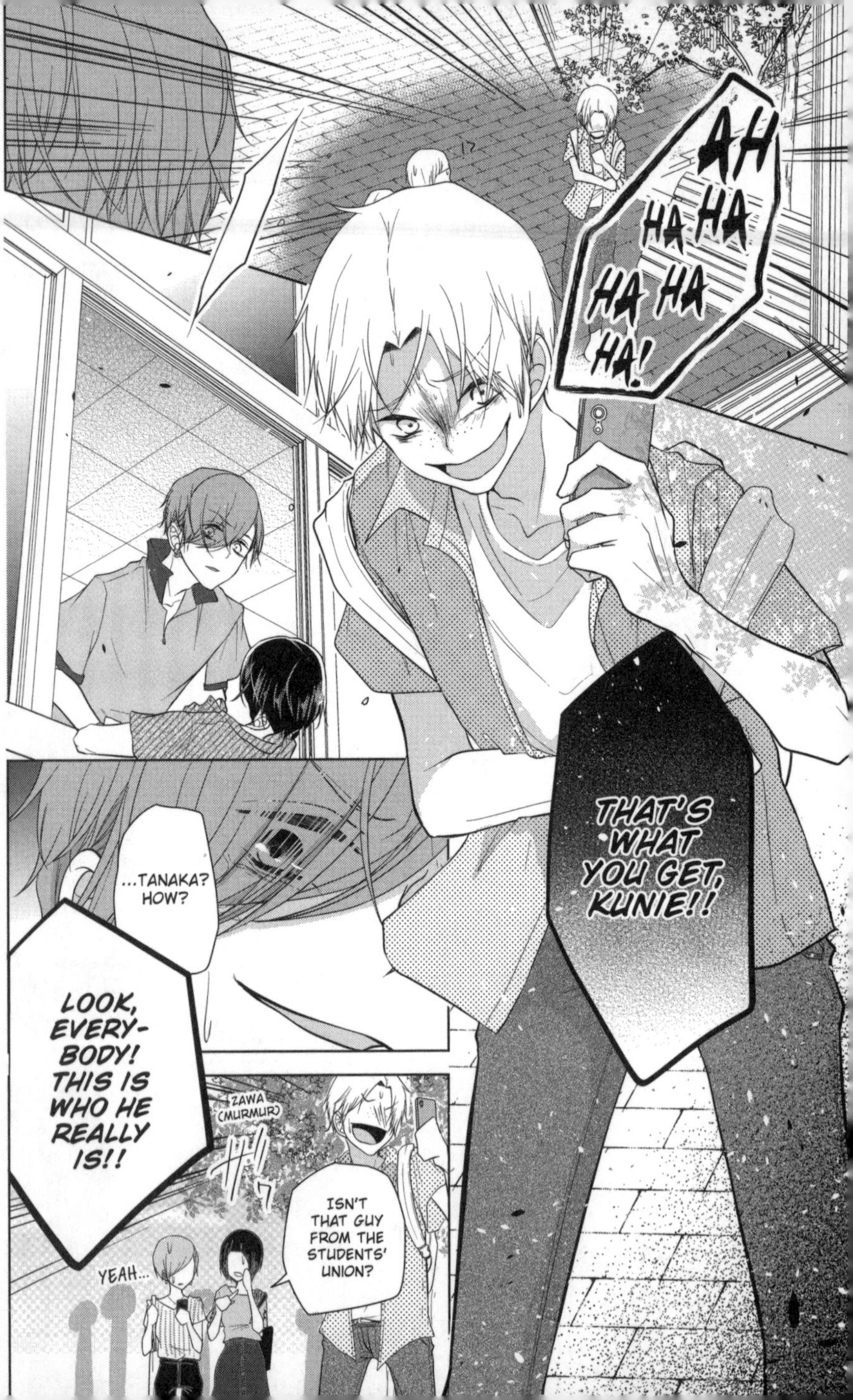
AH HA HA HA HA HA!
THAT'S WHAT YOU GET, KUNIE!!
...TANAKA? HOW?
LOOK, EVERYBODY! THIS IS WHO HE REALLY IS!!
ZAWA (MURMUR)
ISN'T THAT GUY FROM THE STUDENTS' UNION?
YEAH...

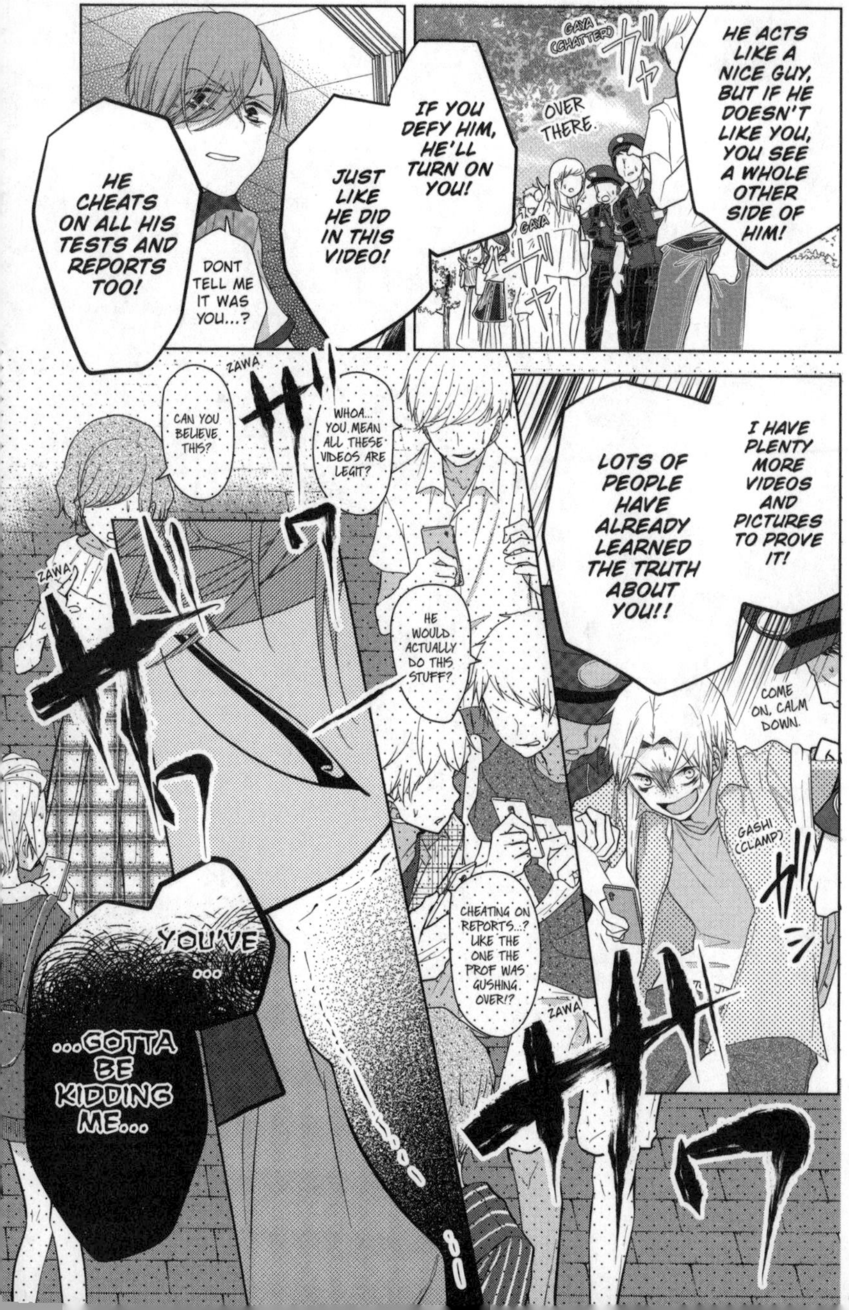
HE ACTS LIKE A NICE GUY, BUT IF HE DOESN'T LIKE YOU, YOU SEE A WHOLE OTHER SIDE OF HIM!
GAYA (CHATTER)
OVER THERE.
GAYA
IF YOU DEFY HIM, HE'LL TURN ON YOU!
JUST LIKE HE DID IN THIS VIDEO!
HE CHEATS ON ALL HIS TESTS AND REPORTS TOO!
DONT TELL ME IT WAS YOU...?
I HAVE PLENTY MORE VIDEOS AND PICTURES TO PROVE IT!
LOTS OF PEOPLE HAVE ALREADY LEARNED THE TRUTH ABOUT YOU!!
COME ON, CALM DOWN.
GASHI (CLAMP)
WHOA... YOU MEAN ALL THESE VIDEOS ARE LEGIT?
ZAWA
CAN YOU BELIEVE THIS?
ZAWA
HE WOULD ACTUALLY DO THIS STUFF?
CHEATING ON REPORTS...? LIKE THE ONE THE PROF WAS GUSHING OVER!?
ZAWA
YOU'VE...
...GOTTA BE KIDDING ME...

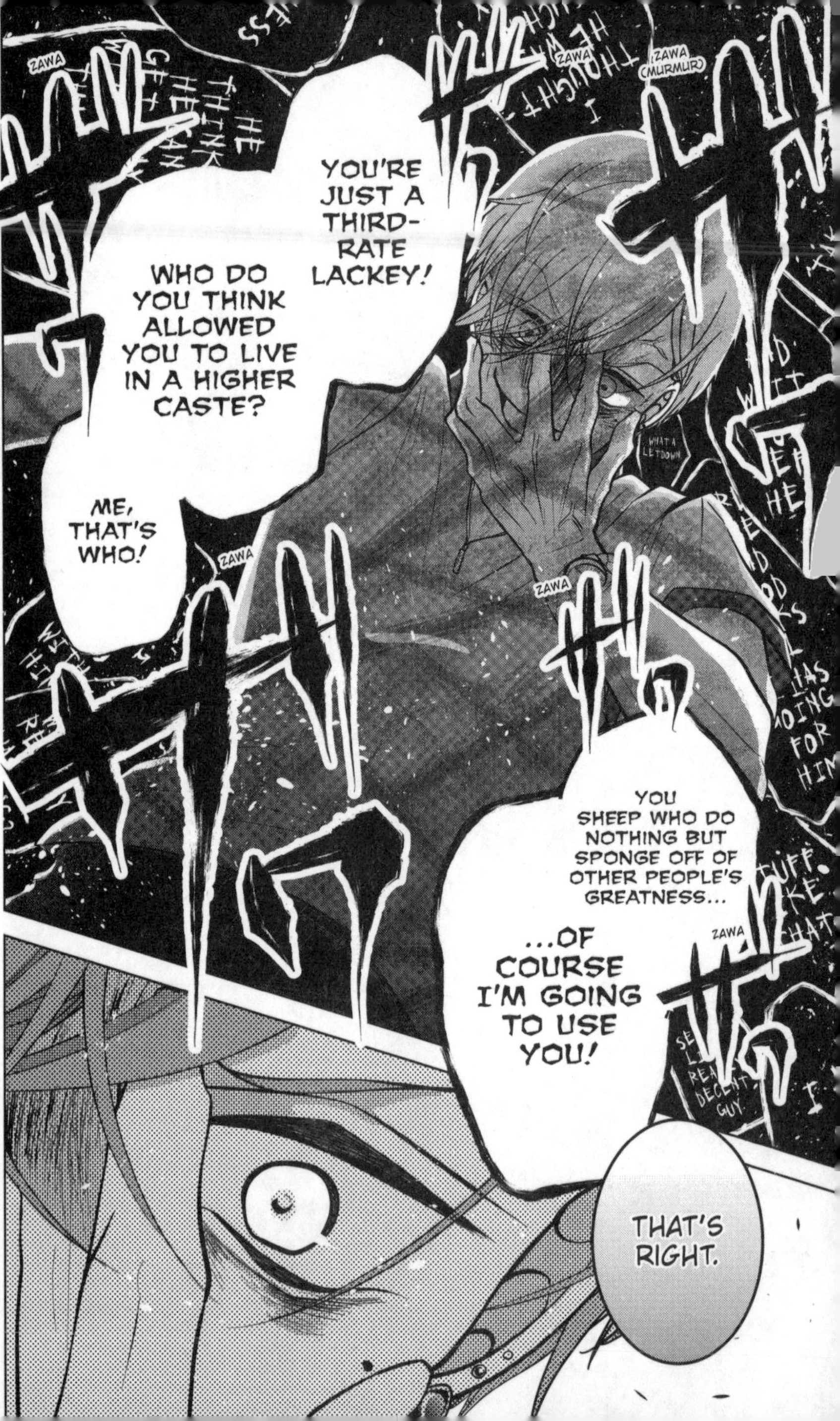
ZAWA
ZAWA (MURMUR)
ZAWA
YOU'RE JUST A THIRD-RATE LACKEY!
WHO DO YOU THINK ALLOWED YOU TO LIVE IN A HIGHER CASTE?
WHAT A LETDOWN.
ME, THAT'S WHO!
ZAWA
ZAWA
YOU SHEEP WHO DO NOTHING BUT SPONGE OFF OF OTHER PEOPLE'S GREATNESS...
...OF COURSE I'M GOING TO USE YOU!
ZAWA
THAT'S RIGHT.

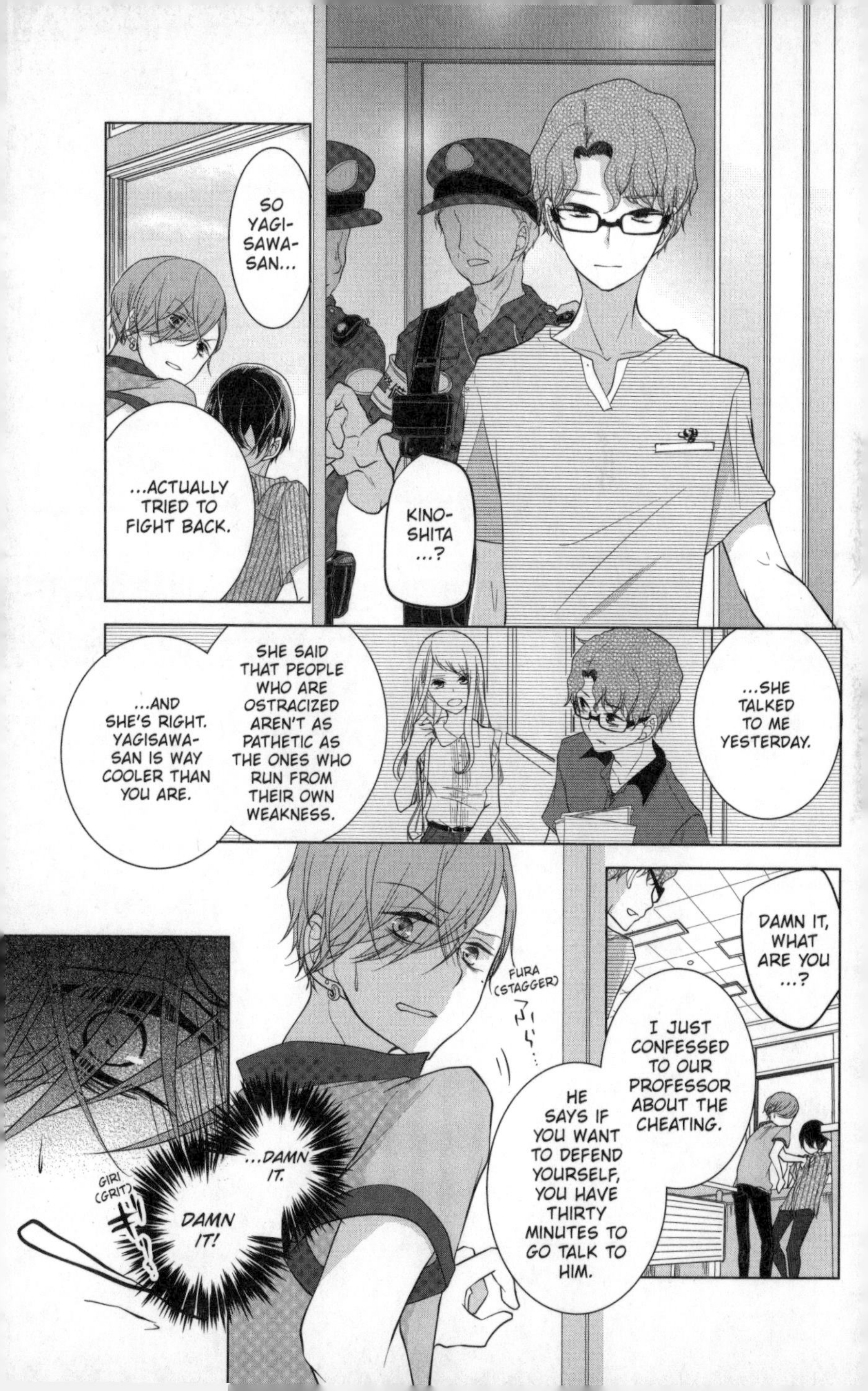
KINO-SHITA ...?
SO YAGI-SAWA-SAN...
...ACTUALLY TRIED TO FIGHT BACK.
...SHE TALKED TO ME YESTERDAY.
SHE SAID THAT PEOPLE WHO ARE OSTRACIZED AREN'T AS PATHETIC AS THE ONES WHO RUN FROM THEIR OWN WEAKNESS.
...AND SHE'S RIGHT. YAGISAWA-SAN IS WAY COOLER THAN YOU ARE.
DAMN IT, WHAT ARE YOU ...?
I JUST CONFESSED TO OUR PROFESSOR ABOUT THE CHEATING.
HE SAYS IF YOU WANT TO DEFEND YOURSELF, YOU HAVE THIRTY MINUTES TO GO TALK TO HIM.
FURA (STAGGER)
...DAMN IT.
DAMN IT!
GIRI (GRIT)

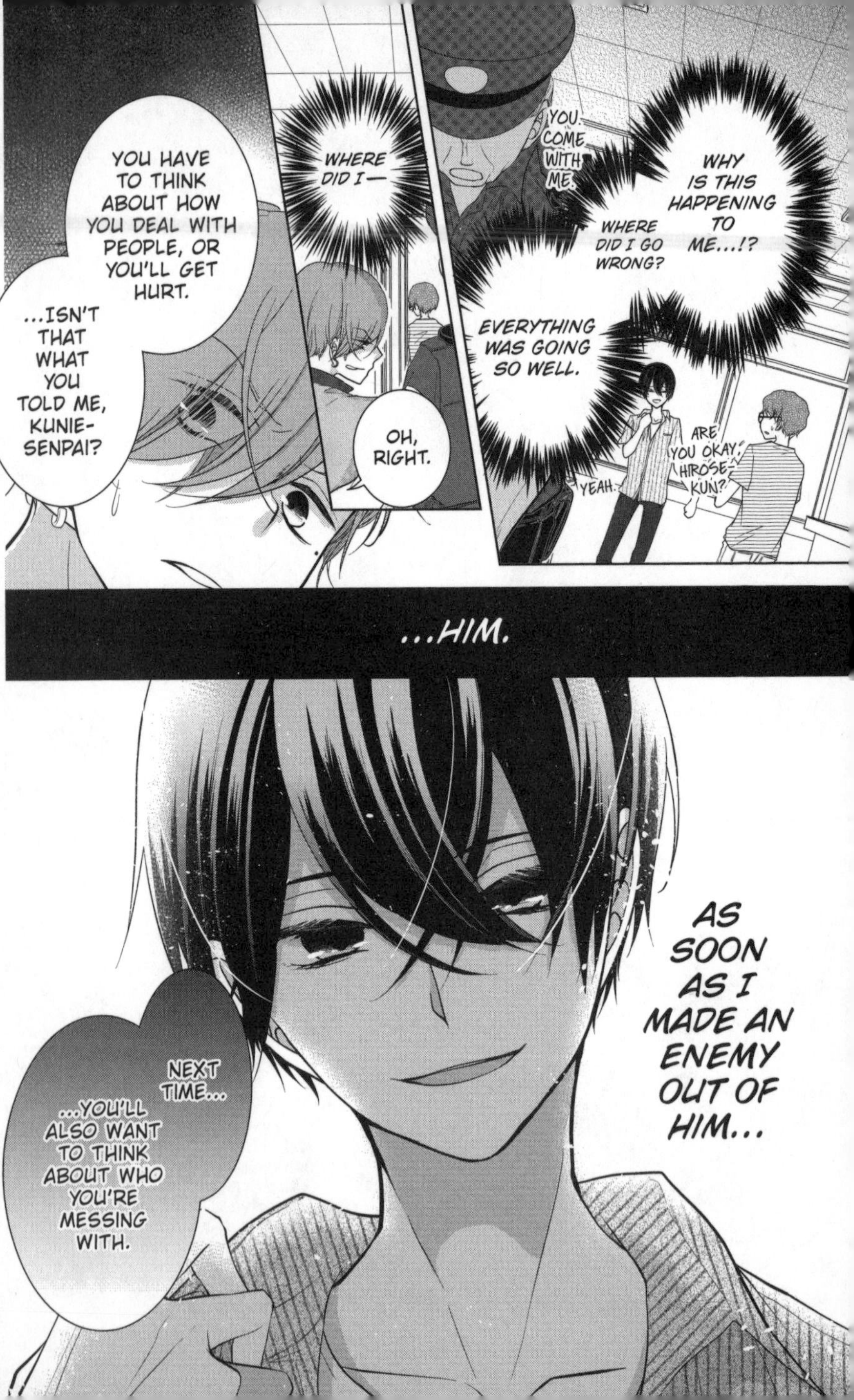
WHY IS THIS HAPPENING TO ME...!?
YOU. COME WITH ME.
WHERE DID I GO WRONG?
EVERYTHING WAS GOING SO WELL.
ARE YOU OKAY, HIROSE-KUN?
YEAH.
WHERE DID I—
OH, RIGHT.
YOU HAVE TO THINK ABOUT HOW YOU DEAL WITH PEOPLE, OR YOU'LL GET HURT.
...ISN'T THAT WHAT YOU TOLD ME, KUNIE-SENPAI?
...HIM.
AS SOON AS I MADE AN ENEMY OUT OF HIM...
NEXT TIME...
...YOU'LL ALSO WANT TO THINK ABOUT WHO YOU'RE MESSING WITH.

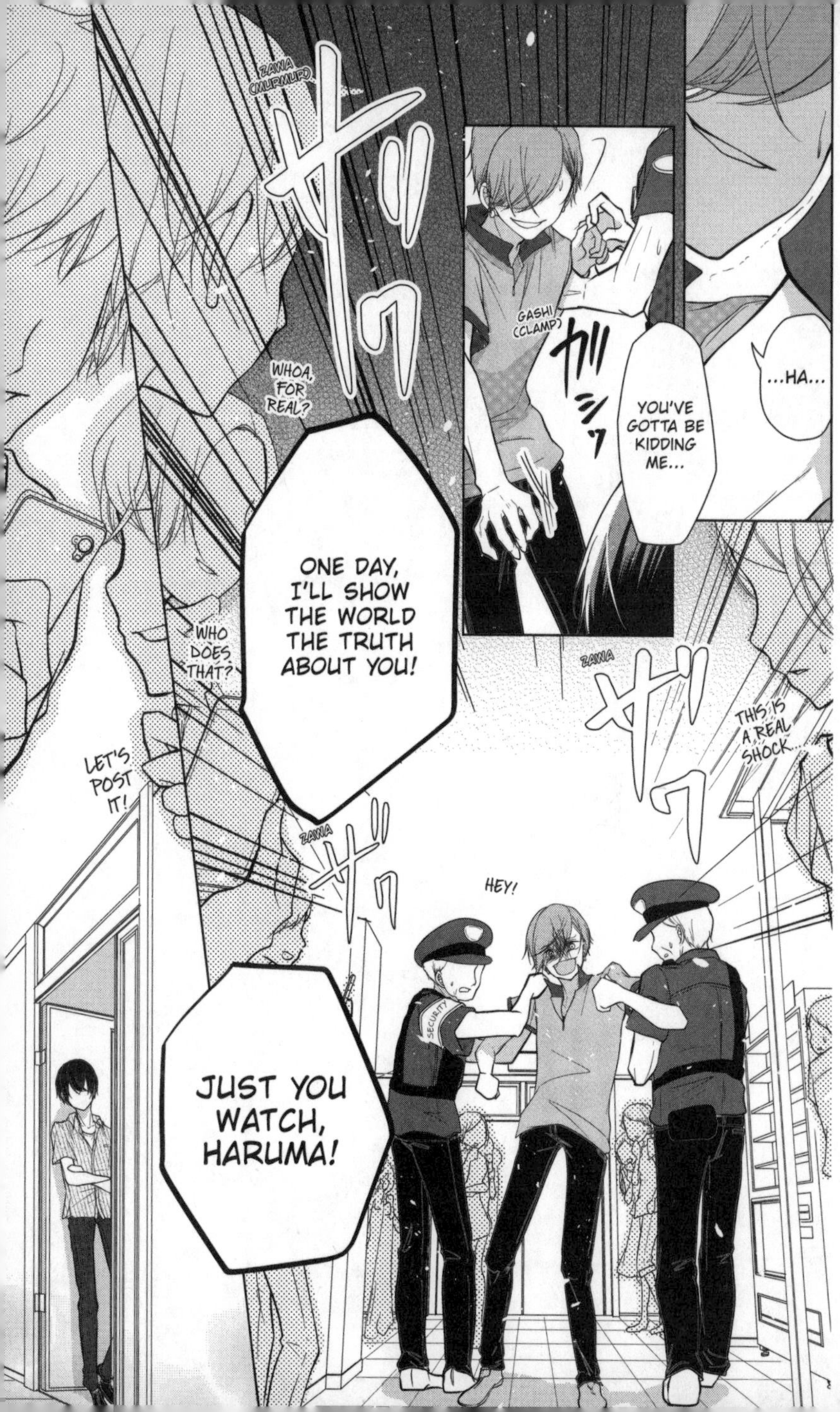
...HA...
GASHI (CLAMP)
YOU'VE GOTTA BE KIDDING ME...
ZAWA (MURMUR)
WHOA, FOR REAL?
ONE DAY, I'LL SHOW THE WORLD THE TRUTH ABOUT YOU!
WHO DOES THAT?
LET'S POST IT!
ZAWA
THIS IS A REAL SHOCK...
ZAWA
HEY!
JUST YOU WATCH, HARUMA!

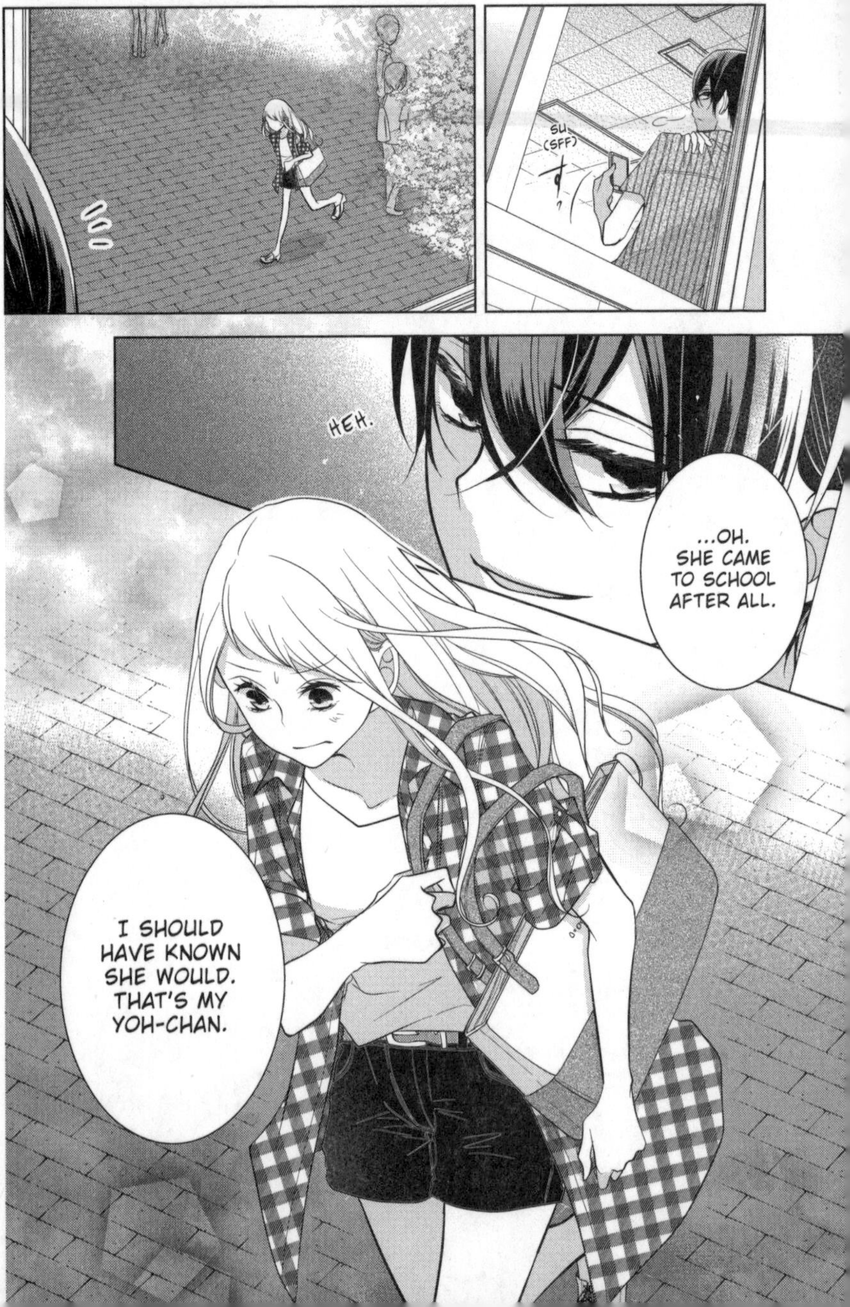
SU (SFF)
HEH.
...OH. SHE CAME TO SCHOOL AFTER ALL.
I SHOULD HAVE KNOWN SHE WOULD. THAT'S MY YOH-CHAN.

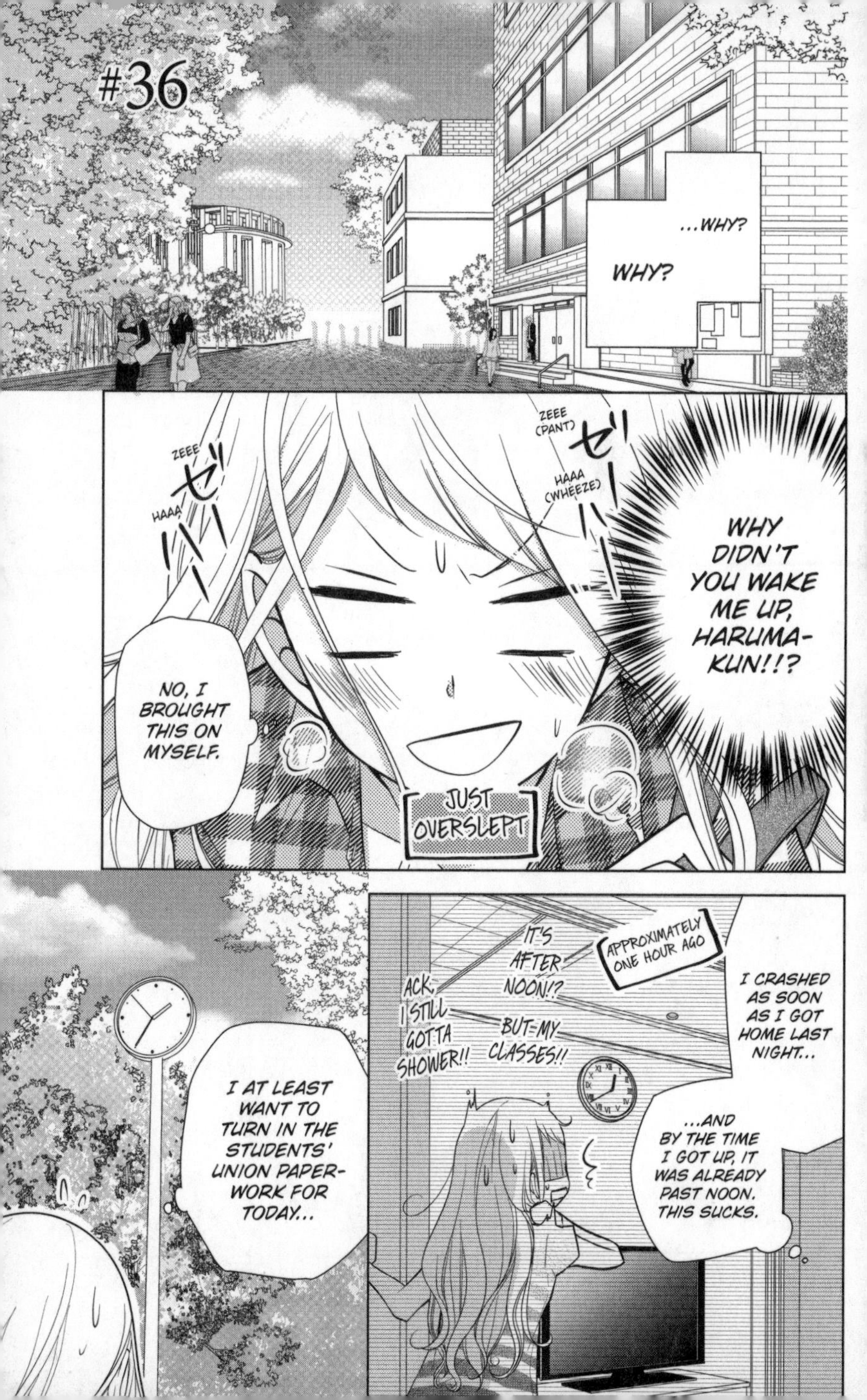
#36
...WHY?
WHY?
WHY DIDN'T YOU WAKE ME UP, HARUMA-KUN!!?
ZEEE (PANT)
HAAA (WHEEZE)
ZEEE
HAAA
JUST OVERSLEPT
NO, I BROUGHT THIS ON MYSELF.
I CRASHED AS SOON AS I GOT HOME LAST NIGHT...
APPROXIMATELY ONE HOUR AGO
IT'S AFTER NOON!?
BUT MY CLASSES!!
ACK, I STILL GOTTA SHOWER!!
...AND BY THE TIME I GOT UP, IT WAS ALREADY PAST NOON. THIS SUCKS.
I AT LEAST WANT TO TURN IN THE STUDENTS' UNION PAPER-WORK FOR TODAY...

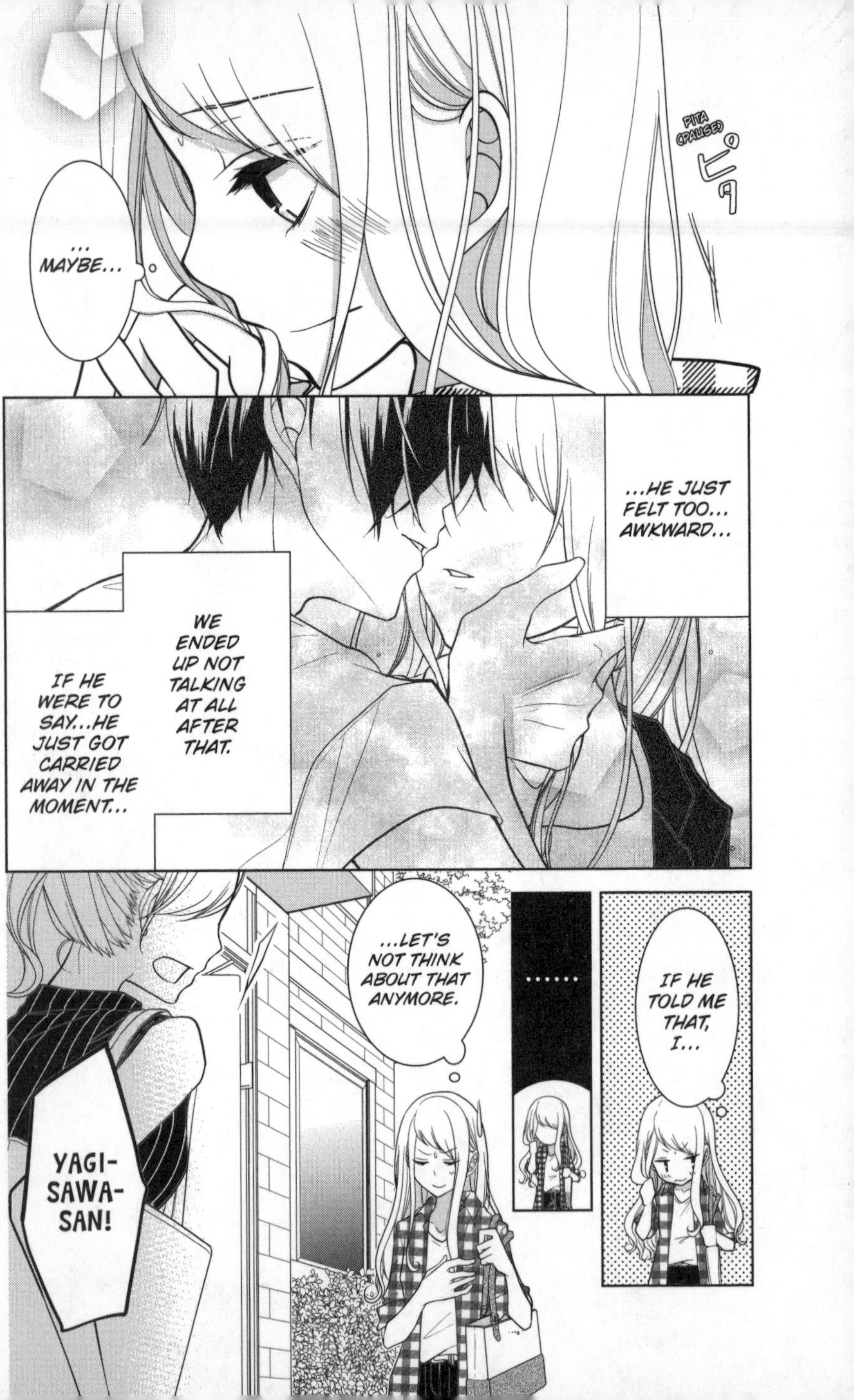
PITA (PAUSE)
ピタ
...MAYBE...
...HE JUST FELT TOO... AWKWARD...
WE ENDED UP NOT TALKING AT ALL AFTER THAT.
IF HE WERE TO SAY...HE JUST GOT CARRIED AWAY IN THE MOMENT...
IF HE TOLD ME THAT, I...
......
...LET'S NOT THINK ABOUT THAT ANYMORE.
YAGI-SAWA-SAN!

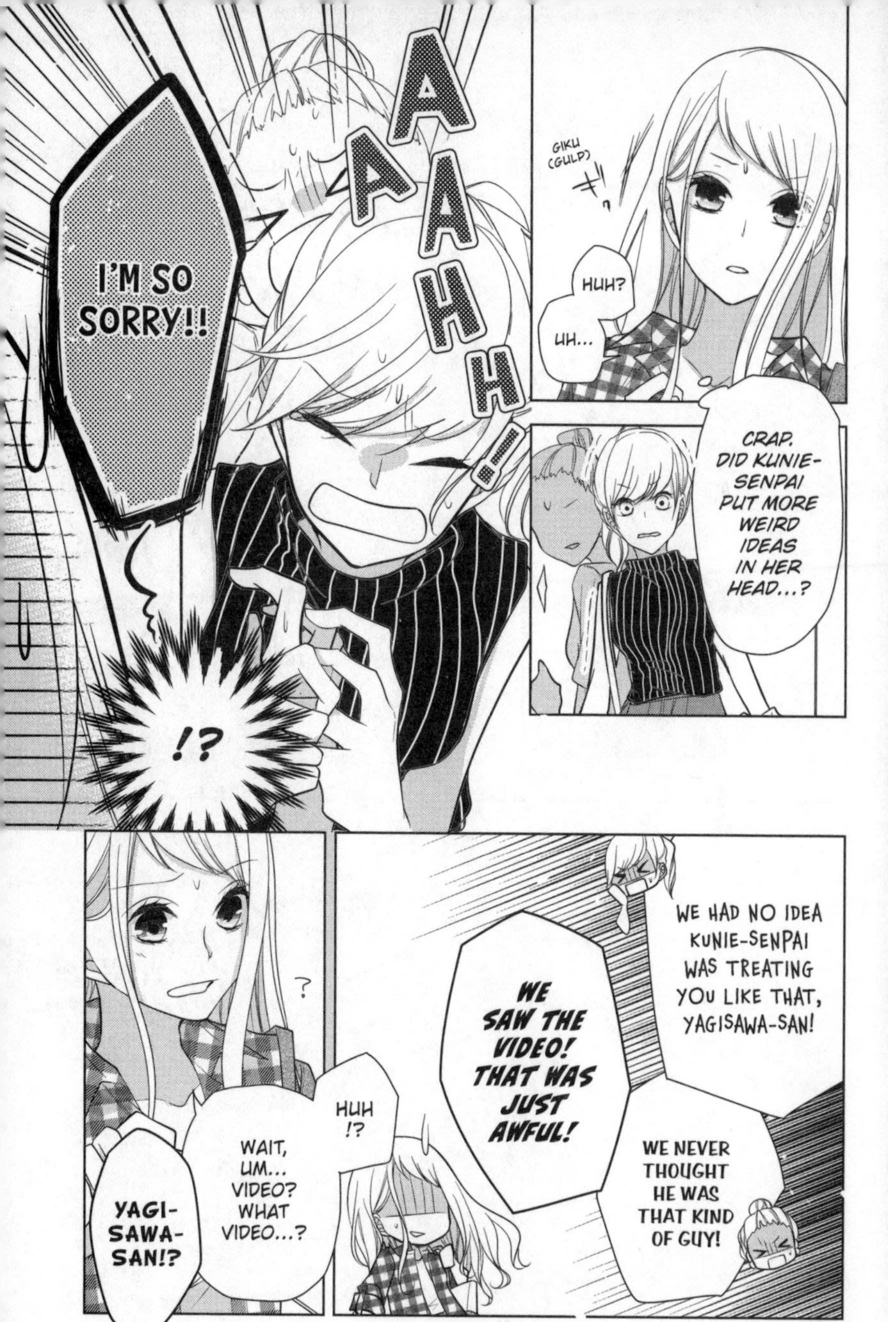
GIKU (GULP)
HUH?
UH...
CRAP. DID KUNIE-SENPAI PUT MORE WEIRD IDEAS IN HER HEAD...?
AAAHH!!
I'M SO SORRY!!
!?
WE HAD NO IDEA KUNIE-SENPAI WAS TREATING YOU LIKE THAT, YAGISAWA-SAN!
WE SAW THE VIDEO! THAT WAS JUST AWFUL!
WE NEVER THOUGHT HE WAS THAT KIND OF GUY!
HUH !?
?
WAIT, UM... VIDEO? WHAT VIDEO...?
YAGI-SAWA-SAN!?

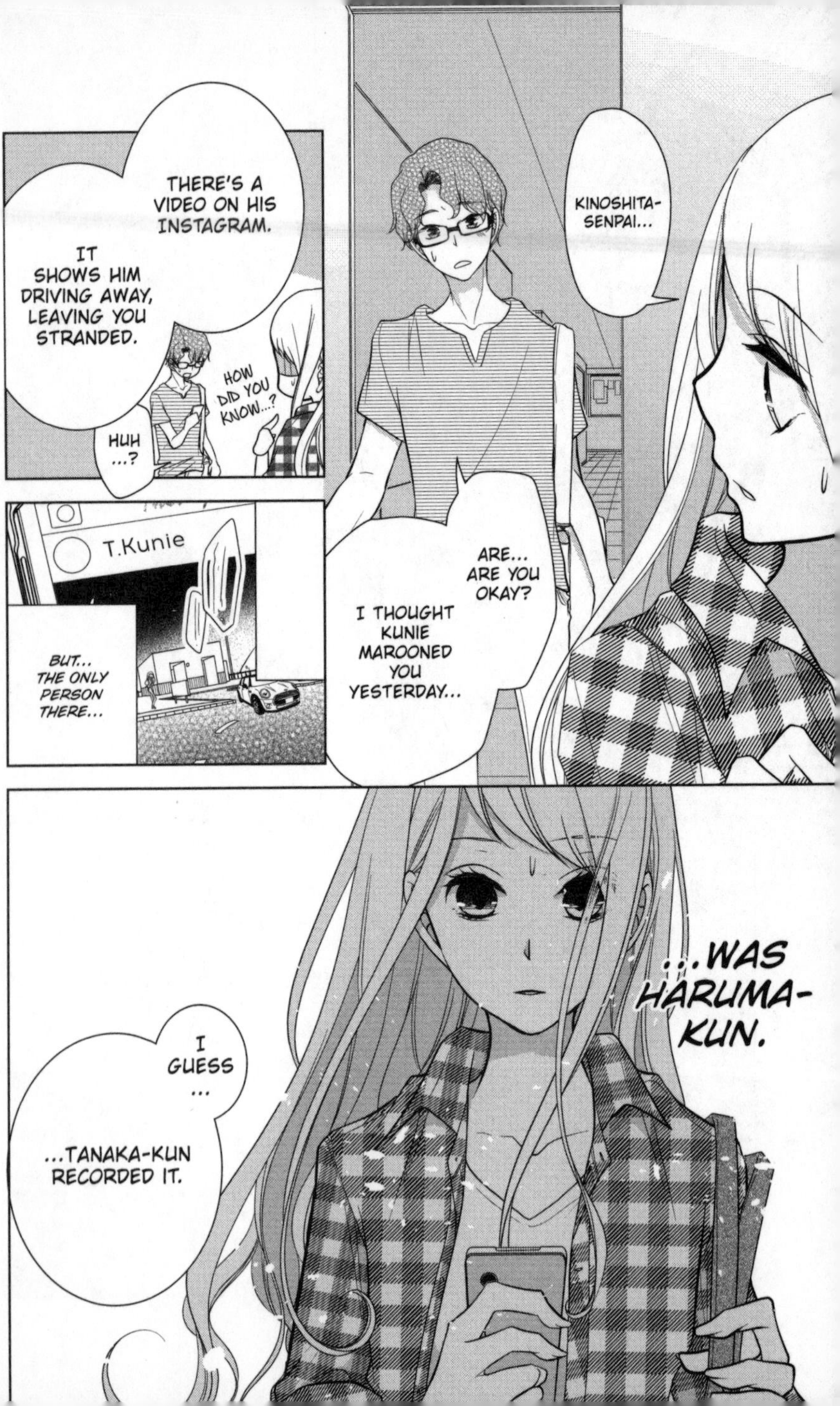
KINOSHITA-SENPAI...
ARE... ARE YOU OKAY?
I THOUGHT KUNIE MAROONED YOU YESTERDAY...
THERE'S A VIDEO ON HIS INSTAGRAM.
IT SHOWS HIM DRIVING AWAY, LEAVING YOU STRANDED.
HOW DID YOU KNOW...?
HUH ...?
T.Kunie
BUT... THE ONLY PERSON THERE...
...WAS HARUMA-KUN.
I GUESS ...
...TANAKA-KUN RECORDED IT.

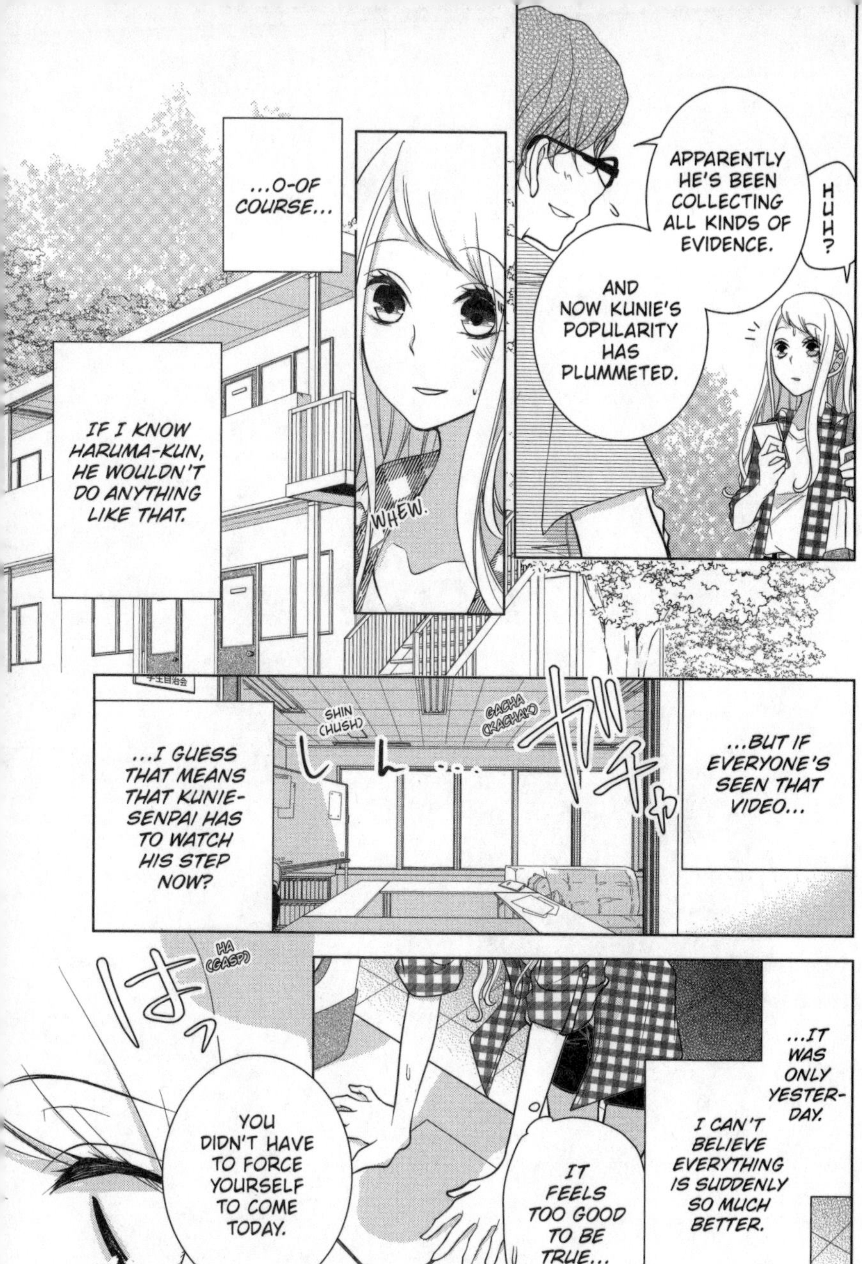
APPARENTLY HE'S BEEN COLLECTING ALL KINDS OF EVIDENCE.
HUH?
AND NOW KUNIE'S POPULARITY HAS PLUMMETED.
...O-OF COURSE...
WHEW.
IF I KNOW HARUMA-KUN, HE WOULDN'T DO ANYTHING LIKE THAT.
...BUT IF EVERYONE'S SEEN THAT VIDEO...
GACHA (KACHAK)
SHIN (HUSH)
...I GUESS THAT MEANS THAT KUNIE-SENPAI HAS TO WATCH HIS STEP NOW?
...IT WAS ONLY YESTERDAY.
I CAN'T BELIEVE EVERYTHING IS SUDDENLY SO MUCH BETTER.
IT FEELS TOO GOOD TO BE TRUE...
HA (GASP)
YOU DIDN'T HAVE TO FORCE YOURSELF TO COME TODAY.

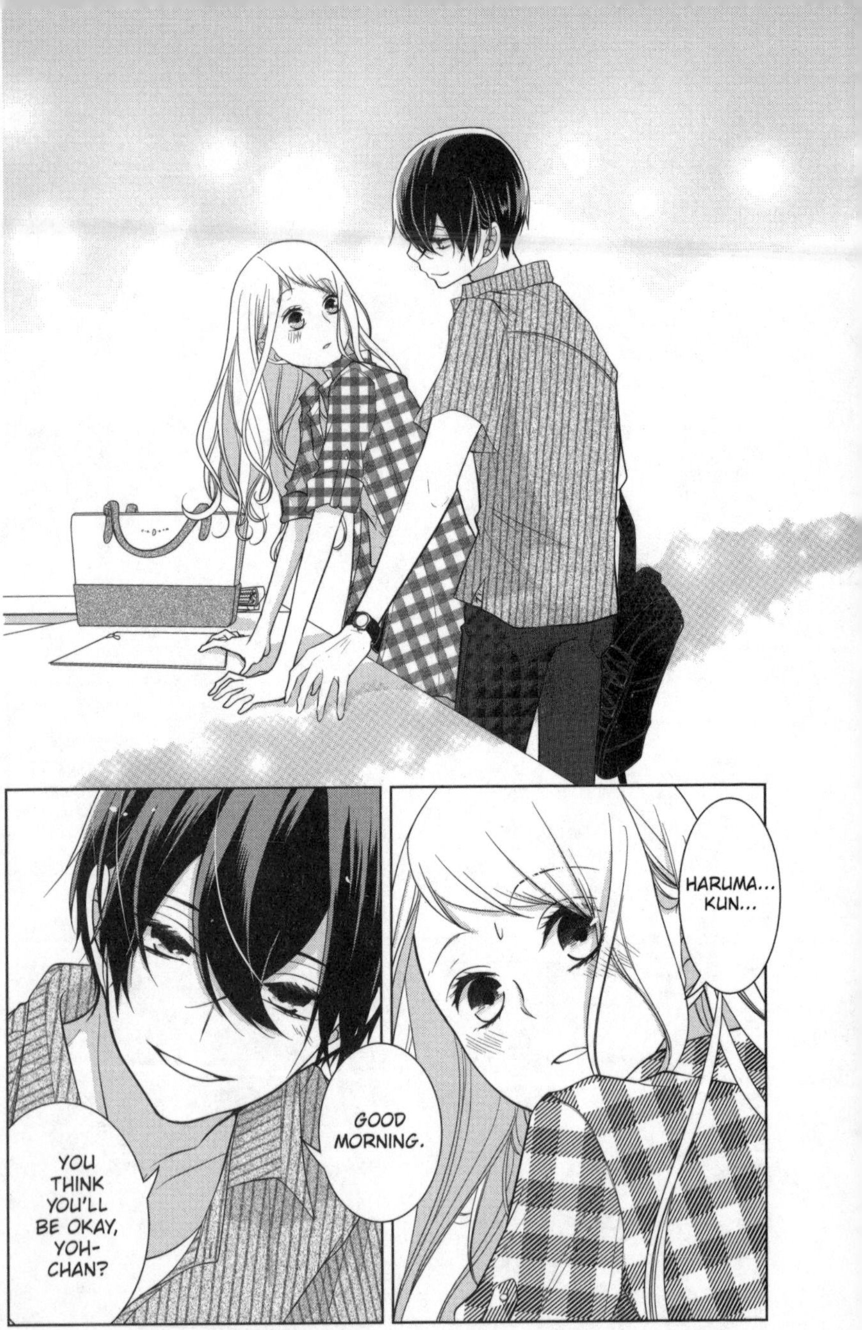
HARUMA... KUN...
GOOD MORNING.
YOU THINK YOU'LL BE OKAY, YOH-CHAN?

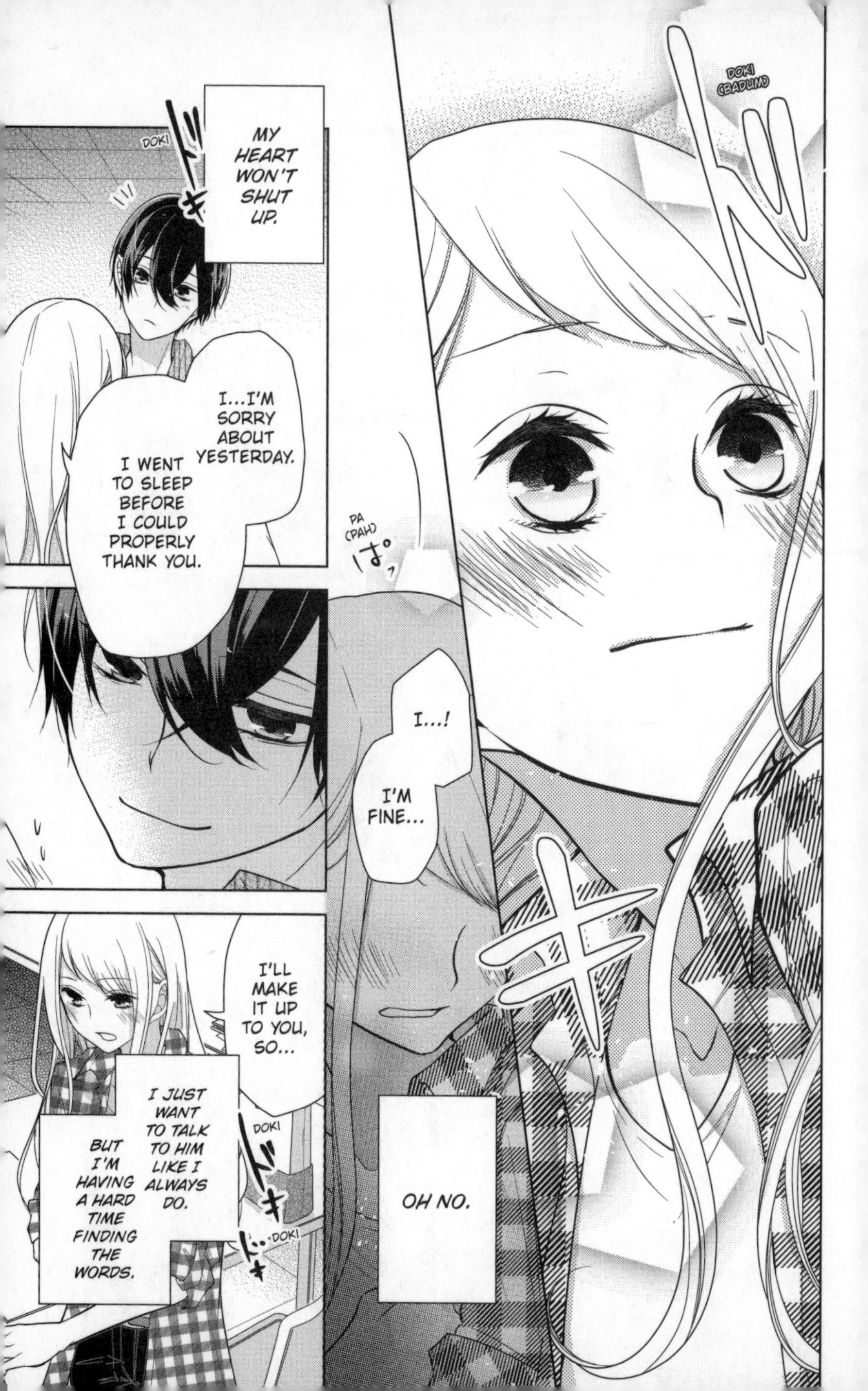
DOKI (BADUMP)
PA (PAH)
ぱっ
I...!
I'M FINE...
OH NO.
DOKI
MY HEART WON'T SHUT UP.
I...I'M SORRY ABOUT YESTERDAY.
I WENT TO SLEEP BEFORE I COULD PROPERLY THANK YOU.
I'LL MAKE IT UP TO YOU, SO...
DOKI
DOKI
I JUST WANT TO TALK TO HIM LIKE I ALWAYS DO.
BUT I'M HAVING A HARD TIME FINDING THE WORDS.

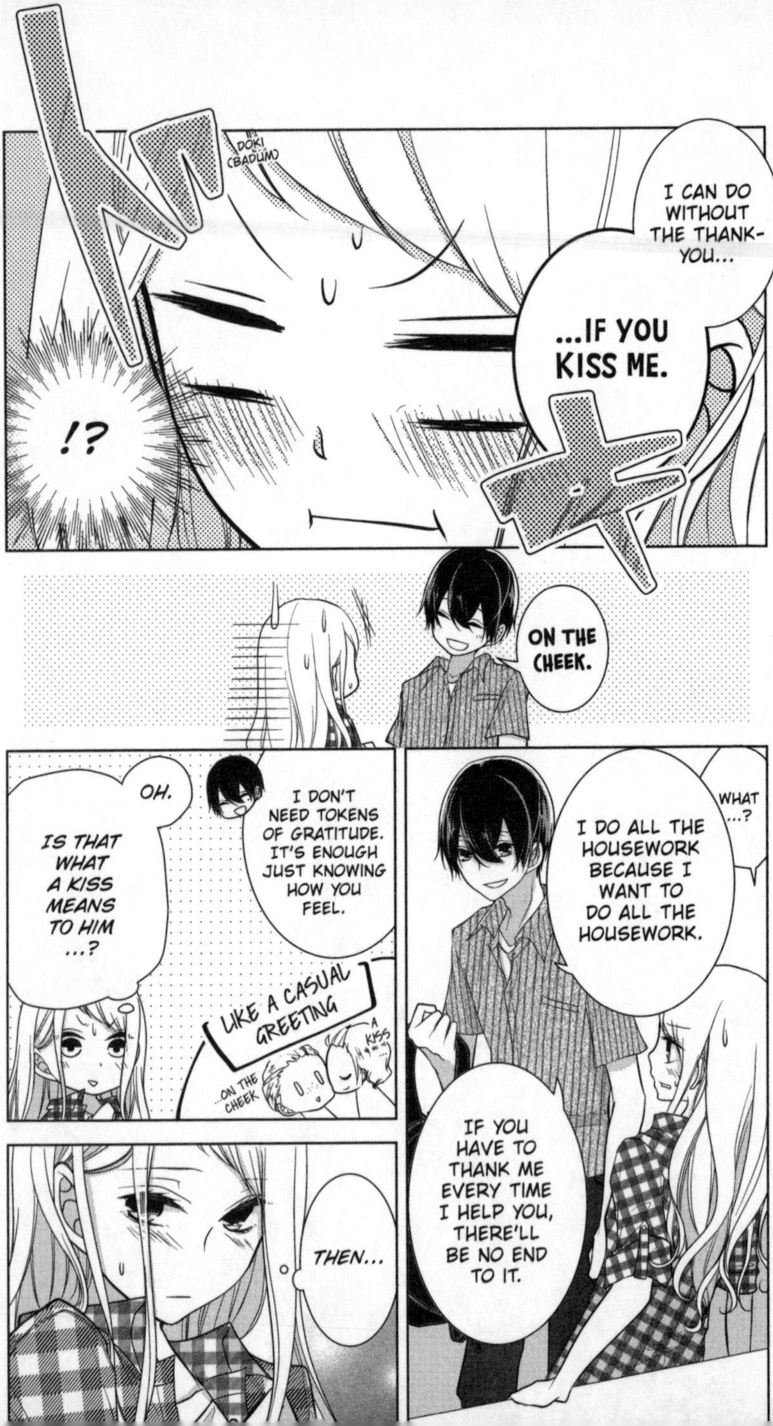
I CAN DO WITHOUT THE THANK-YOU...
...IF YOU KISS ME.
DOKI (BADUM)
!?
ON THE CHEEK.
WHAT ...?
I DO ALL THE HOUSEWORK BECAUSE I WANT TO DO ALL THE HOUSEWORK.
IF YOU HAVE TO THANK ME EVERY TIME I HELP YOU, THERE'LL BE NO END TO IT.
I DON'T NEED TOKENS OF GRATITUDE. IT'S ENOUGH JUST KNOWING HOW YOU FEEL.
OH.
IS THAT WHAT A KISS MEANS TO HIM ...?
LIKE A CASUAL GREETING
A KISS
...ON THE CHEEK
THEN...

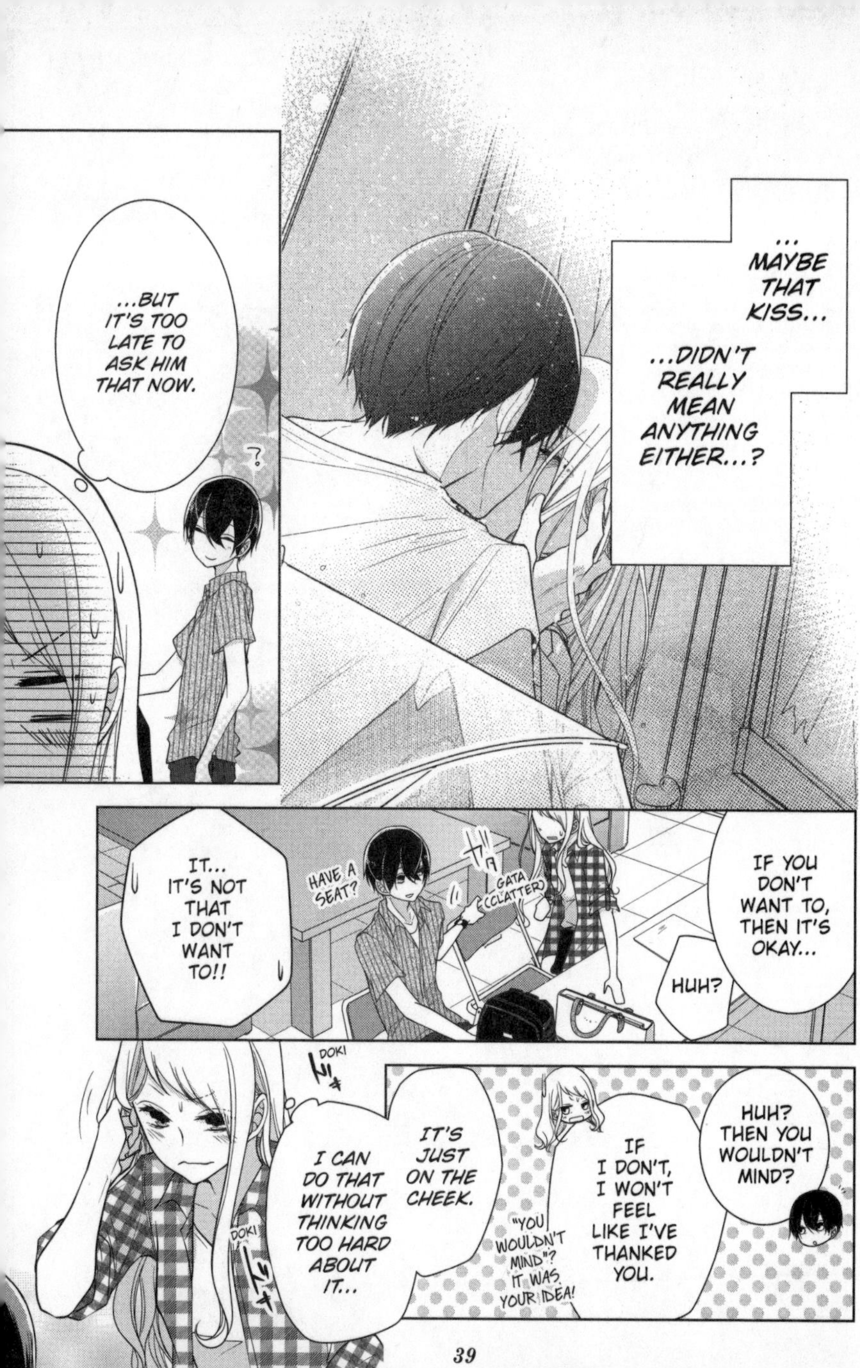
...MAYBE THAT KISS...
...DIDN'T REALLY MEAN ANYTHING EITHER...?
...BUT IT'S TOO LATE TO ASK HIM THAT NOW.
?
IF YOU DON'T WANT TO, THEN IT'S OKAY...
HUH?
GATA (CLATTER)
HAVE A SEAT?
IT... IT'S NOT THAT I DON'T WANT TO!!
HUH? THEN YOU WOULDN'T MIND?
IF I DON'T, I WON'T FEEL LIKE I'VE THANKED YOU.
"YOU WOULDN'T MIND"? IT WAS YOUR IDEA!
DOKI
IT'S JUST ON THE CHEEK.
I CAN DO THAT WITHOUT THINKING TOO HARD ABOUT IT...
DOKI

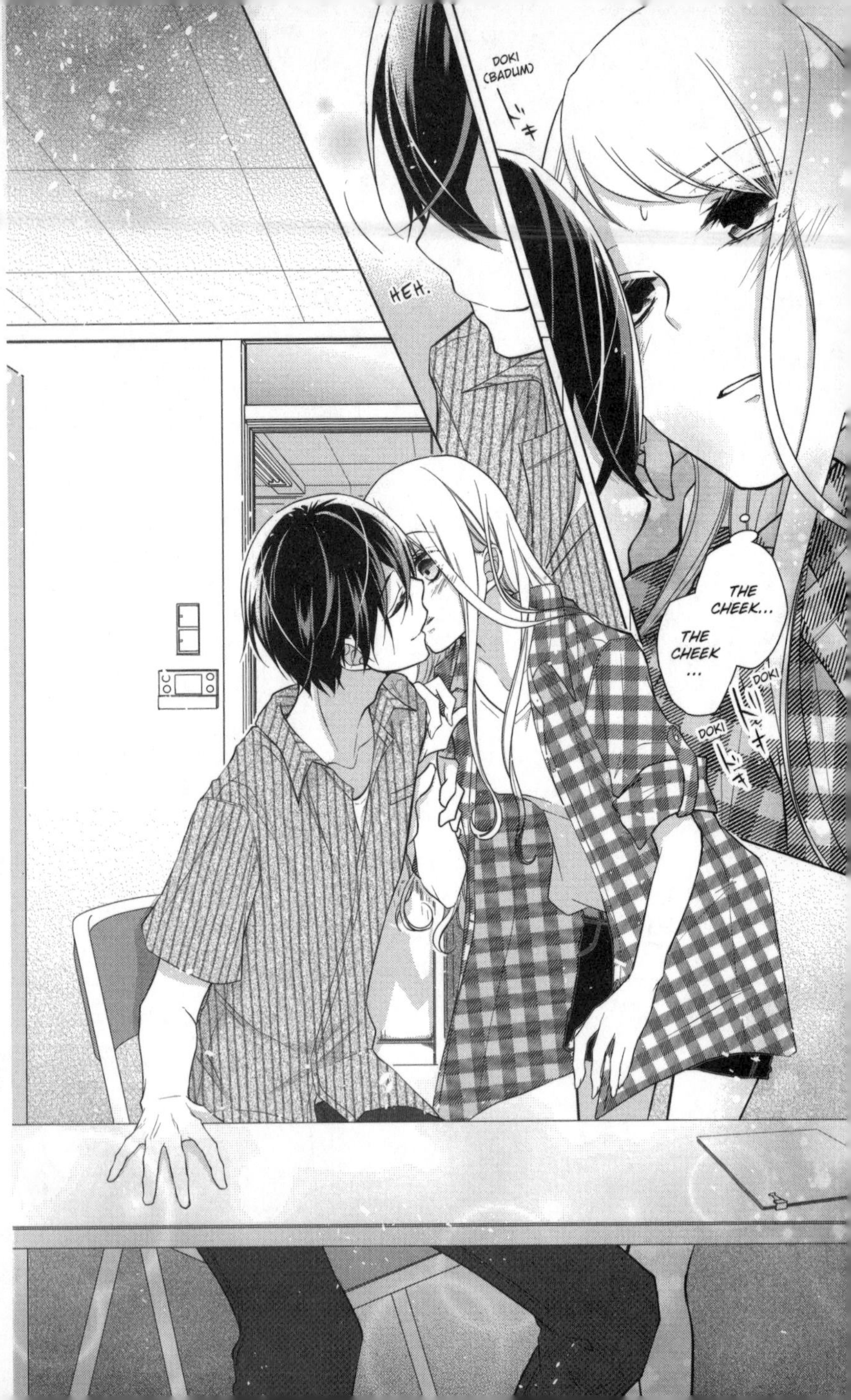
DOKI
(BADUM)
HEH.
THE CHEEK...
THE CHEEK
...
DOKI
DOKI

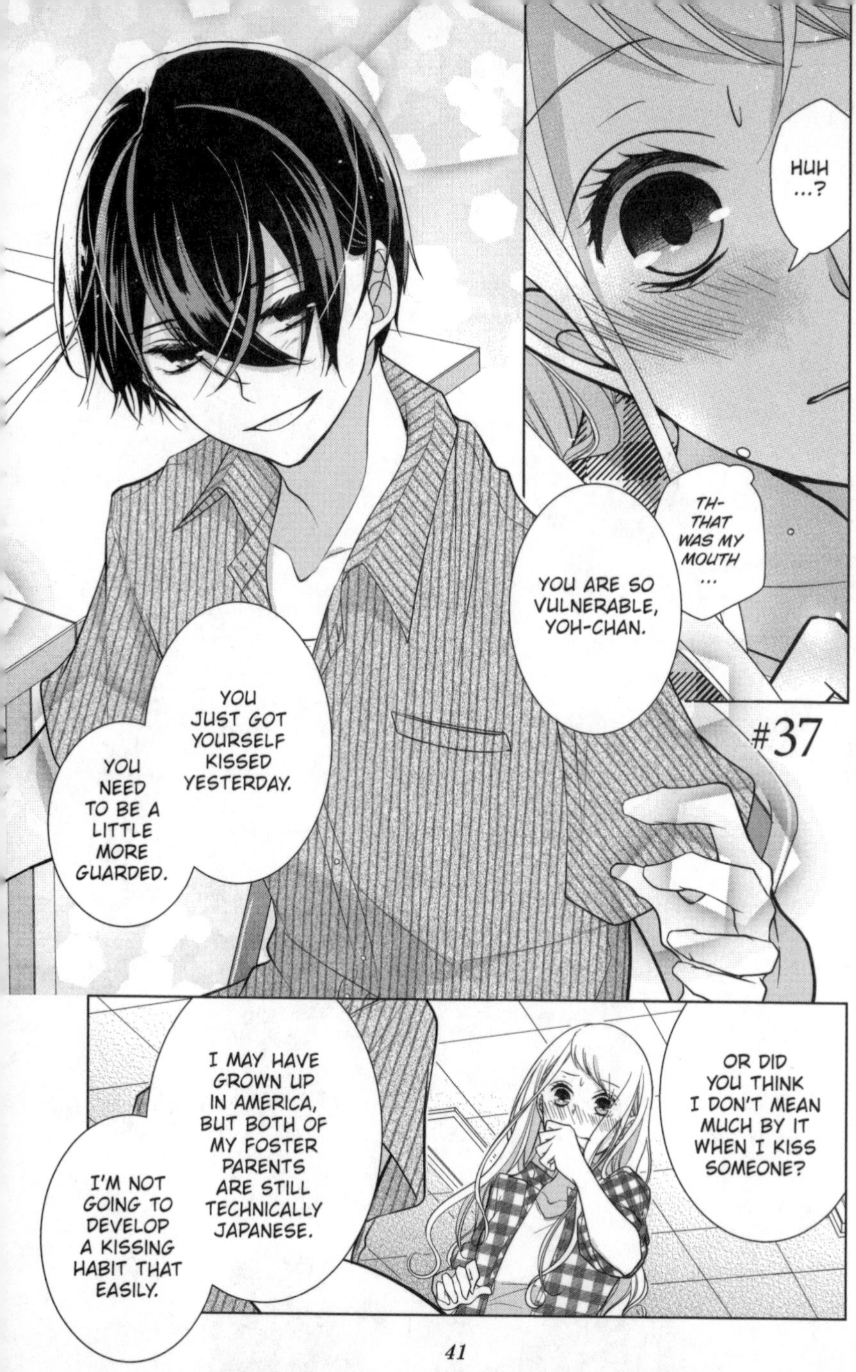
HUH ...?
TH-THAT WAS MY MOUTH ...
YOU ARE SO VULNERABLE, YOH-CHAN.
YOU JUST GOT YOURSELF KISSED YESTERDAY.
YOU NEED TO BE A LITTLE MORE GUARDED.
#37
OR DID YOU THINK I DON'T MEAN MUCH BY IT WHEN I KISS SOMEONE?
I MAY HAVE GROWN UP IN AMERICA, BUT BOTH OF MY FOSTER PARENTS ARE STILL TECHNICALLY JAPANESE.
I'M NOT GOING TO DEVELOP A KISSING HABIT THAT EASILY.

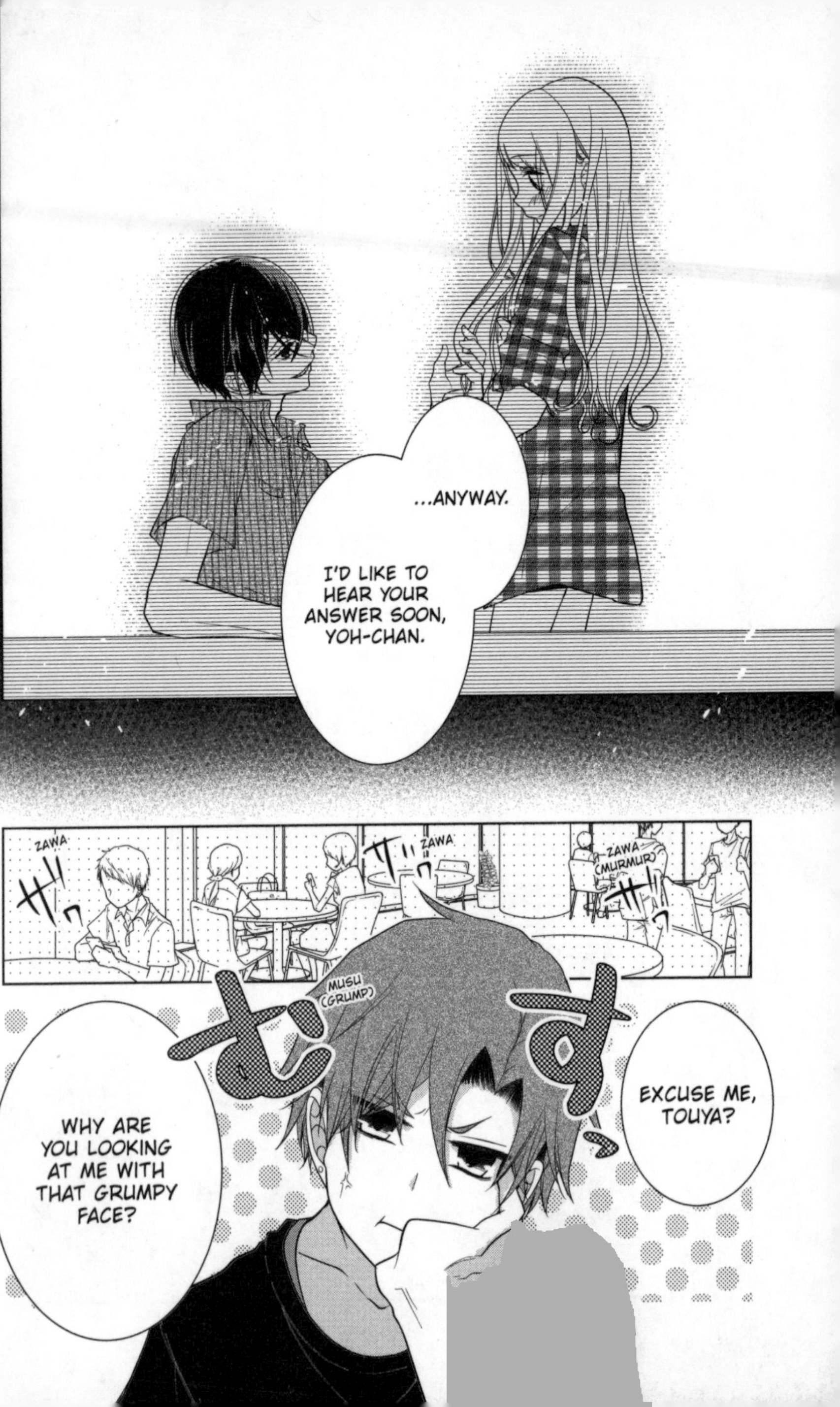
...ANYWAY.
I'D LIKE TO HEAR YOUR ANSWER SOON, YOH-CHAN.
ZAWA (MURMUR)
ZAWA
ZAWA
MUSU (GRUMP)
EXCUSE ME, TOUYA?
WHY ARE YOU LOOKING AT ME WITH THAT GRUMPY FACE?

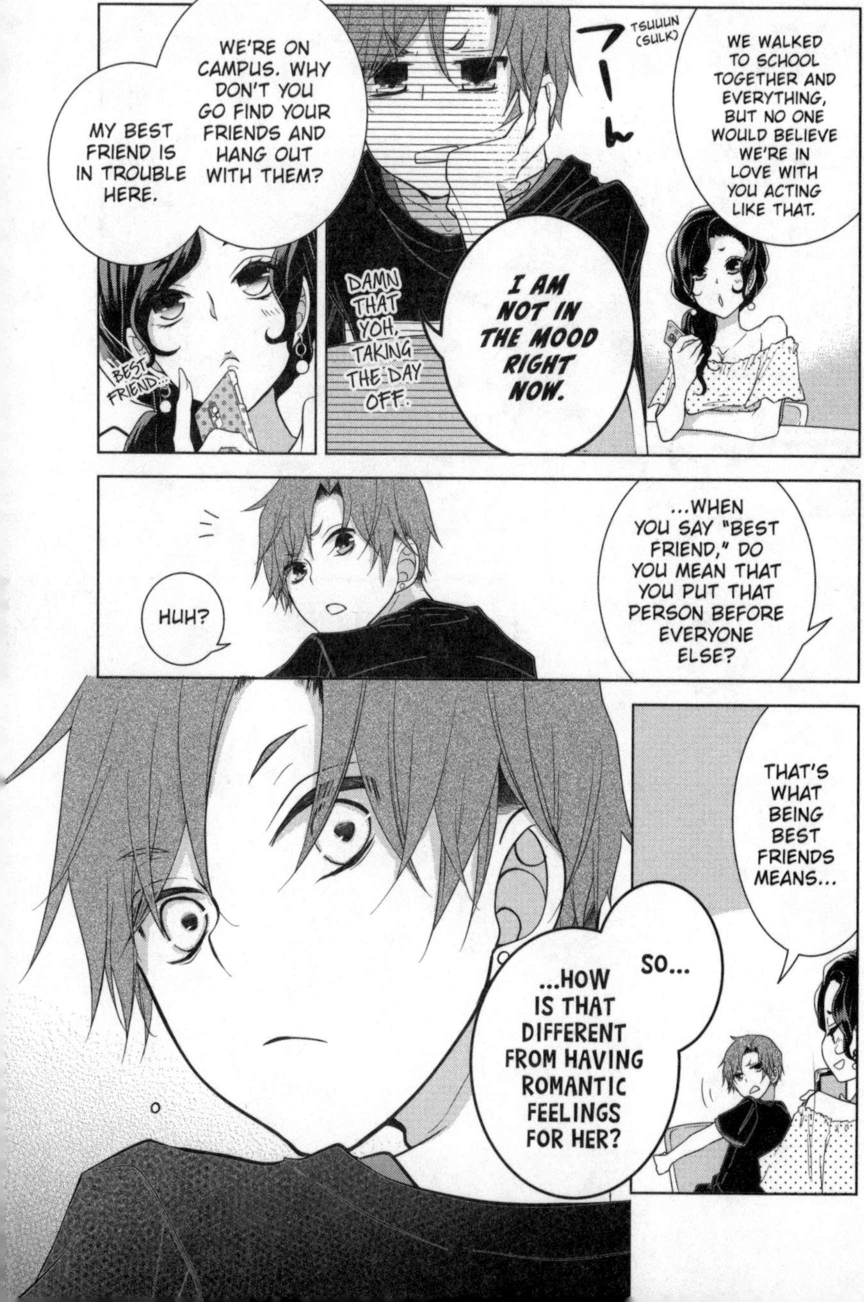
TSUUUN (SULK)
WE WALKED TO SCHOOL TOGETHER AND EVERYTHING, BUT NO ONE WOULD BELIEVE WE'RE IN LOVE WITH YOU ACTING LIKE THAT.
I AM NOT IN THE MOOD RIGHT NOW.
DAMN THAT YOH, TAKING THE DAY OFF.
WE'RE ON CAMPUS. WHY DON'T YOU GO FIND YOUR FRIENDS AND HANG OUT WITH THEM?
MY BEST FRIEND IS IN TROUBLE HERE.
BEST FRIEND...
...WHEN YOU SAY "BEST FRIEND," DO YOU MEAN THAT YOU PUT THAT PERSON BEFORE EVERYONE ELSE?
HUH?
THAT'S WHAT BEING BEST FRIENDS MEANS...
SO...
...HOW IS THAT DIFFERENT FROM HAVING ROMANTIC FEELINGS FOR HER?

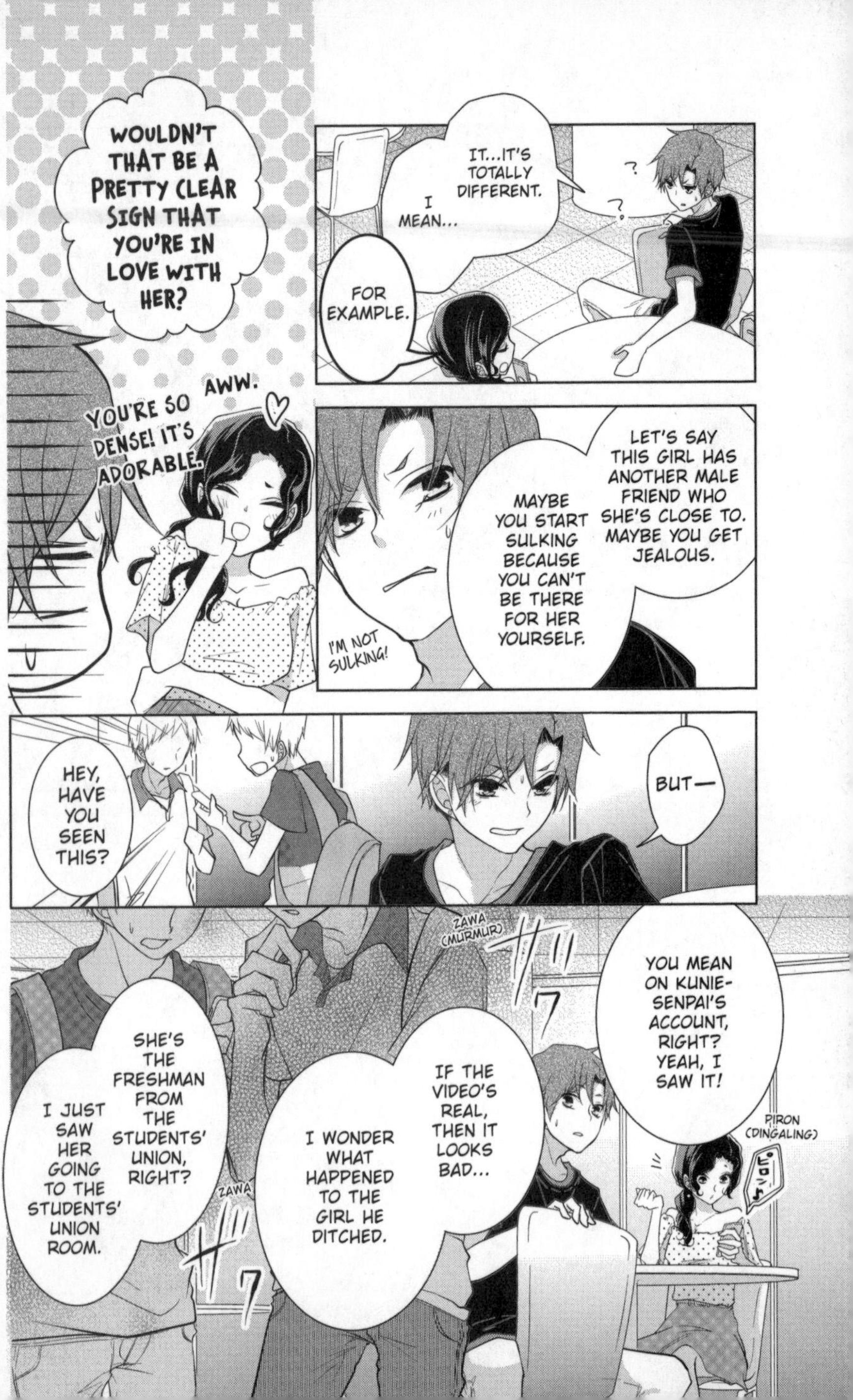
IT...IT'S TOTALLY DIFFERENT.
I MEAN...
FOR EXAMPLE.
LET'S SAY THIS GIRL HAS ANOTHER MALE FRIEND WHO SHE'S CLOSE TO. MAYBE YOU GET JEALOUS.
MAYBE YOU START SULKING BECAUSE YOU CAN'T BE THERE FOR HER YOURSELF.
I'M NOT SULKING!
WOULDN'T THAT BE A PRETTY CLEAR SIGN THAT YOU'RE IN LOVE WITH HER?
AWW.
YOU'RE SO DENSE! IT'S ADORABLE.
BUT—
HEY, HAVE YOU SEEN THIS?
ZAWA (MURMUR)
YOU MEAN ON KUNIE-SENPAI'S ACCOUNT, RIGHT? YEAH, I SAW IT!
PIRON (DINGALING)
IF THE VIDEO'S REAL, THEN IT LOOKS BAD...
I WONDER WHAT HAPPENED TO THE GIRL HE DITCHED.
SHE'S THE FRESHMAN FROM THE STUDENTS' UNION, RIGHT?
ZAWA
I JUST SAW HER GOING TO THE STUDENTS' UNION ROOM.

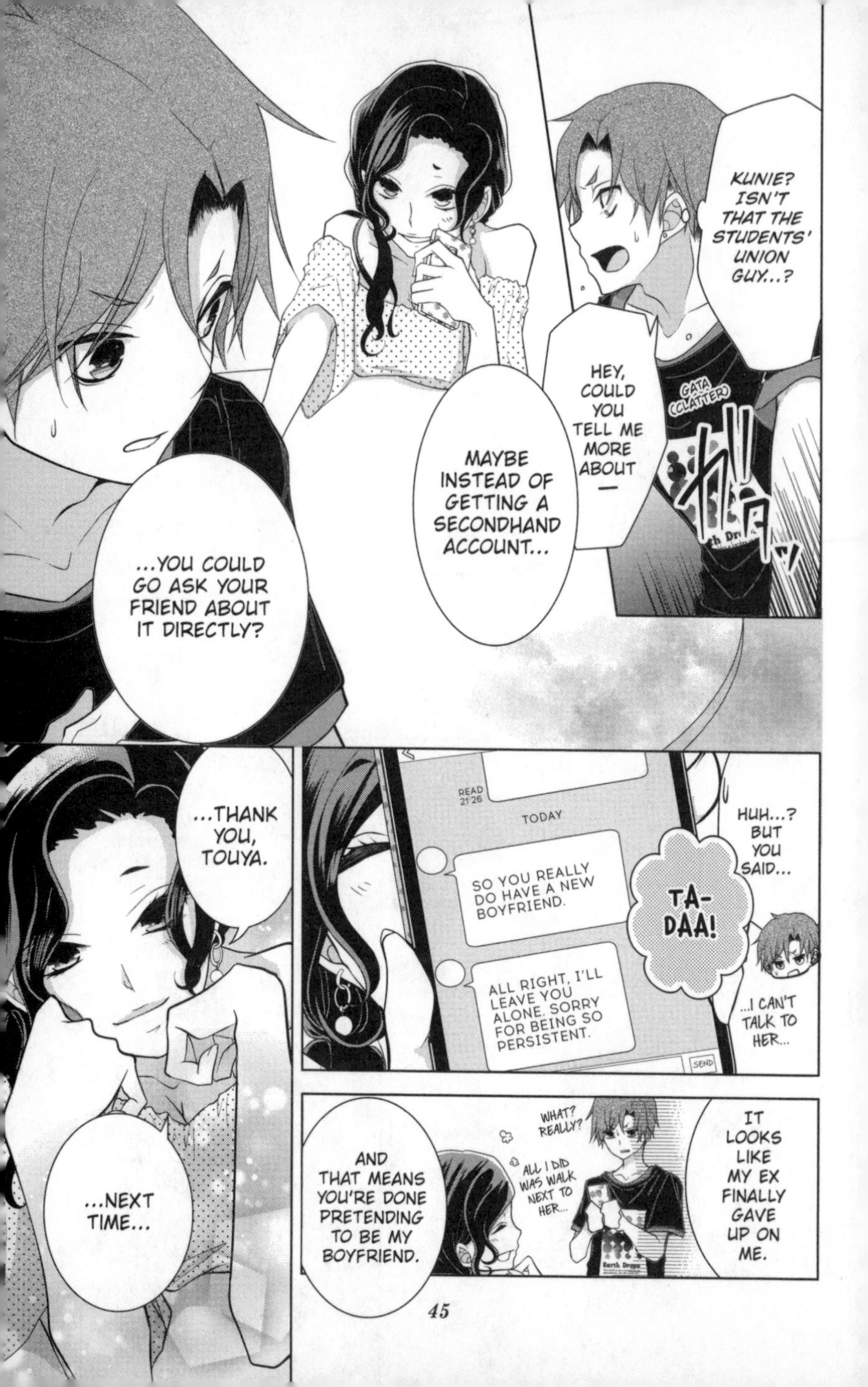
KUNIE? ISN'T THAT THE STUDENTS' UNION GUY...?
HEY, COULD YOU TELL ME MORE ABOUT—
GATA (CLATTER)
MAYBE INSTEAD OF GETTING A SECONDHAND ACCOUNT...
...YOU COULD GO ASK YOUR FRIEND ABOUT IT DIRECTLY?
HUH...? BUT YOU SAID...
READ 21:26
TODAY
SO YOU REALLY DO HAVE A NEW BOYFRIEND.
ALL RIGHT, I'LL LEAVE YOU ALONE. SORRY FOR BEING SO PERSISTENT.
SEND
TA-DAA!
...I CAN'T TALK TO HER...
IT LOOKS LIKE MY EX FINALLY GAVE UP ON ME.
WHAT? REALLY?
ALL I DID WAS WALK NEXT TO HER...
AND THAT MEANS YOU'RE DONE PRETENDING TO BE MY BOYFRIEND.
...THANK YOU, TOUYA.
...NEXT TIME...

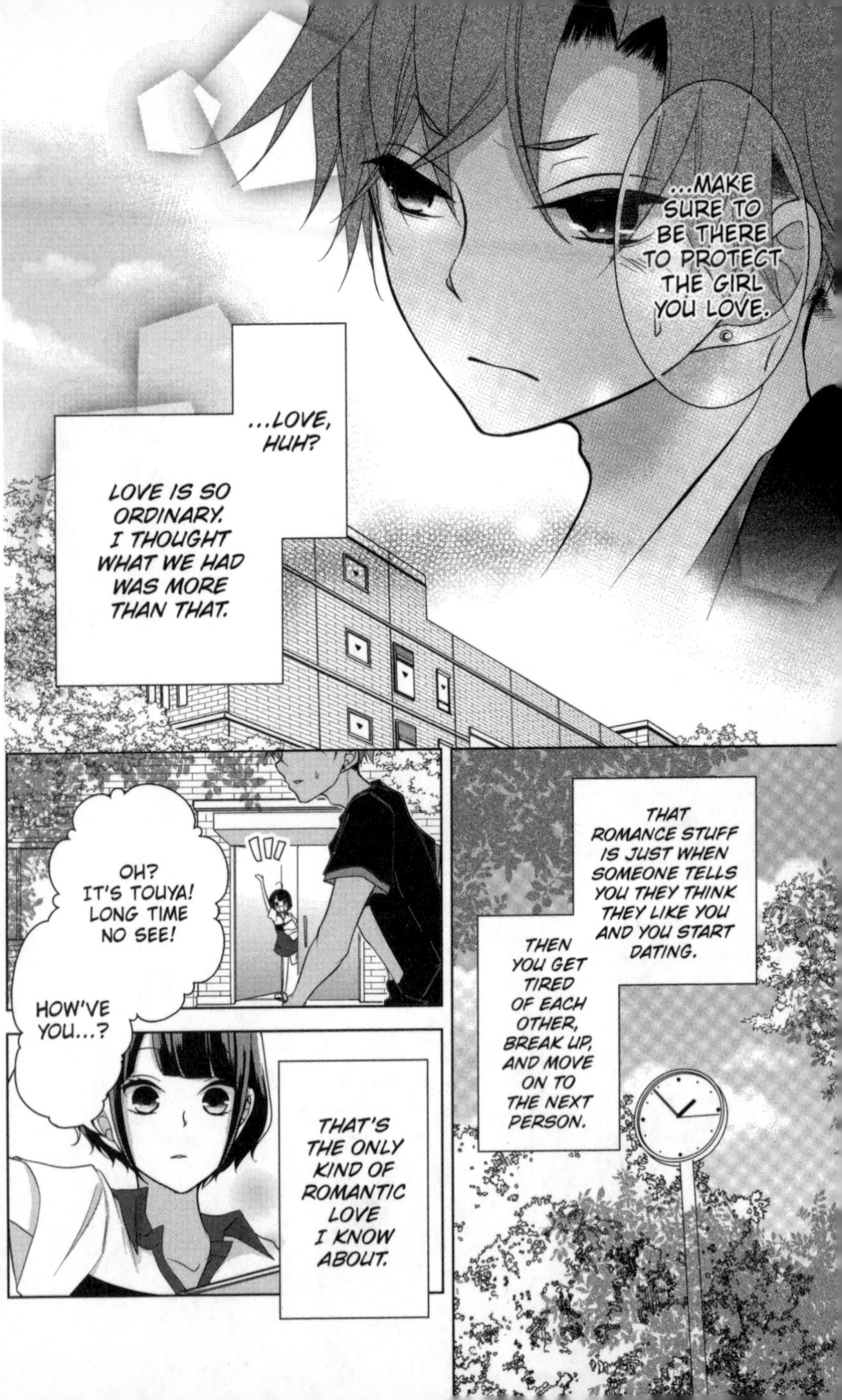
...MAKE SURE TO BE THERE TO PROTECT THE GIRL YOU LOVE.
...LOVE, HUH?
LOVE IS SO ORDINARY. I THOUGHT WHAT WE HAD WAS MORE THAN THAT.
THAT ROMANCE STUFF IS JUST WHEN SOMEONE TELLS YOU THEY THINK THEY LIKE YOU AND YOU START DATING.
THEN YOU GET TIRED OF EACH OTHER, BREAK UP, AND MOVE ON TO THE NEXT PERSON.
OH? IT'S TOUYA! LONG TIME NO SEE!
HOW'VE YOU...?
THAT'S THE ONLY KIND OF ROMANTIC LOVE I KNOW ABOUT.

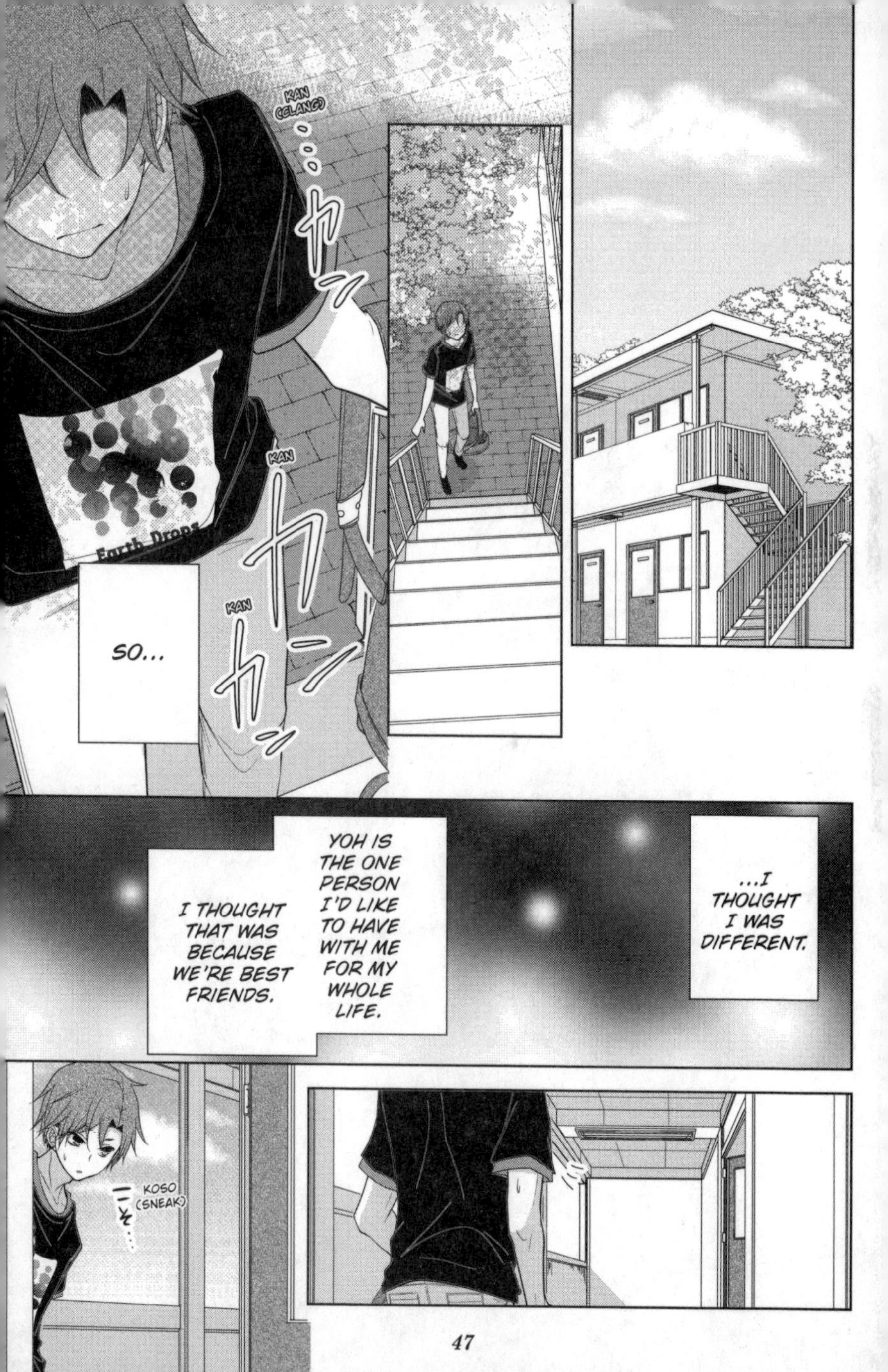
KAN (CLANG)
カッ
KAN
カーン
KAN
カッ
SO...
...I THOUGHT I WAS DIFFERENT.
YOH IS THE ONE PERSON I'D LIKE TO HAVE WITH ME FOR MY WHOLE LIFE.
I THOUGHT THAT WAS BECAUSE WE'RE BEST FRIENDS.
KOSO (SNEAK)
こそ...

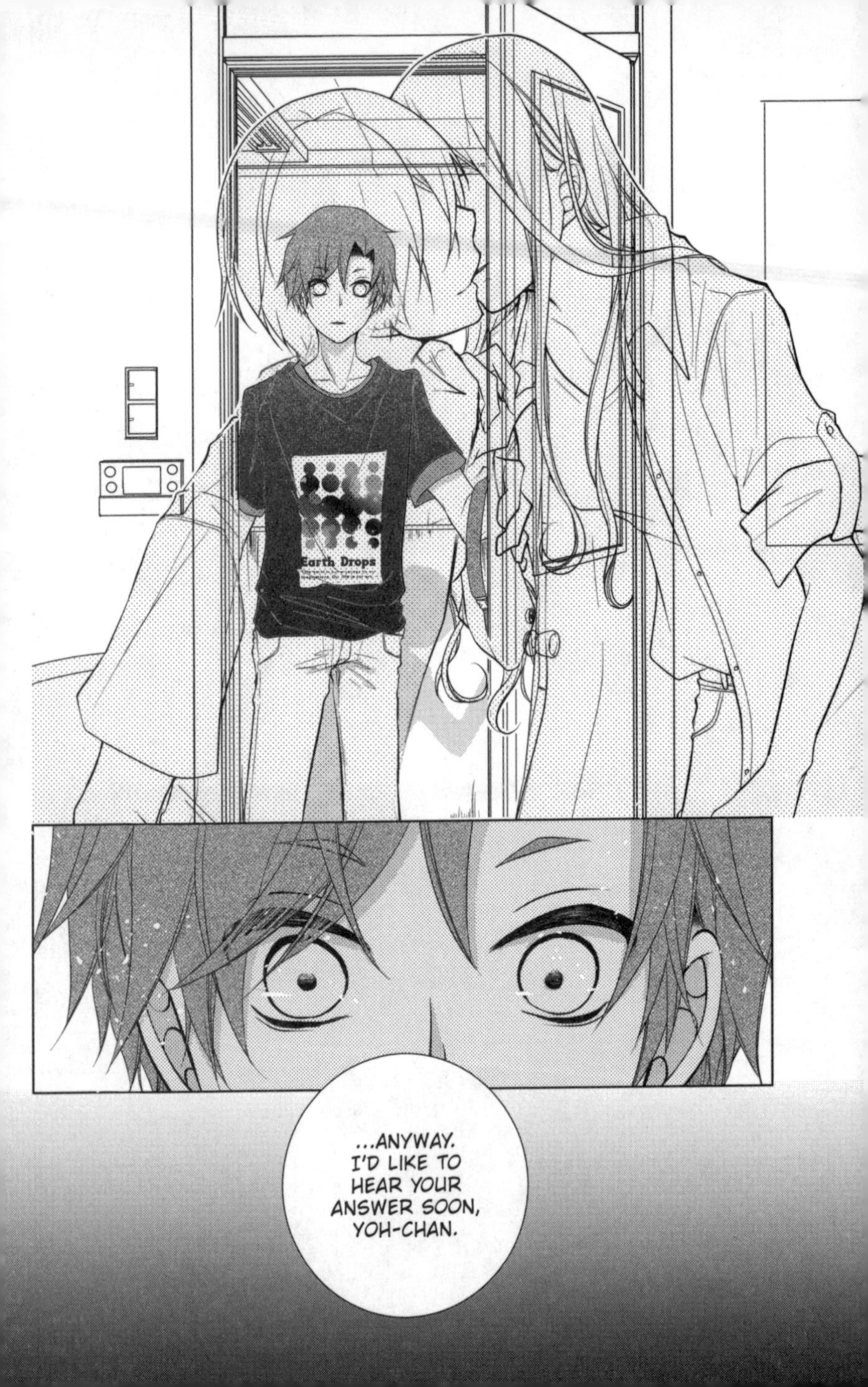
Earth Drops
...ANYWAY. I'D LIKE TO HEAR YOUR ANSWER SOON, YOH-CHAN.

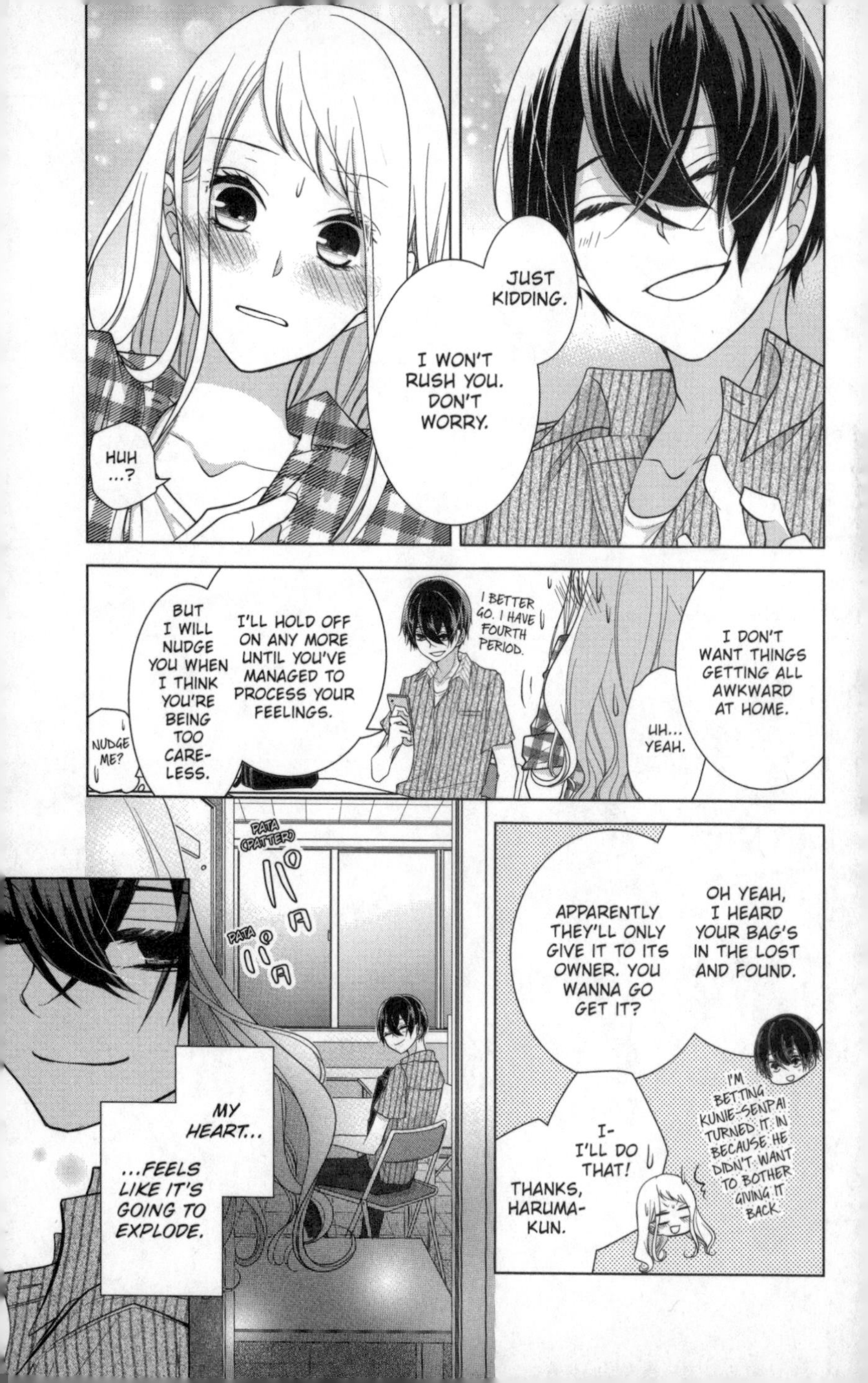
JUST KIDDING.
I WON'T RUSH YOU. DON'T WORRY.
HUH ...?
I DON'T WANT THINGS GETTING ALL AWKWARD AT HOME.
UH... YEAH.
I BETTER GO. I HAVE FOURTH PERIOD.
I'LL HOLD OFF ON ANY MORE UNTIL YOU'VE MANAGED TO PROCESS YOUR FEELINGS.
BUT I WILL NUDGE YOU WHEN I THINK YOU'RE BEING TOO CARELESS.
NUDGE ME?
OH YEAH, I HEARD YOUR BAG'S IN THE LOST AND FOUND.
APPARENTLY THEY'LL ONLY GIVE IT TO ITS OWNER. YOU WANNA GO GET IT?
I'M BETTING KUNIE-SENPAI TURNED IT IN BECAUSE HE DIDN'T WANT TO BOTHER GIVING IT BACK
I-I'LL DO THAT!
THANKS, HARUMA-KUN.
PATA (PATTER)
パタ
PATA
パタ
MY HEART...
...FEELS LIKE IT'S GOING TO EXPLODE.

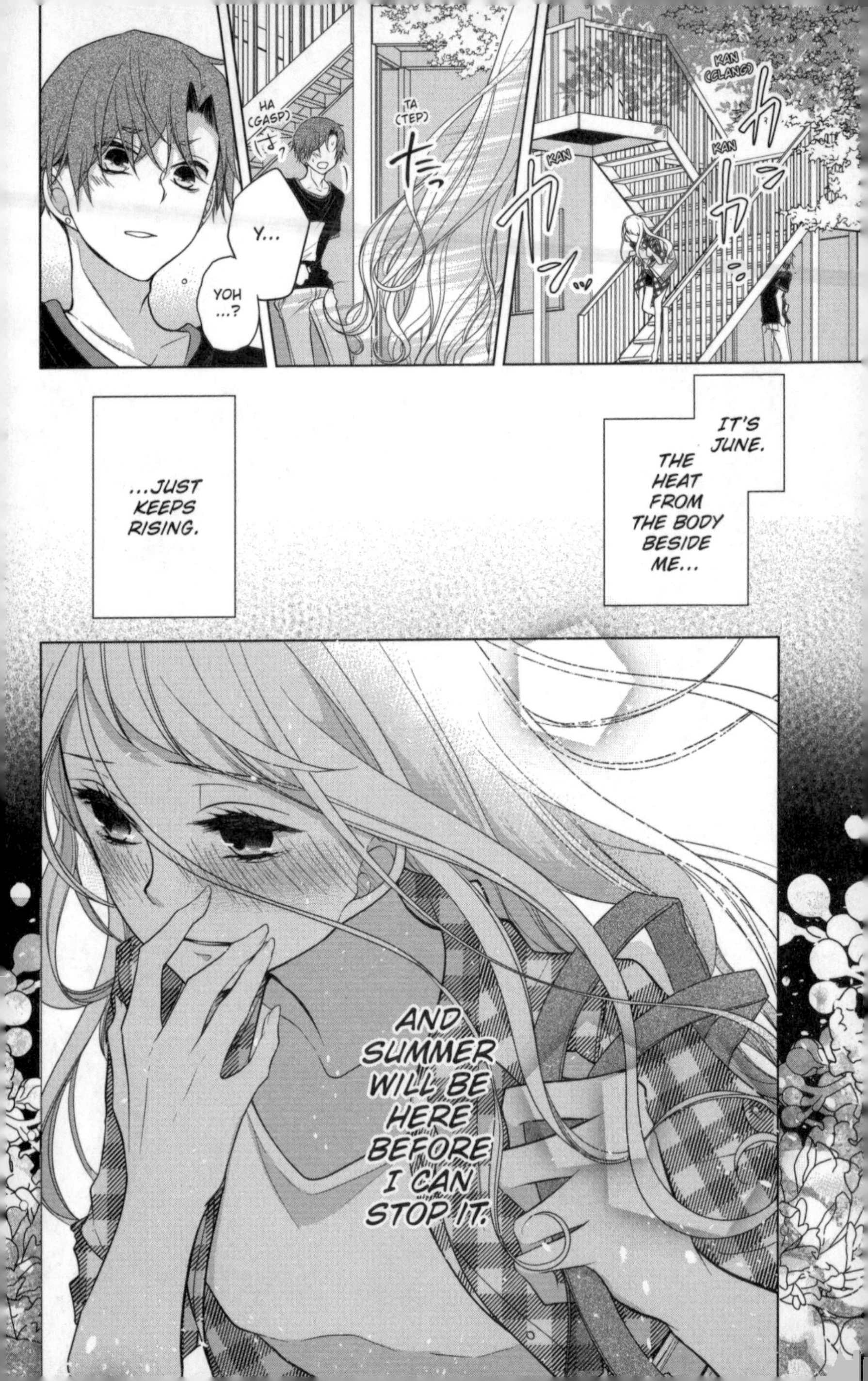
KAN (CLANG)
KAN
KAN
TA (TEP)
HA (GASP)
Y...
YOH ...?
IT'S JUNE.
THE HEAT FROM THE BODY BESIDE ME...
...JUST KEEPS RISING.
AND SUMMER WILL BE HERE BEFORE I CAN STOP IT.

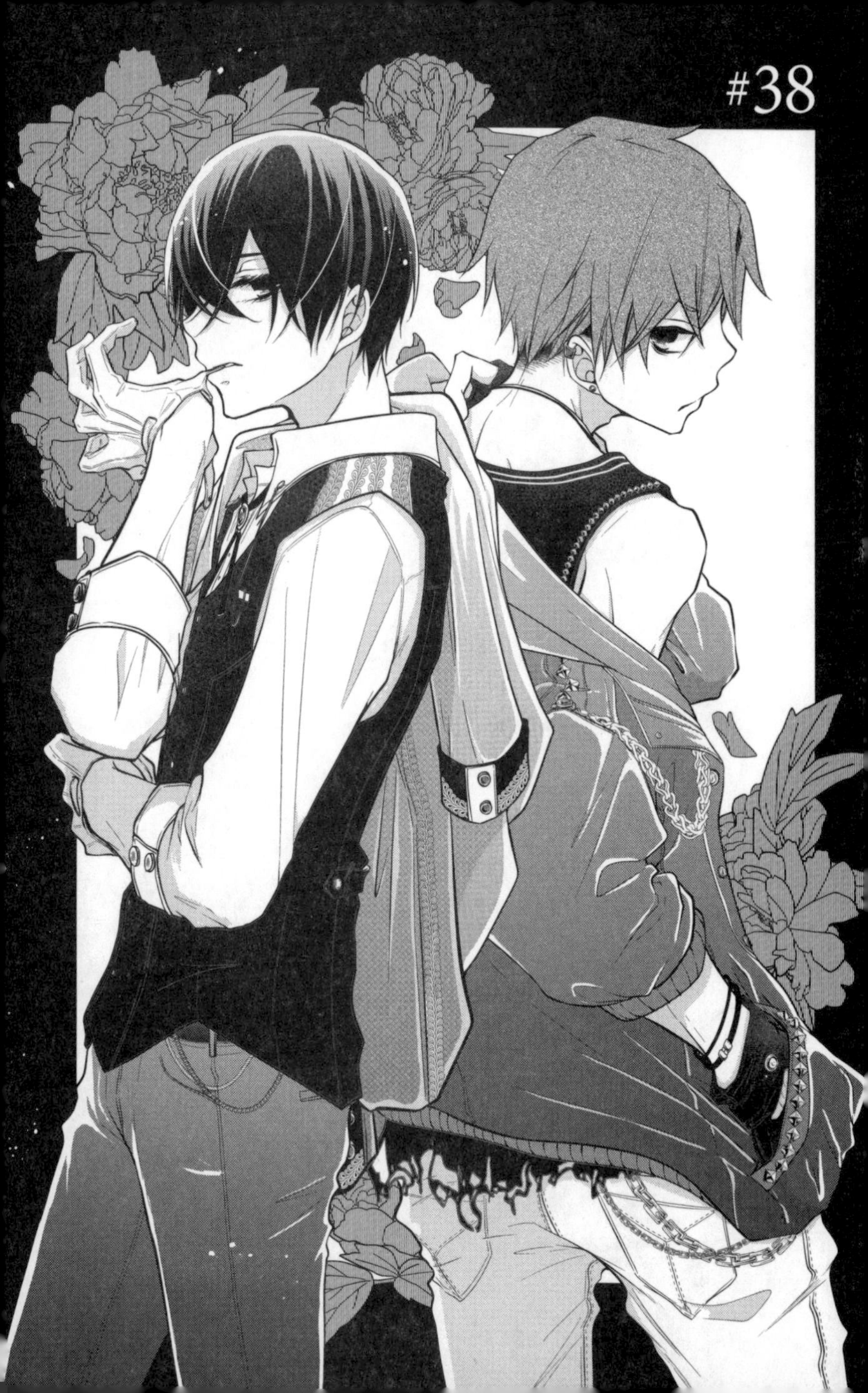
#38

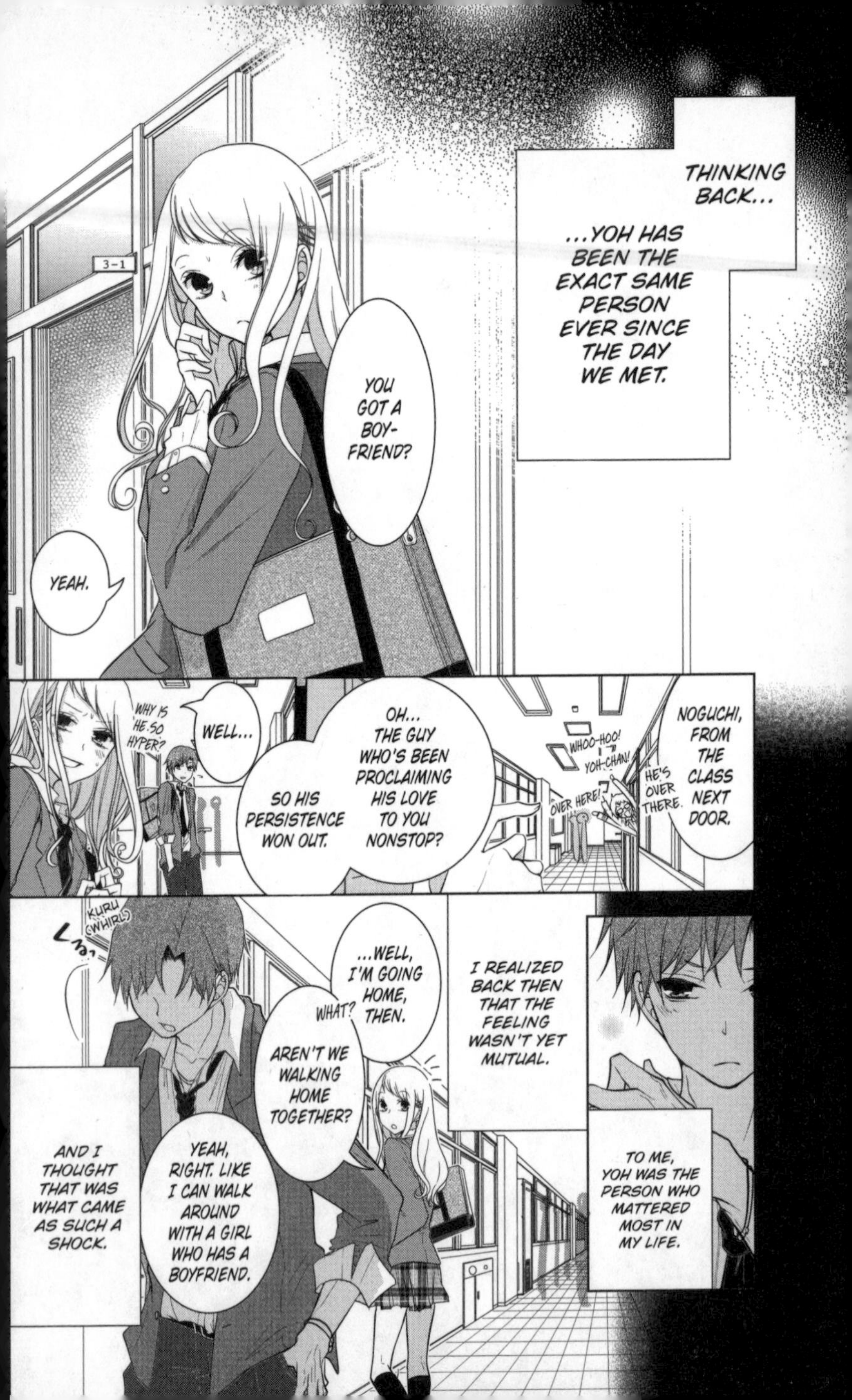
THINKING BACK...
...YOH HAS BEEN THE EXACT SAME PERSON EVER SINCE THE DAY WE MET.
3-1
YOU GOT A BOY-FRIEND?
YEAH.
NOGUCHI, FROM THE CLASS NEXT DOOR.
HE'S OVER THERE.
WHOO-HOO!
YOH-CHAN!
OVER HERE!
OH... THE GUY WHO'S BEEN PROCLAIMING HIS LOVE TO YOU NONSTOP?
SO HIS PERSISTENCE WON OUT.
WELL...
WHY IS HE SO HYPER?
TO ME, YOH WAS THE PERSON WHO MATTERED MOST IN MY LIFE.
I REALIZED BACK THEN THAT THE FEELING WASN'T YET MUTUAL.
...WELL, I'M GOING HOME, THEN.
WHAT?
AREN'T WE WALKING HOME TOGETHER?
くる
KURU (WHIRL)
YEAH, RIGHT. LIKE I CAN WALK AROUND WITH A GIRL WHO HAS A BOYFRIEND.
AND I THOUGHT THAT WAS WHAT CAME AS SUCH A SHOCK.

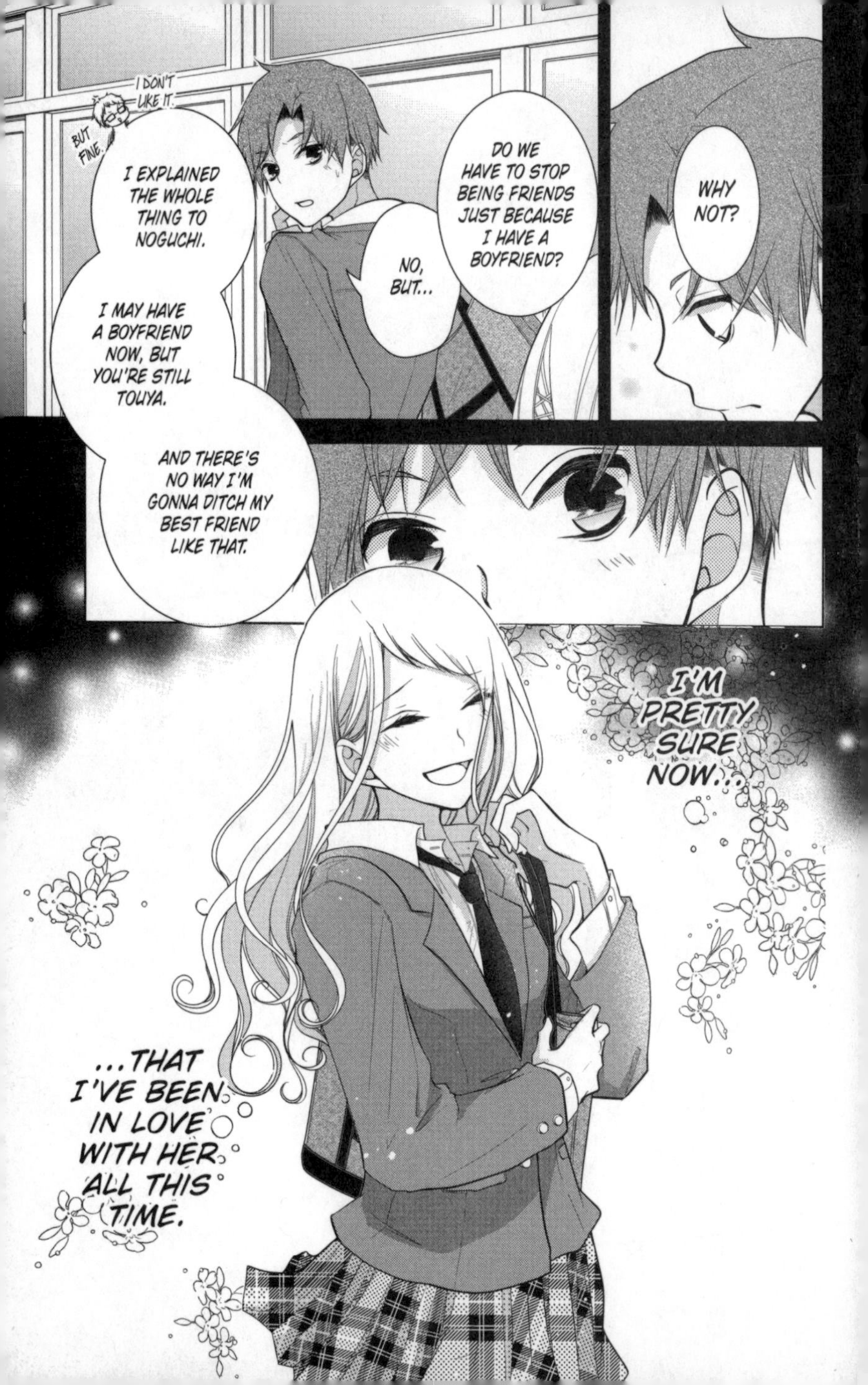
WHY NOT?
DO WE HAVE TO STOP BEING FRIENDS JUST BECAUSE I HAVE A BOYFRIEND?
NO, BUT...
I DON'T LIKE IT.
BUT FINE.
I EXPLAINED THE WHOLE THING TO NOGUCHI.
I MAY HAVE A BOYFRIEND NOW, BUT YOU'RE STILL TOUYA.
AND THERE'S NO WAY I'M GONNA DITCH MY BEST FRIEND LIKE THAT.
I'M PRETTY SURE NOW...
...THAT I'VE BEEN IN LOVE WITH HER ALL THIS TIME.

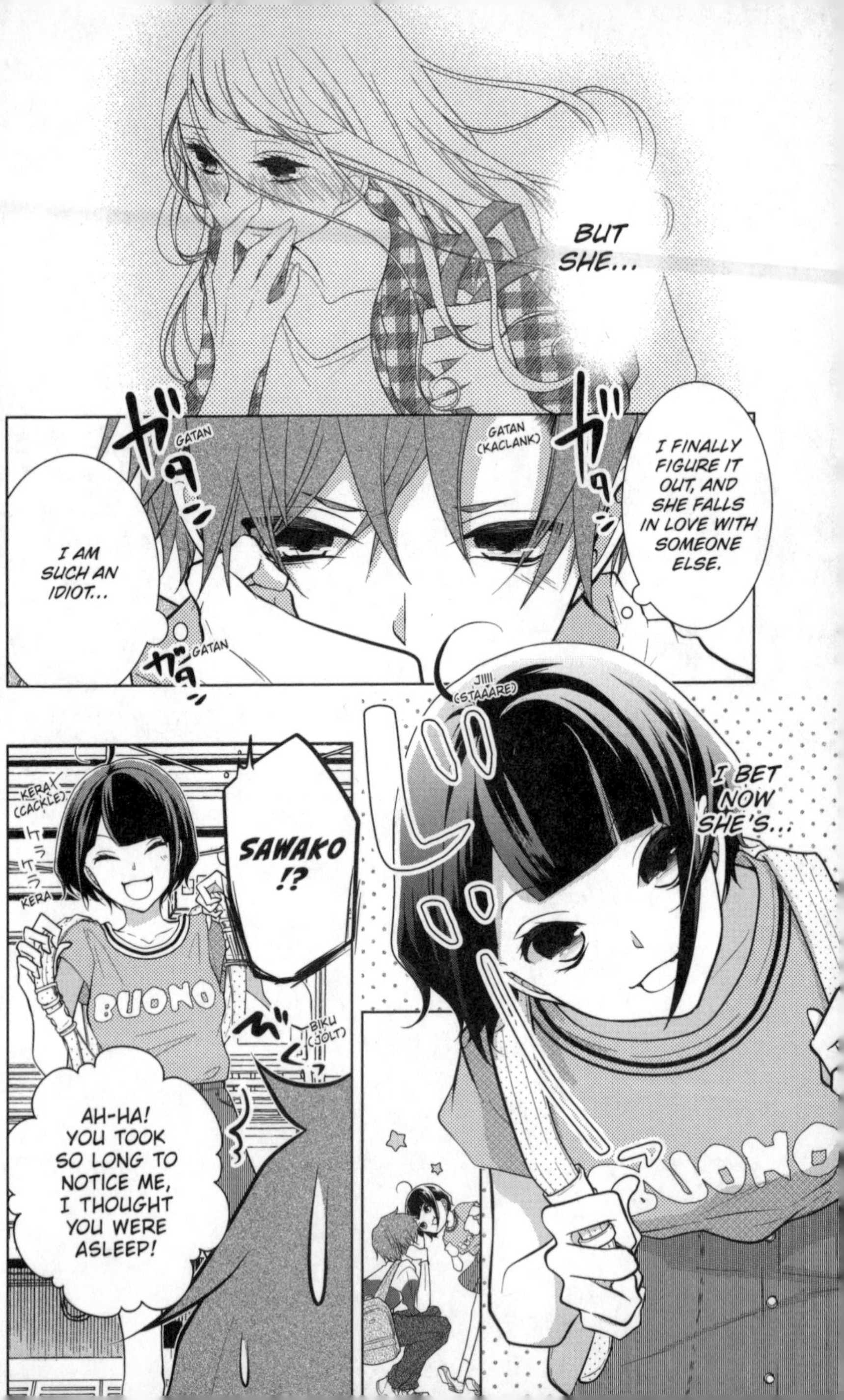
BUT SHE...
GATAN (KACLANK)
GATAN
I FINALLY FIGURE IT OUT, AND SHE FALLS IN LOVE WITH SOMEONE ELSE.
I AM SUCH AN IDIOT...
GATAN
JIIII (STAAARE)
I BET NOW SHE'S...
SAWAKO !?
KERA (CACKLE)
KERA
BIKU (JOLT)
AH-HA! YOU TOOK SO LONG TO NOTICE ME, I THOUGHT YOU WERE ASLEEP!
BUONO
BUONO

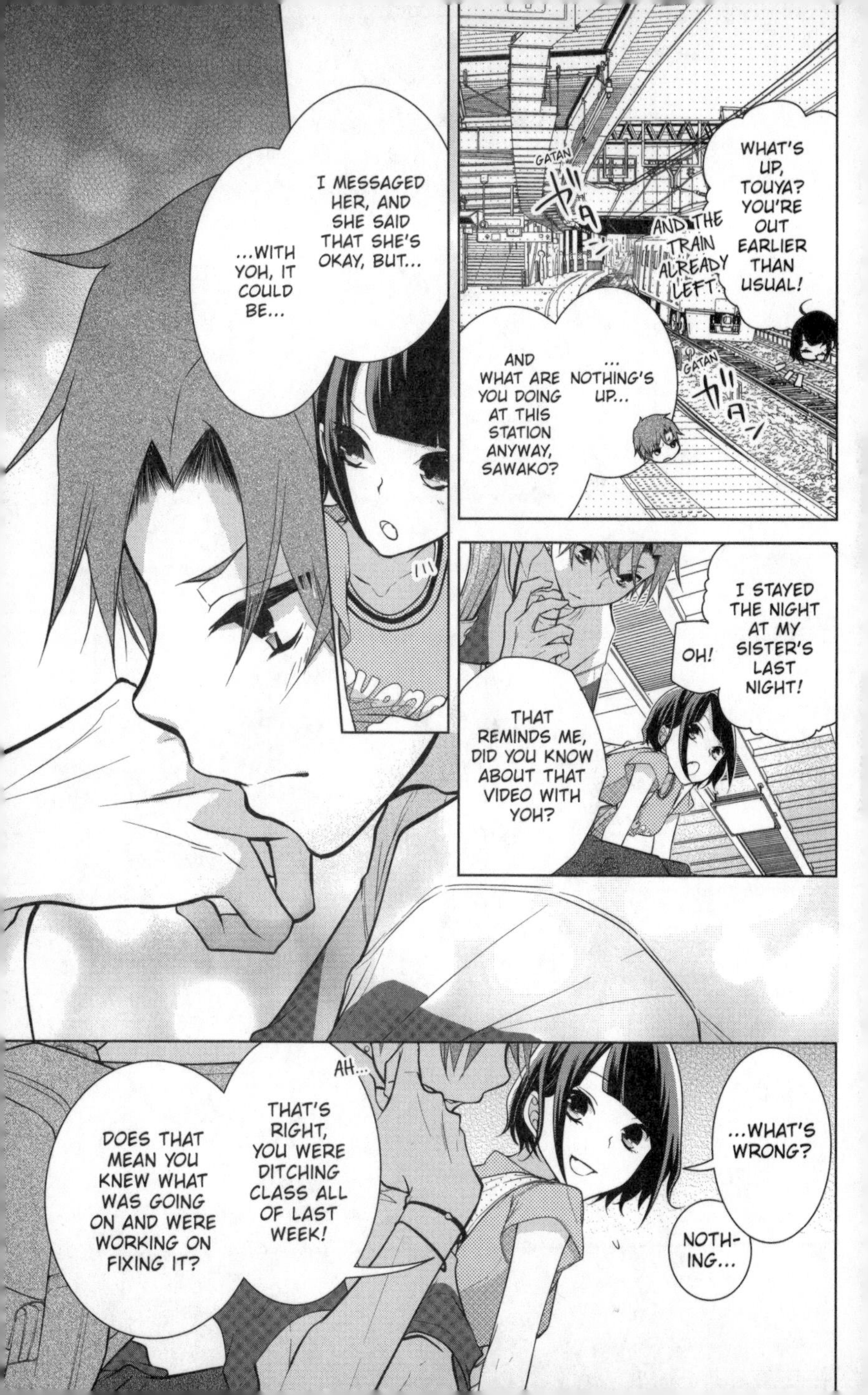
WHAT'S UP, TOUYA? YOU'RE OUT EARLIER THAN USUAL!
GATAN
AND THE TRAIN ALREADY LEFT
GATAN
... NOTHING'S UP...
AND WHAT ARE YOU DOING AT THIS STATION ANYWAY, SAWAKO?
I STAYED THE NIGHT AT MY SISTER'S LAST NIGHT!
OH!
THAT REMINDS ME, DID YOU KNOW ABOUT THAT VIDEO WITH YOH?
I MESSAGED HER, AND SHE SAID THAT SHE'S OKAY, BUT...
...WITH YOH, IT COULD BE...
...WHAT'S WRONG?
NOTH-ING...
AH...
THAT'S RIGHT, YOU WERE DITCHING CLASS ALL OF LAST WEEK!
DOES THAT MEAN YOU KNEW WHAT WAS GOING ON AND WERE WORKING ON FIXING IT?

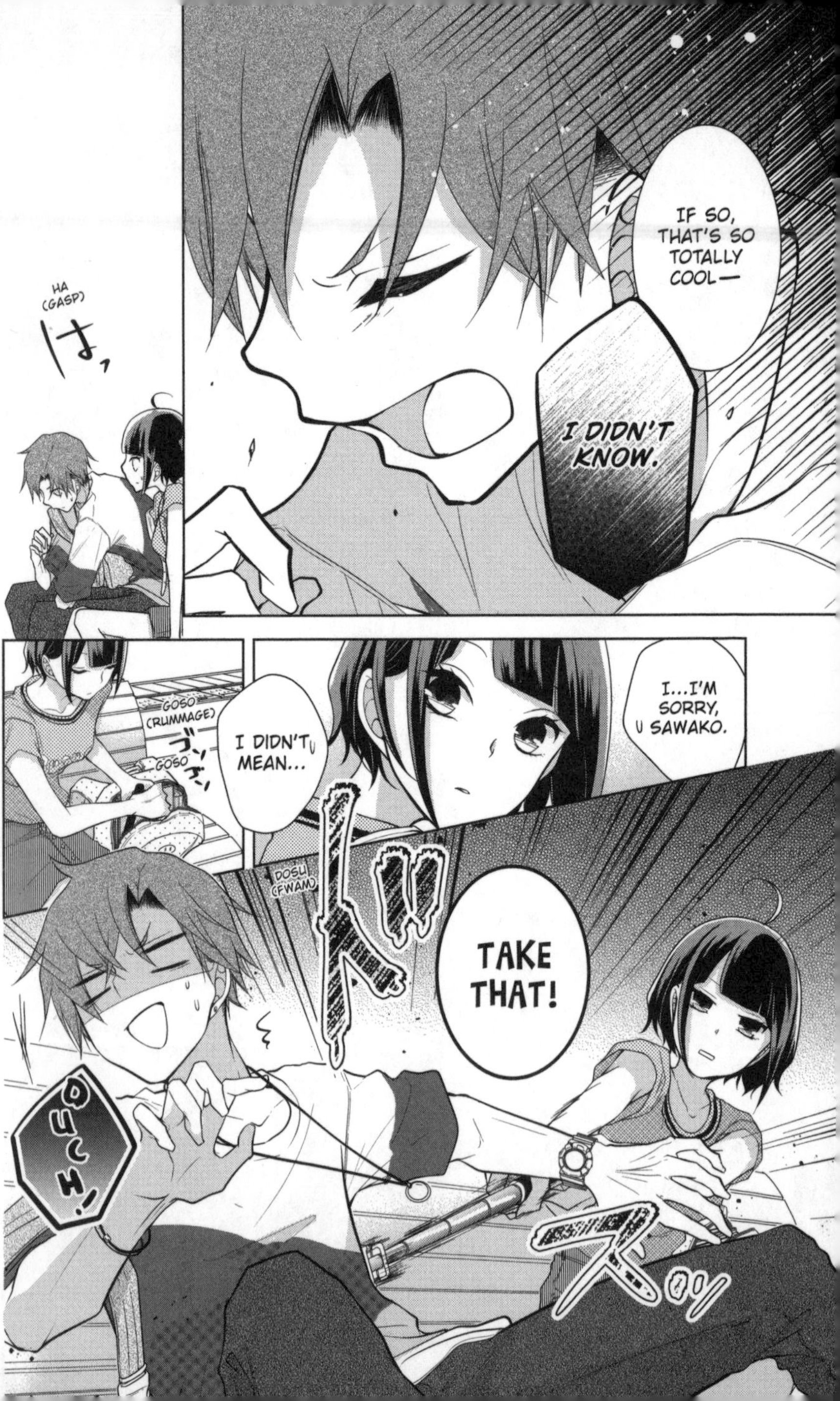
IF SO, THAT'S SO TOTALLY COOL—
I DIDN'T KNOW.
HA (GASP)
はっ
I...I'M SORRY, SAWAKO.
I DIDN'T MEAN...
GOSO (RUMMAGE) GOSO
DOSU (FWAM)
TAKE THAT!
OUCH!

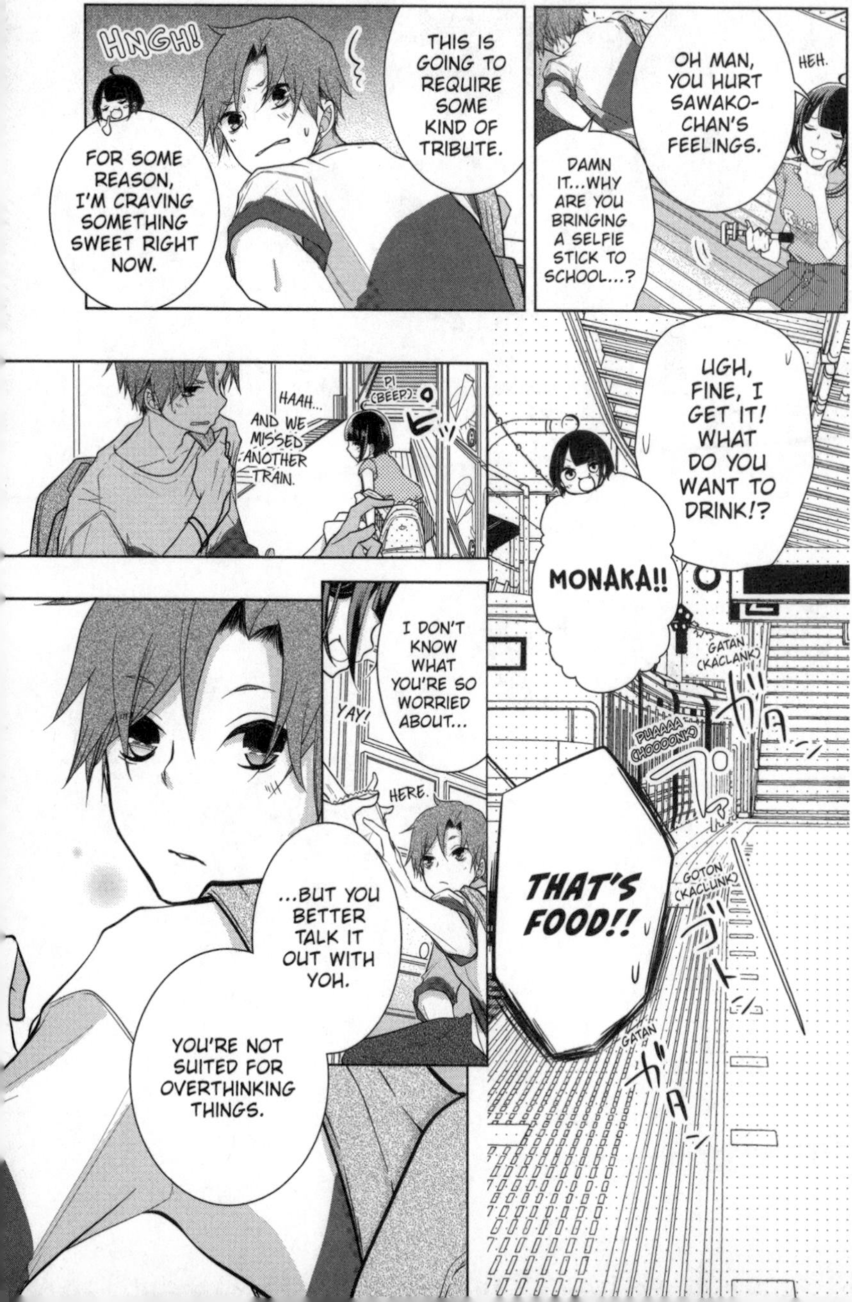
OH MAN, YOU HURT SAWAKO-CHAN'S FEELINGS.
HEH.
DAMN IT...WHY ARE YOU BRINGING A SELFIE STICK TO SCHOOL...?
HNGH!
THIS IS GOING TO REQUIRE SOME KIND OF TRIBUTE.
FOR SOME REASON, I'M CRAVING SOMETHING SWEET RIGHT NOW.
UGH, FINE, I GET IT! WHAT DO YOU WANT TO DRINK!?
MONAKA!!
GATAN (KACLANK)
PUAAAA (CHOOOONK)
THAT'S FOOD!!
GOTON (KACLLINK)
GATAN
HAAH... AND WE MISSED ANOTHER TRAIN.
PI (BEEP)
I DON'T KNOW WHAT YOU'RE SO WORRIED ABOUT...
YAY!
HERE.
...BUT YOU BETTER TALK IT OUT WITH YOH.
YOU'RE NOT SUITED FOR OVERTHINKING THINGS.

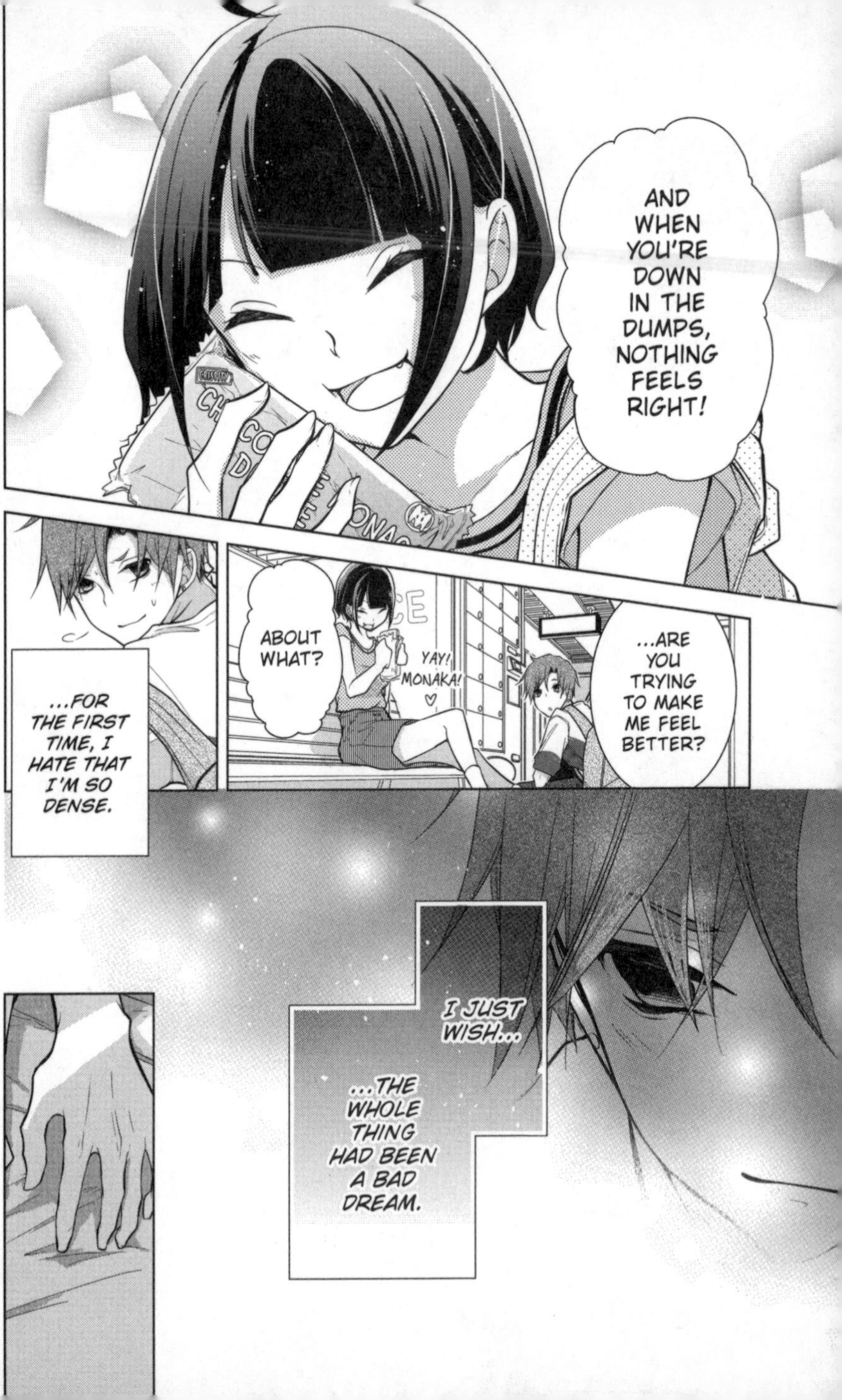
AND WHEN YOU'RE DOWN IN THE DUMPS, NOTHING FEELS RIGHT!
...ARE YOU TRYING TO MAKE ME FEEL BETTER?
YAY! MONAKA! ♡
ABOUT WHAT?
...FOR THE FIRST TIME, I HATE THAT I'M SO DENSE.
I JUST WISH...
...THE WHOLE THING HAD BEEN A BAD DREAM.

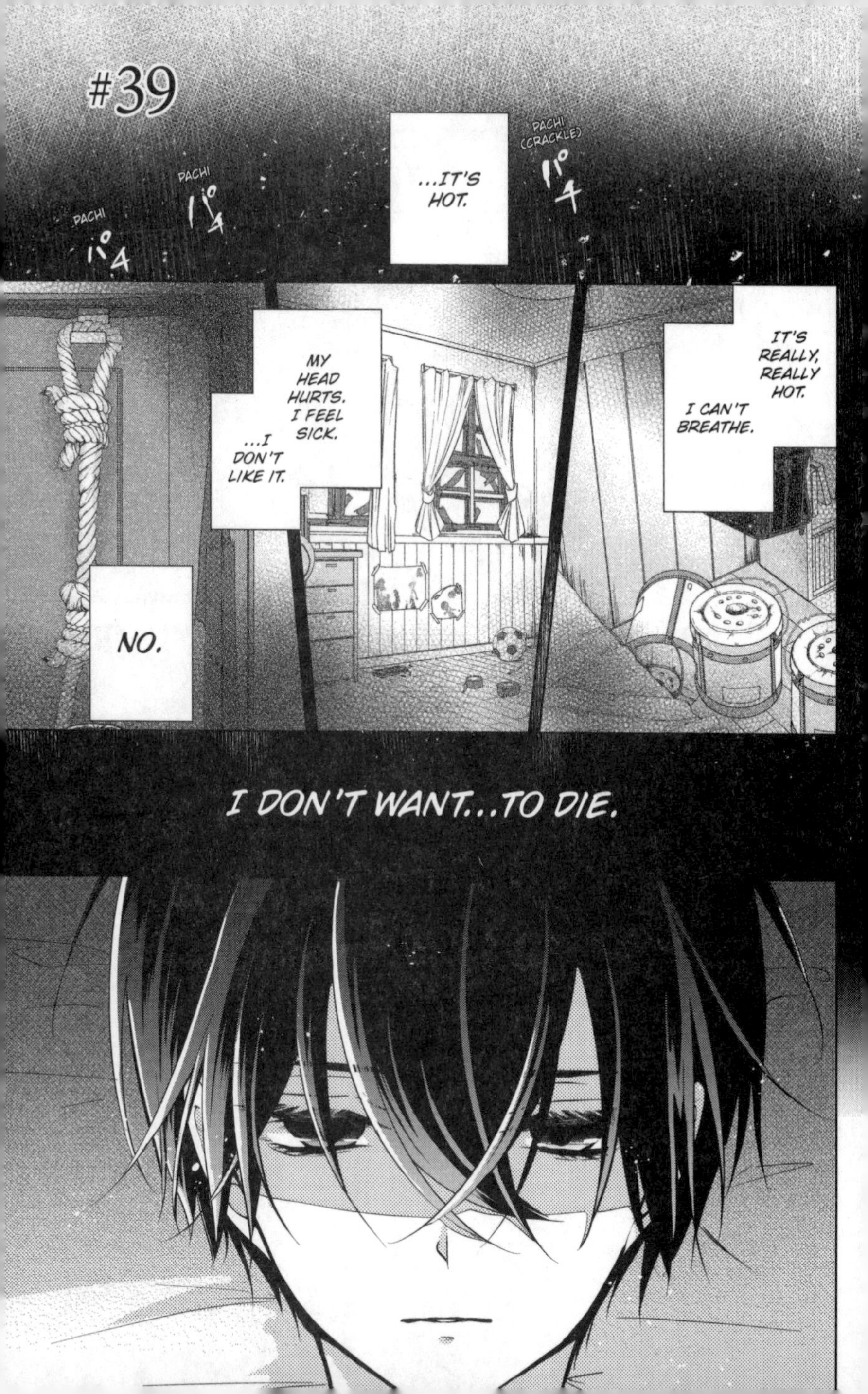
#39
PACHI (CRACKLE)
...IT'S HOT.
PACHI
PACHI
IT'S REALLY, REALLY HOT.
I CAN'T BREATHE.
MY HEAD HURTS. I FEEL SICK.
...I DON'T LIKE IT.
NO.
I DON'T WANT...TO DIE.

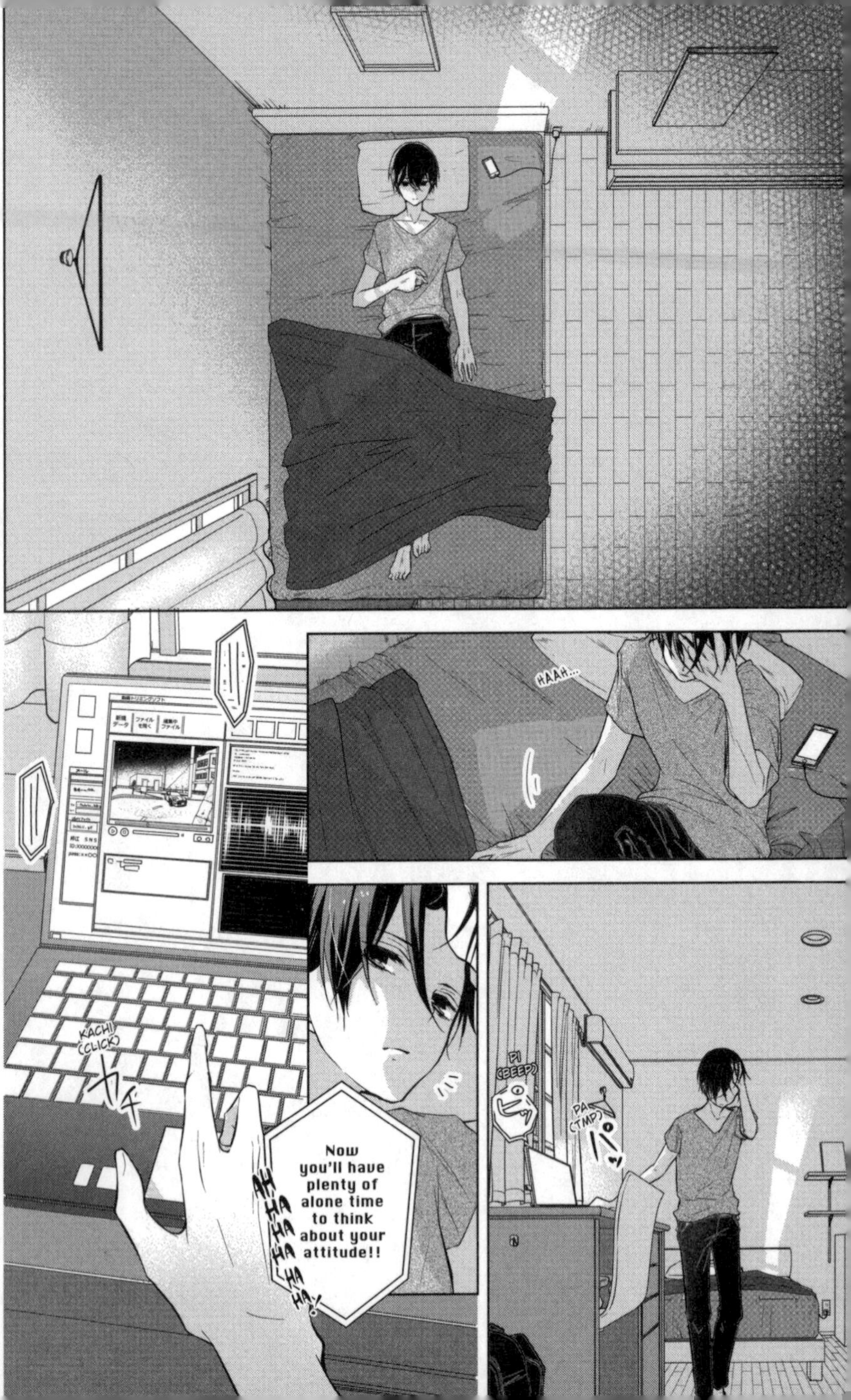
HAAAH...
PI (BEEP)
PA (TMP)
Now you'll have plenty of alone time to think about your attitude!!
AH HA HA HA HA HA!
KACHI (CLICK)

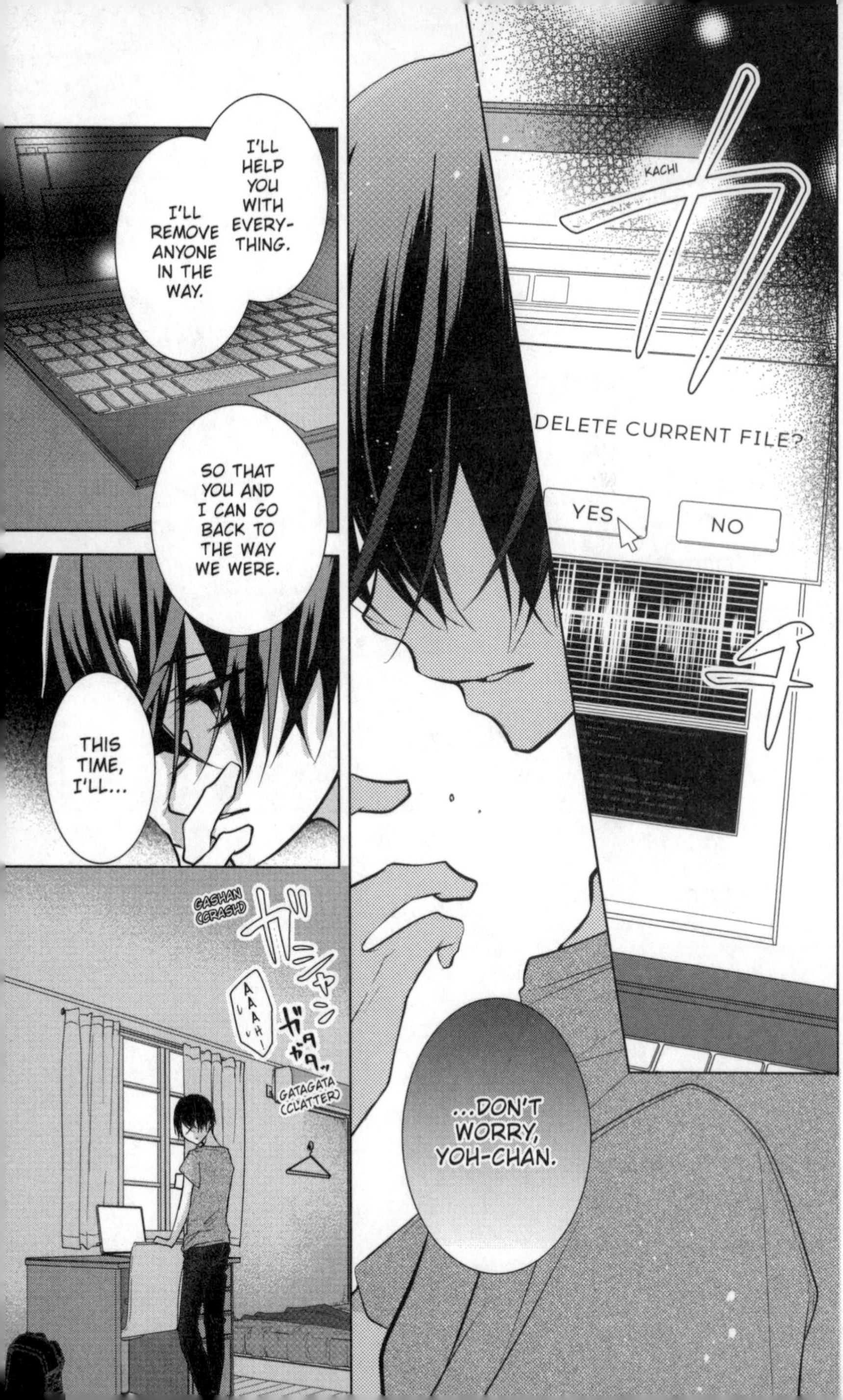

KACHI
DELETE CURRENT FILE?
YES
NO
...DON'T WORRY, YOH-CHAN.
I'LL HELP YOU WITH EVERY-THING.
I'LL REMOVE ANYONE IN THE WAY.
SO THAT YOU AND I CAN GO BACK TO THE WAY WE WERE.
THIS TIME, I'LL...
GASHAN (CRASH)
AAAH!
GATAGATA (CLATTER)

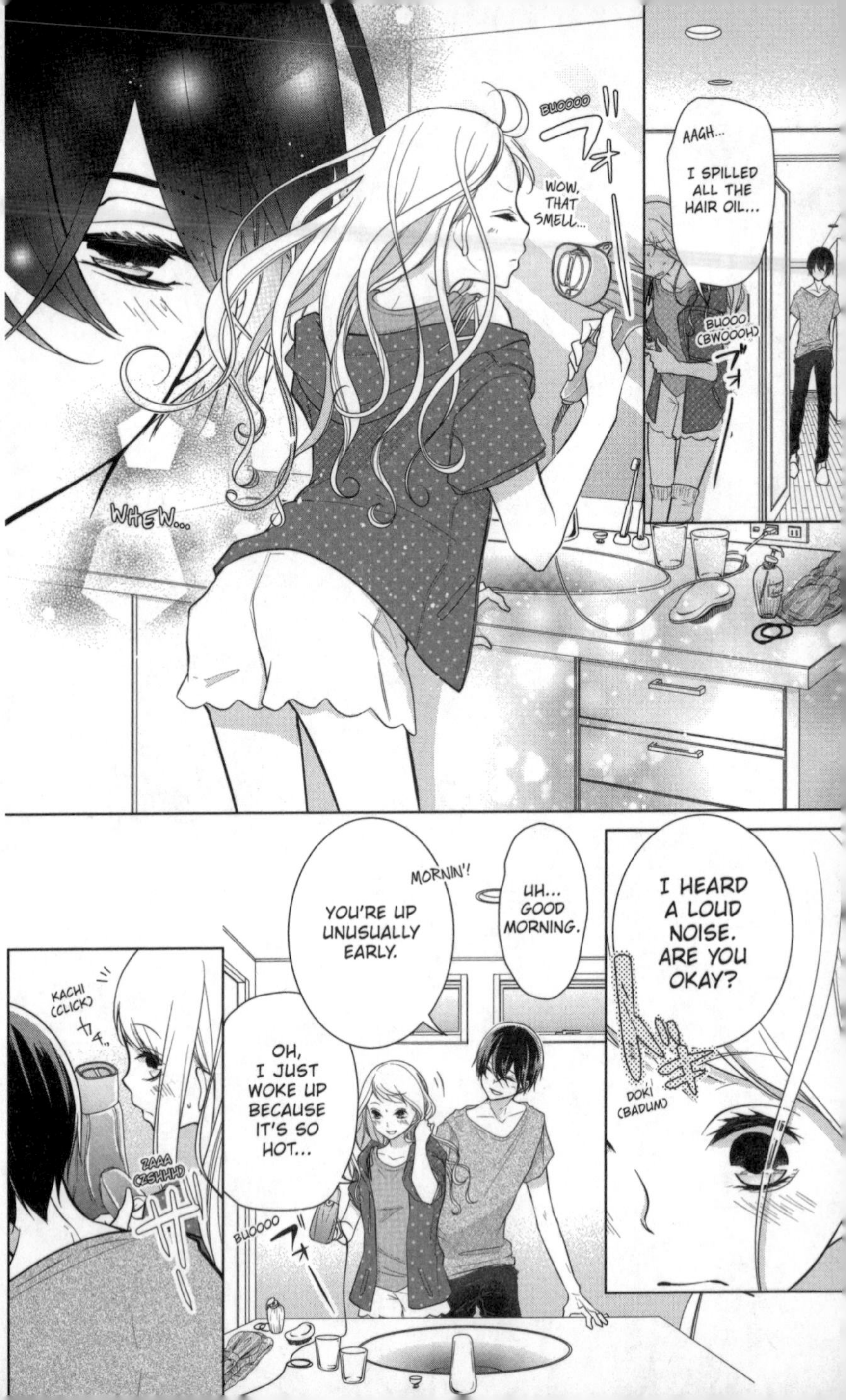
AAGH...
I SPILLED ALL THE HAIR OIL...
BUOOO (BWOOOH)
BUOOOO
WOW, THAT SMELL...
WHEW...
I HEARD A LOUD NOISE. ARE YOU OKAY?
DOKI (BADUM)
UH... GOOD MORNING.
MORNIN'!
YOU'RE UP UNUSUALLY EARLY.
OH, I JUST WOKE UP BECAUSE IT'S SO HOT...
BUOOOO
KACHI (CLICK)
ZAAA (ZSHHHH)

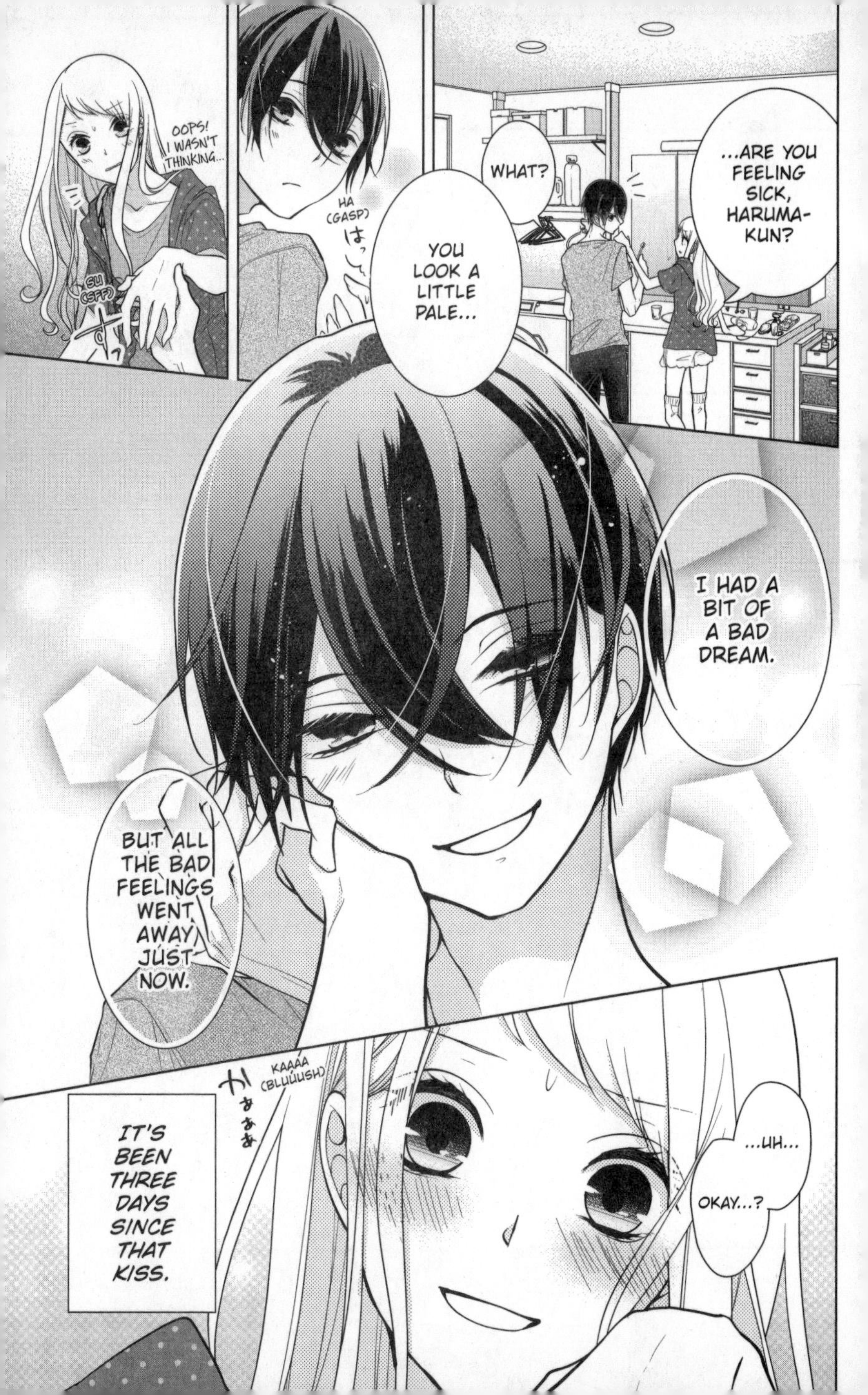
...ARE YOU FEELING SICK, HARUMA-KUN?
WHAT?
YOU LOOK A LITTLE PALE...
HA (GASP)
OOPS! I WASN'T THINKING...
SU (SFF)
I HAD A BIT OF A BAD DREAM.
BUT ALL THE BAD FEELINGS WENT AWAY JUST NOW.
...UH...
OKAY...?
KAAAA (BLUUUSH)
IT'S BEEN THREE DAYS SINCE THAT KISS.

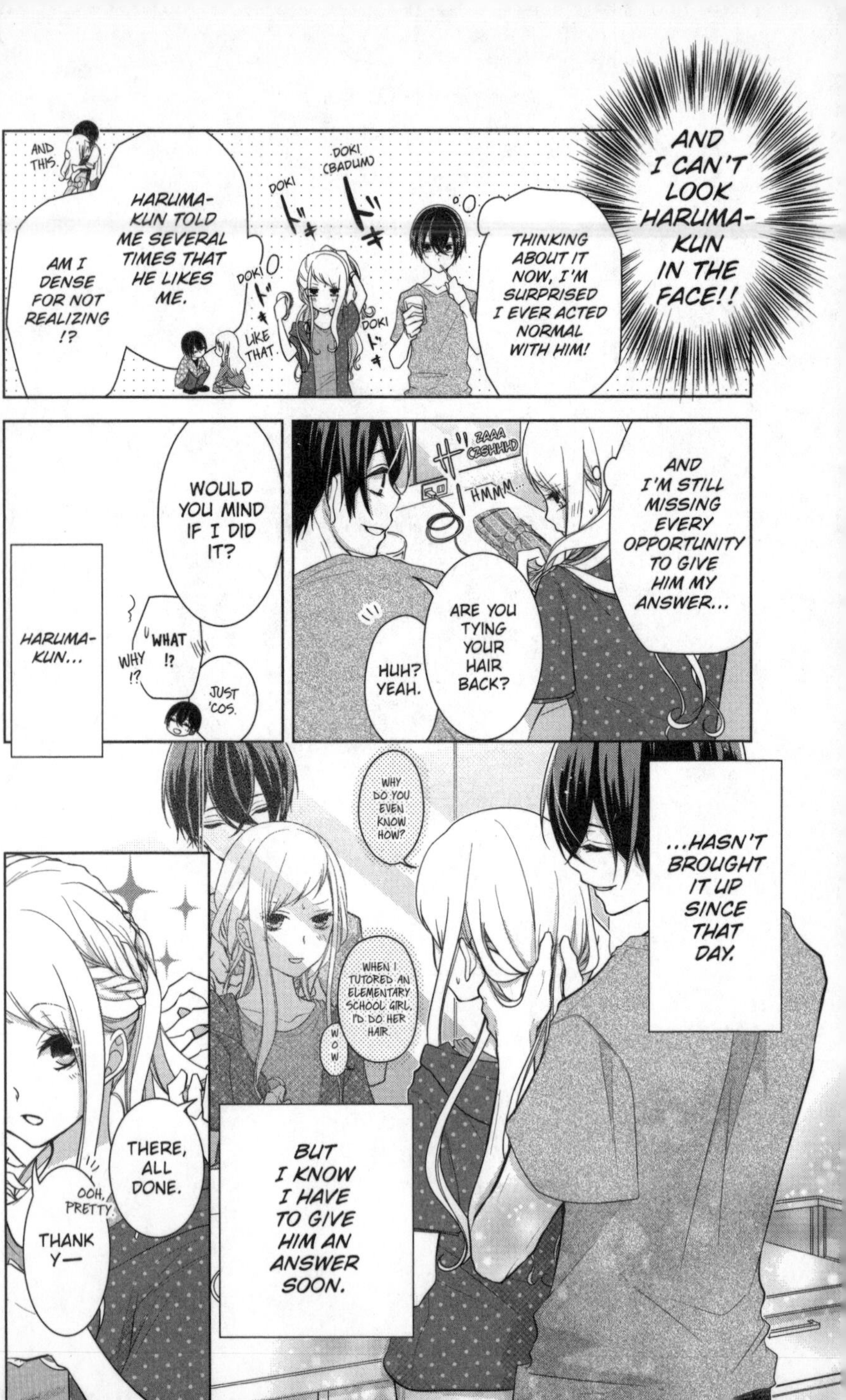
AND I CAN'T LOOK HARUMA-KUN IN THE FACE!!
THINKING ABOUT IT NOW, I'M SURPRISED I EVER ACTED NORMAL WITH HIM!
DOKI (BADUM)
DOKI
DOKI
DOKI
HARUMA-KUN TOLD ME SEVERAL TIMES THAT HE LIKES ME.
AM I DENSE FOR NOT REALIZING!?
AND THIS.
LIKE THAT.
AND I'M STILL MISSING EVERY OPPORTUNITY TO GIVE HIM MY ANSWER...
ZAAA CZSHHHD
HMMM...
ARE YOU TYING YOUR HAIR BACK?
HUH? YEAH.
WOULD YOU MIND IF I DID IT?
WHAT!?
WHY!?
JUST 'COS.
HARUMA-KUN...
...HASN'T BROUGHT IT UP SINCE THAT DAY.
WHY DO YOU EVEN KNOW HOW?
WHEN I TUTORED AN ELEMENTARY SCHOOL GIRL, I'D DO HER HAIR.
WOW
BUT I KNOW I HAVE TO GIVE HIM AN ANSWER SOON.
THERE, ALL DONE.
OOH, PRETTY.
THANK Y—

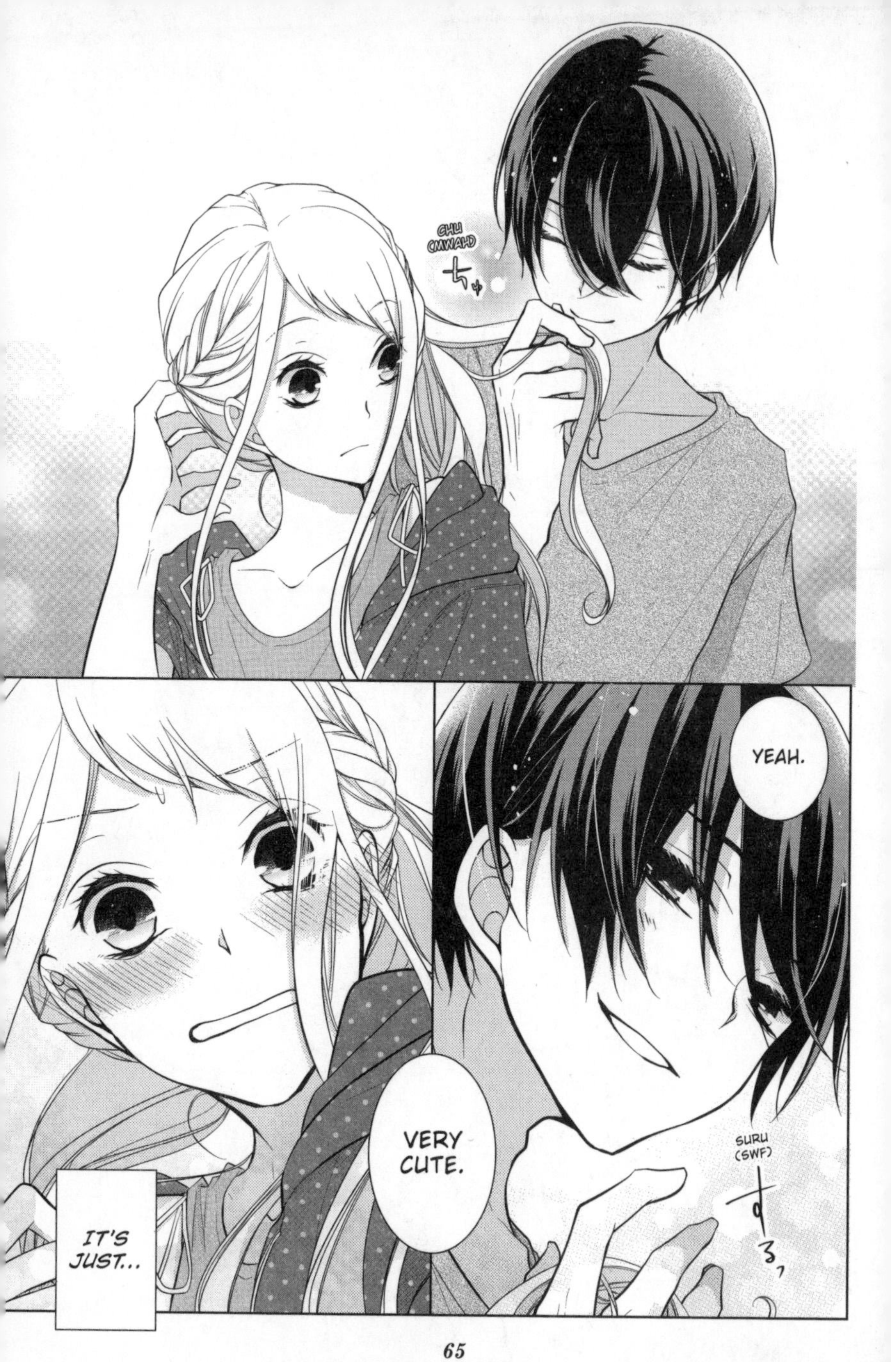
CHU (MWAH)
ちゅ
YEAH.
VERY CUTE.
SURU (SWF)
する
IT'S JUST...

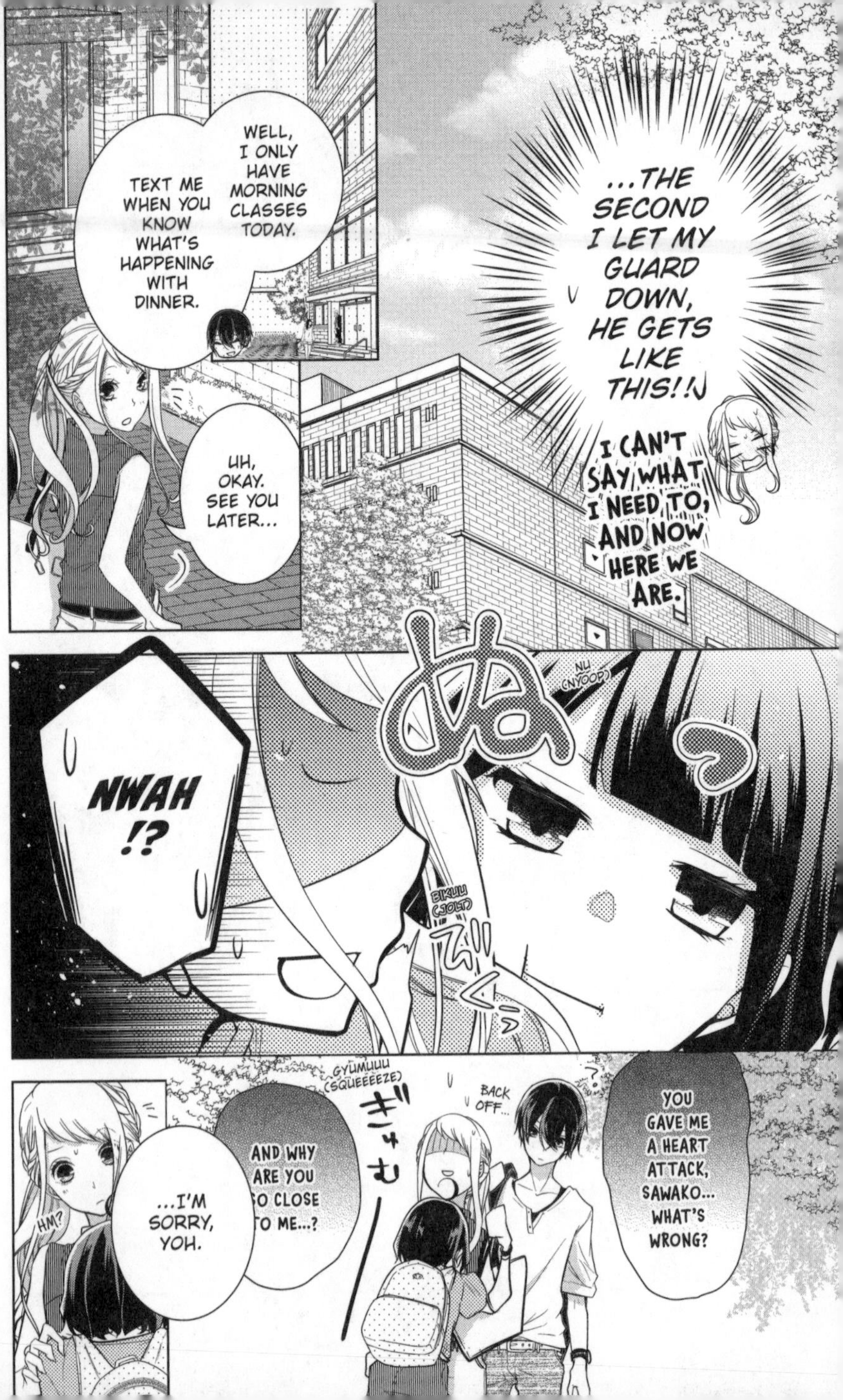

...THE SECOND I LET MY GUARD DOWN, HE GETS LIKE THIS!!
I CAN'T SAY WHAT I NEED TO, AND NOW HERE WE ARE.
WELL, I ONLY HAVE MORNING CLASSES TODAY.
TEXT ME WHEN YOU KNOW WHAT'S HAPPENING WITH DINNER.
UH, OKAY. SEE YOU LATER...
NU (NYOOP)
BIKUU (JOLT)
NWAH!?
YOU GAVE ME A HEART ATTACK, SAWAKO... WHAT'S WRONG?
BACK OFF...
GYUMUUU (SQUEEEEZE)
AND WHY ARE YOU SO CLOSE TO ME...?
...I'M SORRY, YOH.
HM?

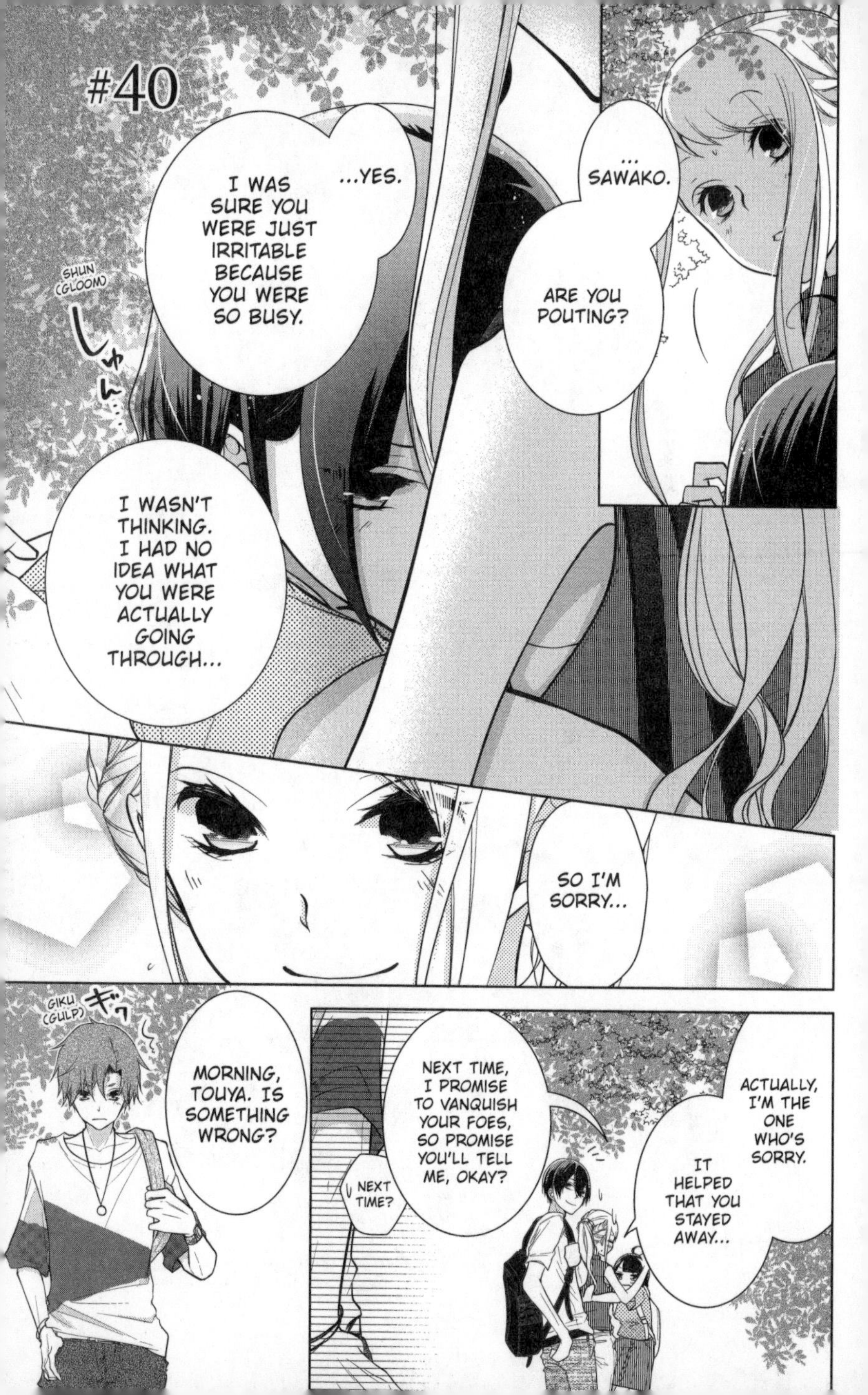
#40
... SAWAKO.
ARE YOU POUTING?
...YES.
I WAS SURE YOU WERE JUST IRRITABLE BECAUSE YOU WERE SO BUSY.
SHUN (GLOOM)
I WASN'T THINKING. I HAD NO IDEA WHAT YOU WERE ACTUALLY GOING THROUGH...
SO I'M SORRY...
ACTUALLY, I'M THE ONE WHO'S SORRY.
IT HELPED THAT YOU STAYED AWAY...
NEXT TIME, I PROMISE TO VANQUISH YOUR FOES, SO PROMISE YOU'LL TELL ME, OKAY?
NEXT TIME?
GIKU (GULP)
MORNING, TOUYA. IS SOMETHING WRONG?

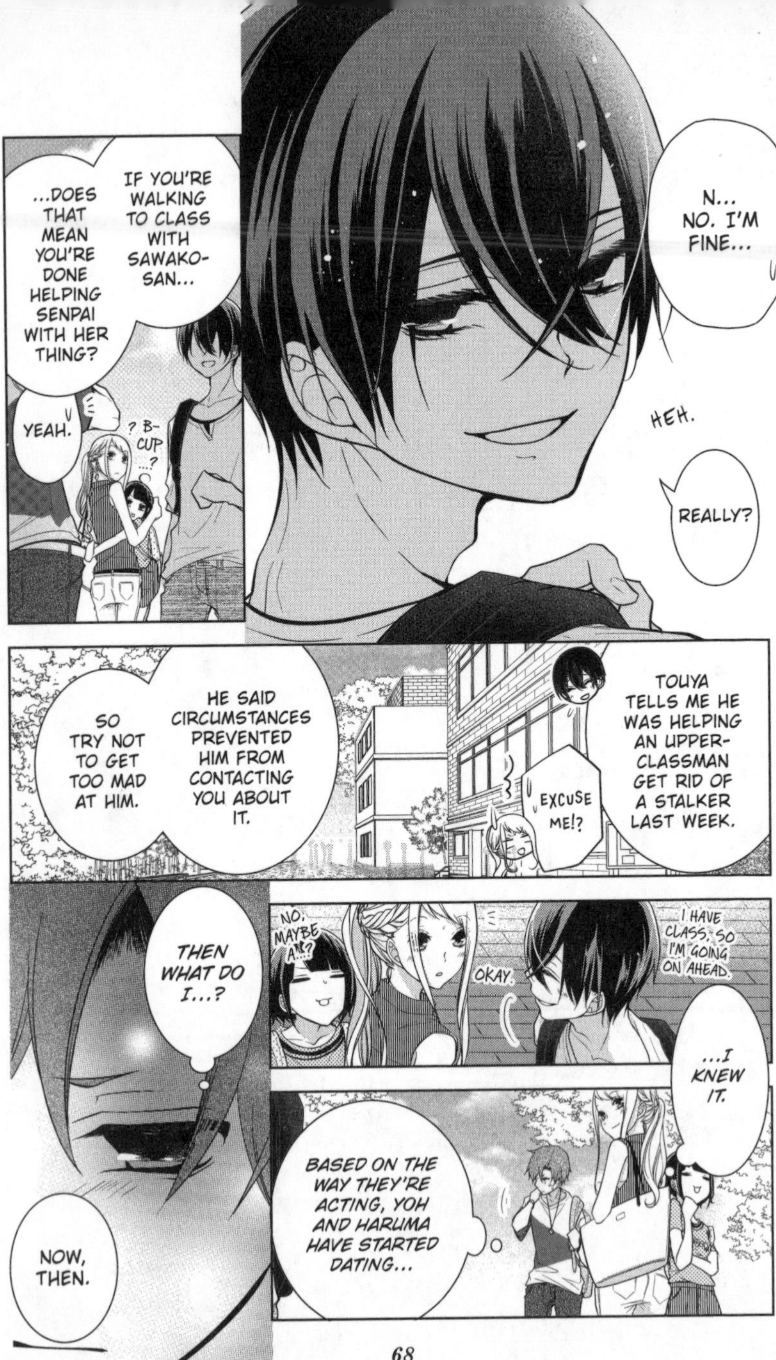
N... NO. I'M FINE...
HEH.
REALLY?
IF YOU'RE WALKING TO CLASS WITH SAWAKO-SAN...
...DOES THAT MEAN YOU'RE DONE HELPING SENPAI WITH HER THING?
YEAH.
? B-CUP ...?
TOUYA TELLS ME HE WAS HELPING AN UPPER-CLASSMAN GET RID OF A STALKER LAST WEEK.
EXCUSE ME!?
HE SAID CIRCUMSTANCES PREVENTED HIM FROM CONTACTING YOU ABOUT IT.
SO TRY NOT TO GET TOO MAD AT HIM.
I HAVE CLASS, SO I'M GOING ON AHEAD.
OKAY.
NO, MAYBE A...?
...I KNEW IT.
BASED ON THE WAY THEY'RE ACTING, YOH AND HARUMA HAVE STARTED DATING...
THEN WHAT DO I...?
NOW, THEN.

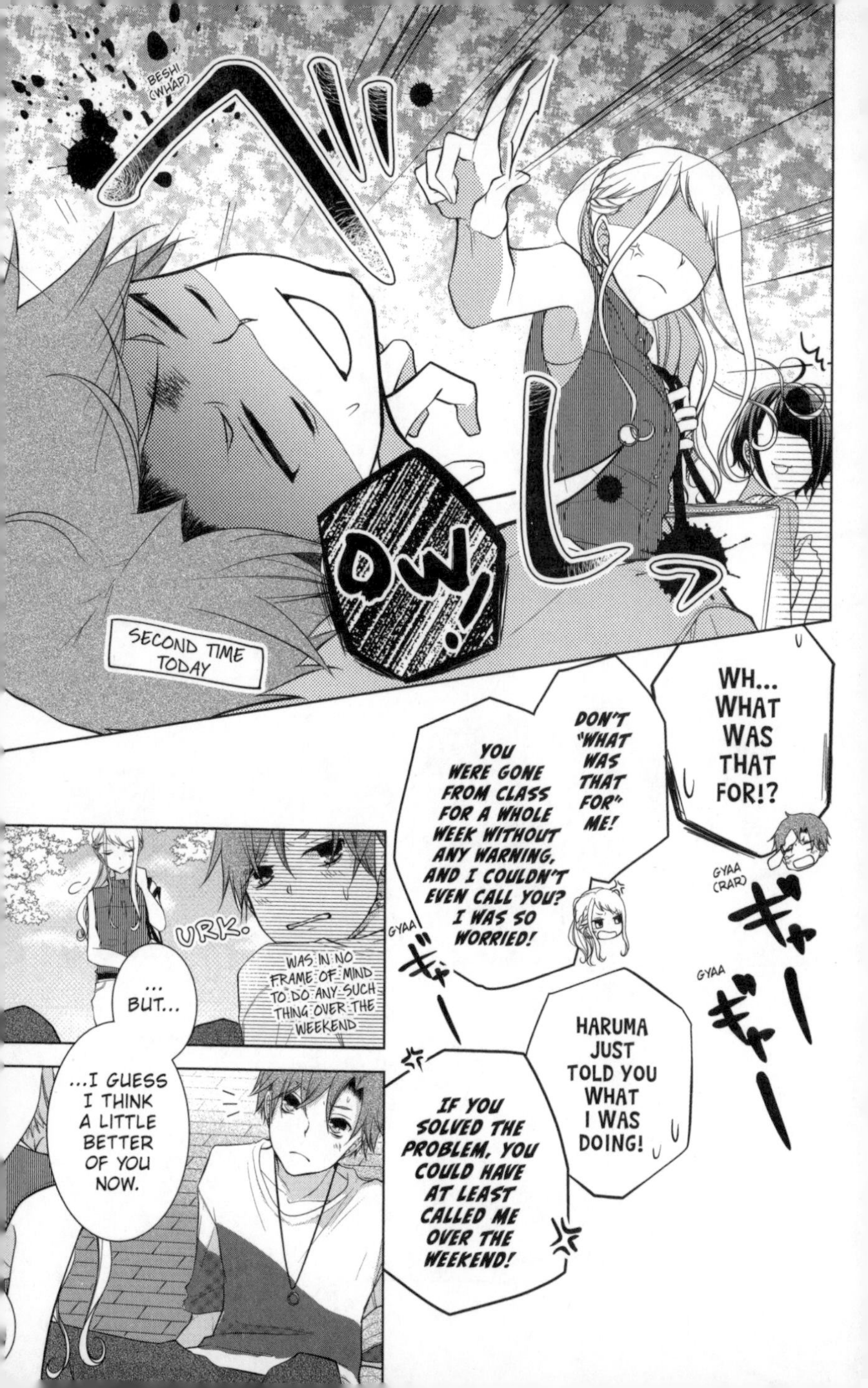
BESHI (WHAP)
OW!
SECOND TIME TODAY
WH... WHAT WAS THAT FOR!?
GYAA (RAR)
DON'T "WHAT WAS THAT FOR" ME!
YOU WERE GONE FROM CLASS FOR A WHOLE WEEK WITHOUT ANY WARNING, AND I COULDN'T EVEN CALL YOU? I WAS SO WORRIED!
GYAA
GYAA
HARUMA JUST TOLD YOU WHAT I WAS DOING!
IF YOU SOLVED THE PROBLEM, YOU COULD HAVE AT LEAST CALLED ME OVER THE WEEKEND!
URK.
WAS IN NO FRAME OF MIND TO DO ANY SUCH THING OVER THE WEEKEND
... BUT...
...I GUESS I THINK A LITTLE BETTER OF YOU NOW.

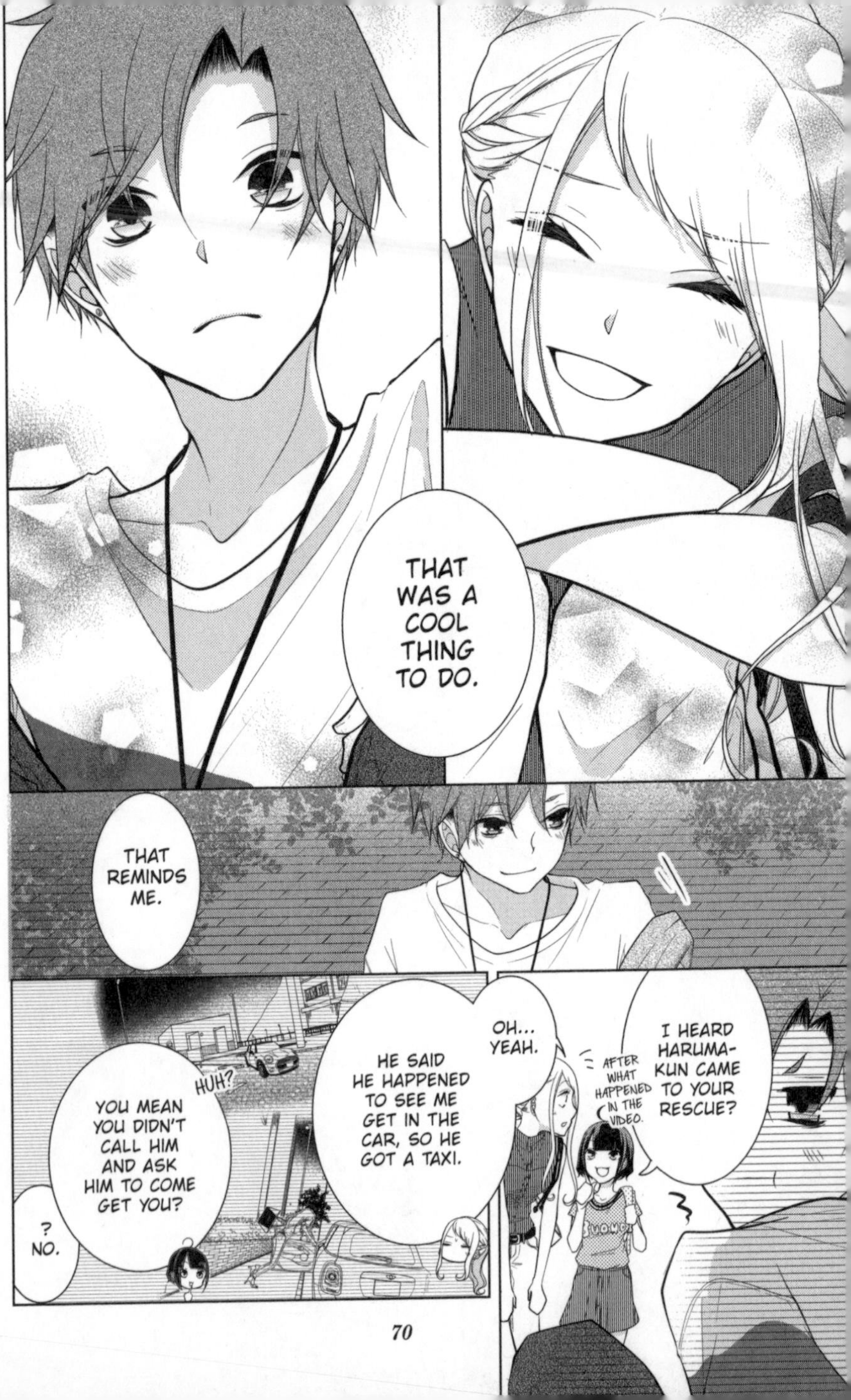
THAT WAS A COOL THING TO DO.
THAT REMINDS ME.
I HEARD HARUMA-KUN CAME TO YOUR RESCUE?
AFTER WHAT HAPPENED IN THE VIDEO.
OH... YEAH.
HE SAID HE HAPPENED TO SEE ME GET IN THE CAR, SO HE GOT A TAXI.
HUH?
YOU MEAN YOU DIDN'T CALL HIM AND ASK HIM TO COME GET YOU?
? NO.

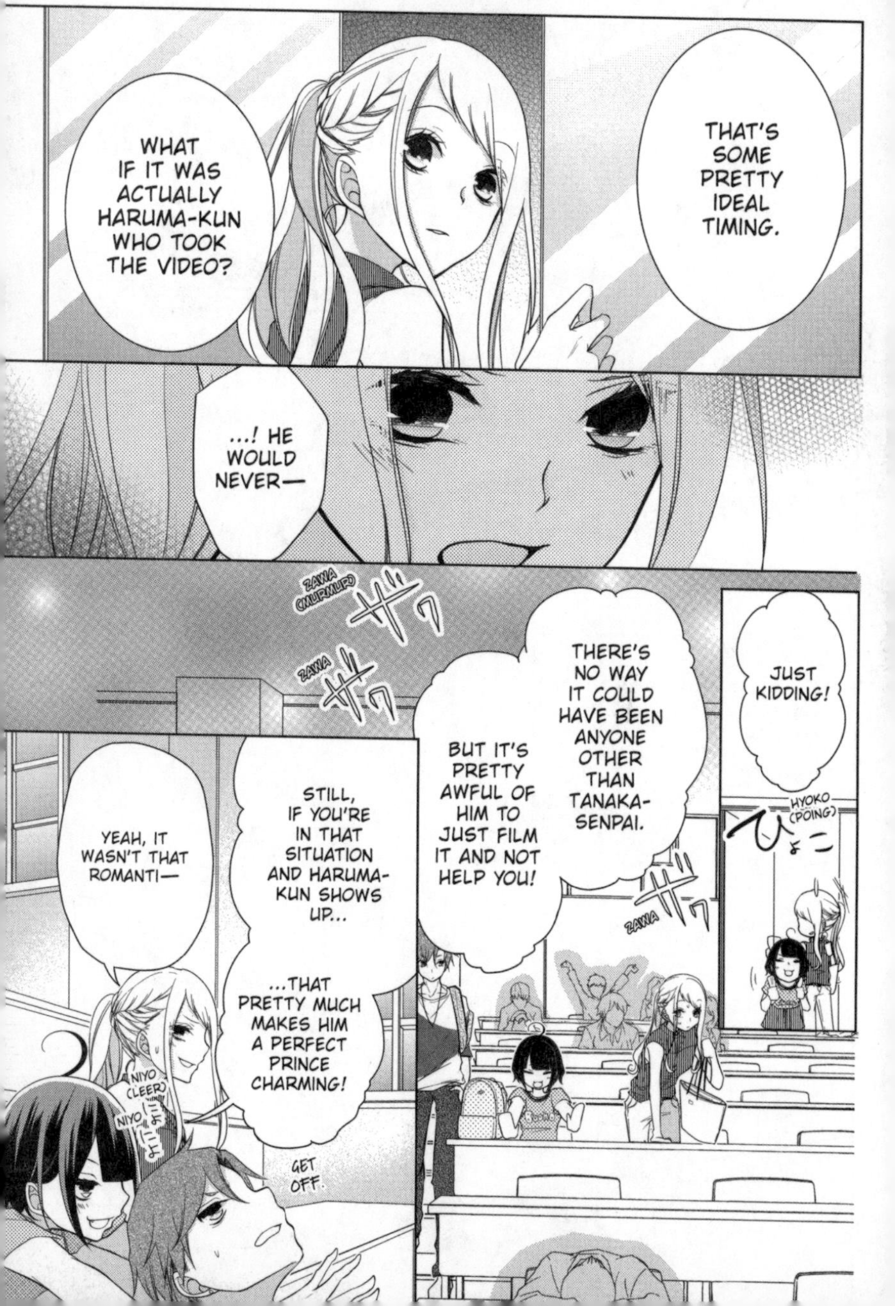
THAT'S SOME PRETTY IDEAL TIMING.
WHAT IF IT WAS ACTUALLY HARUMA-KUN WHO TOOK THE VIDEO?
...! HE WOULD NEVER—
JUST KIDDING!
HYOKO (POING)
ZAWA (MURMUR)
ZAWA
THERE'S NO WAY IT COULD HAVE BEEN ANYONE OTHER THAN TANAKA-SENPAI.
BUT IT'S PRETTY AWFUL OF HIM TO JUST FILM IT AND NOT HELP YOU!
ZAWA
STILL, IF YOU'RE IN THAT SITUATION AND HARUMA-KUN SHOWS UP...
...THAT PRETTY MUCH MAKES HIM A PERFECT PRINCE CHARMING!
YEAH, IT WASN'T THAT ROMANTI—
NIYO (LEER)
NIYO
GET OFF.

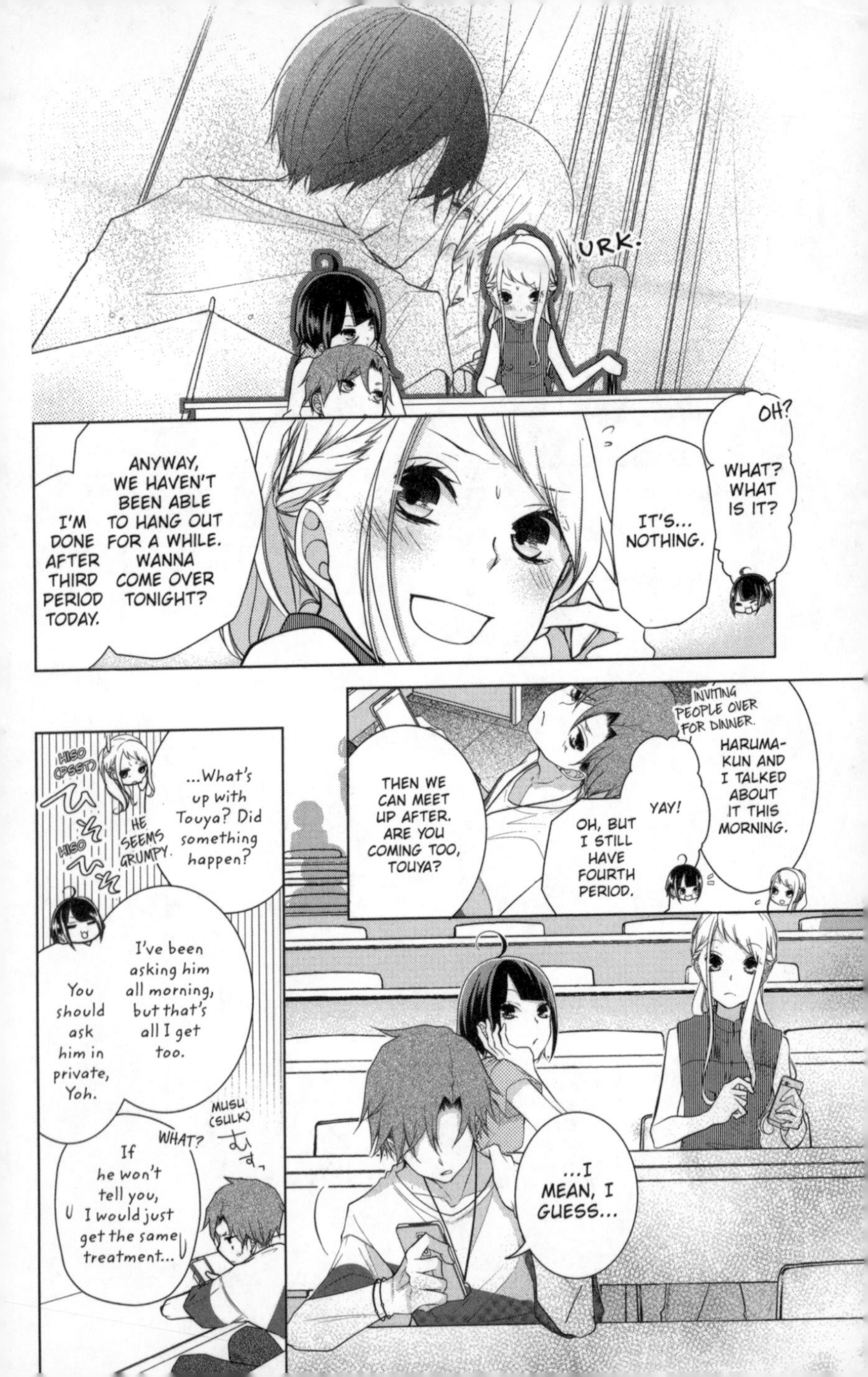
URK.
OH?
WHAT? WHAT IS IT?
IT'S... NOTHING.
ANYWAY, WE HAVEN'T BEEN ABLE TO HANG OUT FOR A WHILE. WANNA COME OVER TONIGHT?
I'M DONE AFTER THIRD PERIOD TODAY.
INVITING PEOPLE OVER FOR DINNER.
HARUMA-KUN AND I TALKED ABOUT IT THIS MORNING.
YAY!
OH, BUT I STILL HAVE FOURTH PERIOD.
THEN WE CAN MEET UP AFTER. ARE YOU COMING TOO, TOUYA?
...I MEAN, I GUESS...
HISO (PSST)
HISO
...What's up with Touya? Did something happen?
HE SEEMS GRUMPY.
I've been asking him all morning, but that's all I get too.
You should ask him in private, Yoh.
MUSU (SULK)
WHAT?
If he won't tell you, I would just get the same treatment...

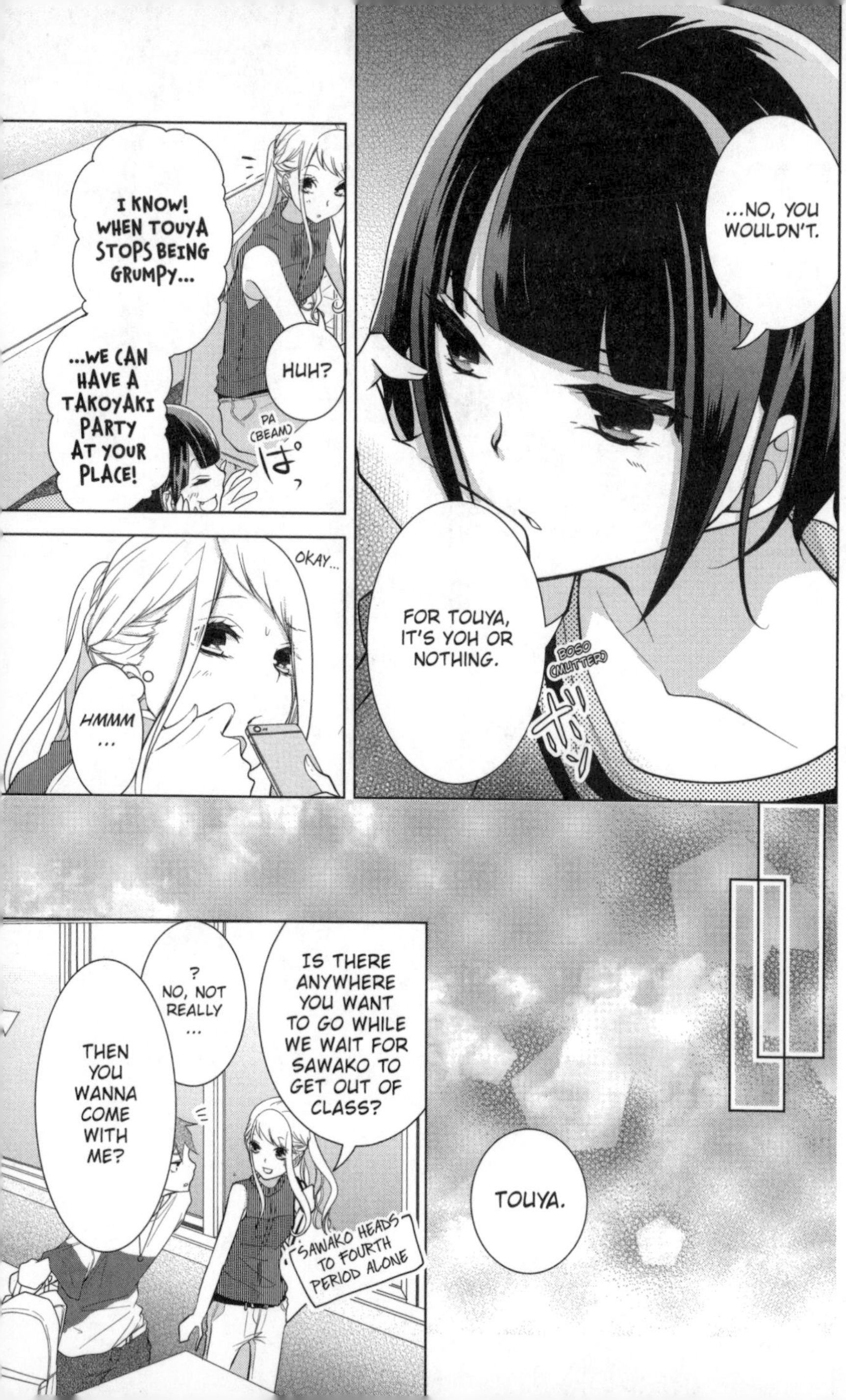
...NO, YOU WOULDN'T.
FOR TOUYA, IT'S YOH OR NOTHING.
BOSO (MUTTER)
I KNOW! WHEN TOUYA STOPS BEING GRUMPY...
HUH?
...WE CAN HAVE A TAKOYAKI PARTY AT YOUR PLACE!
PA (BEAM)
ぱっ
OKAY...
HMMM...
TOUYA.
IS THERE ANYWHERE YOU WANT TO GO WHILE WE WAIT FOR SAWAKO TO GET OUT OF CLASS?
? NO, NOT REALLY...
THEN YOU WANNA COME WITH ME?
SAWAKO HEADS TO FOURTH PERIOD ALONE

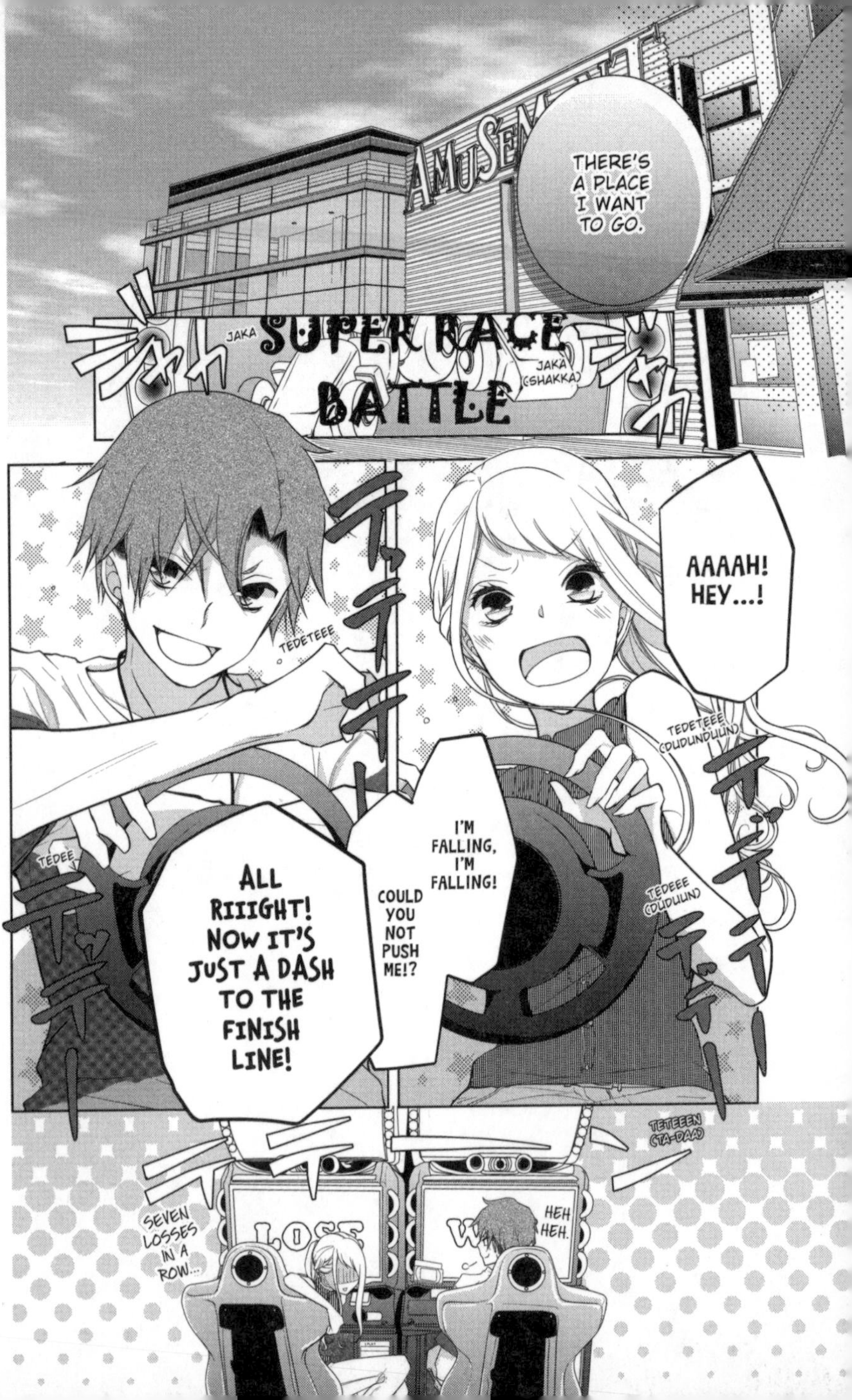
THERE'S A PLACE I WANT TO GO.
JAKA (SHAKKA)
SUPER RACE BATTLE
JAKA
AAAAH! HEY...!
TEDETEEE (DUDUNDUUN)
TEDETEEE
I'M FALLING, I'M FALLING!
COULD YOU NOT PUSH ME!?
TEDEEE (DUDUUN)
TEDEE
ALL RIIIGHT! NOW IT'S JUST A DASH TO THE FINISH LINE!
TETEEEN (TA-DAA)
HEH HEH.
LOSE
SEVEN LOSSES IN A ROW...

#41

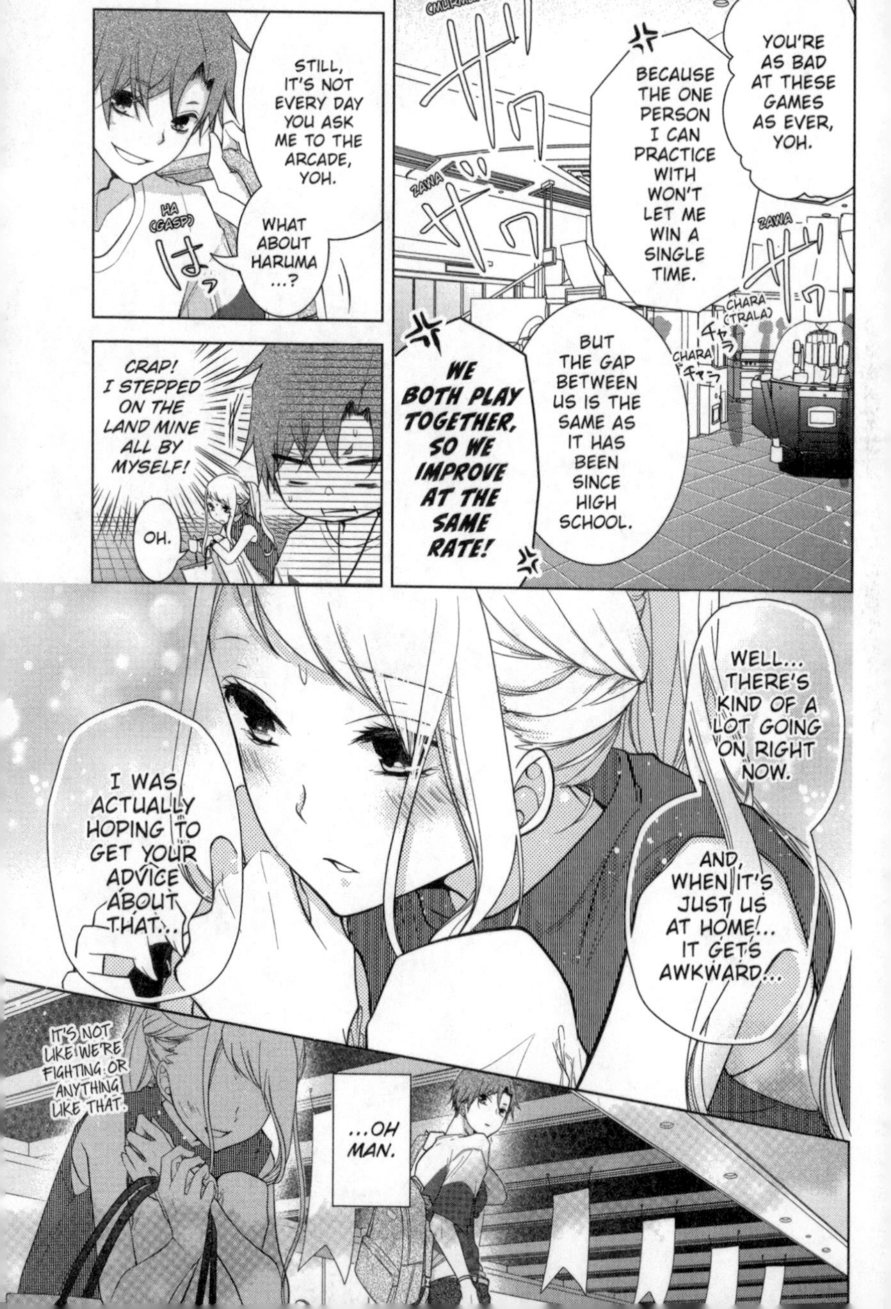
ZAWA (MURMUR)
ザワ
ZAWA
ザワ
YOU'RE AS BAD AT THESE GAMES AS EVER, YOH.
BECAUSE THE ONE PERSON I CAN PRACTICE WITH WON'T LET ME WIN A SINGLE TIME.
ZAWA
ザワ
CHARA (TRALA)
チャラ
CHARA
チャラ
BUT THE GAP BETWEEN US IS THE SAME AS IT HAS BEEN SINCE HIGH SCHOOL.
WE BOTH PLAY TOGETHER, SO WE IMPROVE AT THE SAME RATE!
STILL, IT'S NOT EVERY DAY YOU ASK ME TO THE ARCADE, YOH.
HA (GASP)
はっ
WHAT ABOUT HARUMA ...?
CRAP! I STEPPED ON THE LAND MINE ALL BY MYSELF!
OH.
WELL... THERE'S KIND OF A LOT GOING ON RIGHT NOW.
AND, WHEN IT'S JUST US AT HOME... IT GETS AWKWARD...
I WAS ACTUALLY HOPING TO GET YOUR ADVICE ABOUT THAT...
...OH MAN.
IT'S NOT LIKE WE'RE FIGHTING OR ANYTHING LIKE THAT.

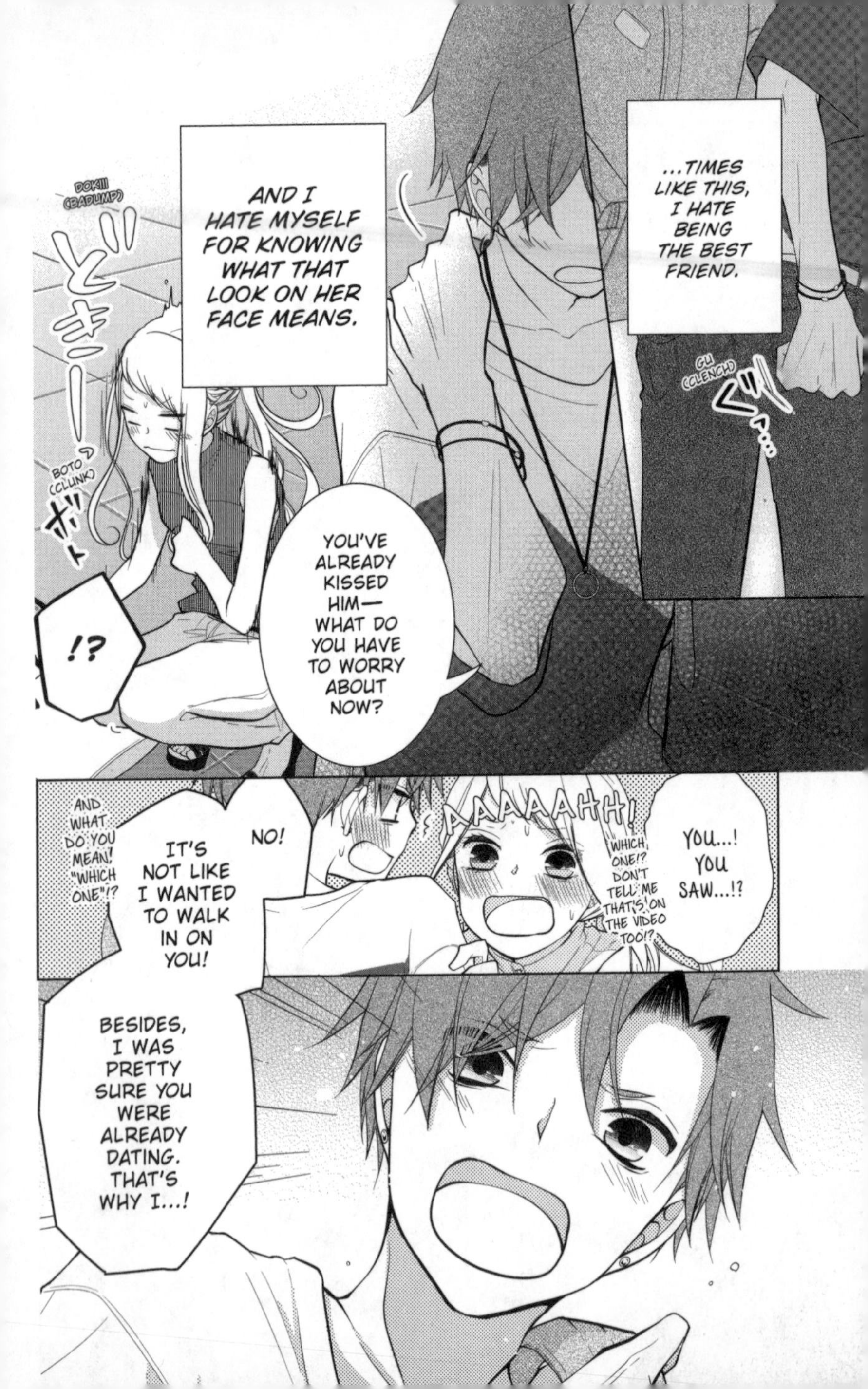
...TIMES LIKE THIS, I HATE BEING THE BEST FRIEND.
GU (CLENCH)
AND I HATE MYSELF FOR KNOWING WHAT THAT LOOK ON HER FACE MEANS.
DOKIII (BADUMP)
BOTO (CLUNK)
YOU'VE ALREADY KISSED HIM—WHAT DO YOU HAVE TO WORRY ABOUT NOW?
!?
YOU...! YOU SAW...!?
WHICH ONE!? DON'T TELL ME THAT'S ON THE VIDEO TOO!?
AAAAAAHH!
NO!
IT'S NOT LIKE I WANTED TO WALK IN ON YOU!
AND WHAT DO YOU MEAN! "WHICH ONE"!?
BESIDES, I WAS PRETTY SURE YOU WERE ALREADY DATING. THAT'S WHY I...!

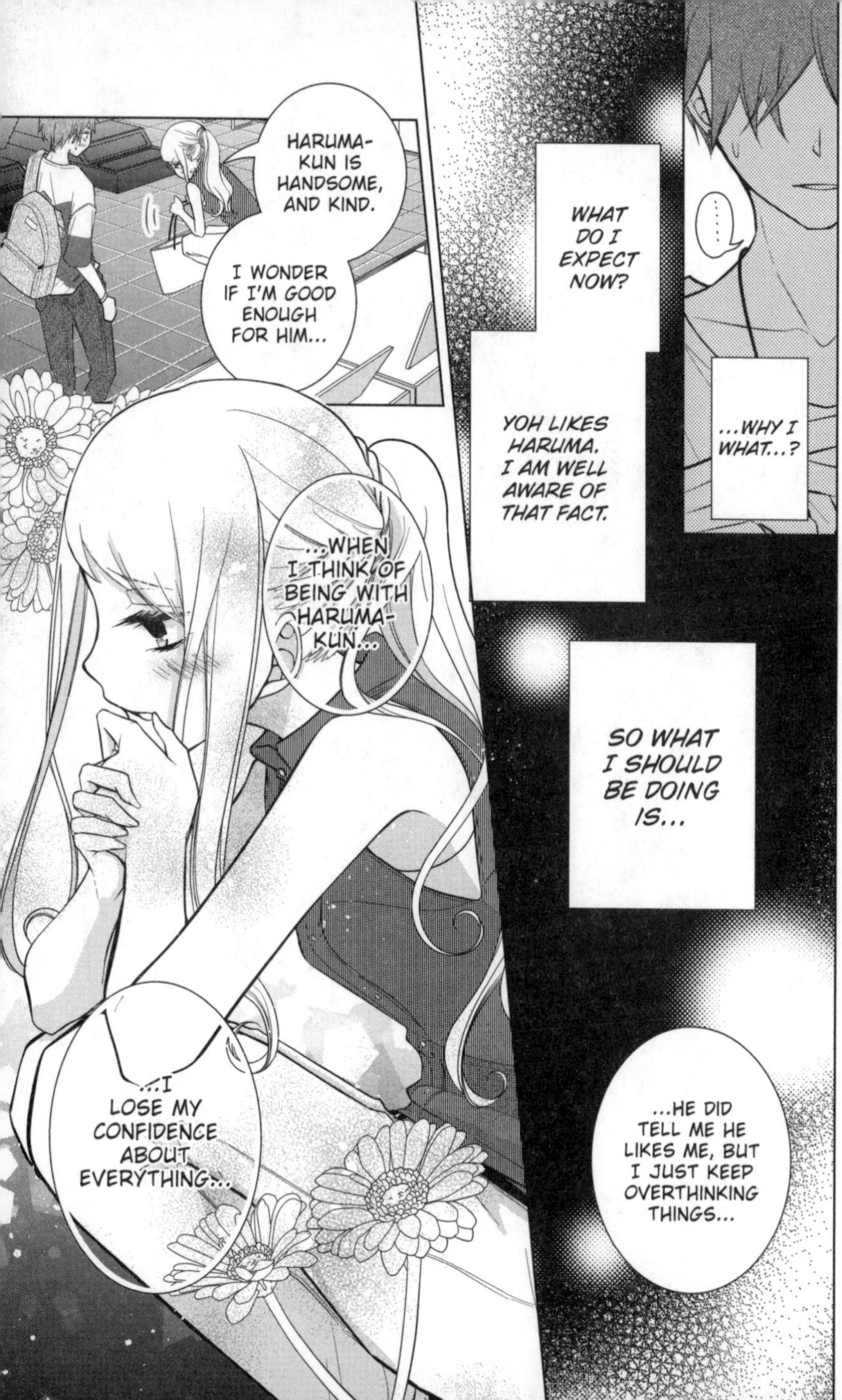

……
WHAT DO I EXPECT NOW?
...WHY I WHAT...?
YOH LIKES HARUMA. I AM WELL AWARE OF THAT FACT.
SO WHAT I SHOULD BE DOING IS...
...HE DID TELL ME HE LIKES ME, BUT I JUST KEEP OVERTHINKING THINGS...
HARUMA-KUN IS HANDSOME, AND KIND.
I WONDER IF I'M GOOD ENOUGH FOR HIM...
...WHEN I THINK OF BEING WITH HARUMA-KUN...
...I LOSE MY CONFIDENCE ABOUT EVERYTHING...

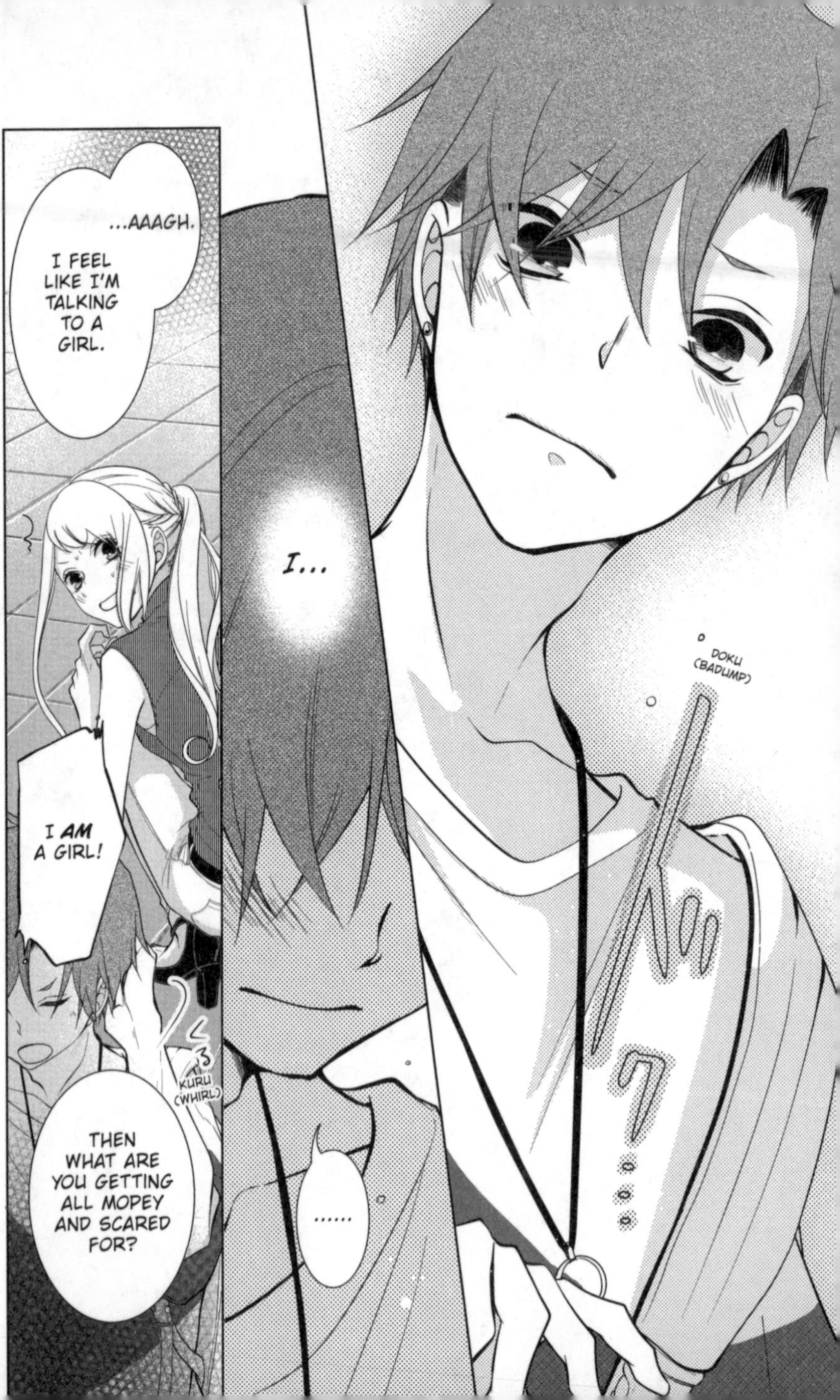
...AAAGH.
I FEEL LIKE I'M TALKING TO A GIRL.
I *AM* A GIRL!
KURU (WHIRL)
THEN WHAT ARE YOU GETTING ALL MOPEY AND SCARED FOR?
I...
DOKU (BADUMP)
......

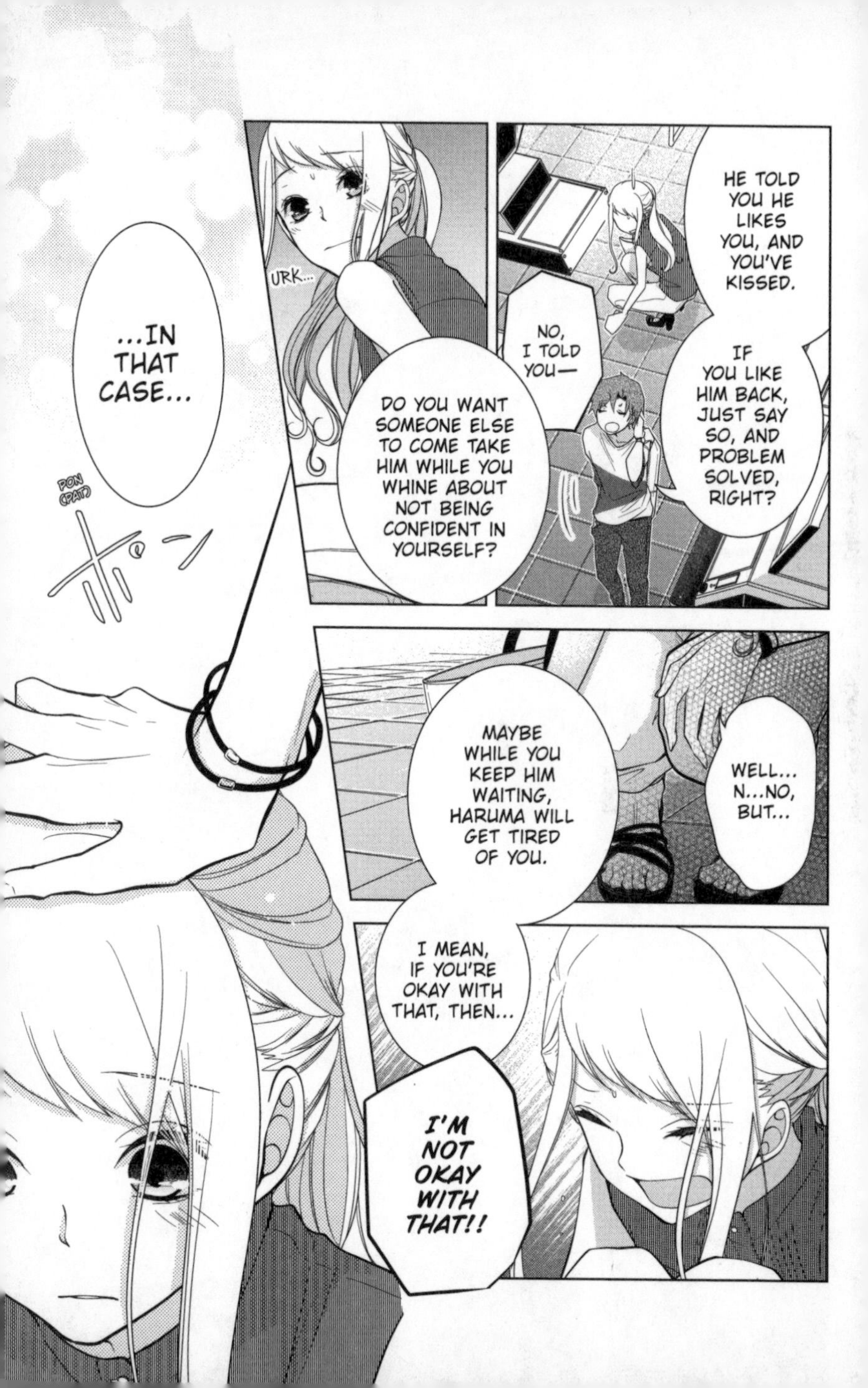
HE TOLD YOU HE LIKES YOU, AND YOU'VE KISSED.
NO, I TOLD YOU—
IF YOU LIKE HIM BACK, JUST SAY SO, AND PROBLEM SOLVED, RIGHT?
URK...
DO YOU WANT SOMEONE ELSE TO COME TAKE HIM WHILE YOU WHINE ABOUT NOT BEING CONFIDENT IN YOURSELF?
WELL... N...NO, BUT...
MAYBE WHILE YOU KEEP HIM WAITING, HARUMA WILL GET TIRED OF YOU.
I MEAN, IF YOU'RE OKAY WITH THAT, THEN...
I'M NOT OKAY WITH THAT!!
...IN THAT CASE...
PON (PAT)

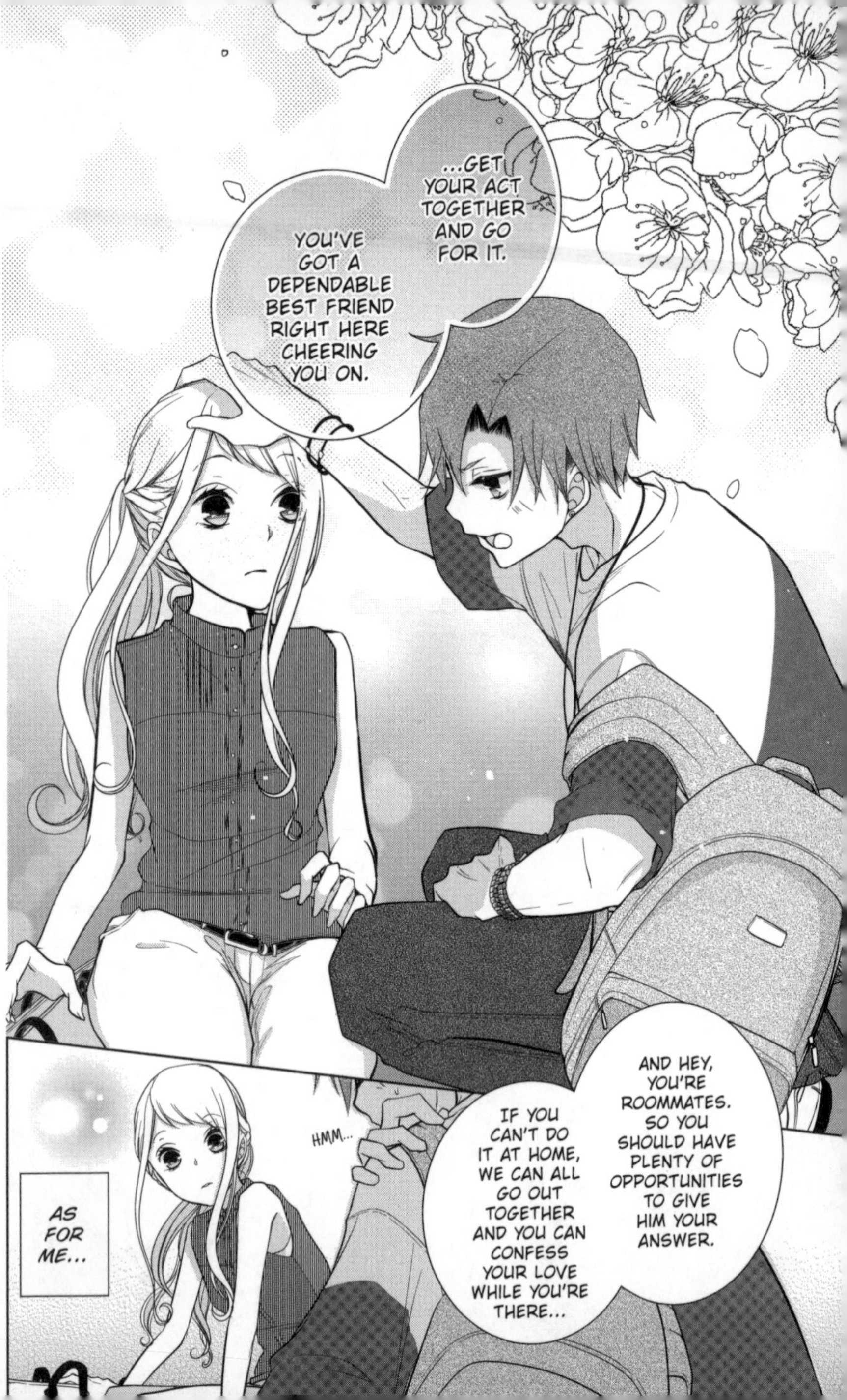
...GET YOUR ACT TOGETHER AND GO FOR IT.
YOU'VE GOT A DEPENDABLE BEST FRIEND RIGHT HERE CHEERING YOU ON.
AND HEY, YOU'RE ROOMMATES. SO YOU SHOULD HAVE PLENTY OF OPPORTUNITIES TO GIVE HIM YOUR ANSWER.
IF YOU CAN'T DO IT AT HOME, WE CAN ALL GO OUT TOGETHER AND YOU CAN CONFESS YOUR LOVE WHILE YOU'RE THERE...
HMM...
AS FOR ME...

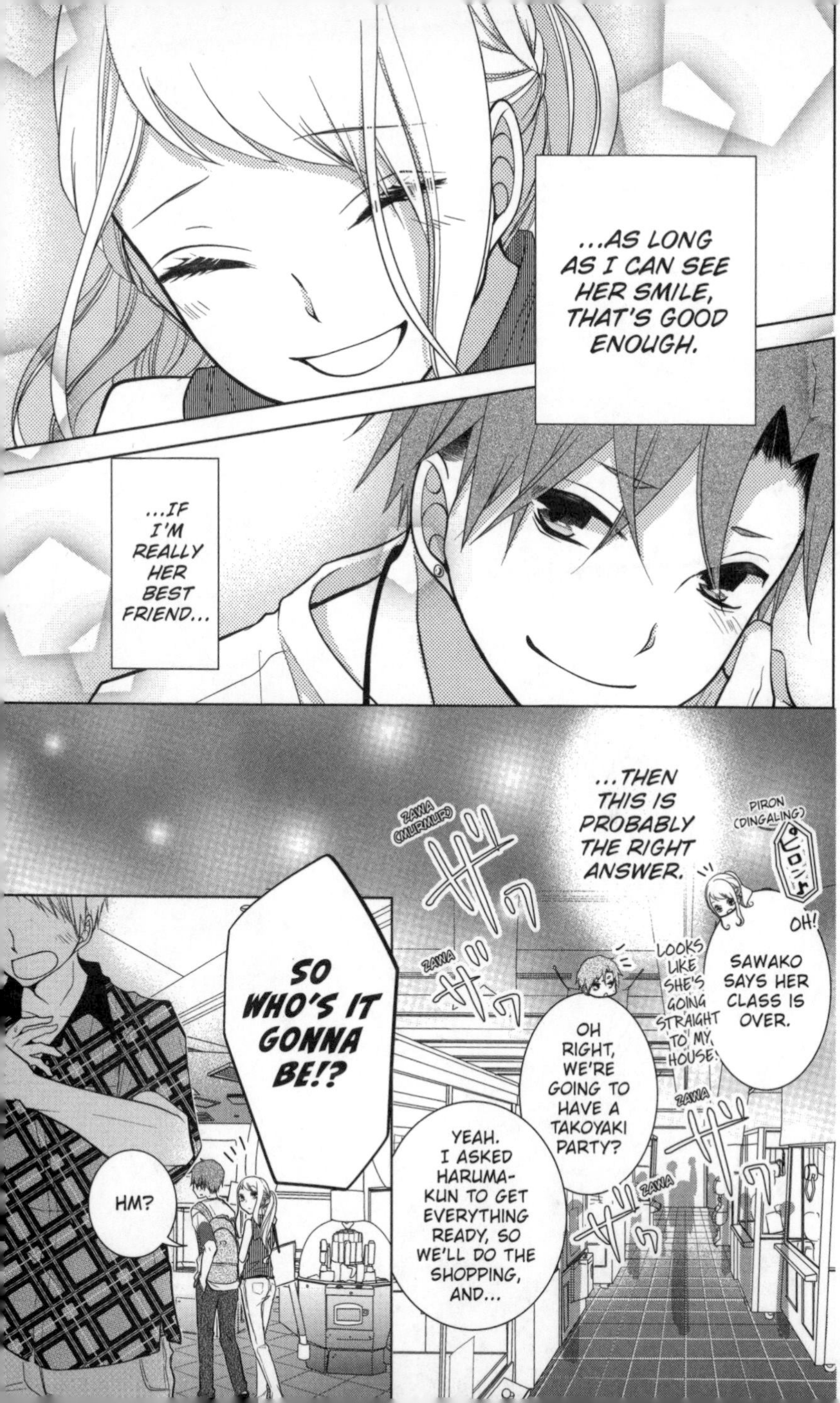
...AS LONG AS I CAN SEE HER SMILE, THAT'S GOOD ENOUGH.
...IF I'M REALLY HER BEST FRIEND...
...THEN THIS IS PROBABLY THE RIGHT ANSWER.
PIRON (DINGALING)
OH!
SAWAKO SAYS HER CLASS IS OVER.
LOOKS LIKE SHE'S GOING STRAIGHT TO MY HOUSE!
ZAWA (MURMUR)
ZAWA
OH RIGHT, WE'RE GOING TO HAVE A TAKOYAKI PARTY?
ZAWA
YEAH. I ASKED HARUMA-KUN TO GET EVERYTHING READY, SO WE'LL DO THE SHOPPING, AND...
ZAWA
SO WHO'S IT GONNA BE!?
HM?

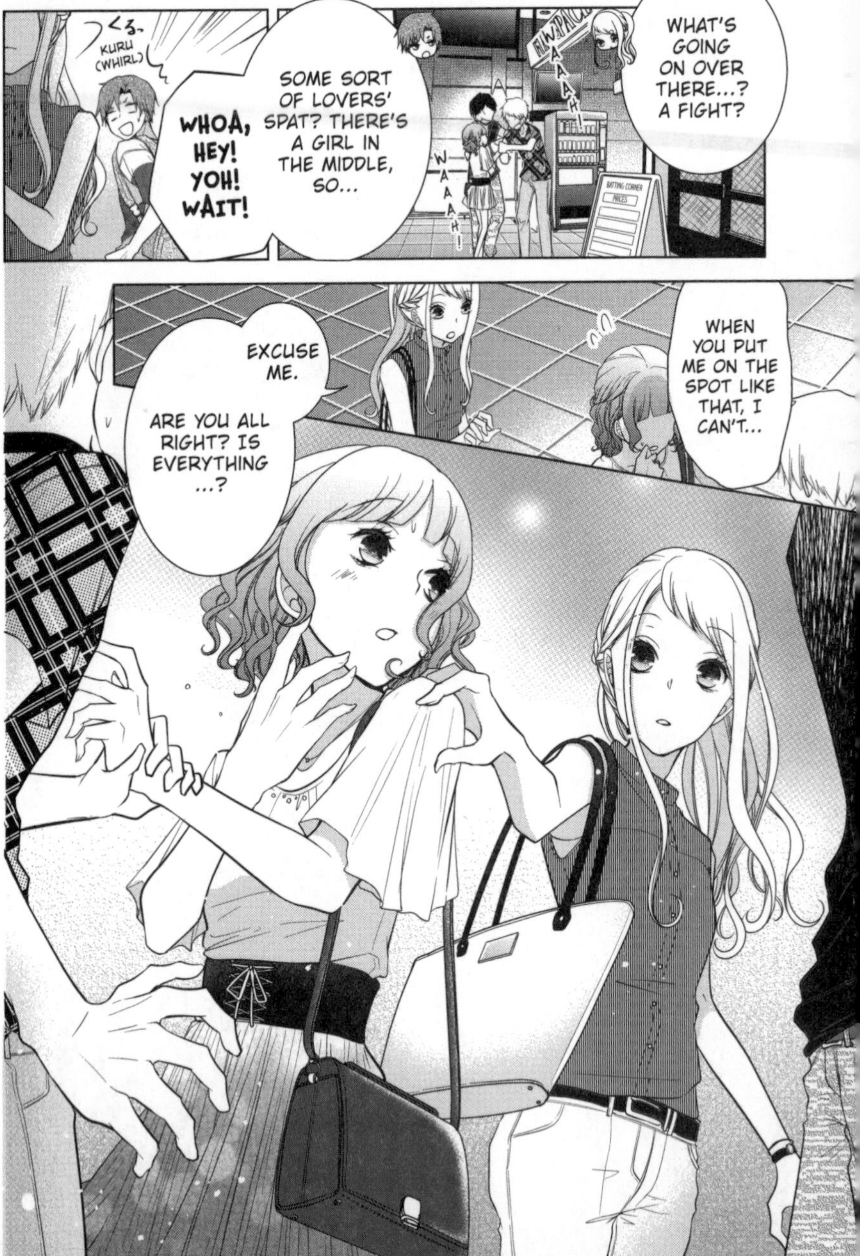
WHAT'S GOING ON OVER THERE...? A FIGHT?
WAAAH!
WAAAH!
BATTING CORNER
PRICES
SOME SORT OF LOVERS' SPAT? THERE'S A GIRL IN THE MIDDLE, SO...
WHOA, HEY! YOH! WAIT!
KURU (WHIRL)
WHEN YOU PUT ME ON THE SPOT LIKE THAT, I CAN'T...
EXCUSE ME.
ARE YOU ALL RIGHT? IS EVERYTHING ...?

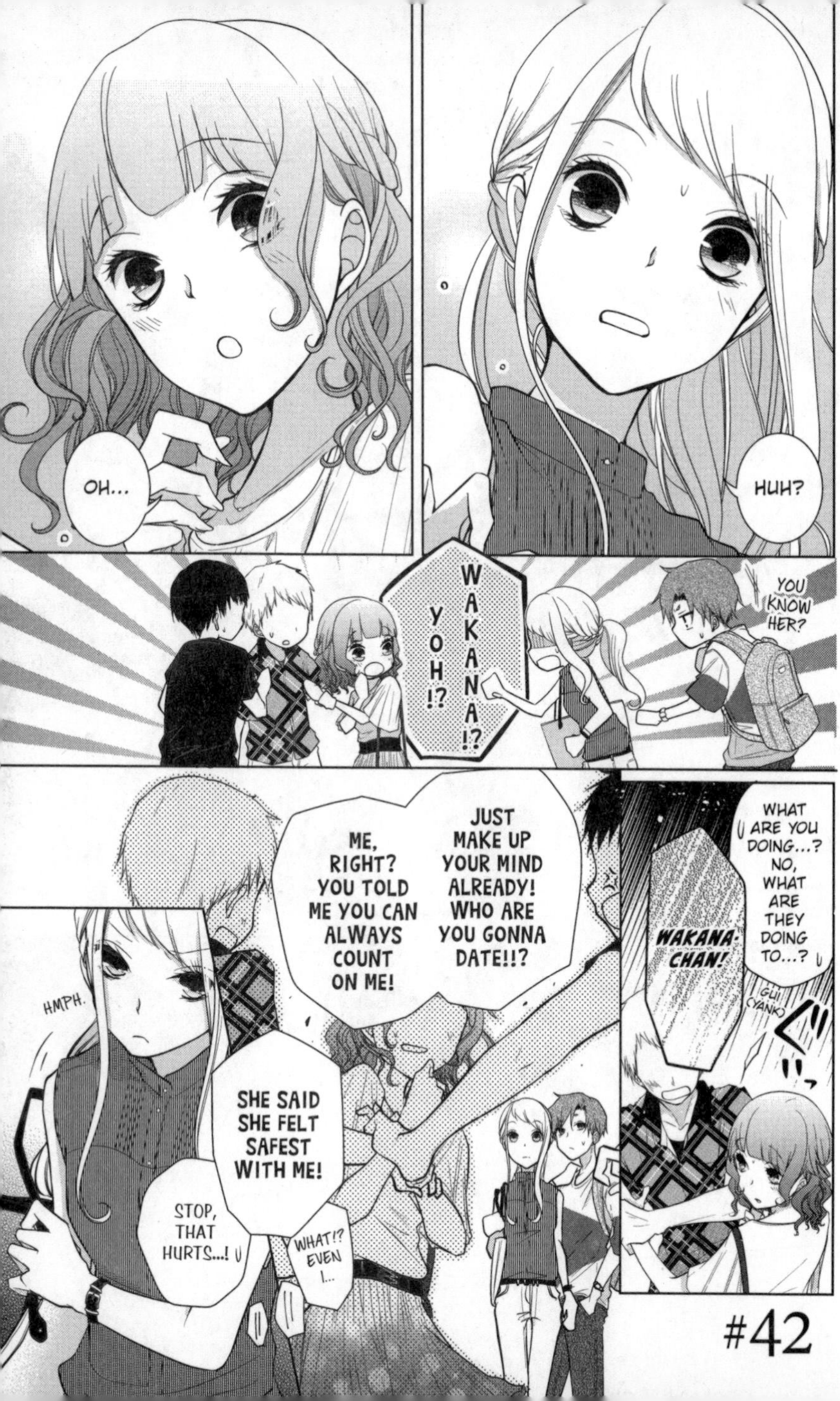
HUH?
OH...
YOU KNOW HER?
WAKANA!?
YOH!?
WHAT ARE YOU DOING...? NO, WHAT ARE THEY DOING TO...?
WAKANA-CHAN!
GUI (YANK)
JUST MAKE UP YOUR MIND ALREADY! WHO ARE YOU GONNA DATE!!?
ME, RIGHT? YOU TOLD ME YOU CAN ALWAYS COUNT ON ME!
HMPH.
SHE SAID SHE FELT SAFEST WITH ME!
WHAT!? EVEN I...
STOP, THAT HURTS...!
#42

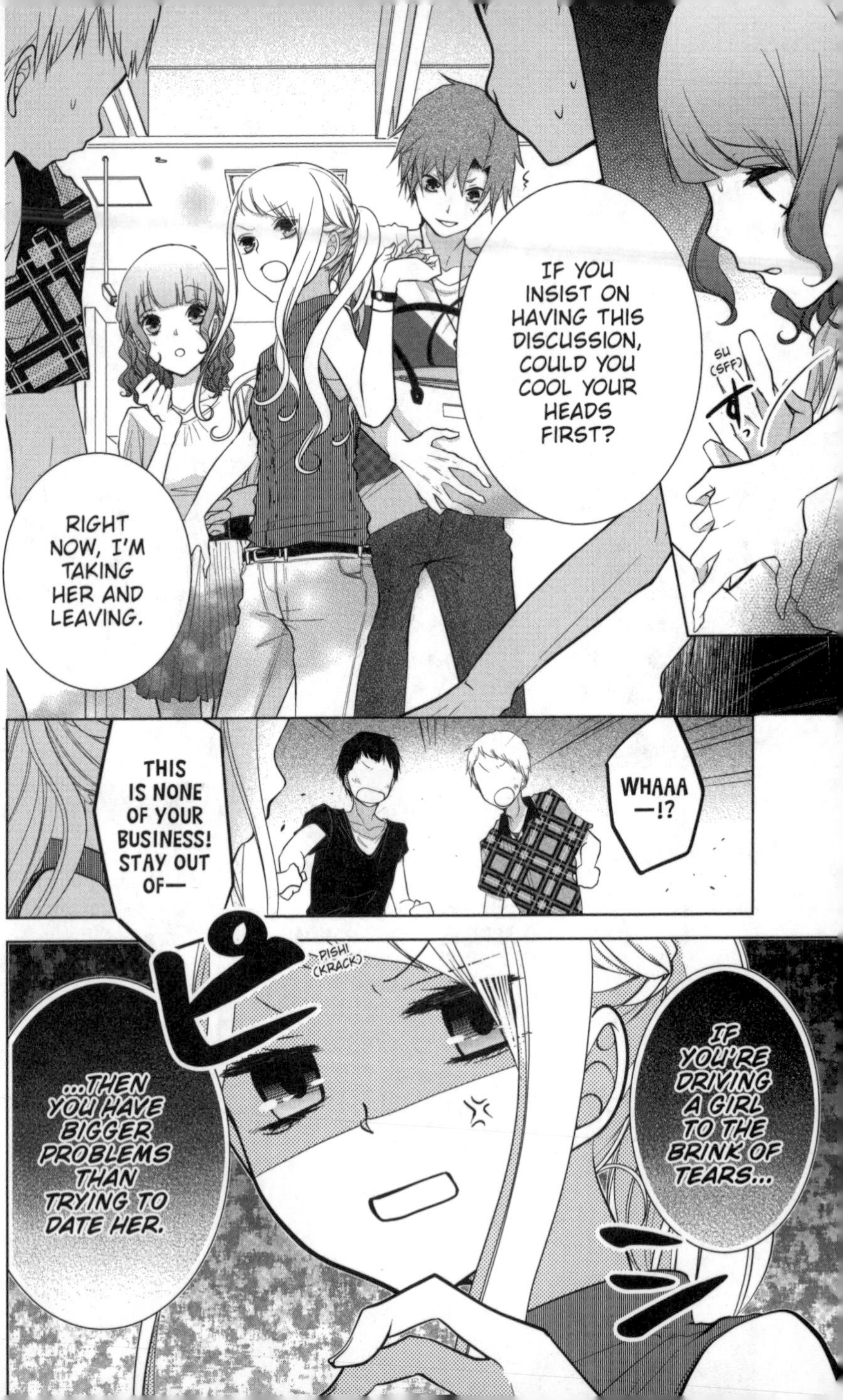
IF YOU INSIST ON HAVING THIS DISCUSSION, COULD YOU COOL YOUR HEADS FIRST?
SU (SFF)
RIGHT NOW, I'M TAKING HER AND LEAVING.
WHAAA—!?
THIS IS NONE OF YOUR BUSINESS! STAY OUT OF—
PISHI (KRACK)
IF YOU'RE DRIVING A GIRL TO THE BRINK OF TEARS...
...THEN YOU HAVE BIGGER PROBLEMS THAN TRYING TO DATE HER.

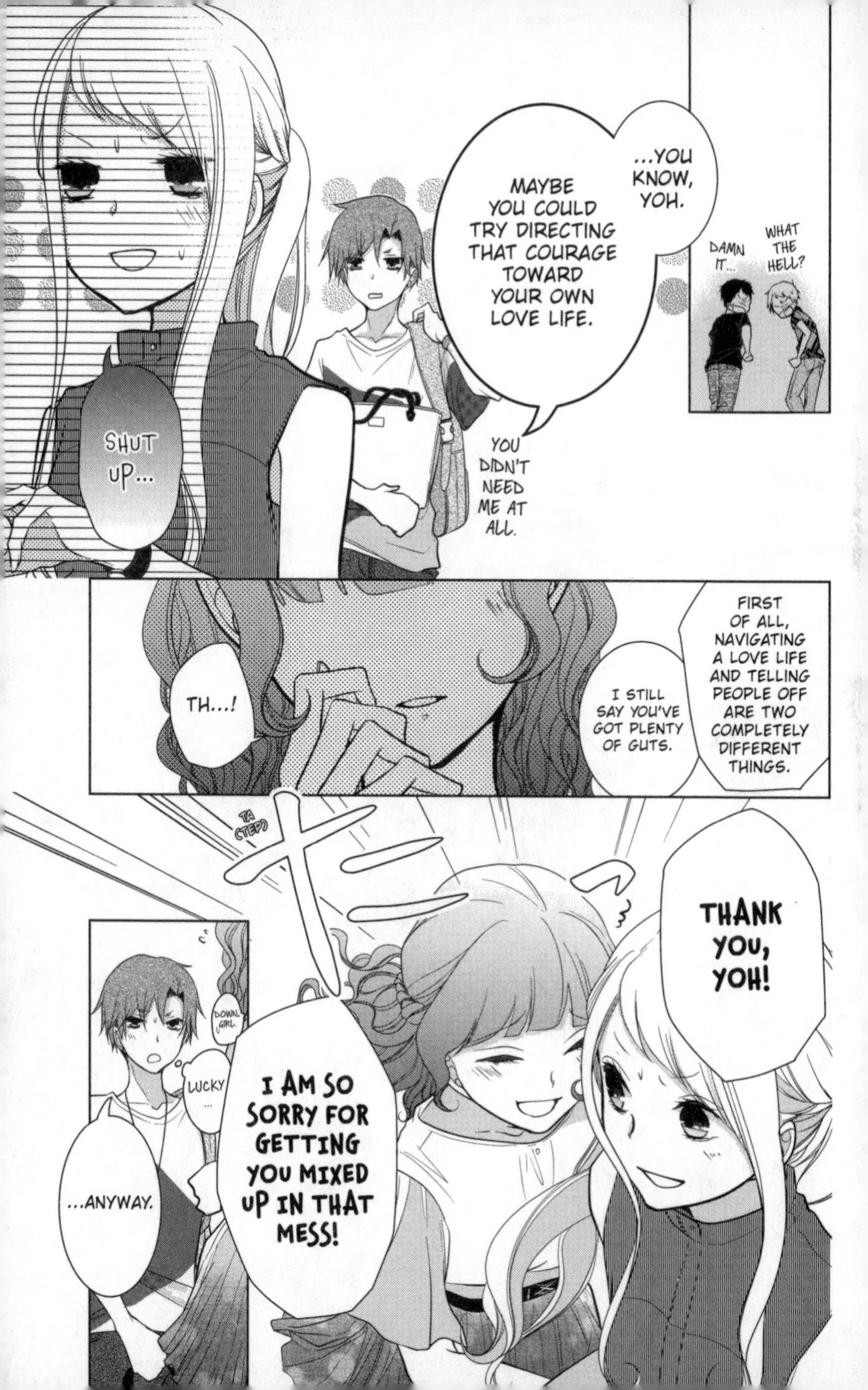
WHAT THE HELL?
DAMN IT...
...YOU KNOW, YOH.
MAYBE YOU COULD TRY DIRECTING THAT COURAGE TOWARD YOUR OWN LOVE LIFE.
YOU DIDN'T NEED ME AT ALL.
SHUT UP...
FIRST OF ALL, NAVIGATING A LOVE LIFE AND TELLING PEOPLE OFF ARE TWO COMPLETELY DIFFERENT THINGS.
I STILL SAY YOU'VE GOT PLENTY OF GUTS.
TH...!
TA (TEP)
THANK YOU, YOH!
I AM SO SORRY FOR GETTING YOU MIXED UP IN THAT MESS!
DOWN, GIRL.
LUCKY...
...ANYWAY.

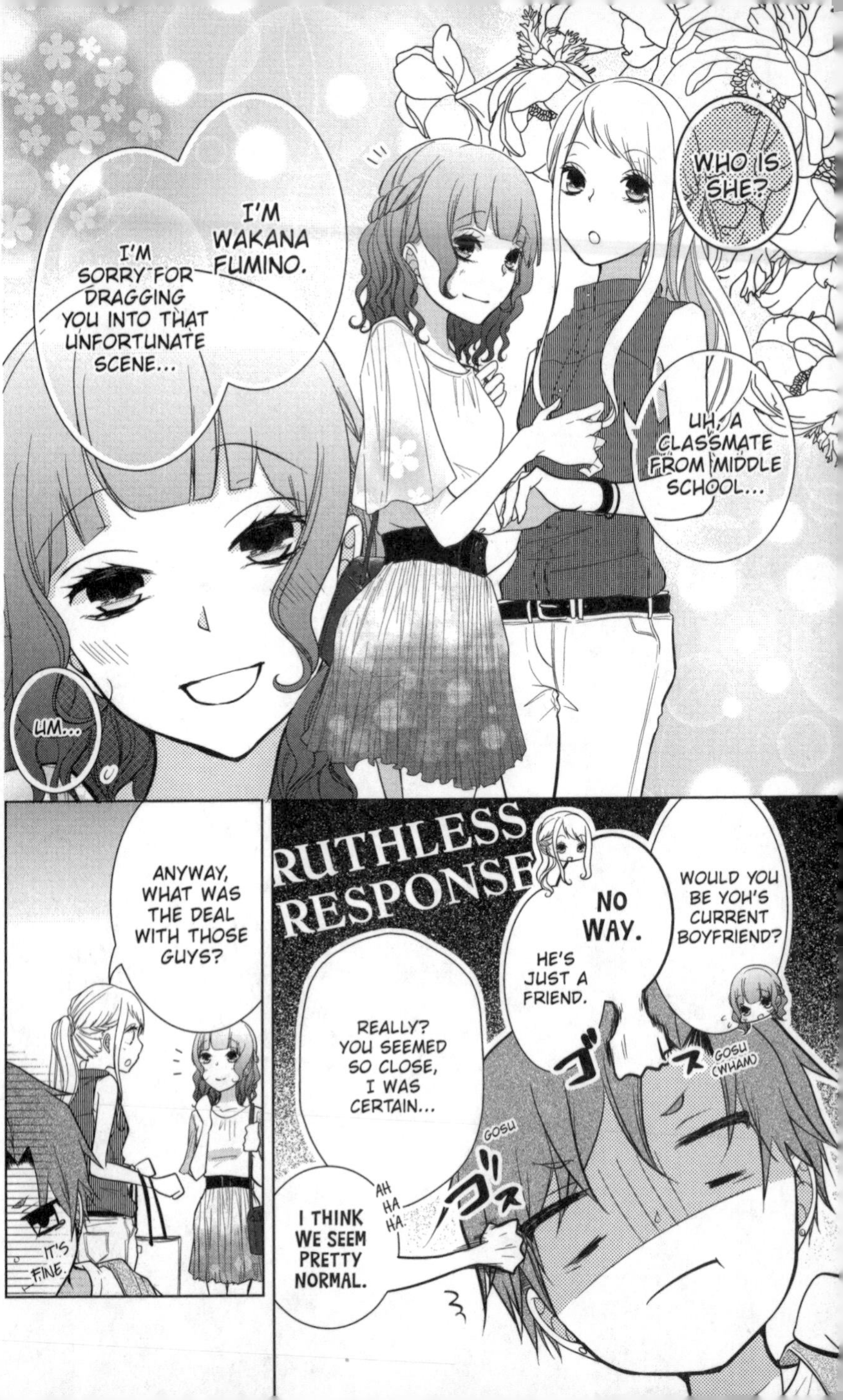
WHO IS SHE?
UH, A CLASSMATE FROM MIDDLE SCHOOL...
I'M WAKANA FUMINO.
I'M SORRY FOR DRAGGING YOU INTO THAT UNFORTUNATE SCENE...
UM...
WOULD YOU BE YOH'S CURRENT BOYFRIEND?
NO WAY.
HE'S JUST A FRIEND.
RUTHLESS RESPONSE
GOSU (WHAM)
REALLY? YOU SEEMED SO CLOSE, I WAS CERTAIN...
GOSU
AH HA HA.
I THINK WE SEEM PRETTY NORMAL.
ANYWAY, WHAT WAS THE DEAL WITH THOSE GUYS?
IT'S FINE.

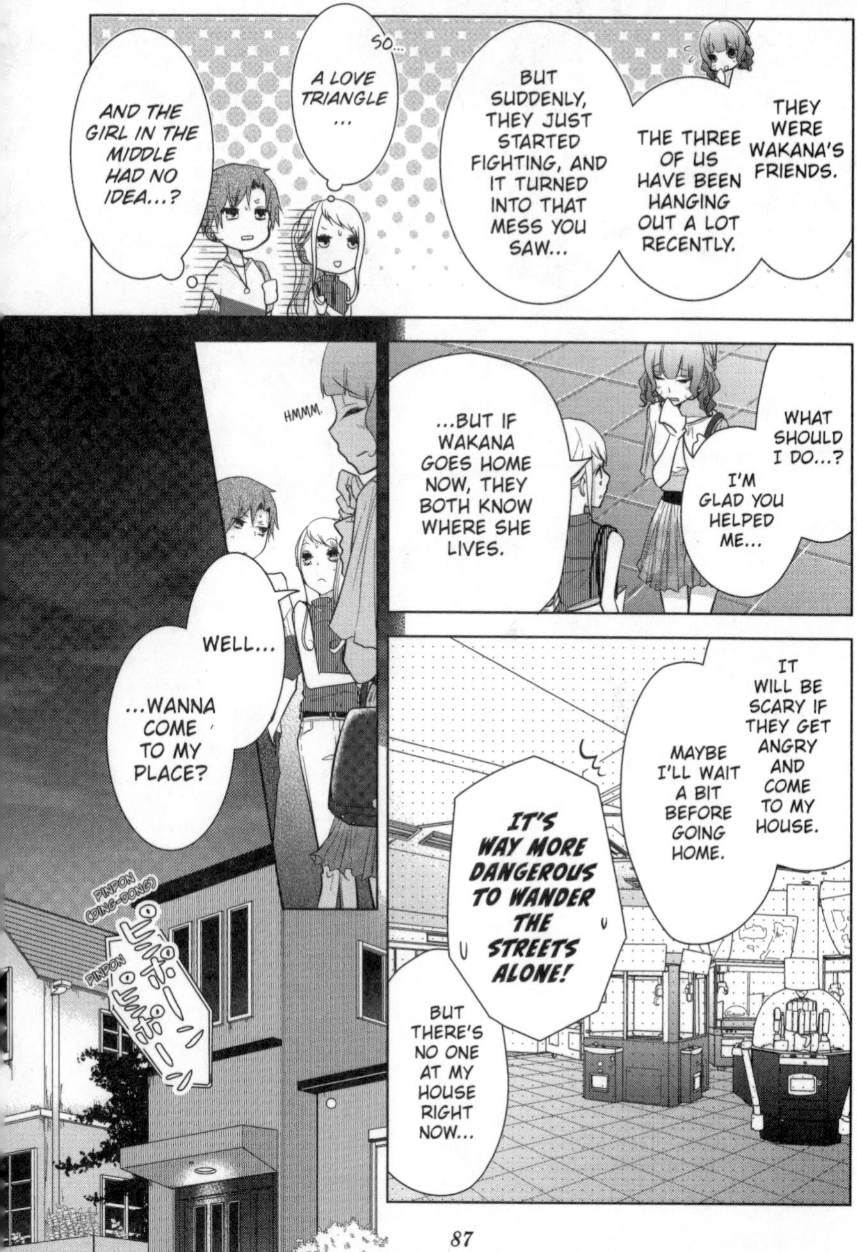
THEY WERE WAKANA'S FRIENDS.
THE THREE OF US HAVE BEEN HANGING OUT A LOT RECENTLY.
BUT SUDDENLY, THEY JUST STARTED FIGHTING, AND IT TURNED INTO THAT MESS YOU SAW...
SO...
A LOVE TRIANGLE...
AND THE GIRL IN THE MIDDLE HAD NO IDEA...?
WHAT SHOULD I DO...?
I'M GLAD YOU HELPED ME...
...BUT IF WAKANA GOES HOME NOW, THEY BOTH KNOW WHERE SHE LIVES.
IT WILL BE SCARY IF THEY GET ANGRY AND COME TO MY HOUSE.
MAYBE I'LL WAIT A BIT BEFORE GOING HOME.
IT'S WAY MORE DANGEROUS TO WANDER THE STREETS ALONE!
BUT THERE'S NO ONE AT MY HOUSE RIGHT NOW...
HMMM.
WELL...
...WANNA COME TO MY PLACE?
PINPON (DING-DONG)
PINPON

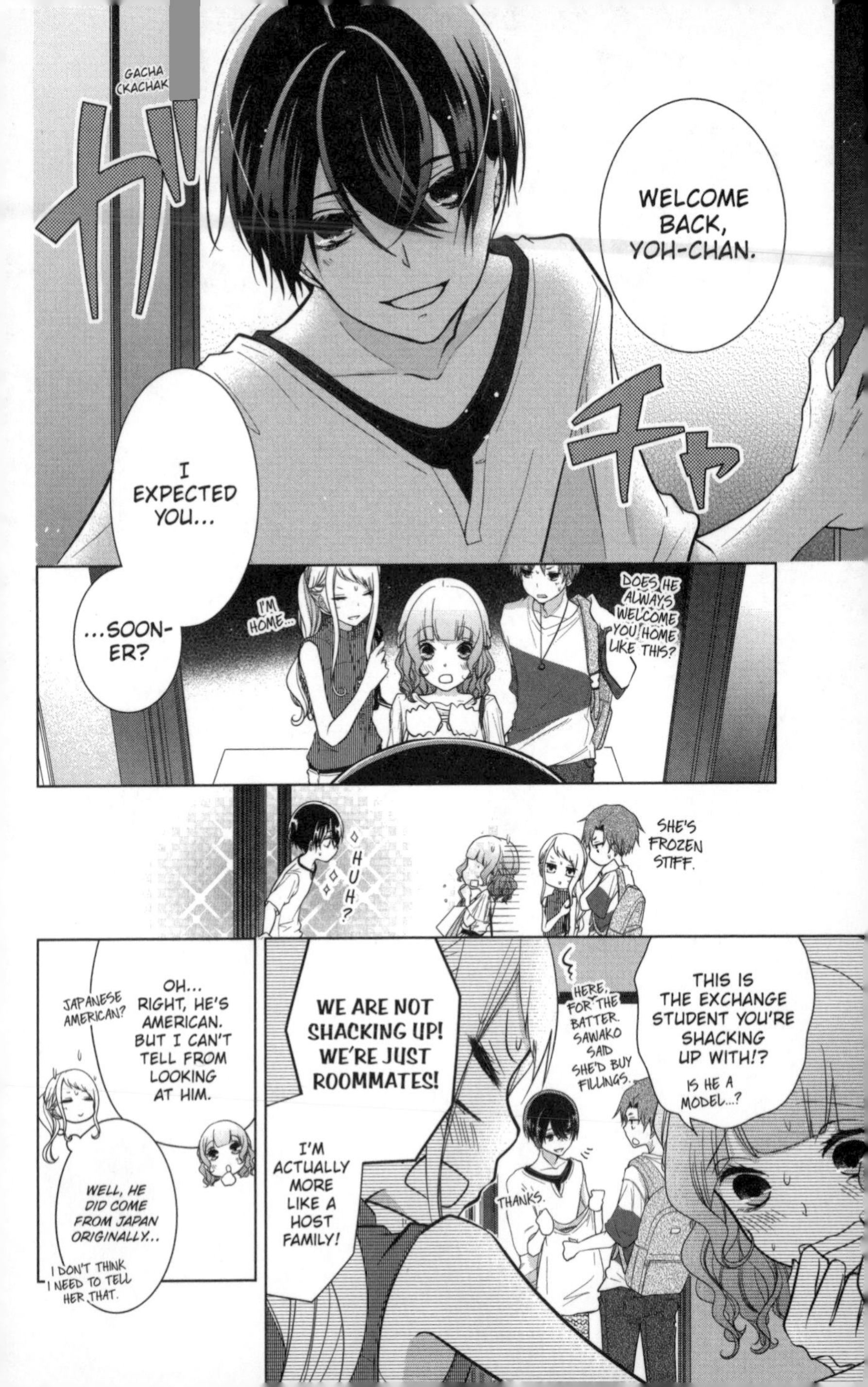
GACHA KACHAK
WELCOME BACK, YOH-CHAN.
I EXPECTED YOU...
...SOON-ER?
DOES HE ALWAYS WELCOME YOU HOME LIKE THIS?
I'M HOME...
SHE'S FROZEN STIFF.
HUH?
THIS IS THE EXCHANGE STUDENT YOU'RE SHACKING UP WITH!?
IS HE A MODEL...?
HERE, FOR THE BATTER. SAWAKO SAID SHE'D BUY FILLINGS.
WE ARE NOT SHACKING UP! WE'RE JUST ROOMMATES!
THANKS.
I'M ACTUALLY MORE LIKE A HOST FAMILY!
OH... RIGHT, HE'S AMERICAN. BUT I CAN'T TELL FROM LOOKING AT HIM.
JAPANESE AMERICAN?
WELL, HE DID COME FROM JAPAN ORIGINALLY...
I DON'T THINK I NEED TO TELL HER THAT.

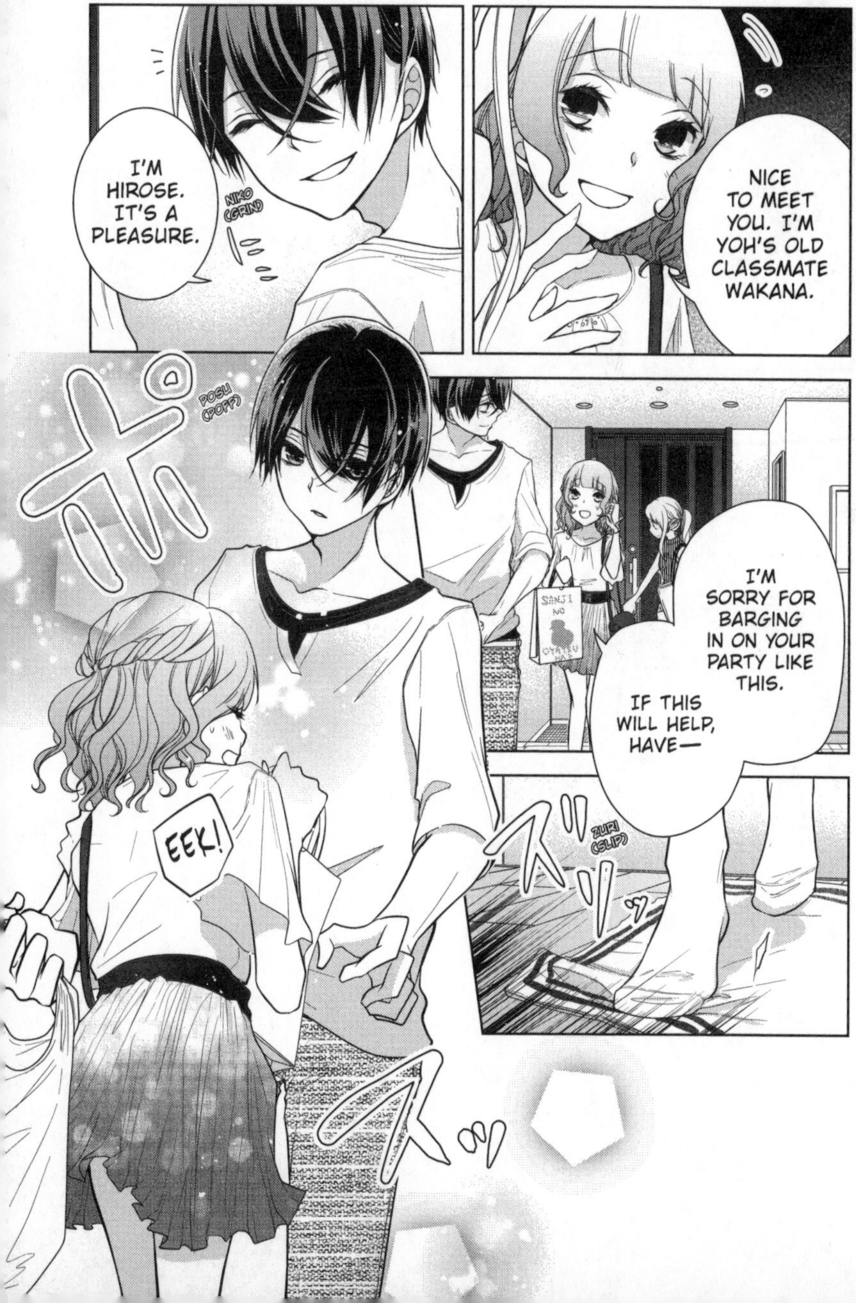
NICE TO MEET YOU. I'M YOH'S OLD CLASSMATE WAKANA.
I'M HIROSE. IT'S A PLEASURE.
NIKO (GRIN)
I'M SORRY FOR BARGING IN ON YOUR PARTY LIKE THIS.
IF THIS WILL HELP, HAVE—
POSU (POFF)
ZURI (SLIP)
EEK!

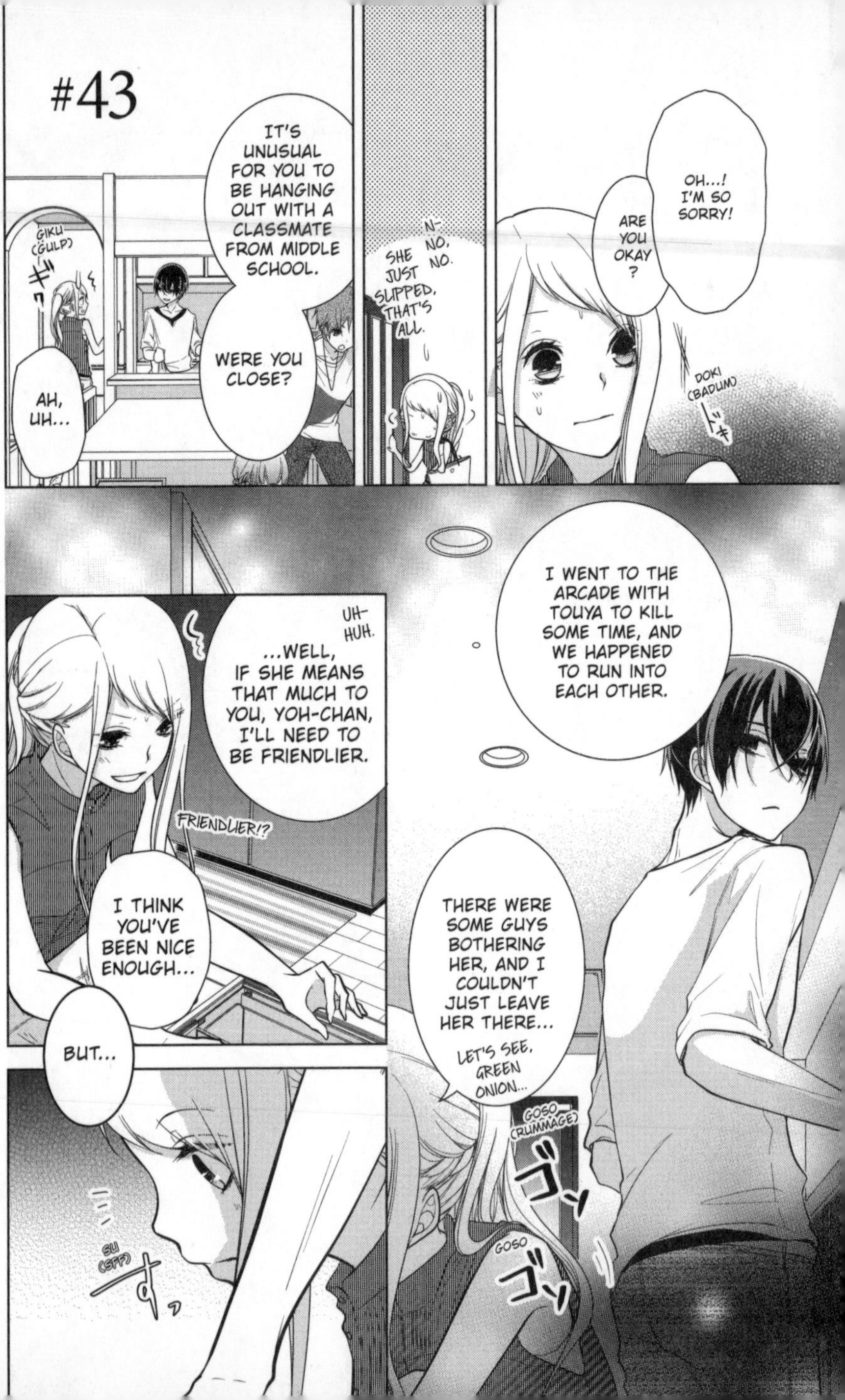
OH...! I'M SO SORRY!
ARE YOU OKAY?
DOKI (BADUM)
N-NO, NO.
SHE JUST SLIPPED, THAT'S ALL.
#43
IT'S UNUSUAL FOR YOU TO BE HANGING OUT WITH A CLASSMATE FROM MIDDLE SCHOOL.
WERE YOU CLOSE?
GIKU (GULP)
AH, UH...
I WENT TO THE ARCADE WITH TOUYA TO KILL SOME TIME, AND WE HAPPENED TO RUN INTO EACH OTHER.
THERE WERE SOME GUYS BOTHERING HER, AND I COULDN'T JUST LEAVE HER THERE...
LET'S SEE, GREEN ONION...
GOSO (RUMMAGE)
GOSO
UH-HUH.
...WELL, IF SHE MEANS THAT MUCH TO YOU, YOH-CHAN, I'LL NEED TO BE FRIENDLIER.
FRIENDLIER!?
I THINK YOU'VE BEEN NICE ENOUGH...
BUT...
SU (SFF)

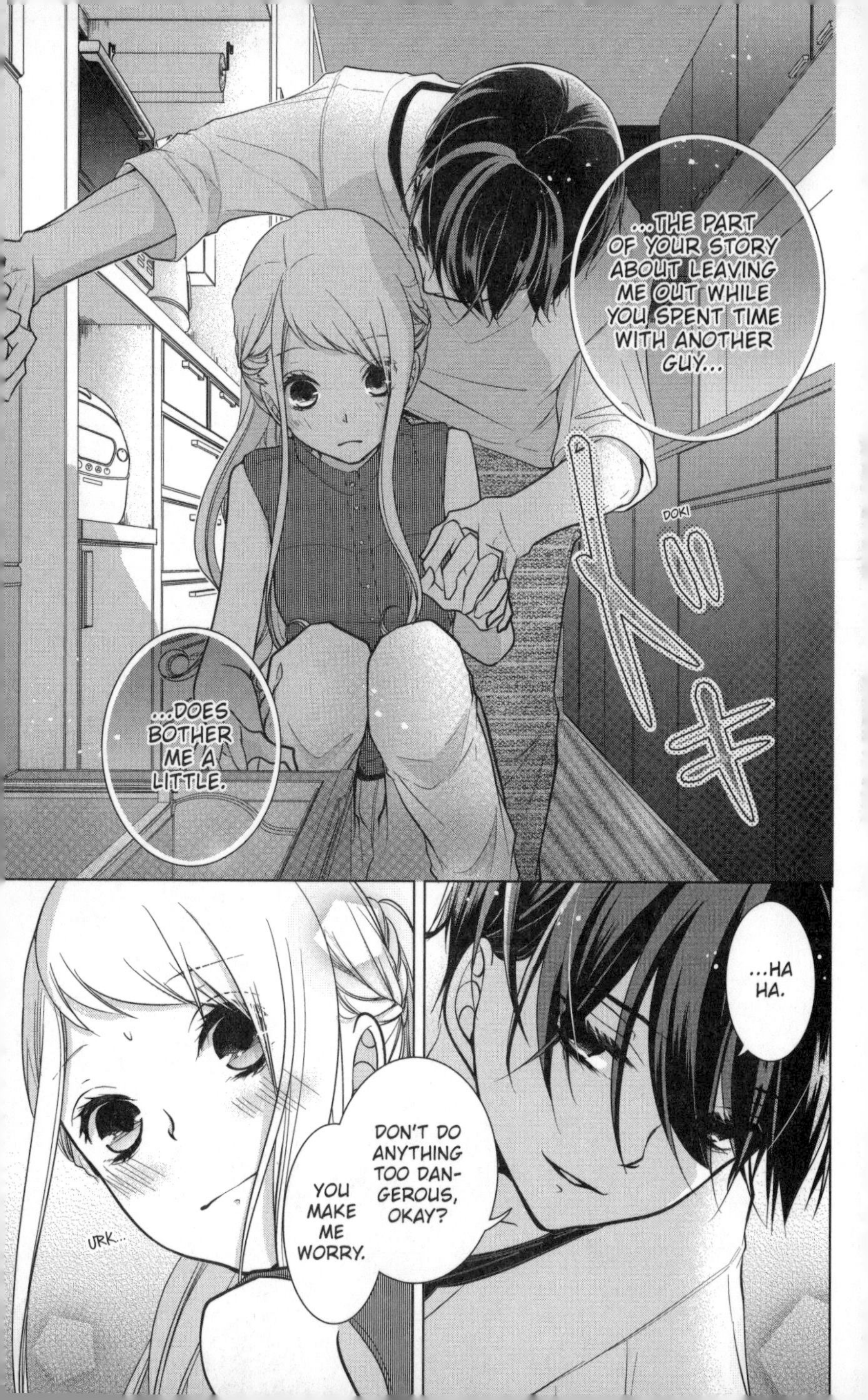
...THE PART OF YOUR STORY ABOUT LEAVING ME OUT WHILE YOU SPENT TIME WITH ANOTHER GUY...
...DOES BOTHER ME A LITTLE.
DOKI
...HA HA.
DON'T DO ANYTHING TOO DAN-GEROUS, OKAY?
YOU MAKE ME WORRY.
URK...

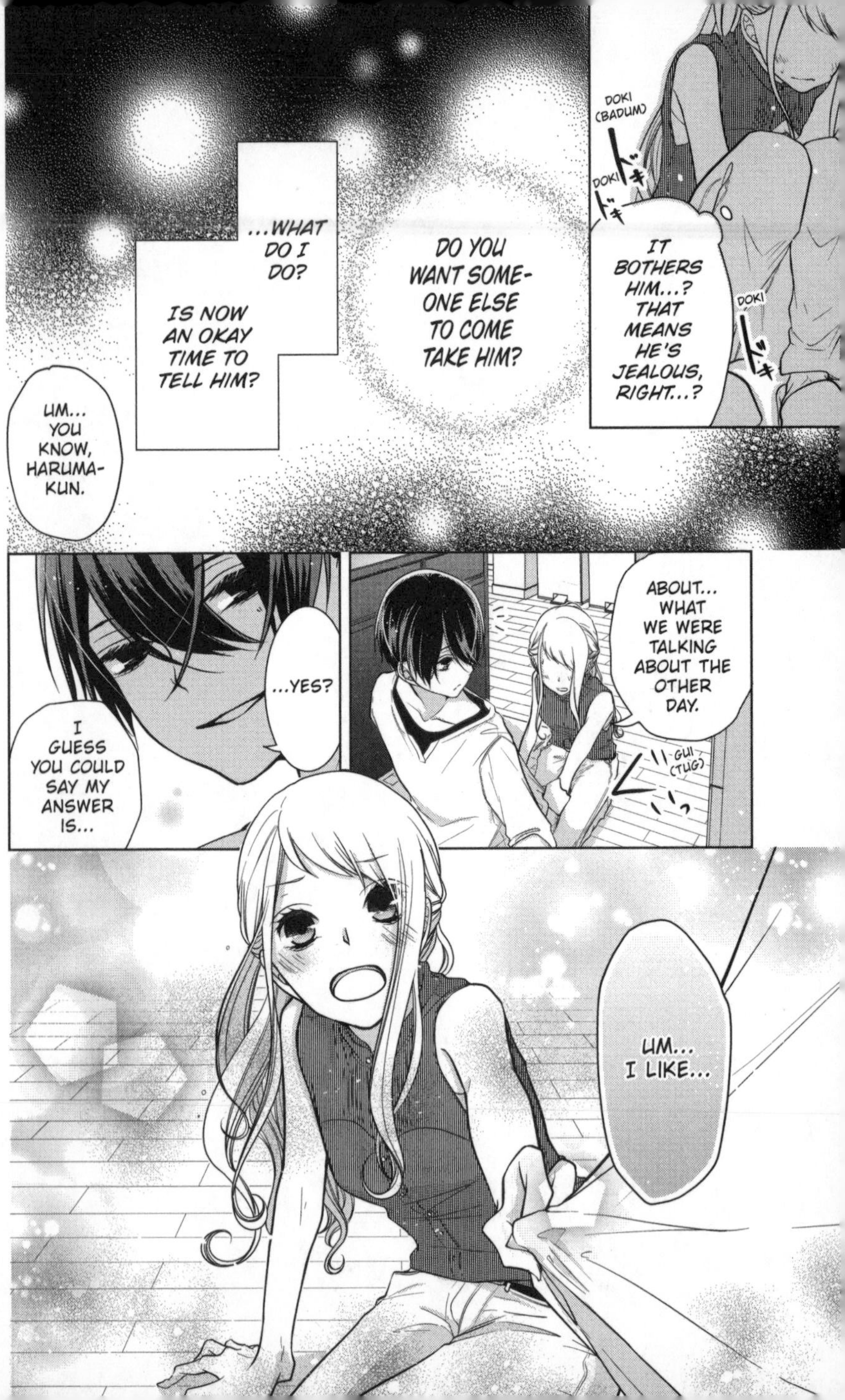
DOKI (BADUM)
ドキ
DOKI
ドキ
IT BOTHERS HIM...? THAT MEANS HE'S JEALOUS, RIGHT...?
DOKI
ドキ
DO YOU WANT SOME-ONE ELSE TO COME TAKE HIM?
...WHAT DO I DO?
IS NOW AN OKAY TIME TO TELL HIM?
UM... YOU KNOW, HARUMA-KUN.
ABOUT... WHAT WE WERE TALKING ABOUT THE OTHER DAY.
GUI (TUG)
...YES?
I GUESS YOU COULD SAY MY ANSWER IS...
UM... I LIKE...

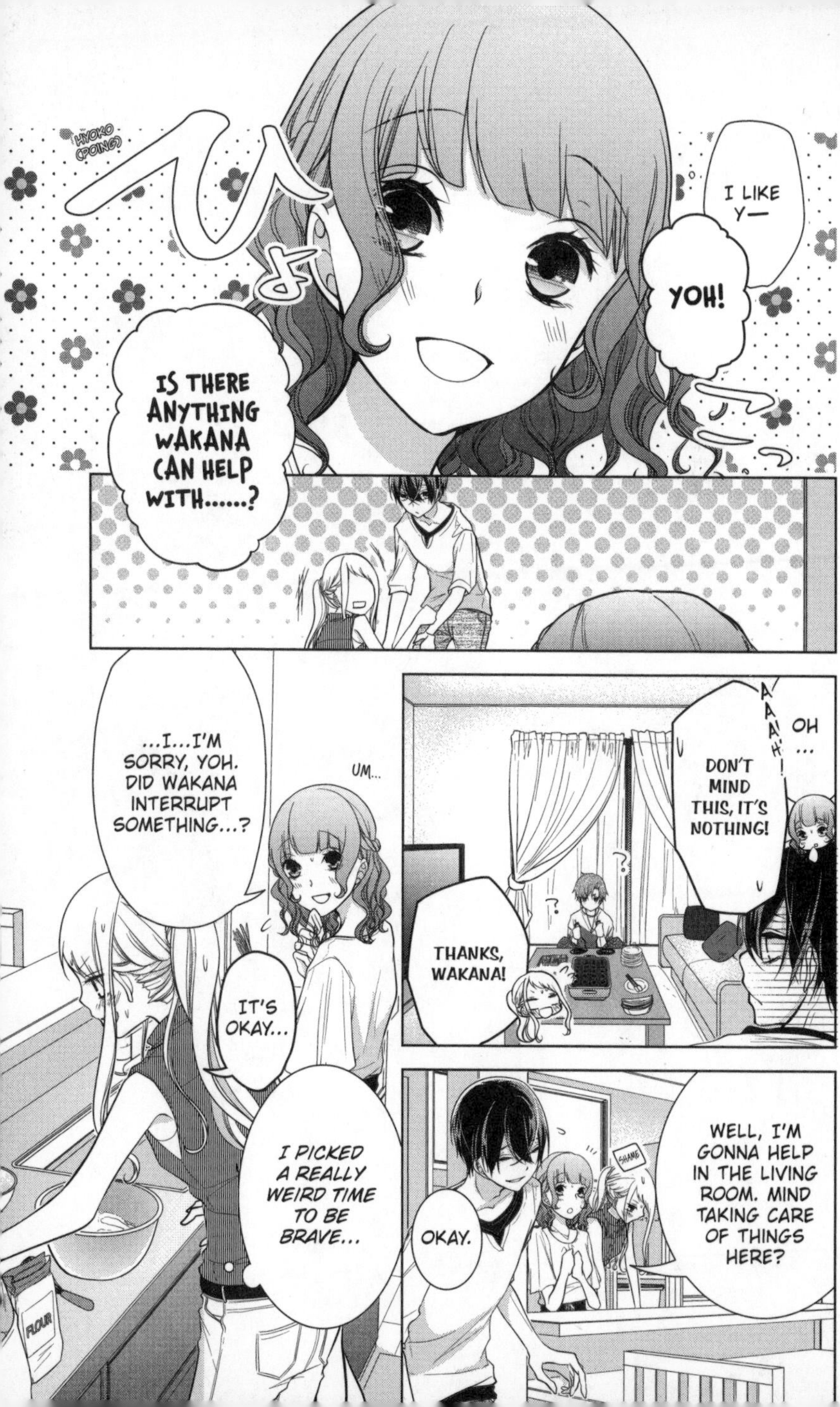
I LIKE Y—
YOH!
HYOKO (POING)
IS THERE ANYTHING WAKANA CAN HELP WITH......?
OH...
AAAH!
DON'T MIND THIS, IT'S NOTHING!
THANKS, WAKANA!
WELL, I'M GONNA HELP IN THE LIVING ROOM. MIND TAKING CARE OF THINGS HERE?
SHAME
OKAY.
...I...I'M SORRY, YOH. DID WAKANA INTERRUPT SOMETHING...?
UM...
IT'S OKAY...
I PICKED A REALLY WEIRD TIME TO BE BRAVE...
FLOUR

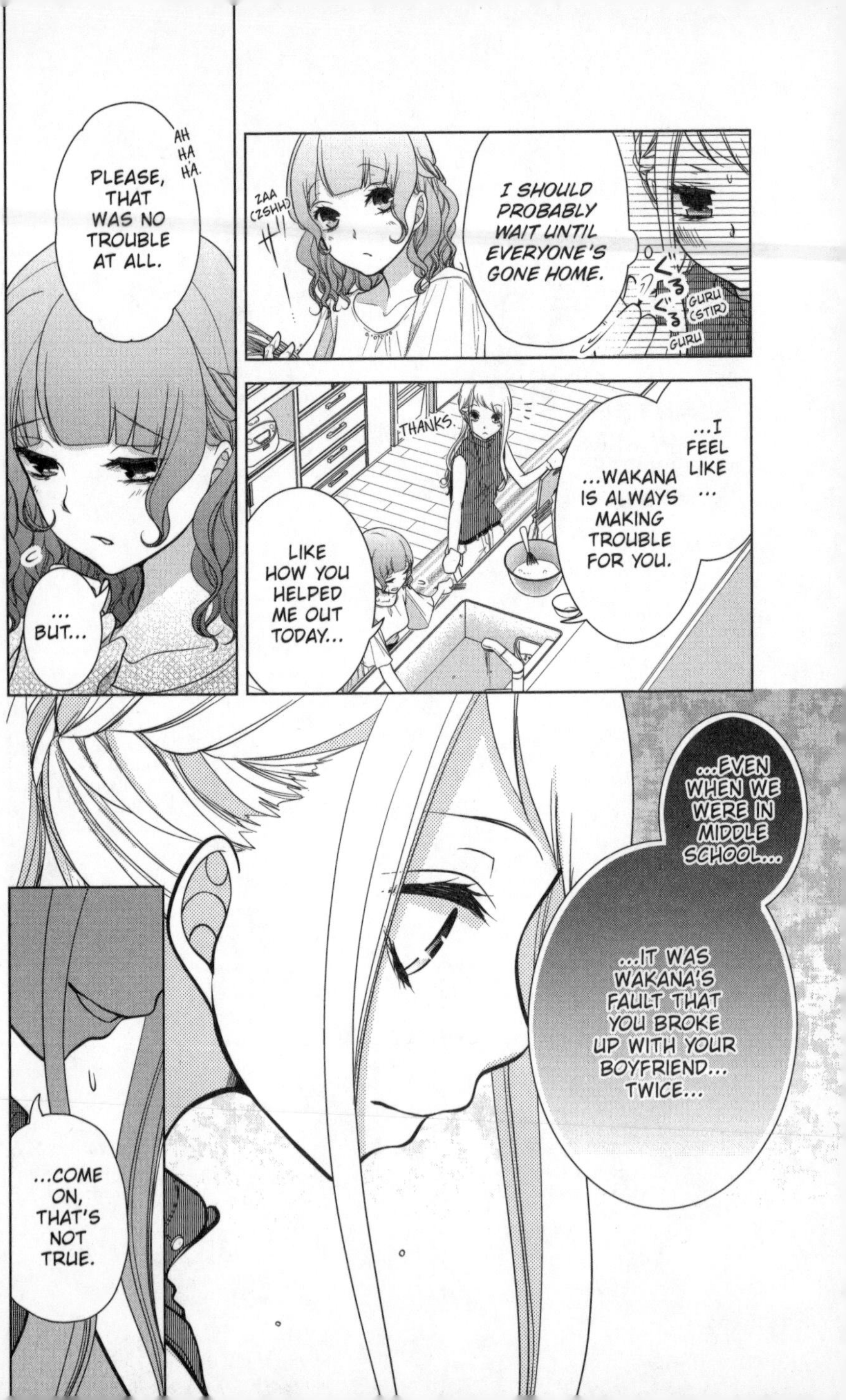
I SHOULD PROBABLY WAIT UNTIL EVERYONE'S GONE HOME.
GURU (STIR) GURU
ZAA (ZSHH)
...I FEEL LIKE...
...WAKANA IS ALWAYS MAKING TROUBLE FOR YOU.
THANKS.
LIKE HOW YOU HELPED ME OUT TODAY...
AH HA HA.
PLEASE, THAT WAS NO TROUBLE AT ALL.
... BUT...
...EVEN WHEN WE WERE IN MIDDLE SCHOOL...
...IT WAS WAKANA'S FAULT THAT YOU BROKE UP WITH YOUR BOYFRIEND... TWICE...
...COME ON, THAT'S NOT TRUE.

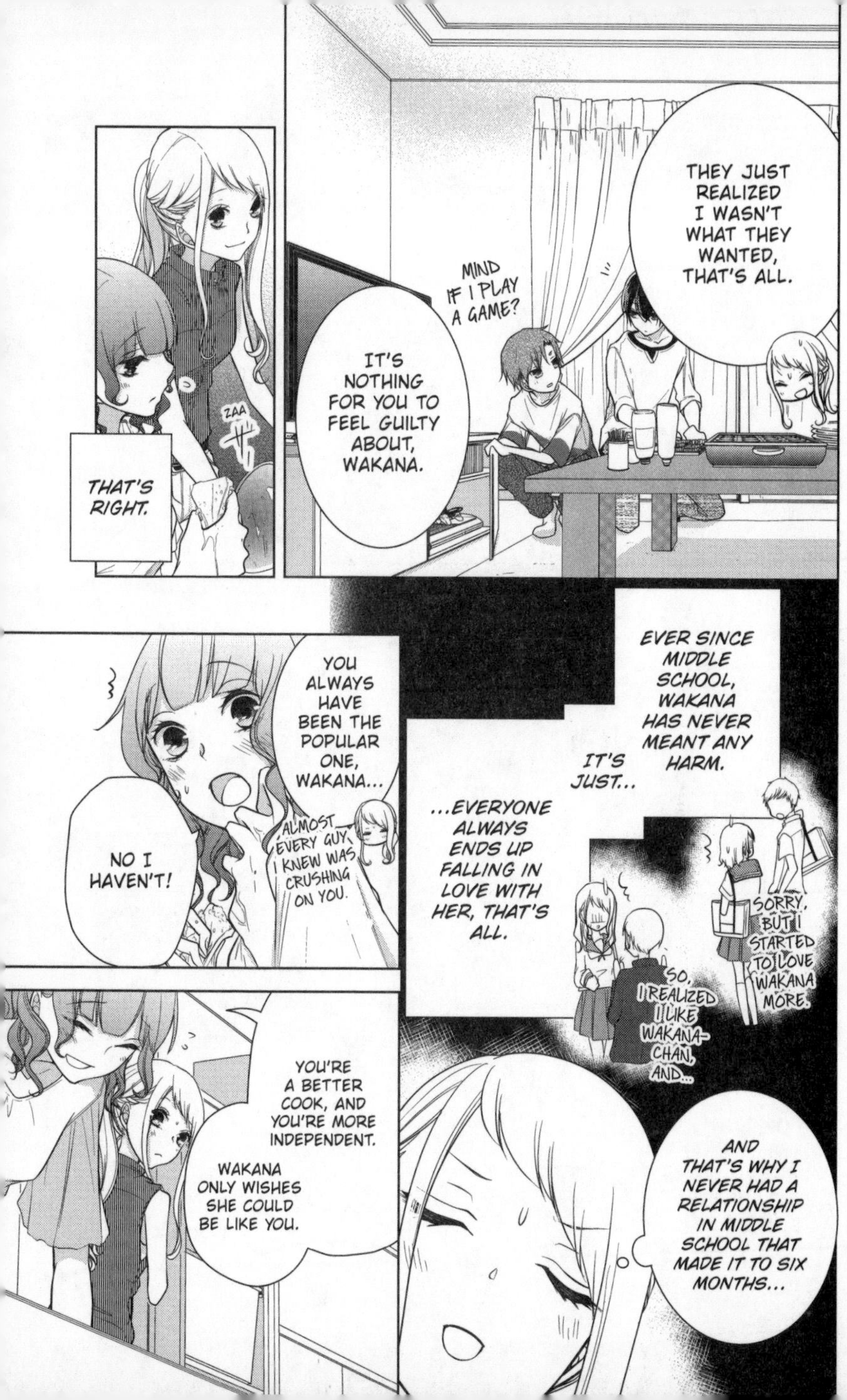
THEY JUST REALIZED I WASN'T WHAT THEY WANTED, THAT'S ALL.
MIND IF I PLAY A GAME?
IT'S NOTHING FOR YOU TO FEEL GUILTY ABOUT, WAKANA.
ZAA
THAT'S RIGHT.
EVER SINCE MIDDLE SCHOOL, WAKANA HAS NEVER MEANT ANY HARM.
IT'S JUST...
...EVERYONE ALWAYS ENDS UP FALLING IN LOVE WITH HER, THAT'S ALL.
SORRY, BUT I STARTED TO LOVE WAKANA MORE.
SO, I REALIZED I LIKE WAKANA-CHAN, AND...
AND THAT'S WHY I NEVER HAD A RELATIONSHIP IN MIDDLE SCHOOL THAT MADE IT TO SIX MONTHS...
YOU ALWAYS HAVE BEEN THE POPULAR ONE, WAKANA...
ALMOST EVERY GUY I KNEW WAS CRUSHING ON YOU.
NO I HAVEN'T!
YOU'RE A BETTER COOK, AND YOU'RE MORE INDEPENDENT.
WAKANA ONLY WISHES SHE COULD BE LIKE YOU.

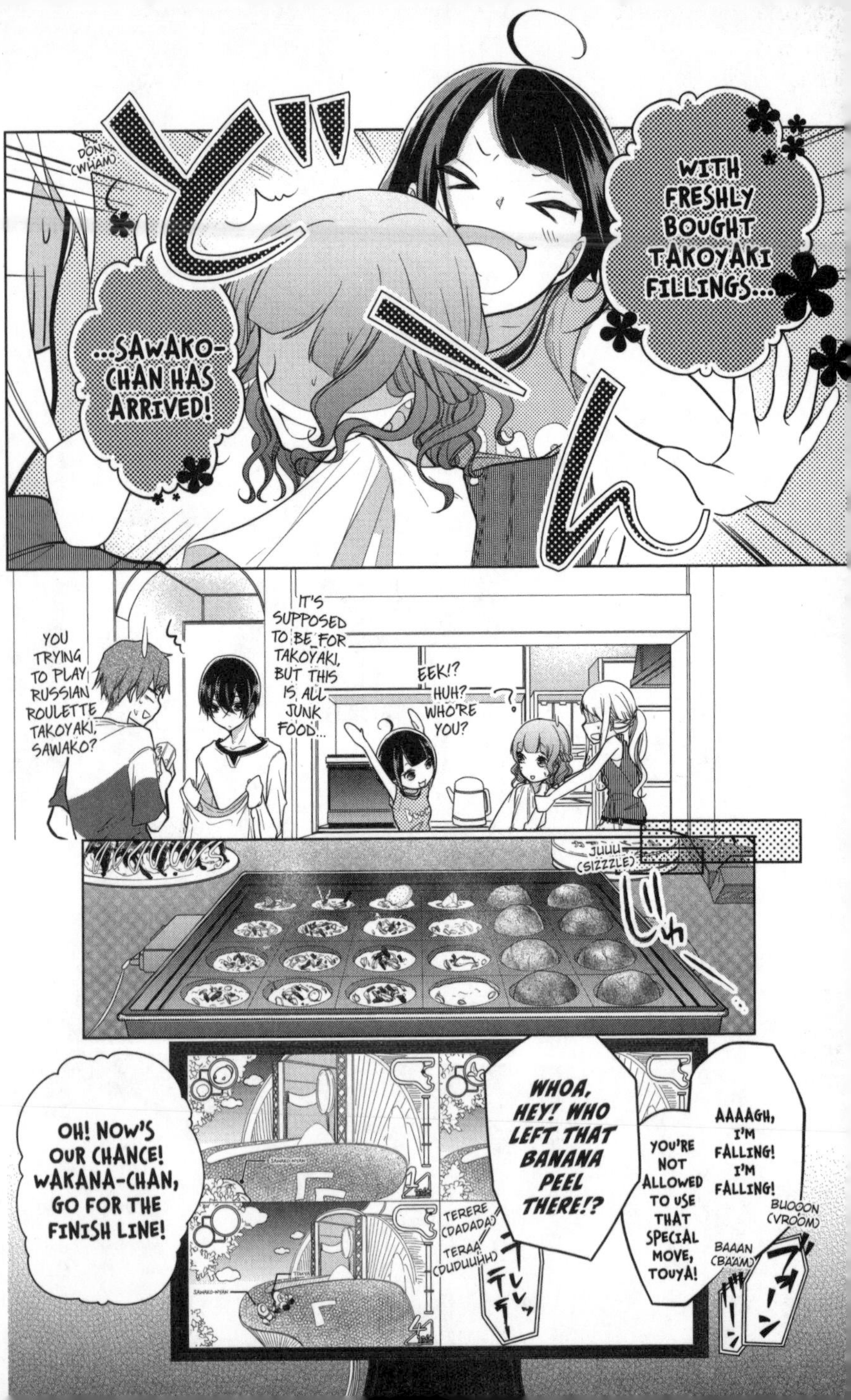
WITH FRESHLY BOUGHT TAKOYAKI FILLINGS...
...SAWAKO-CHAN HAS ARRIVED!
DON (WHAM)
EEK!?
HUH? WHO'RE YOU?
IT'S SUPPOSED TO BE FOR TAKOYAKI, BUT THIS IS ALL JUNK FOOD...
YOU TRYING TO PLAY RUSSIAN ROULETTE TAKOYAKI, SAWAKO?
JUUU (SIZZLE)
BUOOON (VROOM)
BAAAN (BAAM)
AAAAGH, I'M FALLING! I'M FALLING!
YOU'RE NOT ALLOWED TO USE THAT SPECIAL MOVE, TOUYA!
WHOA, HEY! WHO LEFT THAT BANANA PEEL THERE!?
TERERE (DADADA)
TERAA (DUDUUHH)
OH! NOW'S OUR CHANCE! WAKANA-CHAN, GO FOR THE FINISH LINE!

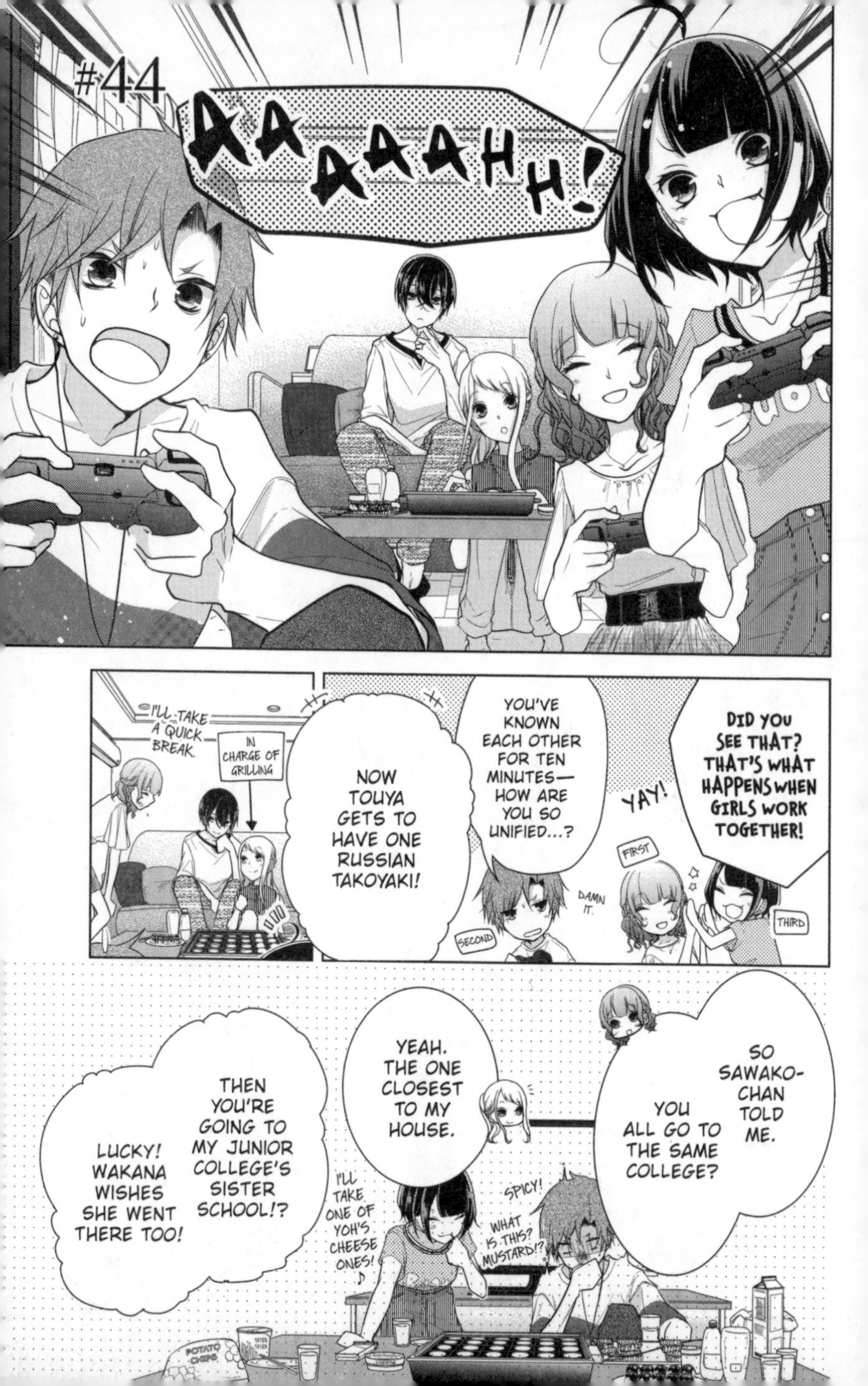

#44
AAAAAAH!
DID YOU SEE THAT? THAT'S WHAT HAPPENS WHEN GIRLS WORK TOGETHER!
YAY!
FIRST
THIRD
YOU'VE KNOWN EACH OTHER FOR TEN MINUTES—HOW ARE YOU SO UNIFIED...?
DAMN IT.
SECOND
NOW TOUYA GETS TO HAVE ONE RUSSIAN TAKOYAKI!
IN CHARGE OF GRILLING
I'LL TAKE A QUICK BREAK.
SO SAWAKO-CHAN TOLD ME.
YOU ALL GO TO THE SAME COLLEGE?
YEAH. THE ONE CLOSEST TO MY HOUSE.
SPICY!
WHAT IS THIS? MUSTARD!?
I'LL TAKE ONE OF YOH'S CHEESE ONES! ♪
THEN YOU'RE GOING TO MY JUNIOR COLLEGE'S SISTER SCHOOL!?
LUCKY! WAKANA WISHES SHE WENT THERE TOO!
POTATO CHIPS

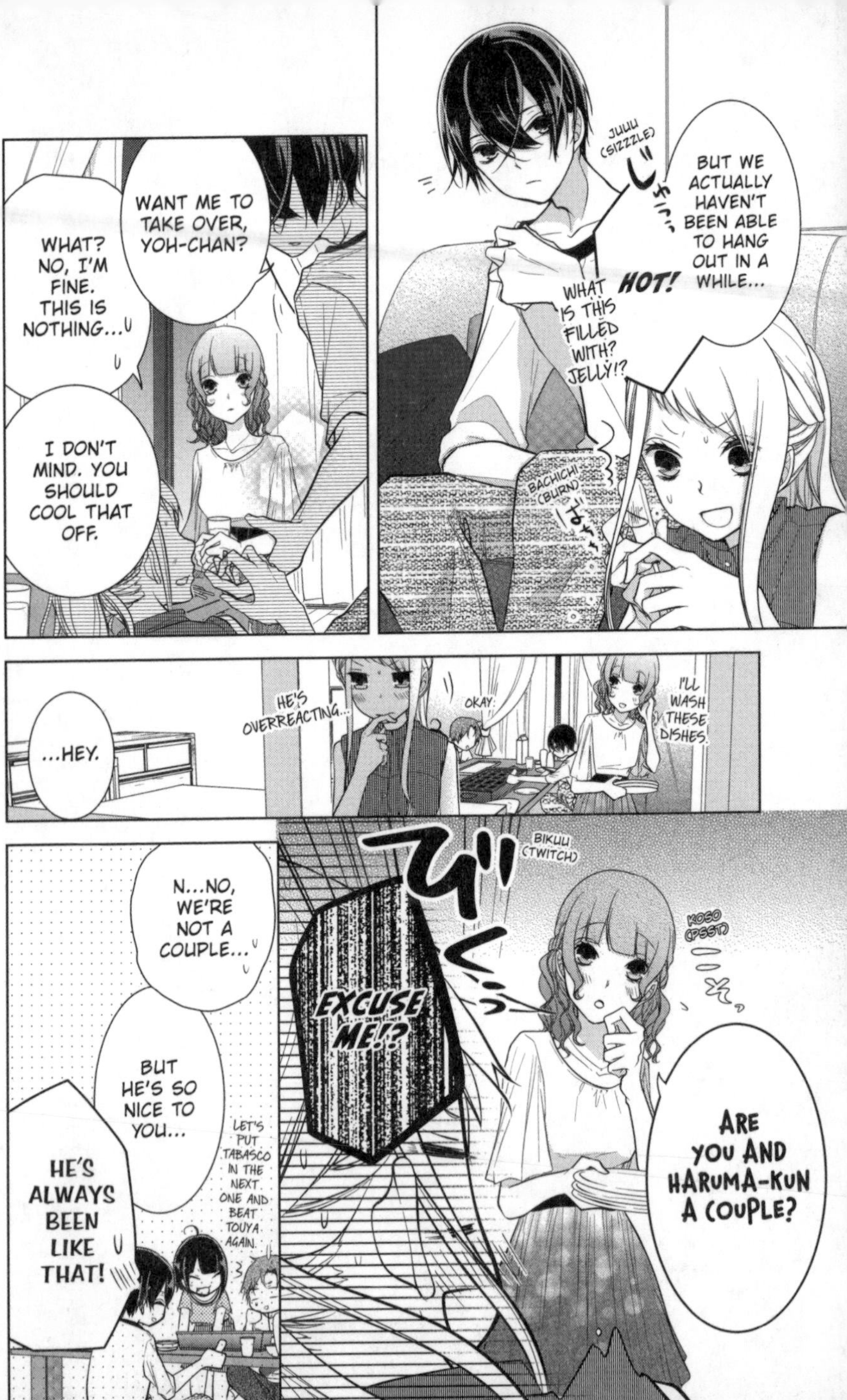
JUUU (SIZZZLE)
BUT WE ACTUALLY HAVEN'T BEEN ABLE TO HANG OUT IN A WHILE...
HOT!
WHAT IS THIS FILLED WITH? JELLY!?
BACHICHI (BURN)
WANT ME TO TAKE OVER, YOH-CHAN?
WHAT? NO, I'M FINE. THIS IS NOTHING...
I DON'T MIND. YOU SHOULD COOL THAT OFF.
I'LL WASH THESE DISHES.
OKAY.
HE'S OVERREACTING...
...HEY.
BIKUU (TWITCH)
KOSO (PSST)
ARE YOU AND HARUMA-KUN A COUPLE?
EXCUSE ME!?
N...NO, WE'RE NOT A COUPLE...
BUT HE'S SO NICE TO YOU...
HE'S ALWAYS BEEN LIKE THAT!
LET'S PUT TABASCO IN THE NEXT ONE AND BEAT TOUYA AGAIN.

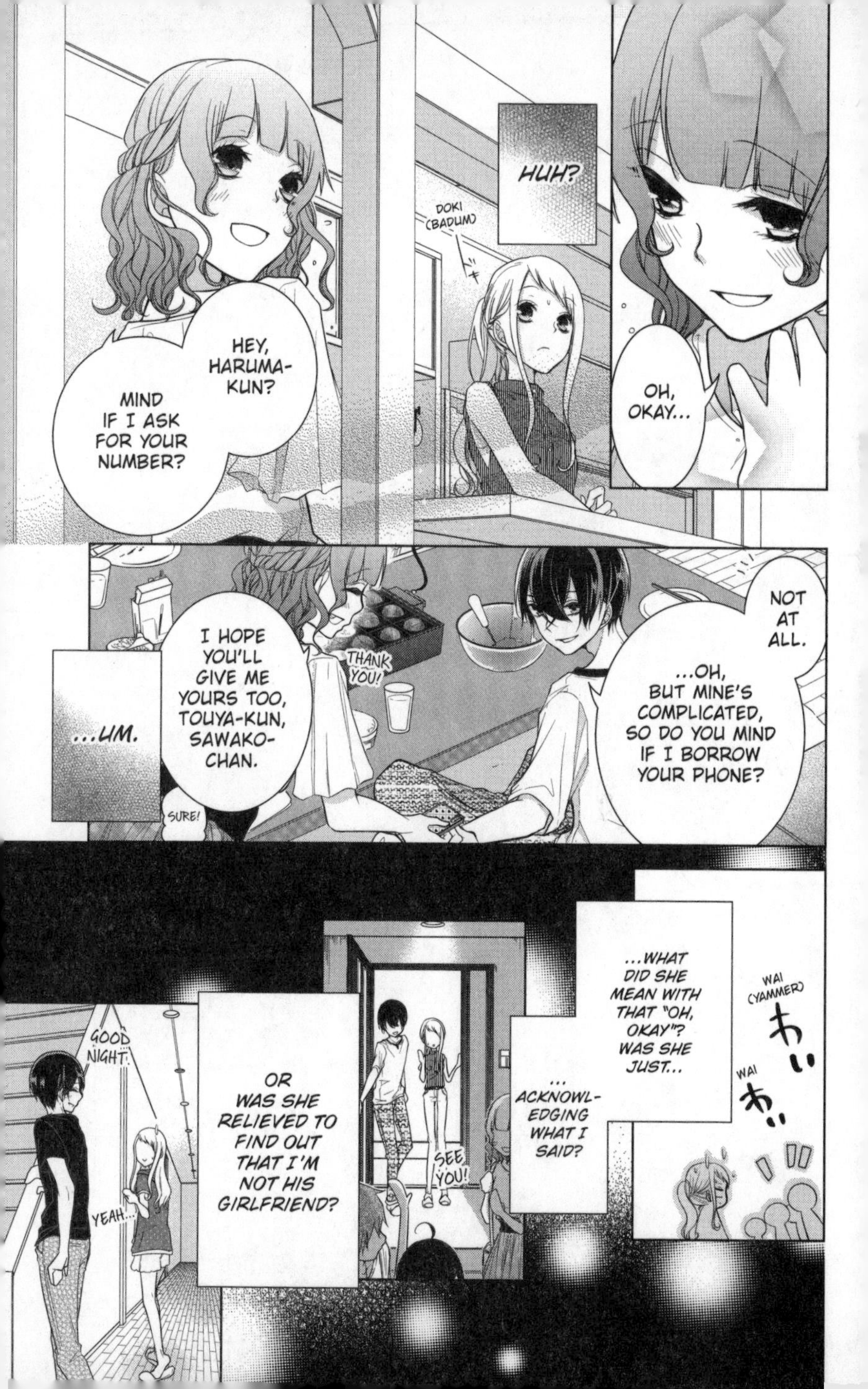
OH, OKAY...
HUH?
DOKI (BADUM)
HEY, HARUMA-KUN?
MIND IF I ASK FOR YOUR NUMBER?
NOT AT ALL.
...OH, BUT MINE'S COMPLICATED, SO DO YOU MIND IF I BORROW YOUR PHONE?
THANK YOU!
I HOPE YOU'LL GIVE ME YOURS TOO, TOUYA-KUN, SAWAKO-CHAN.
SURE!
...UM.
WAI (YAMMER)
WAI
...WHAT DID SHE MEAN WITH THAT "OH, OKAY"? WAS SHE JUST...
... ACKNOWL-EDGING WHAT I SAID?
SEE YOU!
OR WAS SHE RELIEVED TO FIND OUT THAT I'M NOT HIS GIRLFRIEND?
GOOD NIGHT.
YEAH...

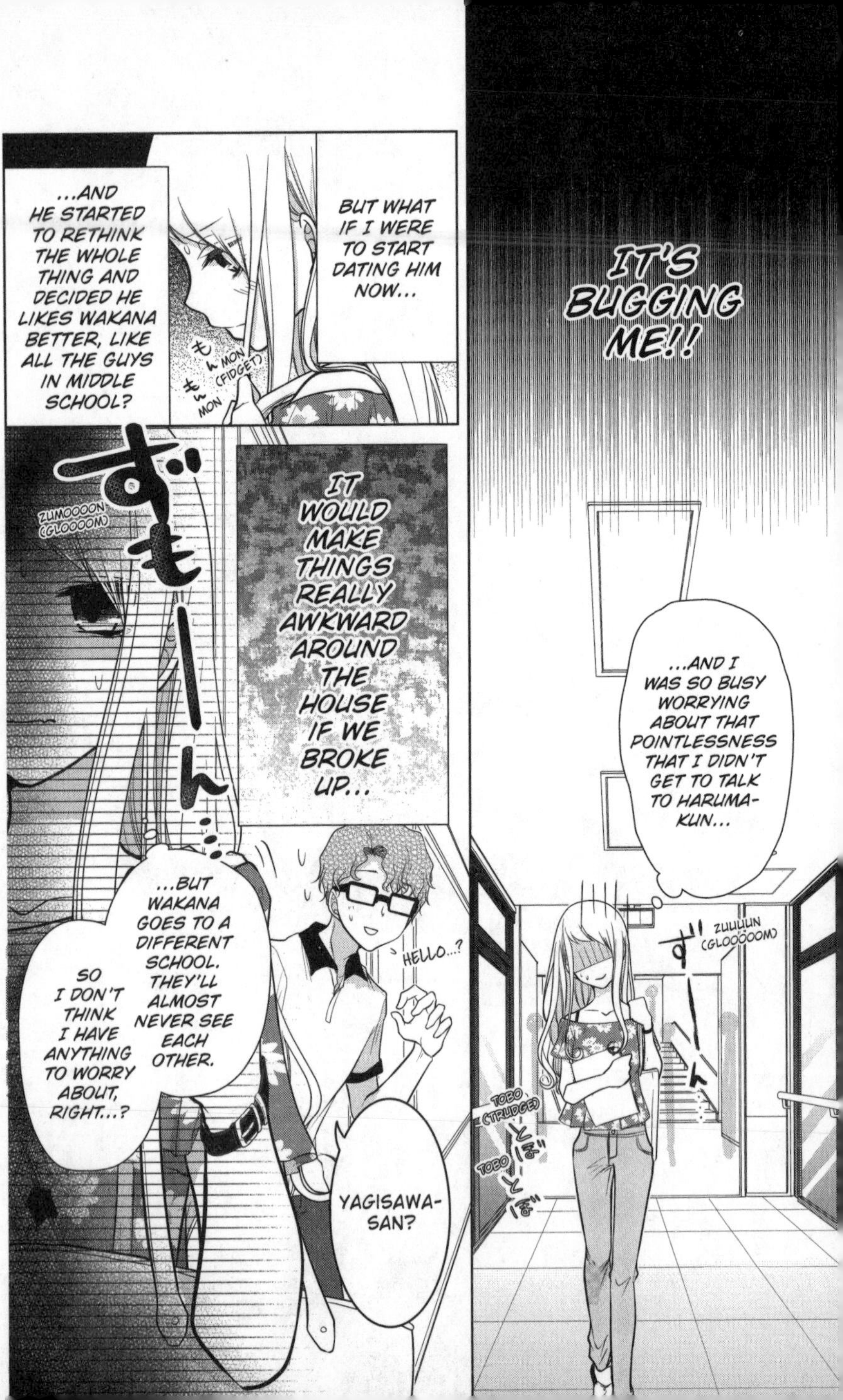
IT'S BUGGING ME!!
...AND I WAS SO BUSY WORRYING ABOUT THAT POINTLESSNESS THAT I DIDN'T GET TO TALK TO HARUMA-KUN...
ZUUUUN (GLOOOOOM)
TOBO (TRUDGE) TOBO
BUT WHAT IF I WERE TO START DATING HIM NOW...
MON (FIDGET) MON
...AND HE STARTED TO RETHINK THE WHOLE THING AND DECIDED HE LIKES WAKANA BETTER, LIKE ALL THE GUYS IN MIDDLE SCHOOL?
IT WOULD MAKE THINGS REALLY AWKWARD AROUND THE HOUSE IF WE BROKE UP...
ZUMOOOON (GLOOOOM)
...BUT WAKANA GOES TO A DIFFERENT SCHOOL. THEY'LL ALMOST NEVER SEE EACH OTHER.
SO I DON'T THINK I HAVE ANYTHING TO WORRY ABOUT, RIGHT...?
HELLO...?
YAGISAWA-SAN?

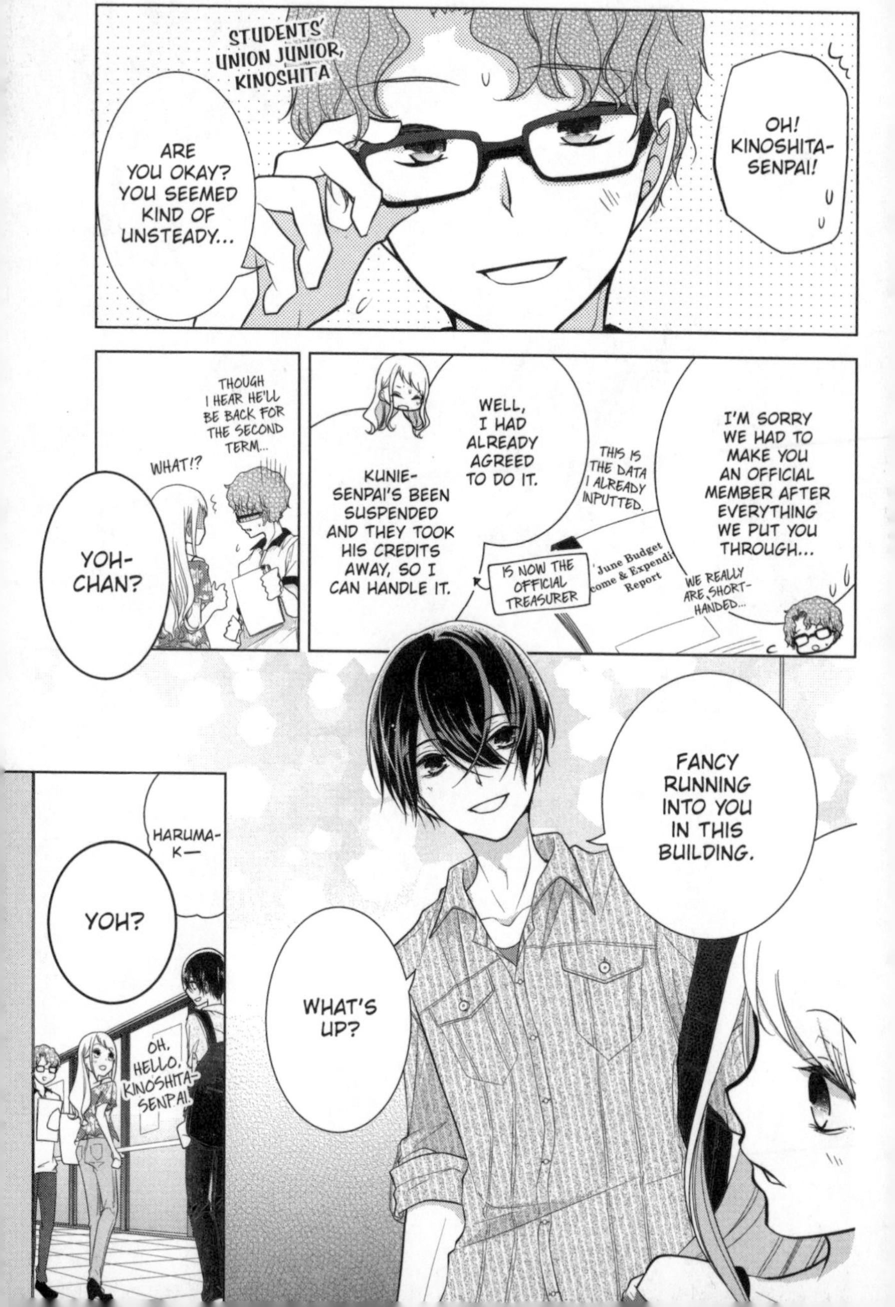
OH! KINOSHITA-SENPAI!
STUDENTS' UNION JUNIOR, KINOSHITA
ARE YOU OKAY? YOU SEEMED KIND OF UNSTEADY...
I'M SORRY WE HAD TO MAKE YOU AN OFFICIAL MEMBER AFTER EVERYTHING WE PUT YOU THROUGH...
WE REALLY ARE SHORT-HANDED...
THIS IS THE DATA I ALREADY INPUTTED.
June Budget
come & Expendi
Report
WELL, I HAD ALREADY AGREED TO DO IT.
IS NOW THE OFFICIAL TREASURER
KUNIE-SENPAI'S BEEN SUSPENDED AND THEY TOOK HIS CREDITS AWAY, SO I CAN HANDLE IT.
THOUGH I HEAR HE'LL BE BACK FOR THE SECOND TERM...
WHAT!?
YOH-CHAN?
FANCY RUNNING INTO YOU IN THIS BUILDING.
WHAT'S UP?
HARUMA-K—
YOH?
OH, HELLO, KINOSHITA-SENPAI!

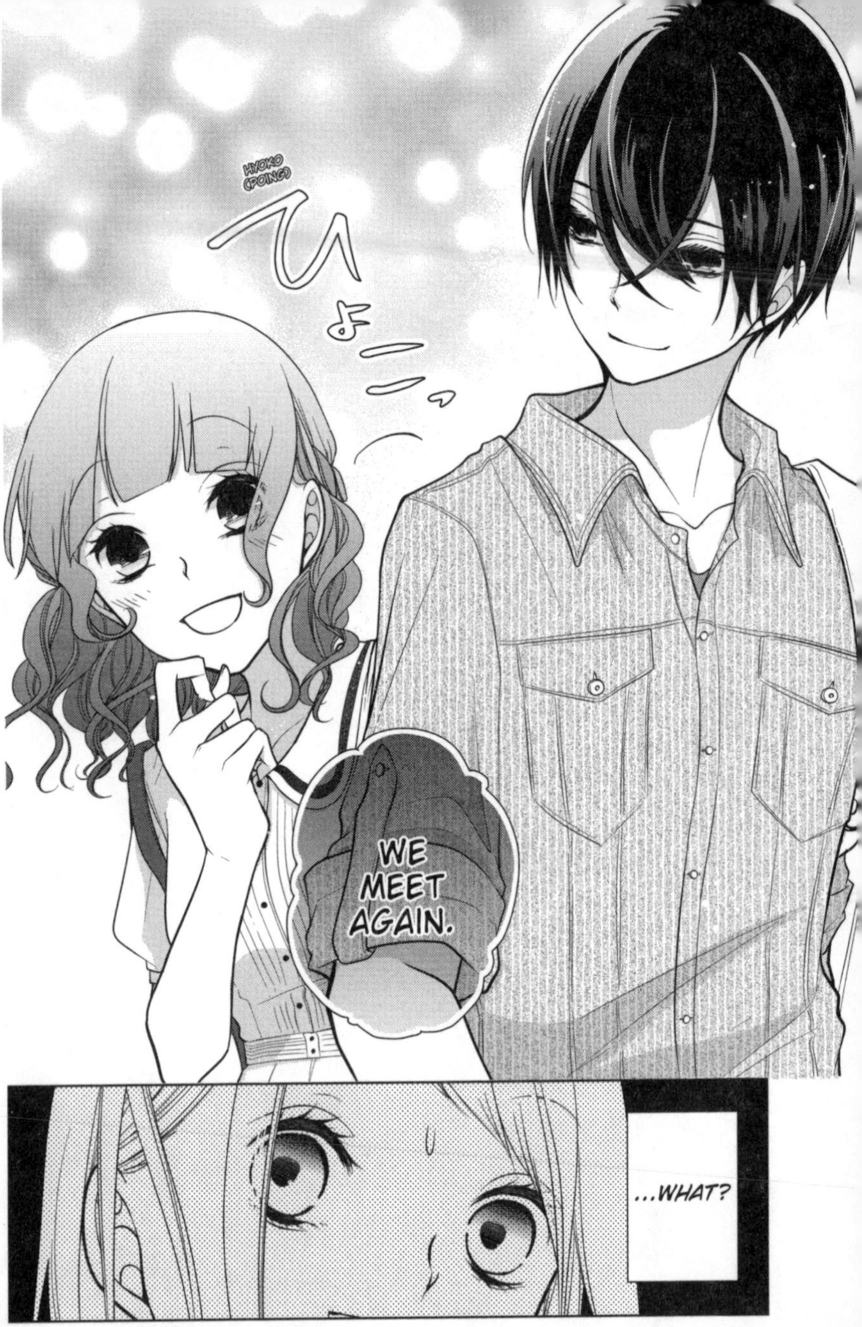
HYOKO (POING)
ひょーー
WE MEET AGAIN.
...WHAT?

#45

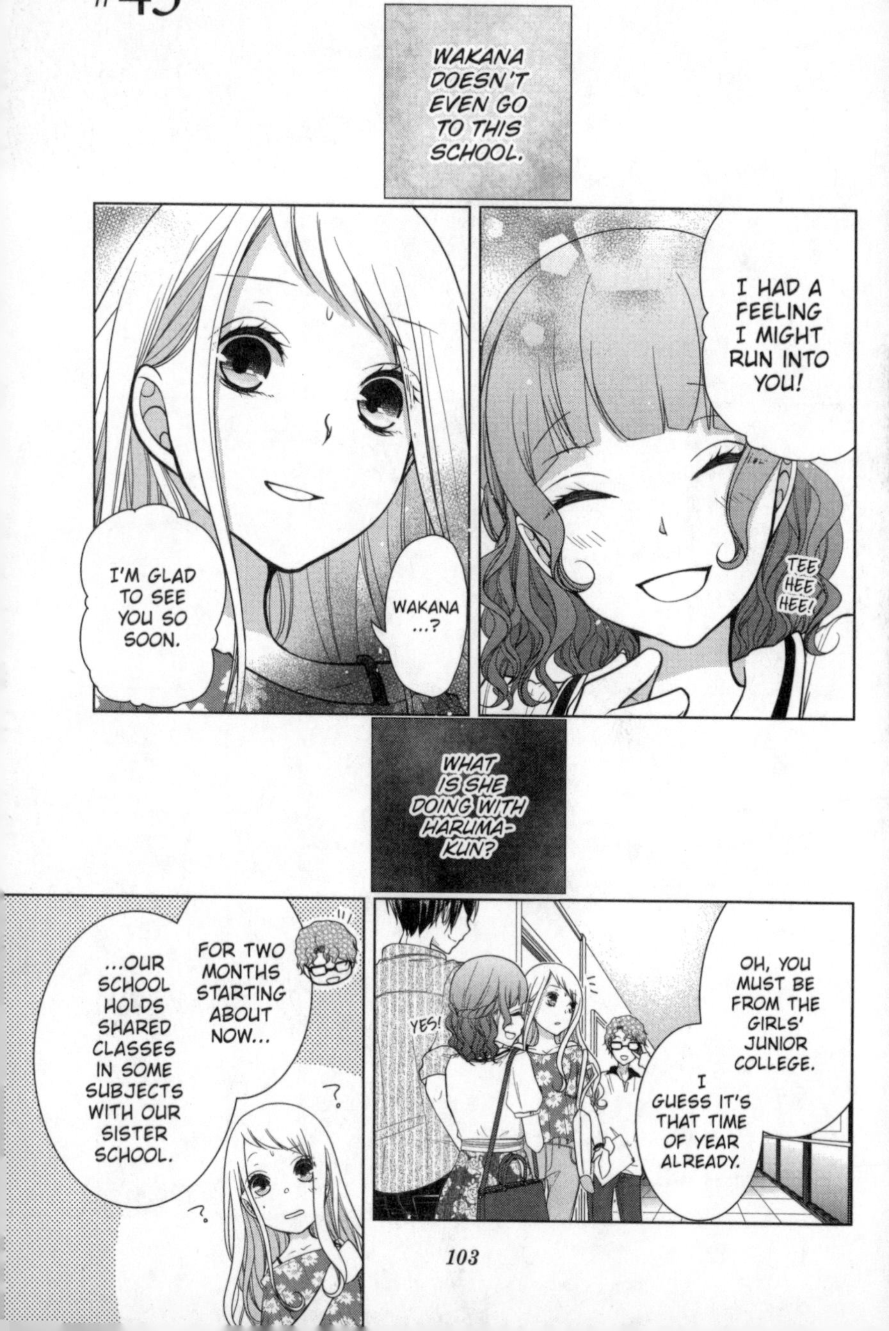
WAKANA DOESN'T EVEN GO TO THIS SCHOOL.
I HAD A FEELING I MIGHT RUN INTO YOU!
TEE HEE HEE!
WAKANA ...?
I'M GLAD TO SEE YOU SO SOON.
WHAT IS SHE DOING WITH HARUMA-KUN?
OH, YOU MUST BE FROM THE GIRLS' JUNIOR COLLEGE.
I GUESS IT'S THAT TIME OF YEAR ALREADY.
YES!
FOR TWO MONTHS STARTING ABOUT NOW...
...OUR SCHOOL HOLDS SHARED CLASSES IN SOME SUBJECTS WITH OUR SISTER SCHOOL.

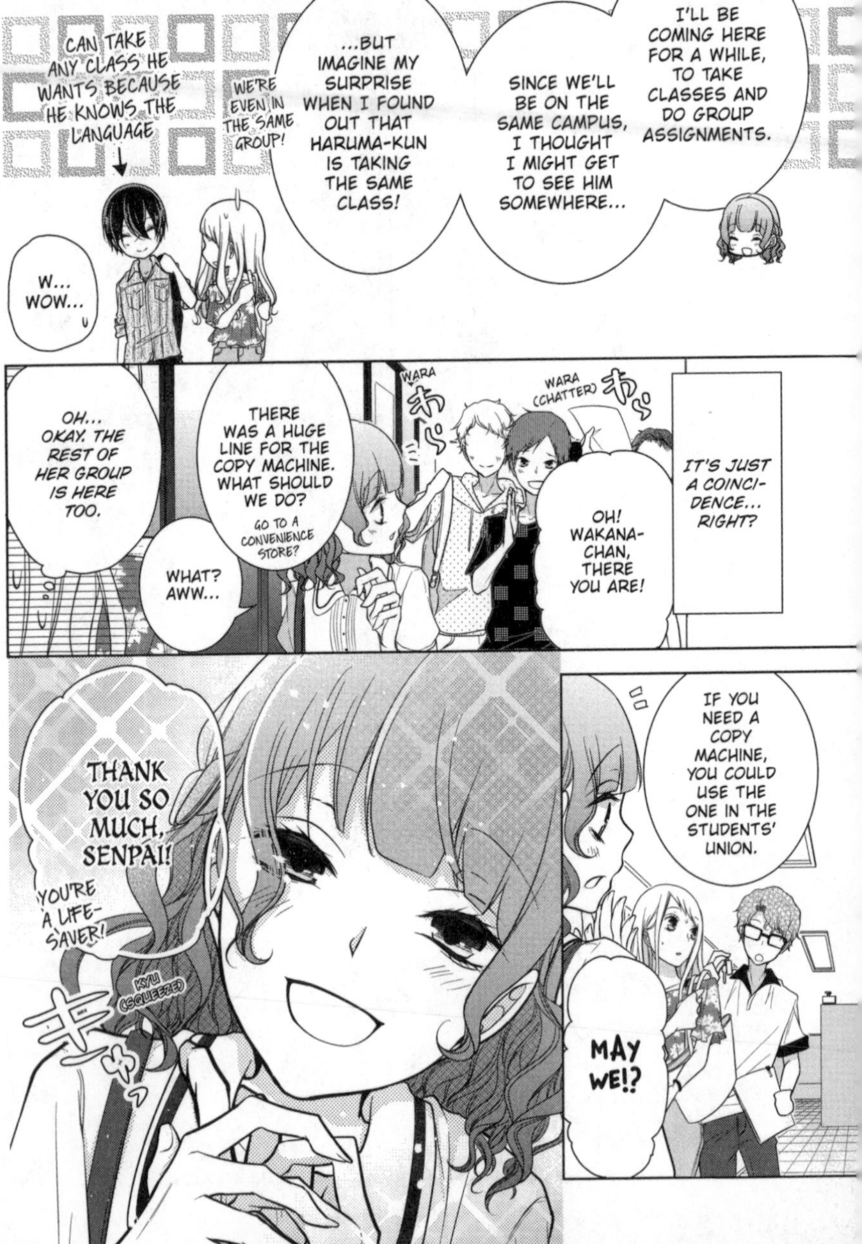
I'LL BE COMING HERE FOR A WHILE, TO TAKE CLASSES AND DO GROUP ASSIGNMENTS.
SINCE WE'LL BE ON THE SAME CAMPUS, I THOUGHT I MIGHT GET TO SEE HIM SOMEWHERE...
...BUT IMAGINE MY SURPRISE WHEN I FOUND OUT THAT HARUMA-KUN IS TAKING THE SAME CLASS!
WE'RE EVEN IN THE SAME GROUP!
CAN TAKE ANY CLASS HE WANTS BECAUSE HE KNOWS THE LANGUAGE
W... WOW...
IT'S JUST A COINCIDENCE... RIGHT?
WARA (CHATTER)
WARA
OH! WAKANA-CHAN, THERE YOU ARE!
THERE WAS A HUGE LINE FOR THE COPY MACHINE. WHAT SHOULD WE DO?
GO TO A CONVENIENCE STORE?
WHAT? AWW...
OH... OKAY. THE REST OF HER GROUP IS HERE TOO.
IF YOU NEED A COPY MACHINE, YOU COULD USE THE ONE IN THE STUDENTS' UNION.
MAY WE!?
THANK YOU SO MUCH, SENPAI!
YOU'RE A LIFE-SAVER!
KYU (SQUEEZE)

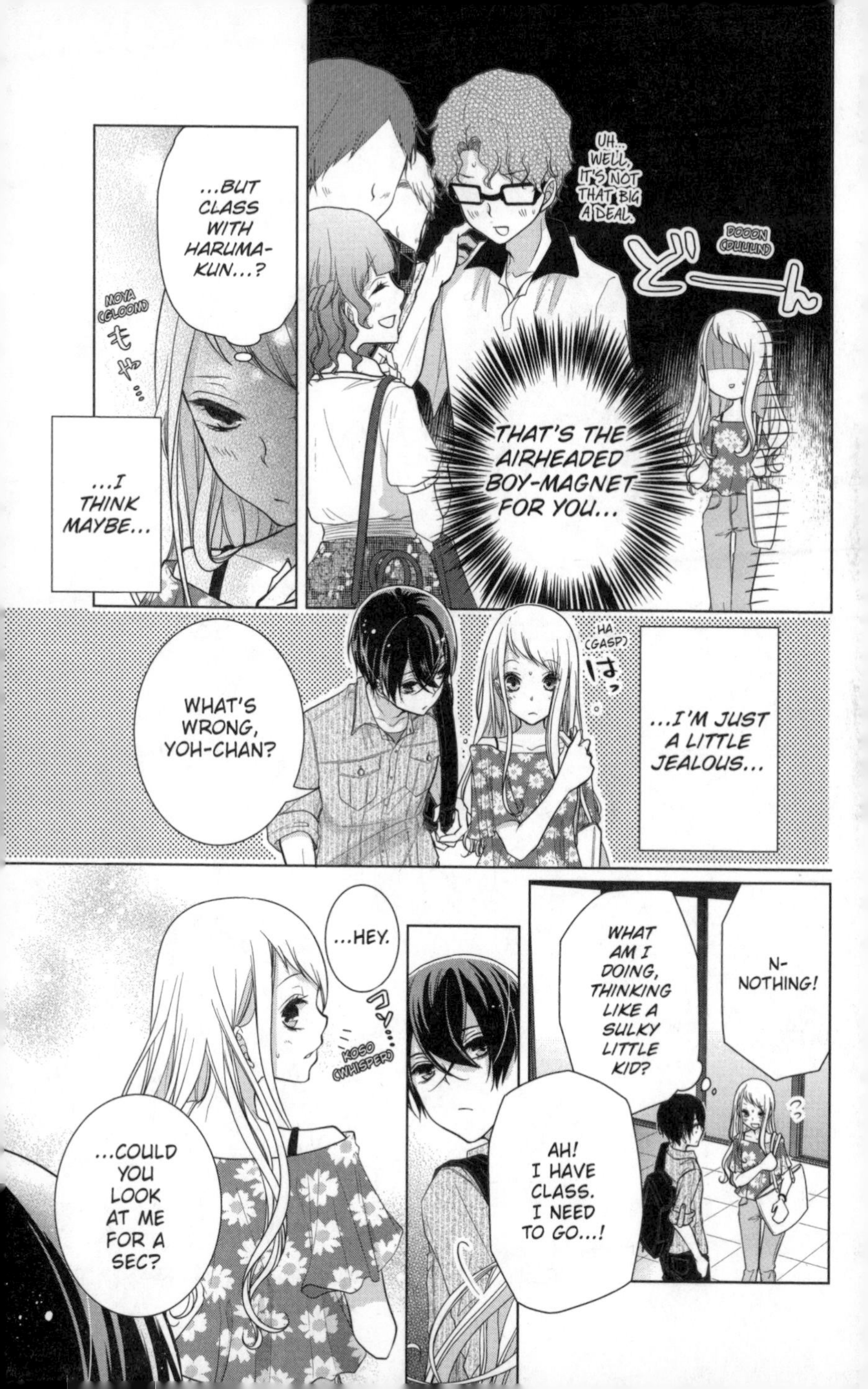
UH... WELL, IT'S NOT THAT BIG A DEAL.
DOOON (DUUUN)
どーん
THAT'S THE AIRHEADED BOY-MAGNET FOR YOU...
...BUT CLASS WITH HARUMA-KUN...?
MOYA (GLOOM)
もや...
...I THINK MAYBE...
...I'M JUST A LITTLE JEALOUS...
HA (GASP)
はっ
WHAT'S WRONG, YOH-CHAN?
N-NOTHING!
WHAT AM I DOING, THINKING LIKE A SULKY LITTLE KID?
AH! I HAVE CLASS. I NEED TO GO...!
...HEY.
KOSO (WHISPER)
コソ...
...COULD YOU LOOK AT ME FOR A SEC?

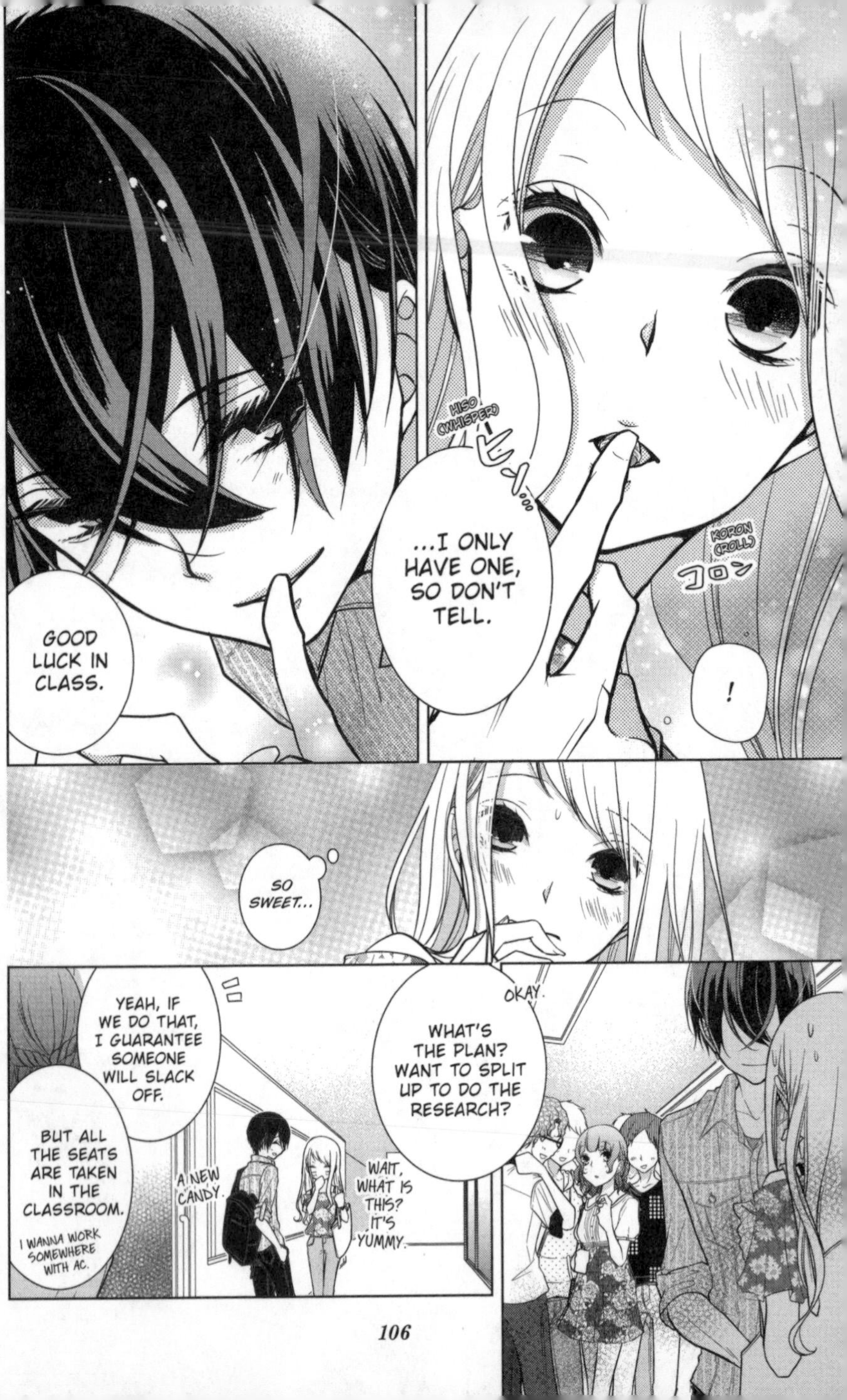
HISO (WHISPER)
ヒソ…
...I ONLY HAVE ONE, SO DON'T TELL.
KORON (ROLL)
コロン
!
GOOD LUCK IN CLASS.
SO SWEET...
OKAY.
WHAT'S THE PLAN? WANT TO SPLIT UP TO DO THE RESEARCH?
YEAH, IF WE DO THAT, I GUARANTEE SOMEONE WILL SLACK OFF.
WAIT, WHAT IS THIS? IT'S YUMMY.
A NEW CANDY.
BUT ALL THE SEATS ARE TAKEN IN THE CLASSROOM.
I WANNA WORK SOMEWHERE WITH AC.

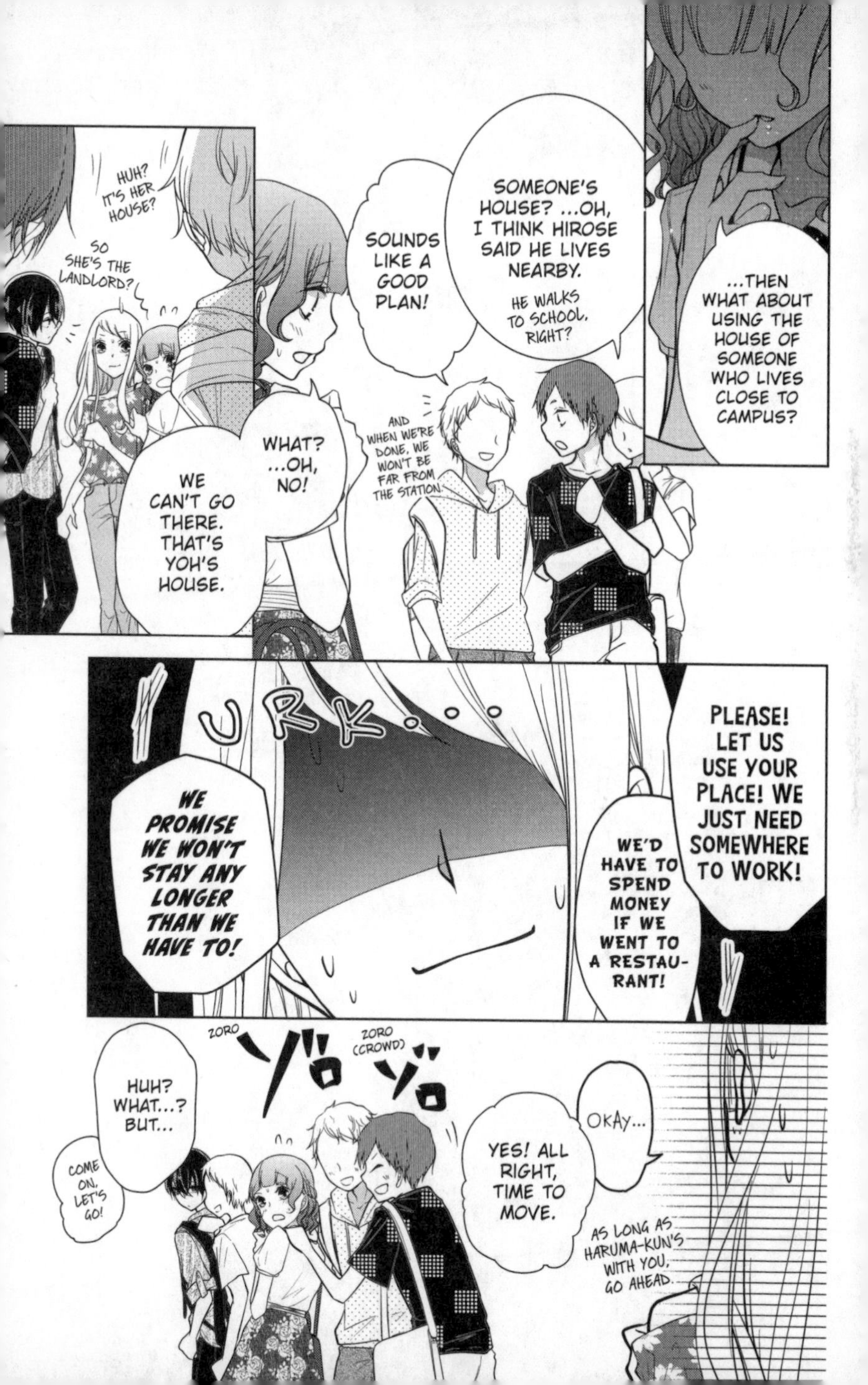
...THEN WHAT ABOUT USING THE HOUSE OF SOMEONE WHO LIVES CLOSE TO CAMPUS?
SOMEONE'S HOUSE? ...OH, I THINK HIROSE SAID HE LIVES NEARBY.
HE WALKS TO SCHOOL, RIGHT?
SOUNDS LIKE A GOOD PLAN!
AND WHEN WE'RE DONE, WE WON'T BE FAR FROM THE STATION
WHAT? ...OH, NO!
WE CAN'T GO THERE. THAT'S YOH'S HOUSE.
HUH? IT'S HER HOUSE?
SO SHE'S THE LANDLORD?
URK...
PLEASE! LET US USE YOUR PLACE! WE JUST NEED SOMEWHERE TO WORK!
WE'D HAVE TO SPEND MONEY IF WE WENT TO A RESTAURANT!
WE PROMISE WE WON'T STAY ANY LONGER THAN WE HAVE TO!
OKAY...
AS LONG AS HARUMA-KUN'S WITH YOU, GO AHEAD.
YES! ALL RIGHT, TIME TO MOVE.
ZORO
ZORO (CROWD)
HUH? WHAT...? BUT...
COME ON, LET'S GO!

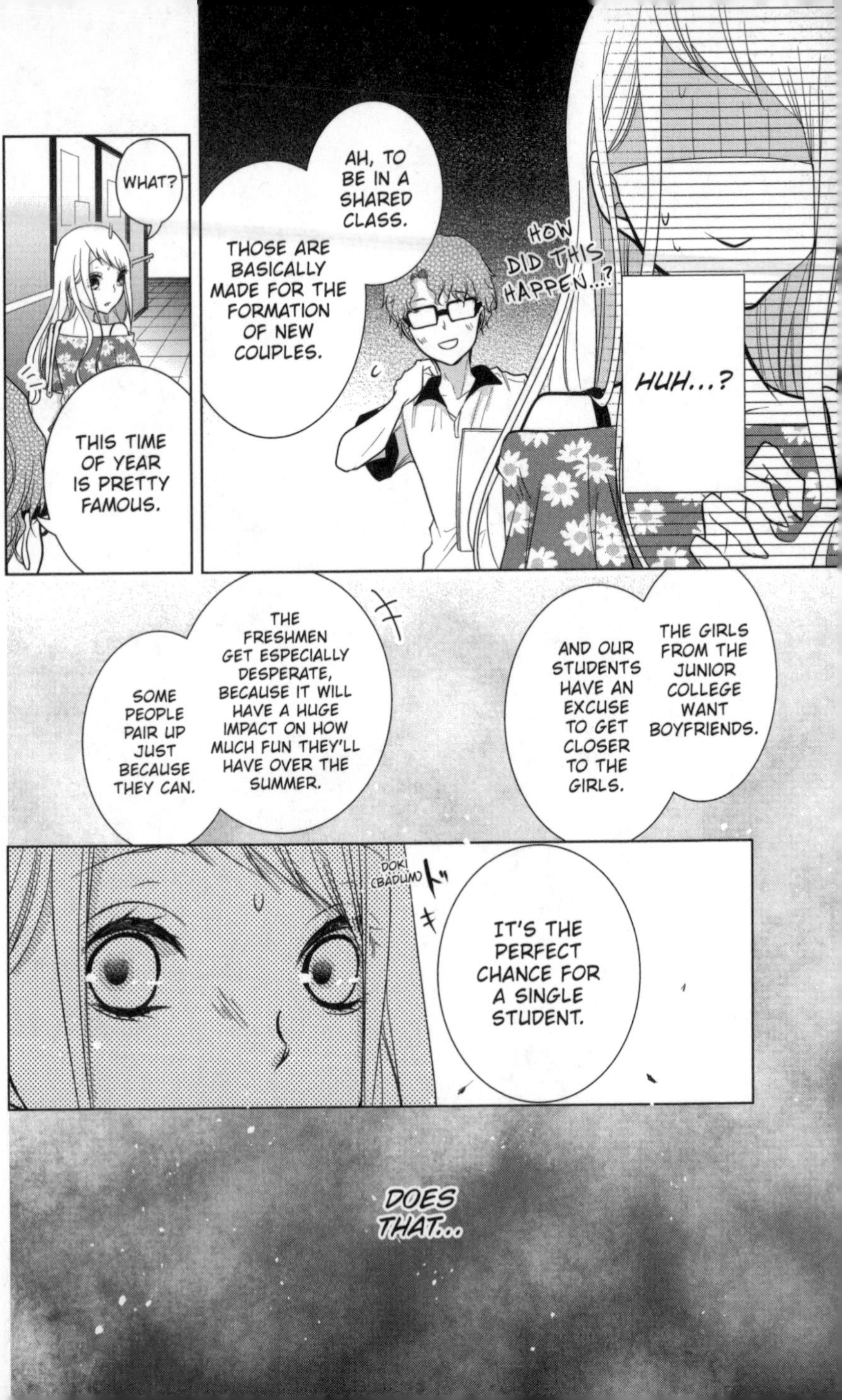

AH, TO BE IN A SHARED CLASS.
THOSE ARE BASICALLY MADE FOR THE FORMATION OF NEW COUPLES.
HOW DID THIS HAPPEN...?
HUH...?
WHAT?
THIS TIME OF YEAR IS PRETTY FAMOUS.
THE GIRLS FROM THE JUNIOR COLLEGE WANT BOYFRIENDS.
AND OUR STUDENTS HAVE AN EXCUSE TO GET CLOSER TO THE GIRLS.
THE FRESHMEN GET ESPECIALLY DESPERATE, BECAUSE IT WILL HAVE A HUGE IMPACT ON HOW MUCH FUN THEY'LL HAVE OVER THE SUMMER.
SOME PEOPLE PAIR UP JUST BECAUSE THEY CAN.
DOKI (BADUM)
IT'S THE PERFECT CHANCE FOR A SINGLE STUDENT.
DOES THAT...

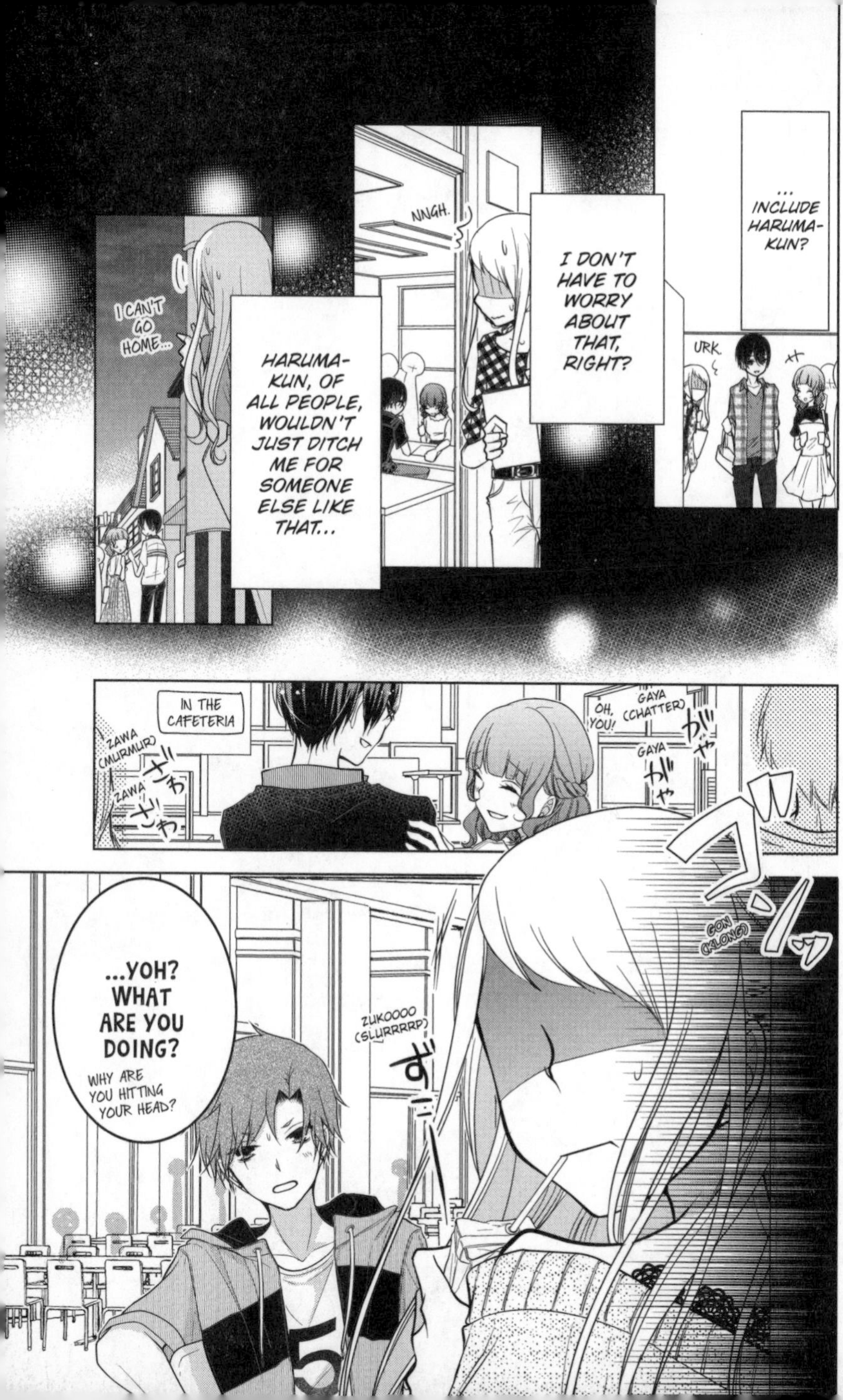

... INCLUDE HARUMA-KUN?
URK.
I DON'T HAVE TO WORRY ABOUT THAT, RIGHT?
NNGH.
HARUMA-KUN, OF ALL PEOPLE, WOULDN'T JUST DITCH ME FOR SOMEONE ELSE LIKE THAT...
I CAN'T GO HOME...
GAYA (CHATTER)
OH, YOU!
GAYA
IN THE CAFETERIA
ZAWA (MURMUR)
ZAWA
GON (KLONG)
ZUKOOOO (SLURRRRP)
...YOH? WHAT ARE YOU DOING?
WHY ARE YOU HITTING YOUR HEAD?

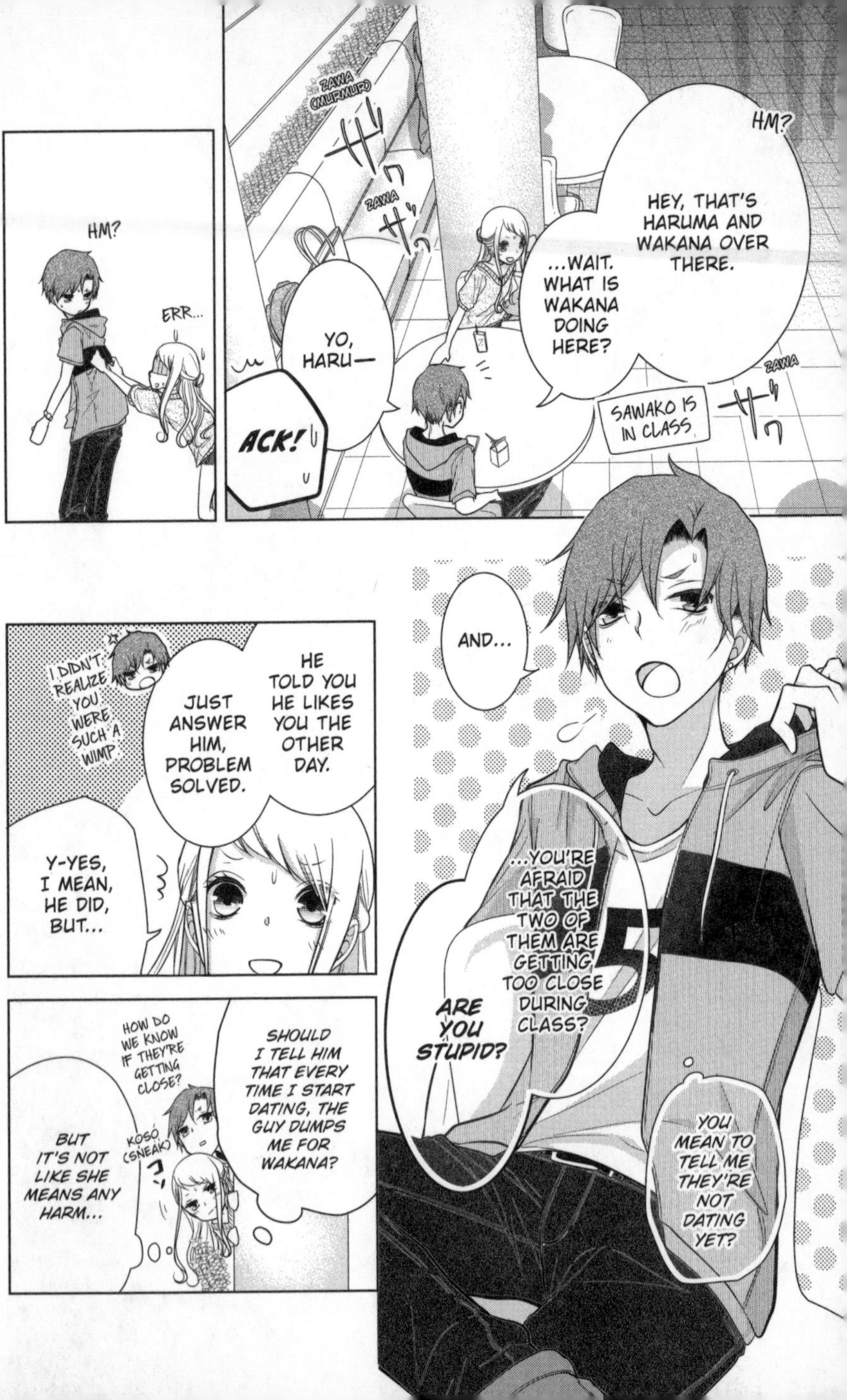
HM?
HEY, THAT'S HARUMA AND WAKANA OVER THERE.
...WAIT. WHAT IS WAKANA DOING HERE?
ZAWA
SAWAKO IS IN CLASS
ZAWA (MURMUR)
ZAWA
YO, HARU—
ACK!
HM?
ERR...
AND...
...YOU'RE AFRAID THAT THE TWO OF THEM ARE GETTING TOO CLOSE DURING CLASS?
YOU MEAN TO TELL ME THEY'RE NOT DATING YET?
ARE YOU STUPID?
HE TOLD YOU HE LIKES YOU THE OTHER DAY.
JUST ANSWER HIM, PROBLEM SOLVED.
I DIDN'T REALIZE YOU WERE SUCH A WIMP.
Y-YES, I MEAN, HE DID, BUT...
SHOULD I TELL HIM THAT EVERY TIME I START DATING, THE GUY DUMPS ME FOR WAKANA?
HOW DO WE KNOW IF THEY'RE GETTING CLOSE?
KOSO (SNEAK)
BUT IT'S NOT LIKE SHE MEANS ANY HARM...

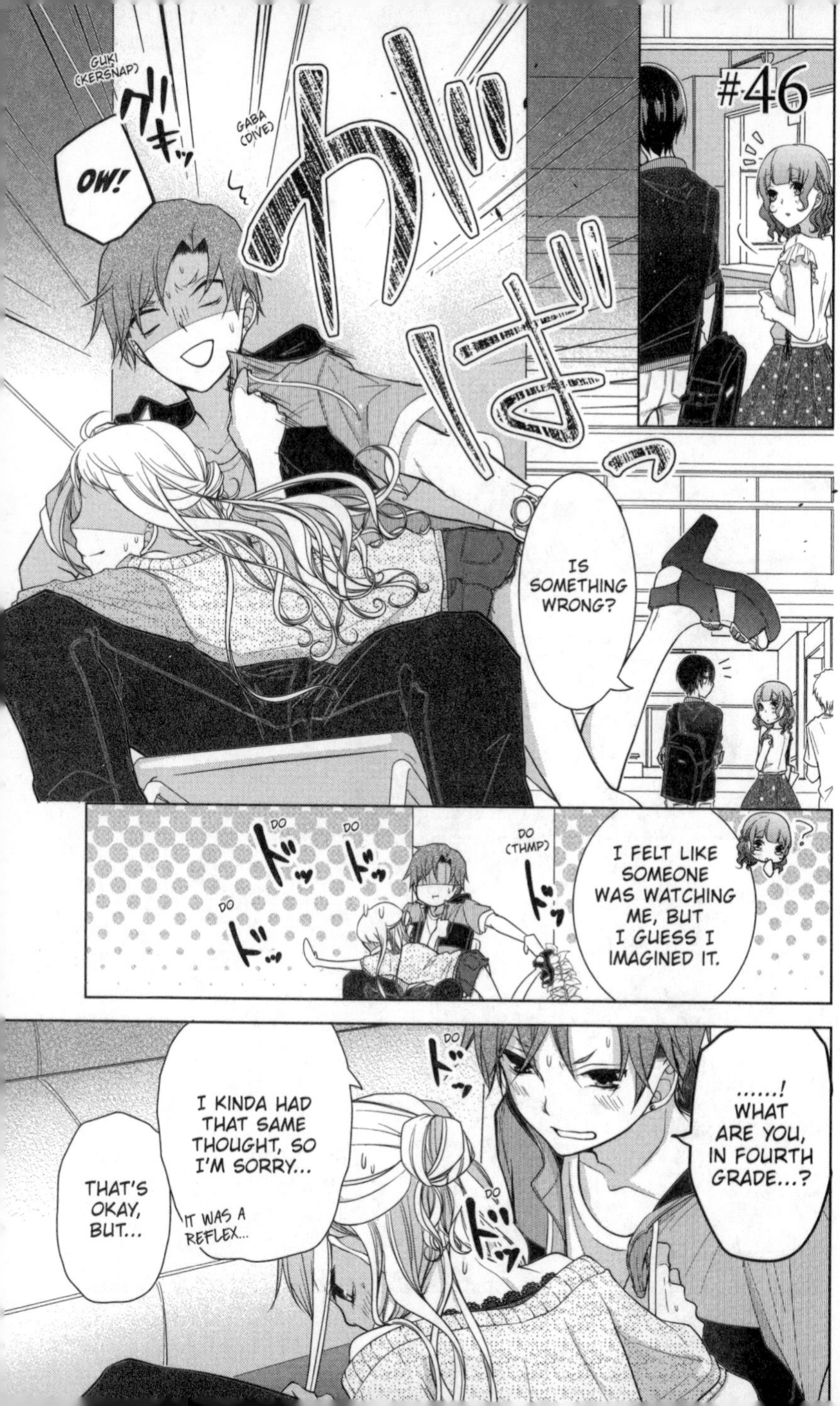
#46
IS SOMETHING WRONG?
GUKI (KERSNAP)
OW!
GABA (DIVE)
I FELT LIKE SOMEONE WAS WATCHING ME, BUT I GUESS I IMAGINED IT.
DO (THMP)
DO
DO
DO
......! WHAT ARE YOU, IN FOURTH GRADE...?
DO
DO
I KINDA HAD THAT SAME THOUGHT, SO I'M SORRY...
IT WAS A REFLEX...
THAT'S OKAY, BUT...

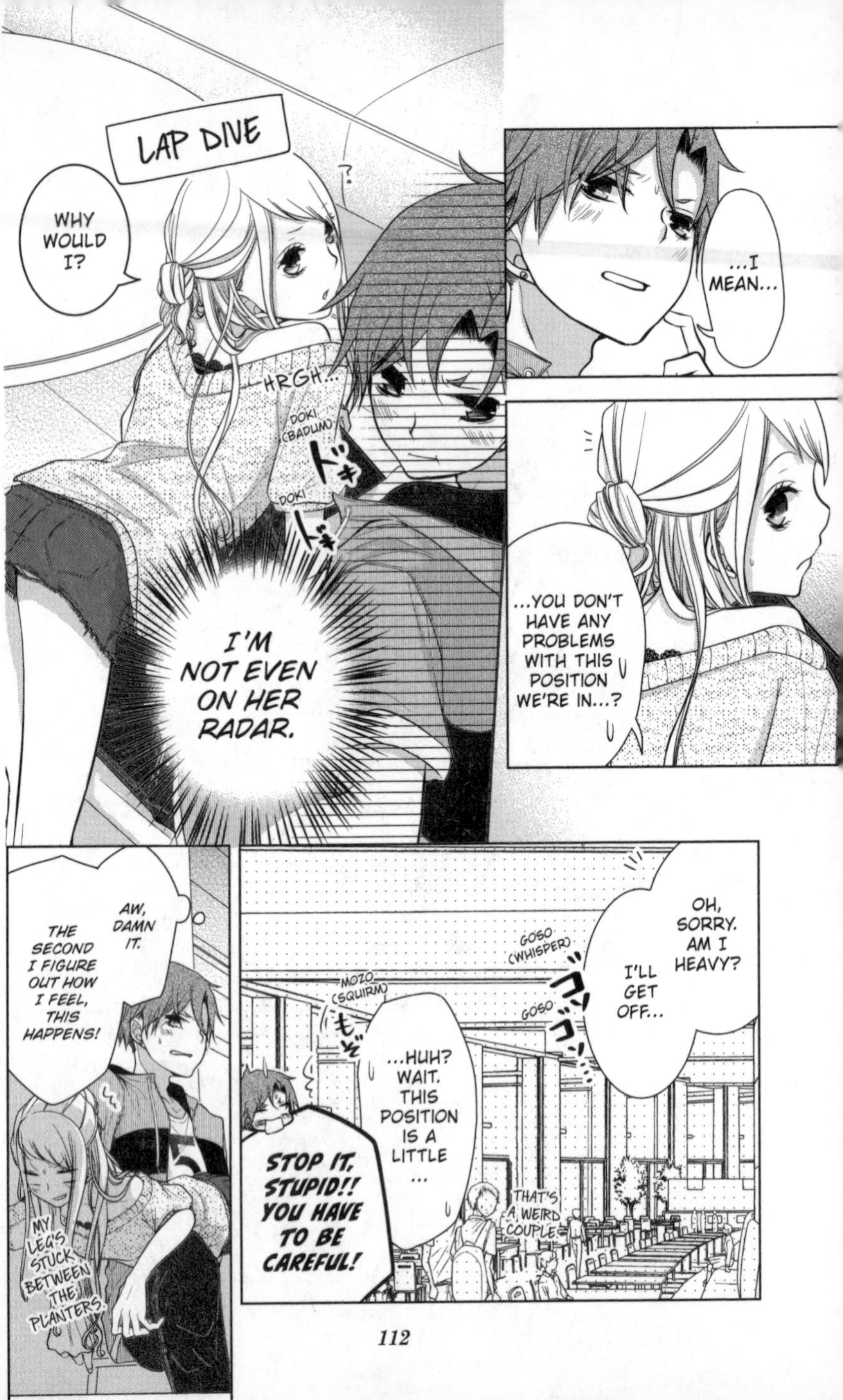
...I MEAN...
...YOU DON'T HAVE ANY PROBLEMS WITH THIS POSITION WE'RE IN...?
LAP DIVE
WHY WOULD I?
HRGH...
DOKI (BADUM)
DOKI
I'M NOT EVEN ON HER RADAR.
OH, SORRY. AM I HEAVY?
I'LL GET OFF...
GOSO (WHISPER)
GOSO
MOZO (SQUIRM)
...HUH? WAIT. THIS POSITION IS A LITTLE ...
STOP IT, STUPID!! YOU HAVE TO BE CAREFUL!
THAT'S A WEIRD COUPLE.
AW, DAMN IT.
THE SECOND I FIGURE OUT HOW I FEEL, THIS HAPPENS!
MY LEG'S STUCK BETWEEN THE PLANTERS.

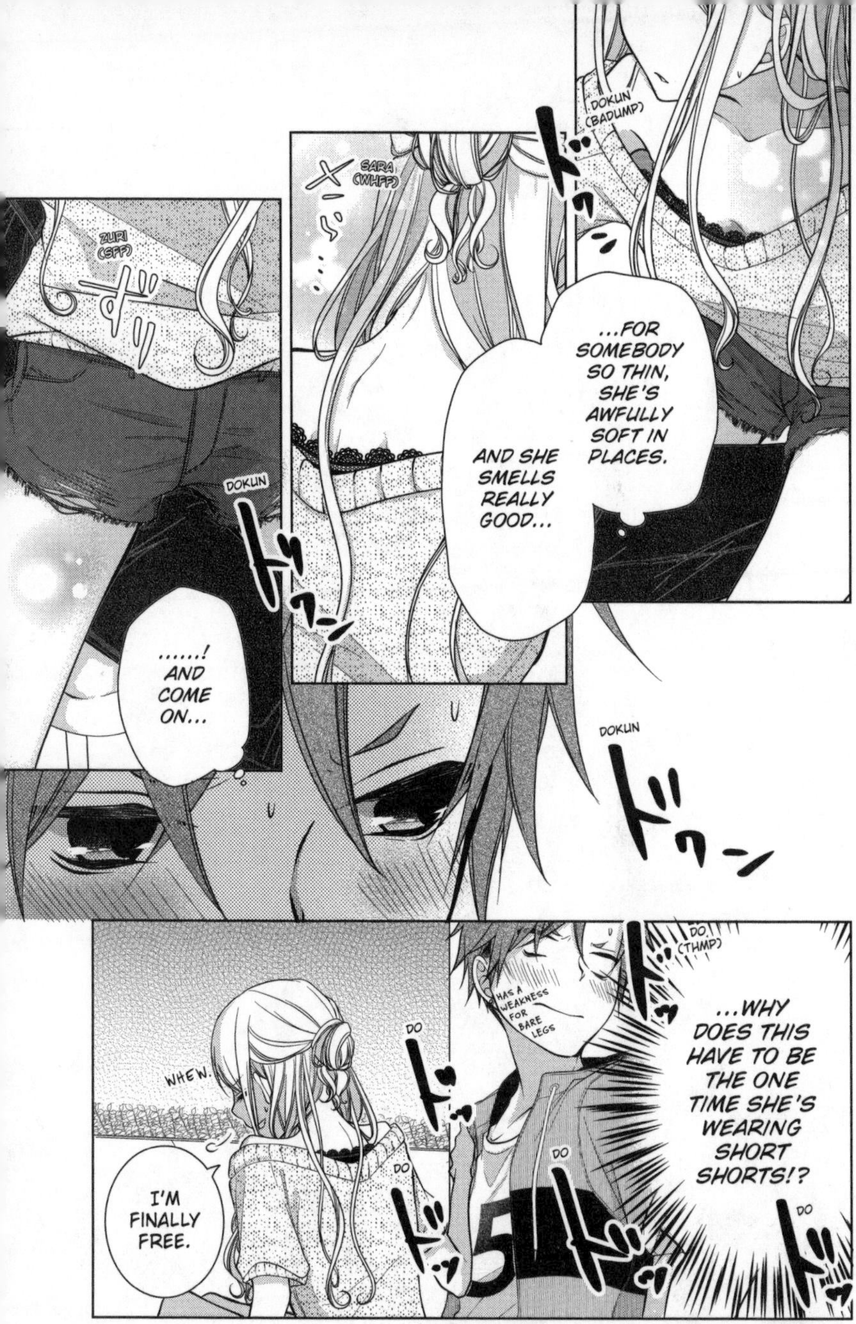
DOKUN (BADUMP)
...FOR SOMEBODY SO THIN, SHE'S AWFULLY SOFT IN PLACES.
AND SHE SMELLS REALLY GOOD...
SARA (WHFF)
ZURI (SFF)
DOKUN
......! AND COME ON...
DOKUN
DO (THMP)
HAS A WEAKNESS FOR BARE LEGS
...WHY DOES THIS HAVE TO BE THE ONE TIME SHE'S WEARING SHORT SHORTS!?
DO
DO
DO
DO
WHEW.
I'M FINALLY FREE.

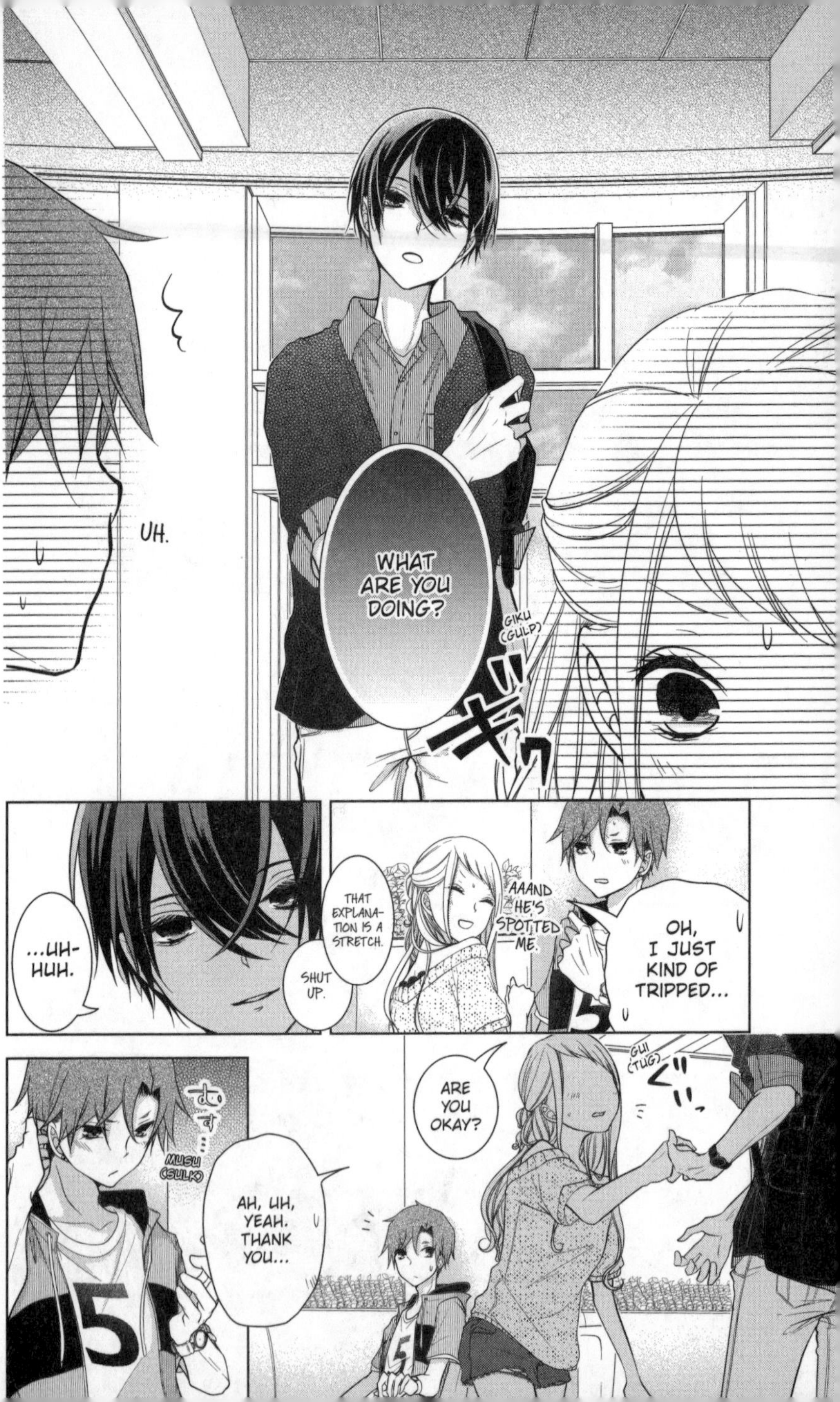
WHAT ARE YOU DOING?
GIKU (GULP)
UH.
OH, I JUST KIND OF TRIPPED...
AAAND HE'S SPOTTED ME.
THAT EXPLANATION IS A STRETCH.
SHUT UP.
...UH-HUH.
GUI (TUG)
ARE YOU OKAY?
むす…
MUSU (SULK)
AH, UH, YEAH. THANK YOU...

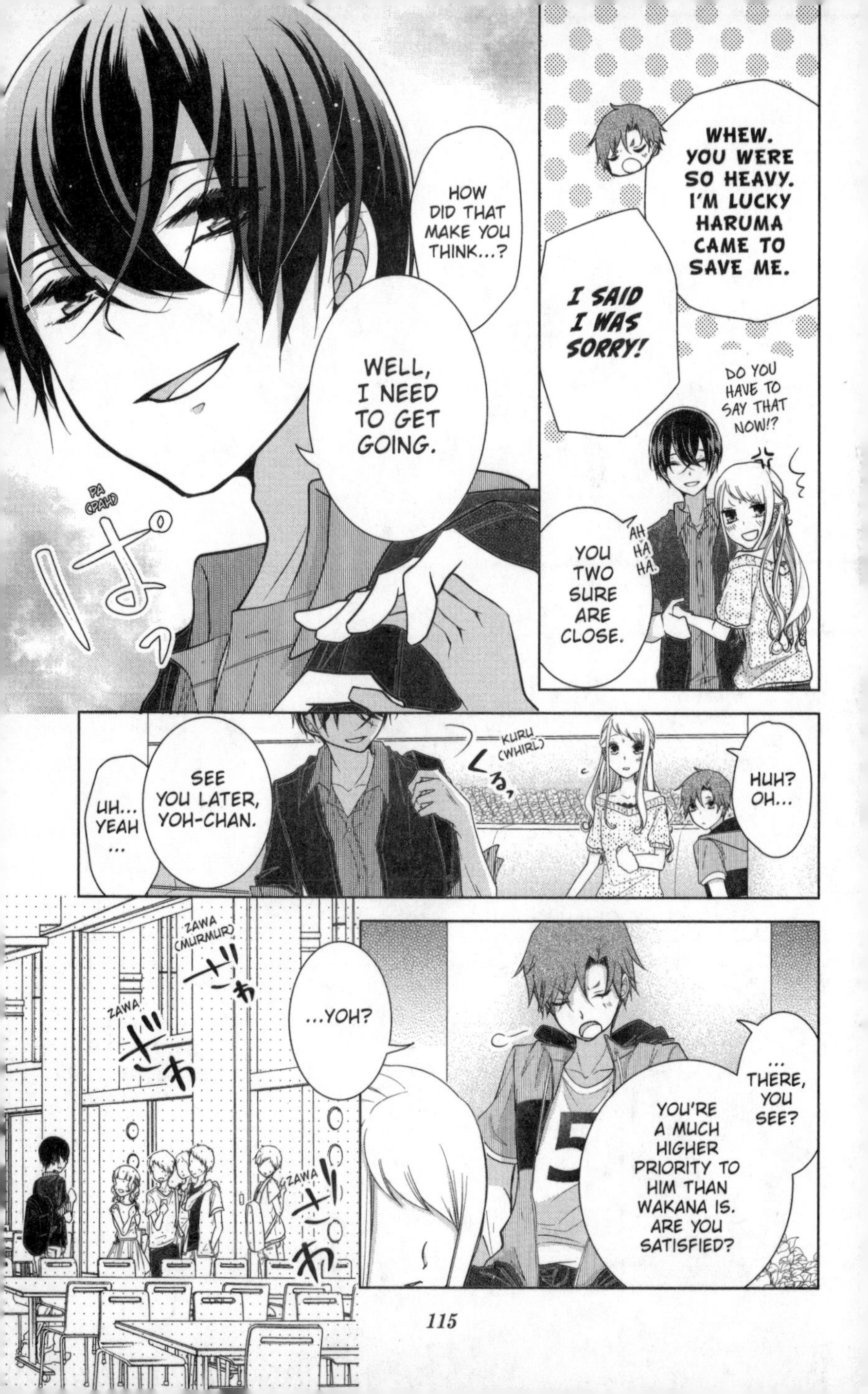
WHEW. YOU WERE SO HEAVY. I'M LUCKY HARUMA CAME TO SAVE ME.
I SAID I WAS SORRY!
DO YOU HAVE TO SAY THAT NOW!?
AH HA HA.
YOU TWO SURE ARE CLOSE.
HOW DID THAT MAKE YOU THINK...?
WELL, I NEED TO GET GOING.
PA (PAH)
HUH? OH...
KURU (WHIRL)
SEE YOU LATER, YOH-CHAN.
UH... YEAH ...
... THERE, YOU SEE?
YOU'RE A MUCH HIGHER PRIORITY TO HIM THAN WAKANA IS. ARE YOU SATISFIED?
...YOH?
ZAWA (MURMUR)
ZAWA
ZAWA

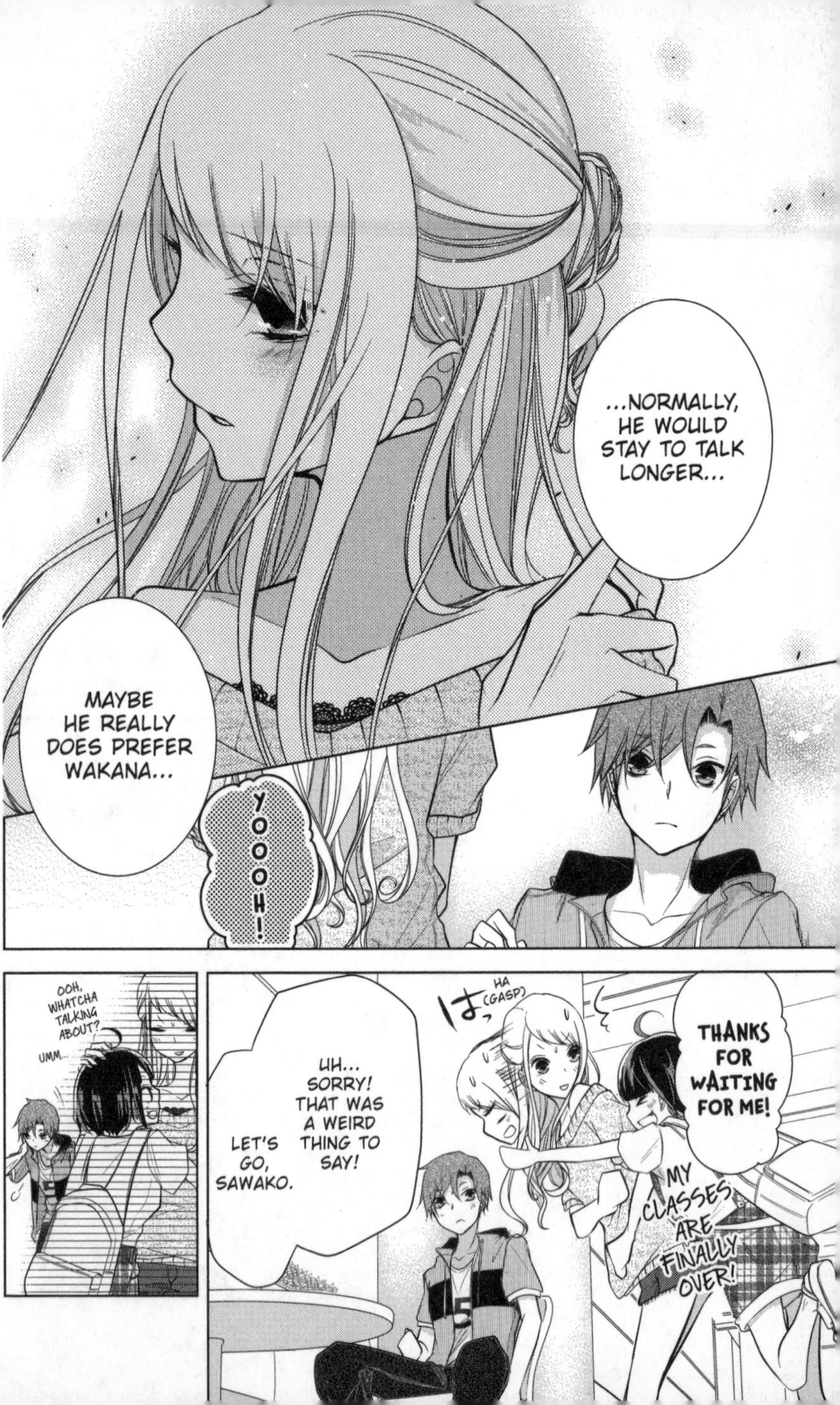
...NORMALLY, HE WOULD STAY TO TALK LONGER...
MAYBE HE REALLY DOES PREFER WAKANA...
YOOOOH!
THANKS FOR WAITING FOR ME!
MY CLASSES ARE FINALLY OVER!
は HA (GASP)
UH... SORRY! THAT WAS A WEIRD THING TO SAY!
LET'S GO, SAWAKO.
OOH, WHATCHA TALKING ABOUT?
UMM...

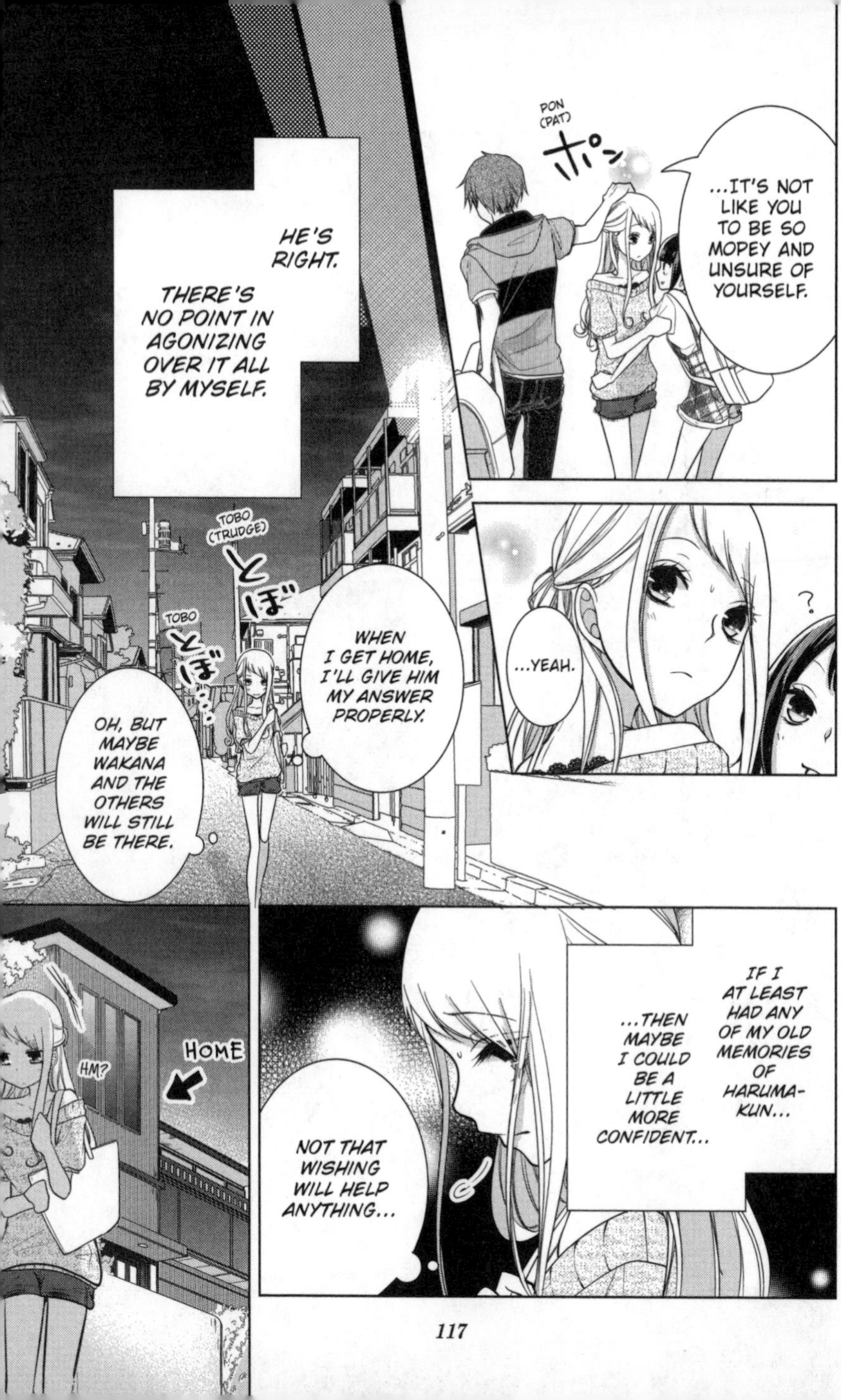
PON (PAT)
...IT'S NOT LIKE YOU TO BE SO MOPEY AND UNSURE OF YOURSELF.
?
...YEAH.
HE'S RIGHT.
THERE'S NO POINT IN AGONIZING OVER IT ALL BY MYSELF.
TOBO (TRUDGE)
TOBO
WHEN I GET HOME, I'LL GIVE HIM MY ANSWER PROPERLY.
OH, BUT MAYBE WAKANA AND THE OTHERS WILL STILL BE THERE.
IF I AT LEAST HAD ANY OF MY OLD MEMORIES OF HARUMA-KUN...
...THEN MAYBE I COULD BE A LITTLE MORE CONFIDENT...
NOT THAT WISHING WILL HELP ANYTHING...
HOME
HM?

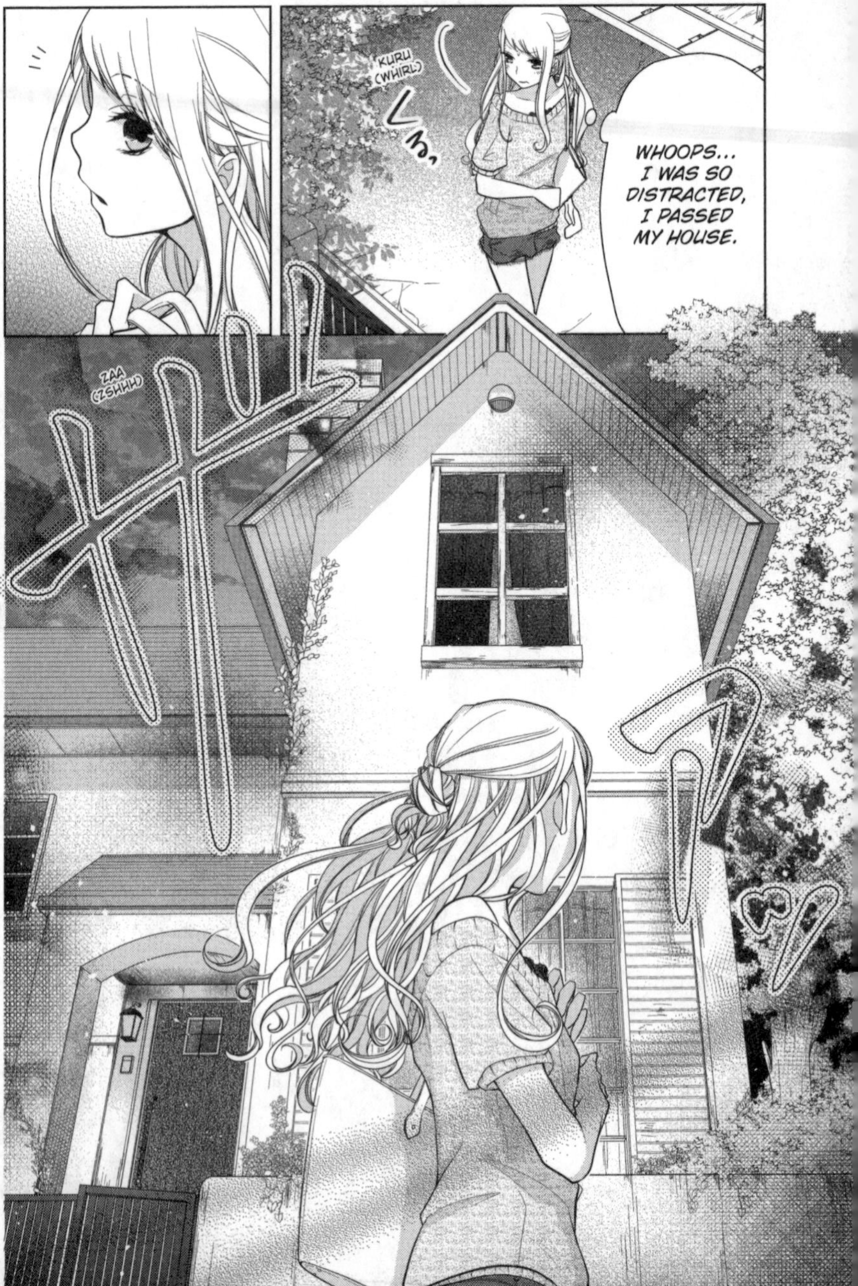
WHOOPS... I WAS SO DISTRACTED, I PASSED MY HOUSE.
KURU (WHIRL)
ZAA (ZSHHH)

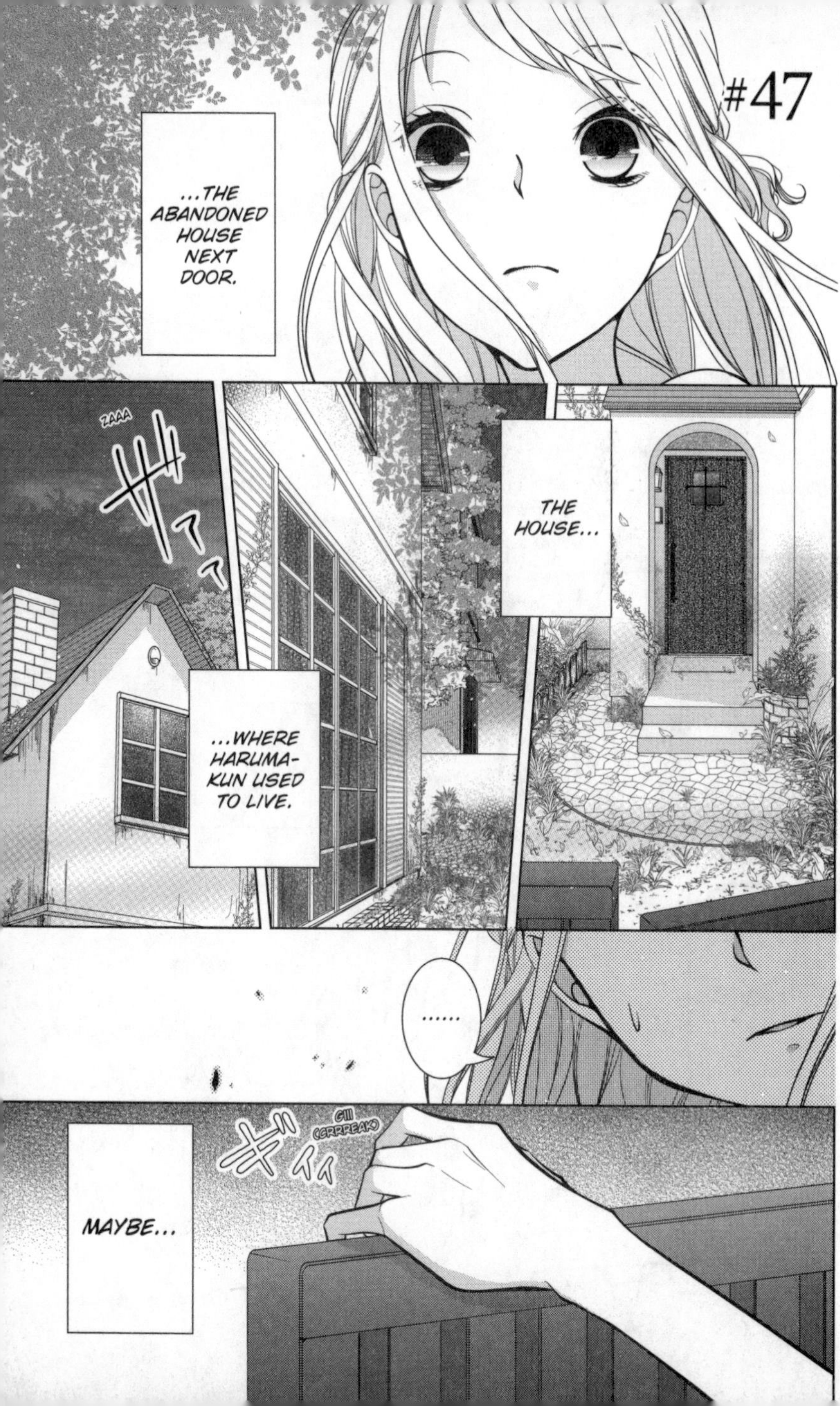
#47
...THE ABANDONED HOUSE NEXT DOOR.
THE HOUSE...
...WHERE HARUMA-KUN USED TO LIVE.
ZAAA
......
GIII (CRRREAK)
MAYBE...

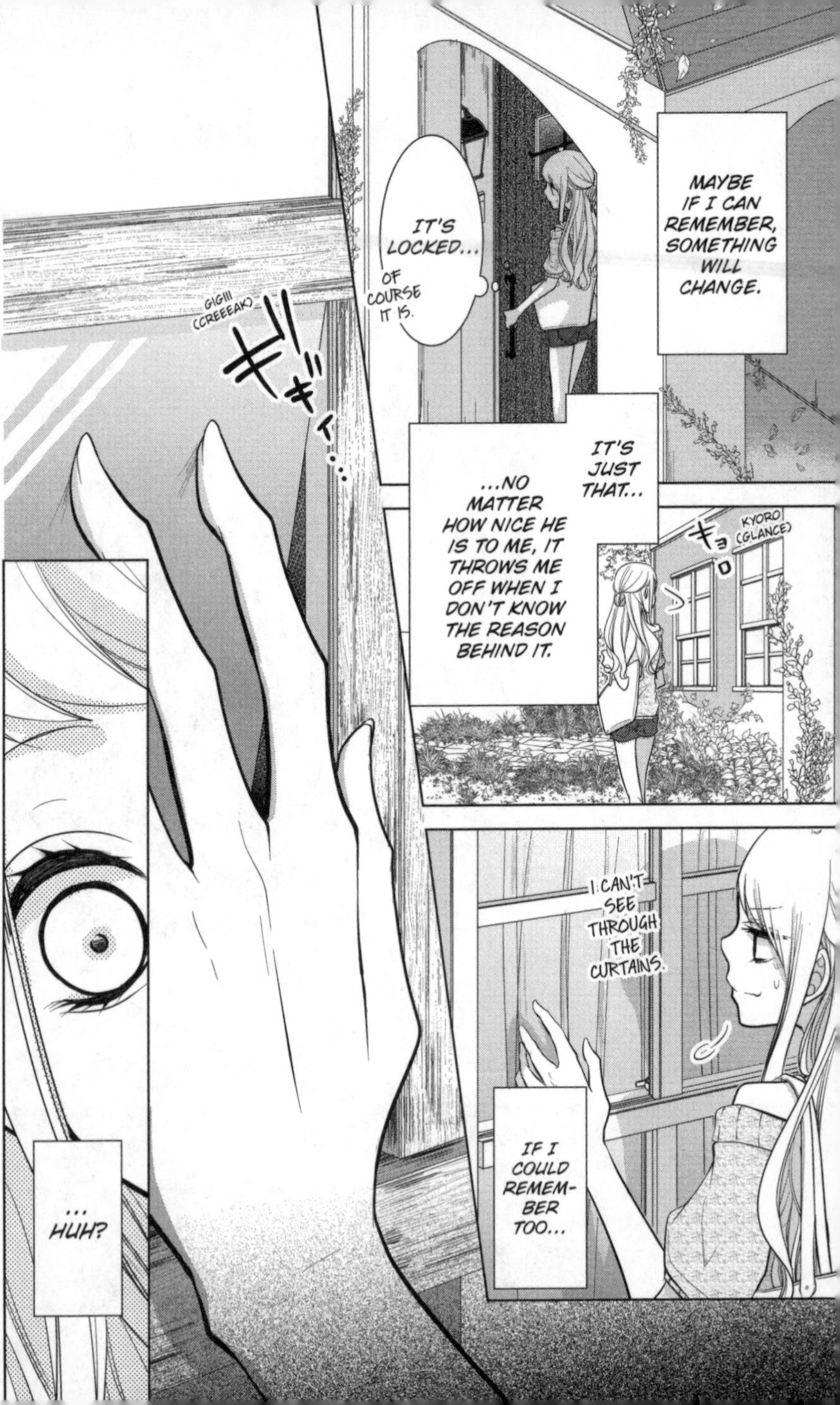
MAYBE IF I CAN REMEMBER, SOMETHING WILL CHANGE.
IT'S LOCKED...
OF COURSE IT IS.
IT'S JUST THAT...
...NO MATTER HOW NICE HE IS TO ME, IT THROWS ME OFF WHEN I DON'T KNOW THE REASON BEHIND IT.
KYORO (GLANCE)
I CAN'T SEE THROUGH THE CURTAINS.
IF I COULD REMEMBER TOO...
GIGIII (CREEEAK)
... HUH?

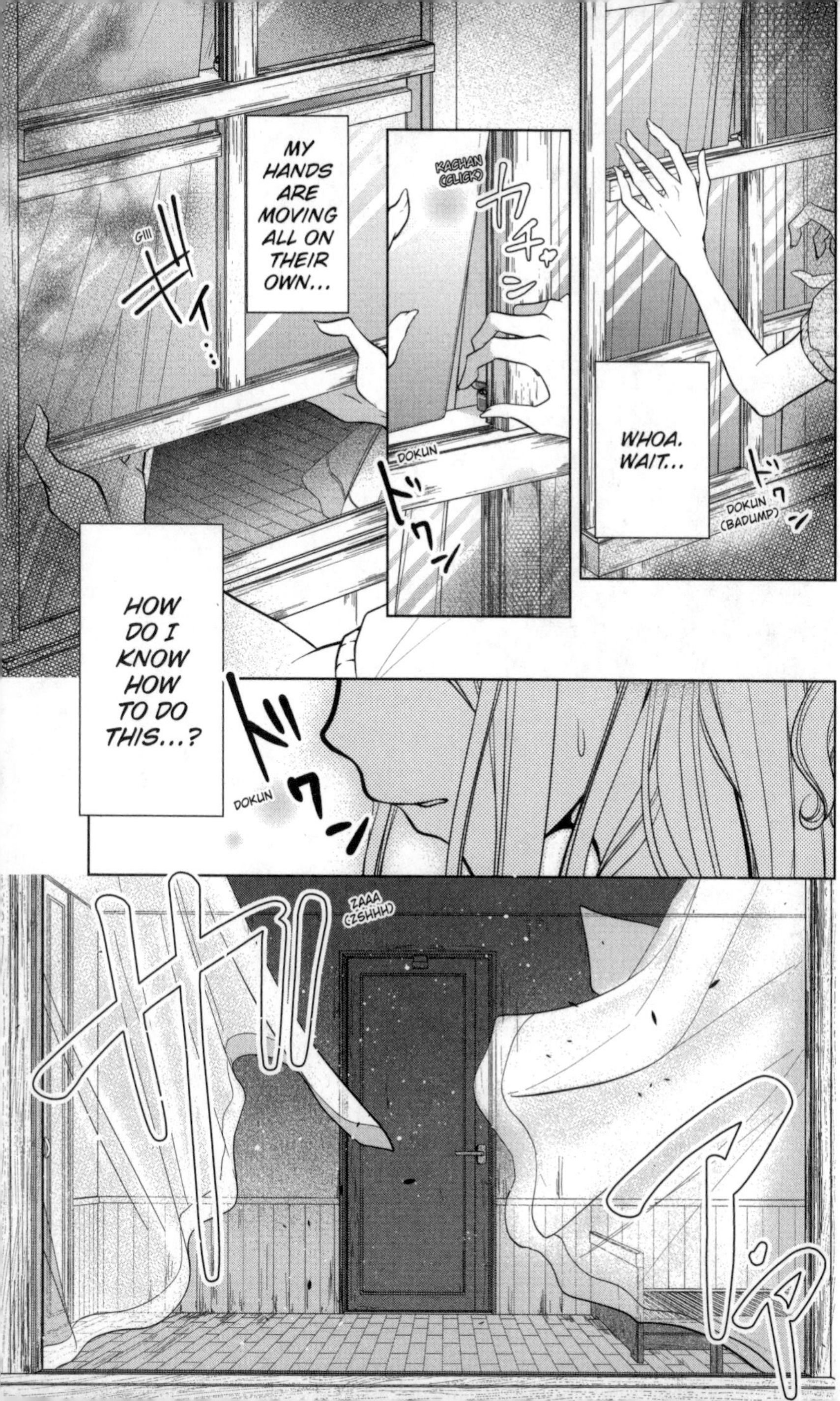
WHOA. WAIT...
DOKUN (BADUMP)
KACHAN (CLICK)
DOKUN
MY HANDS ARE MOVING ALL ON THEIR OWN...
GIII
HOW DO I KNOW HOW TO DO THIS...?
DOKUN
ZAAA (ZSHHH)

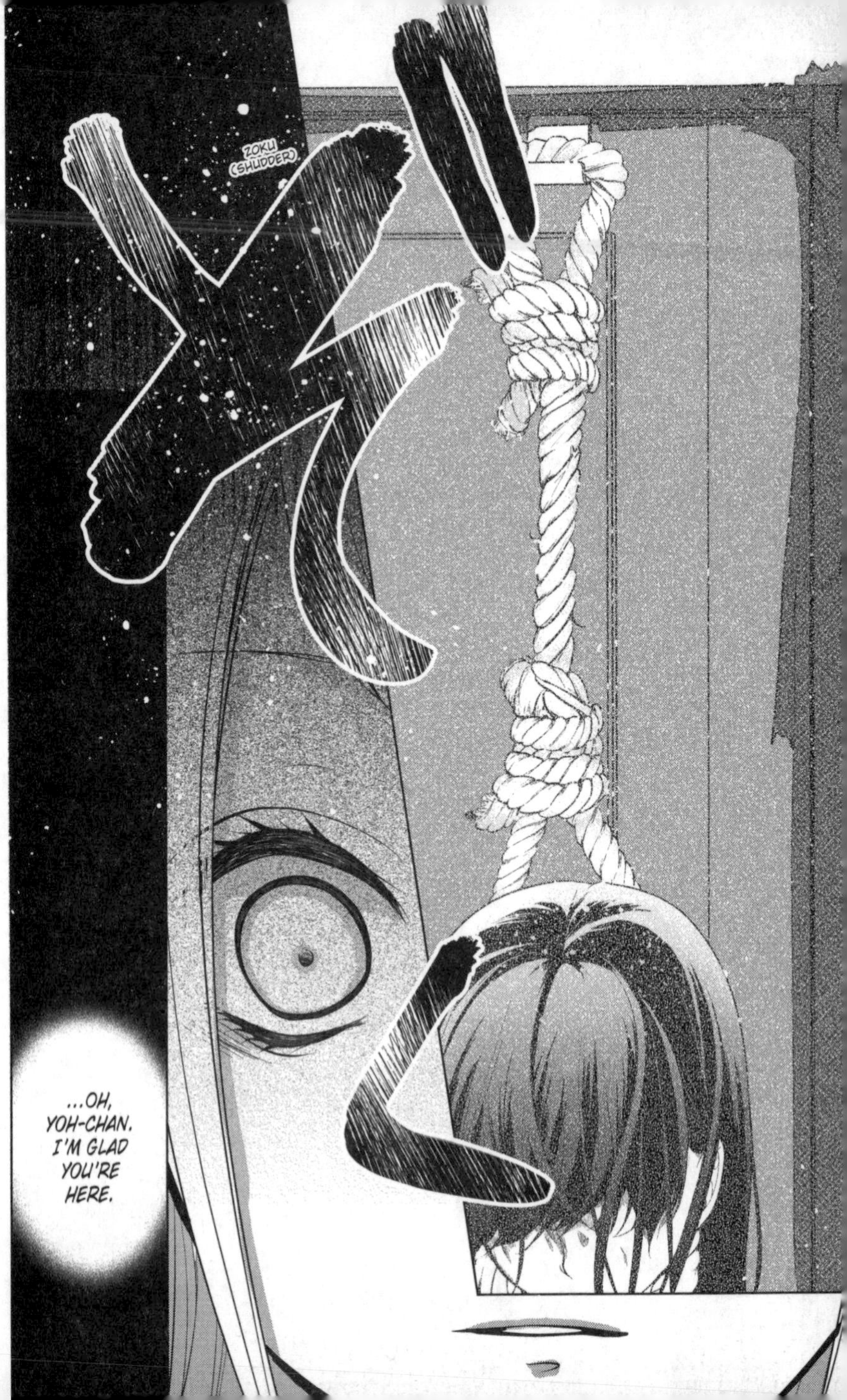
ZOKU (SHUDDER)
...OH, YOH-CHAN. I'M GLAD YOU'RE HERE.

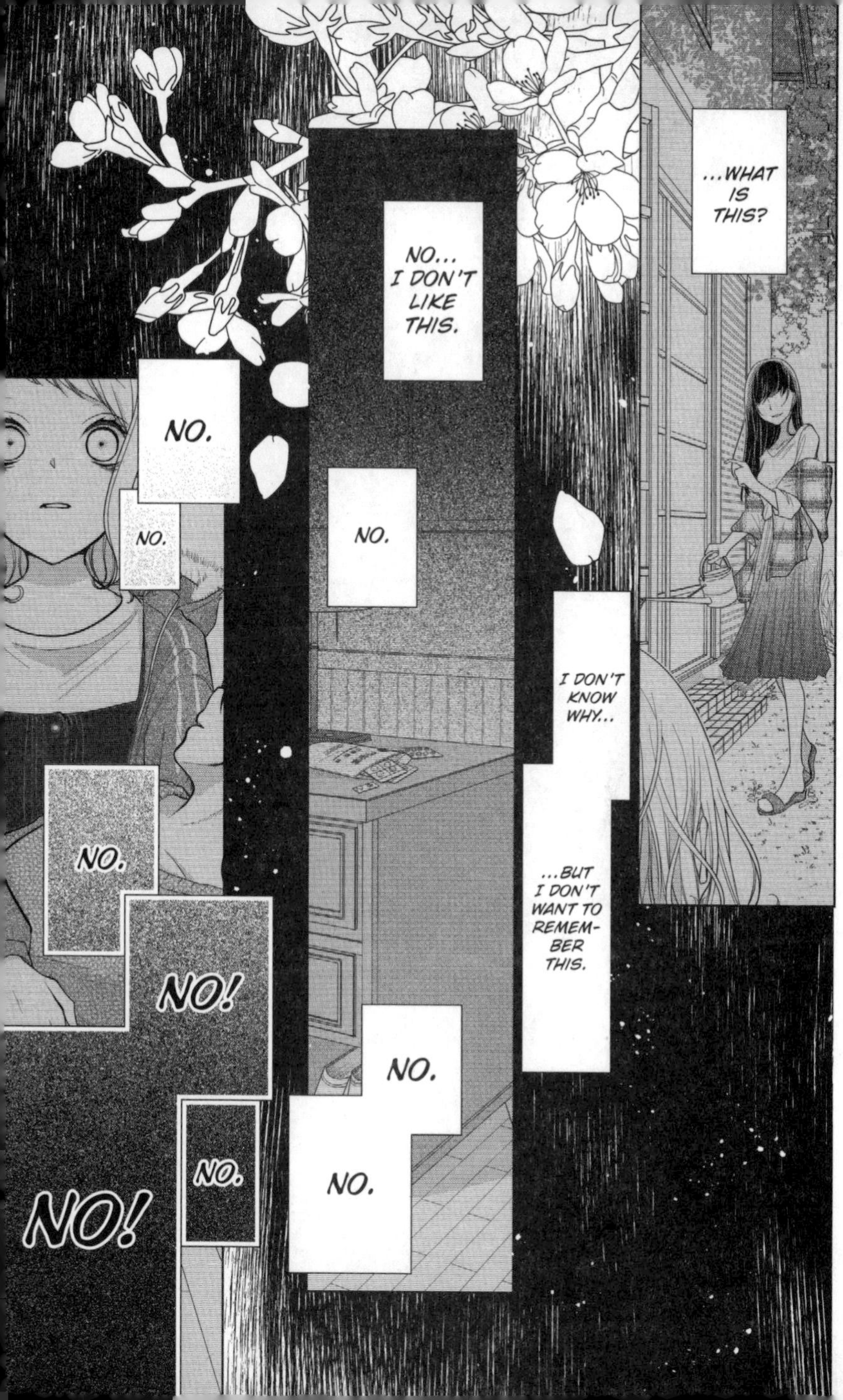
...WHAT IS THIS?
I DON'T KNOW WHY...
...BUT I DON'T WANT TO REMEMBER THIS.
NO... I DON'T LIKE THIS.
NO.
NO.
NO.
NO.
NO.
NO.
NO!
NO.
NO!

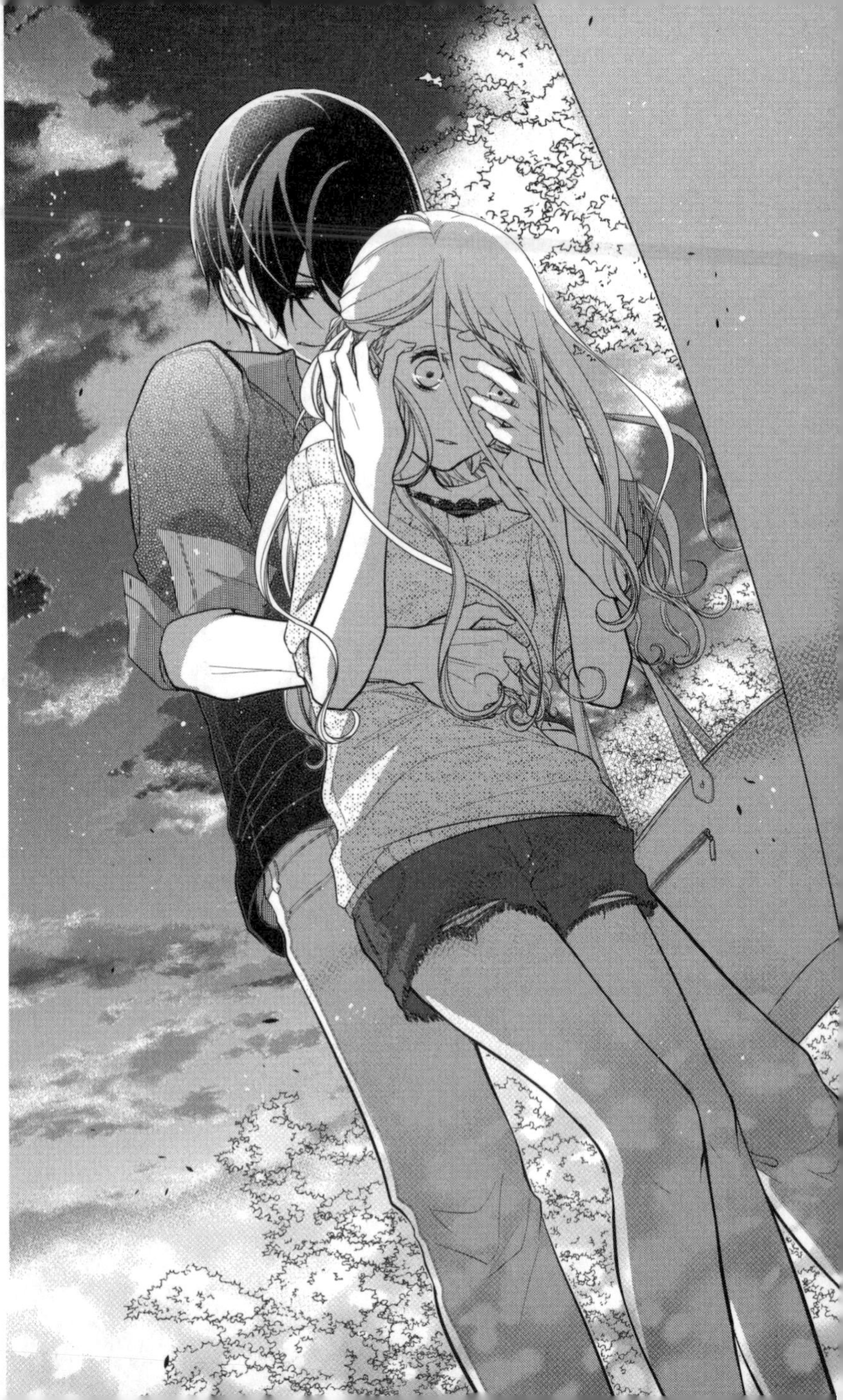

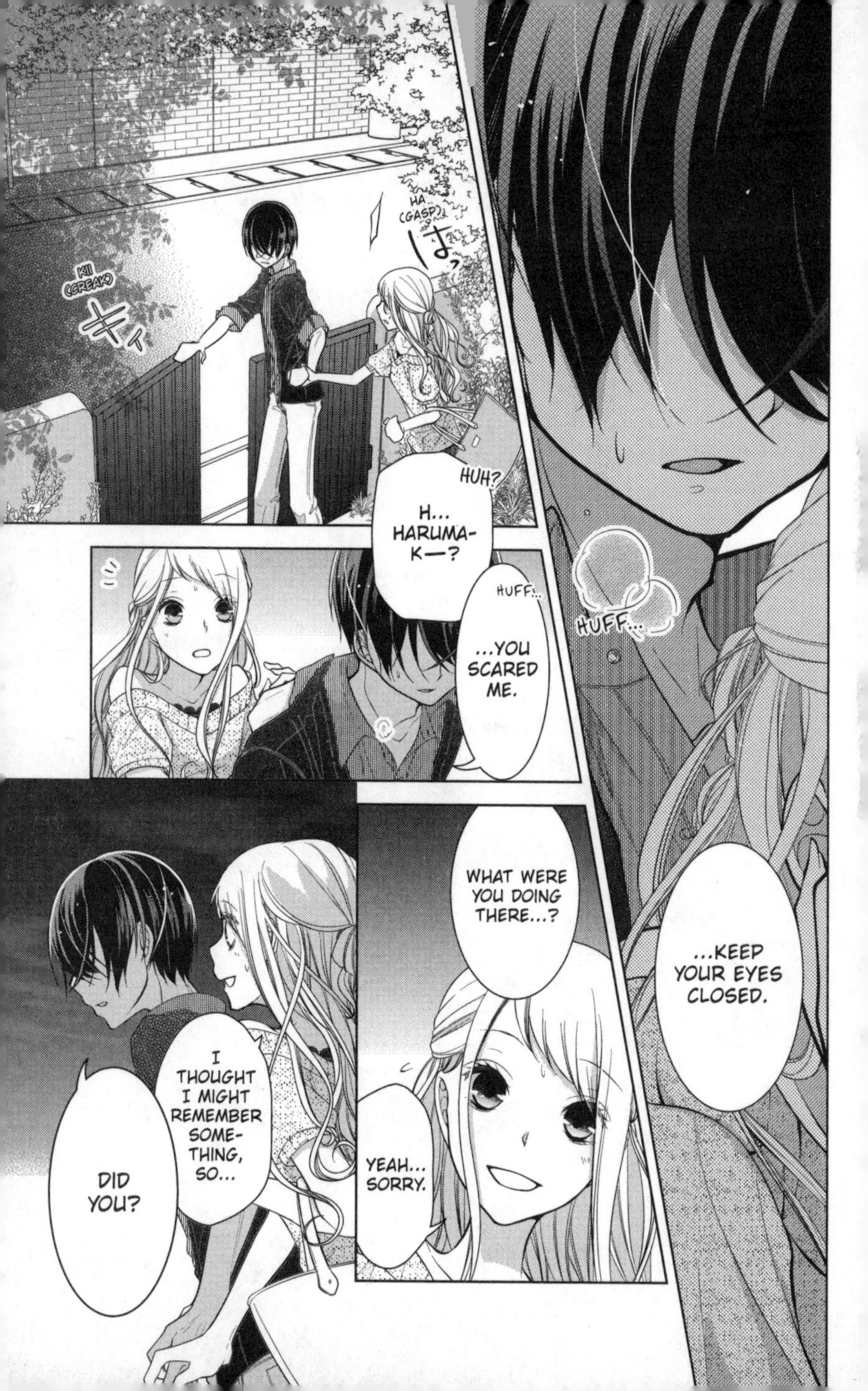
HUFF...
...KEEP YOUR EYES CLOSED.
HA (GASP)
は
KII (CREAK)
キィ
HUH?
H... HARUMA-K—?
HUFF...
...YOU SCARED ME.
WHAT WERE YOU DOING THERE...?
YEAH... SORRY.
I THOUGHT I MIGHT REMEMBER SOME-THING, SO...
DID YOU?

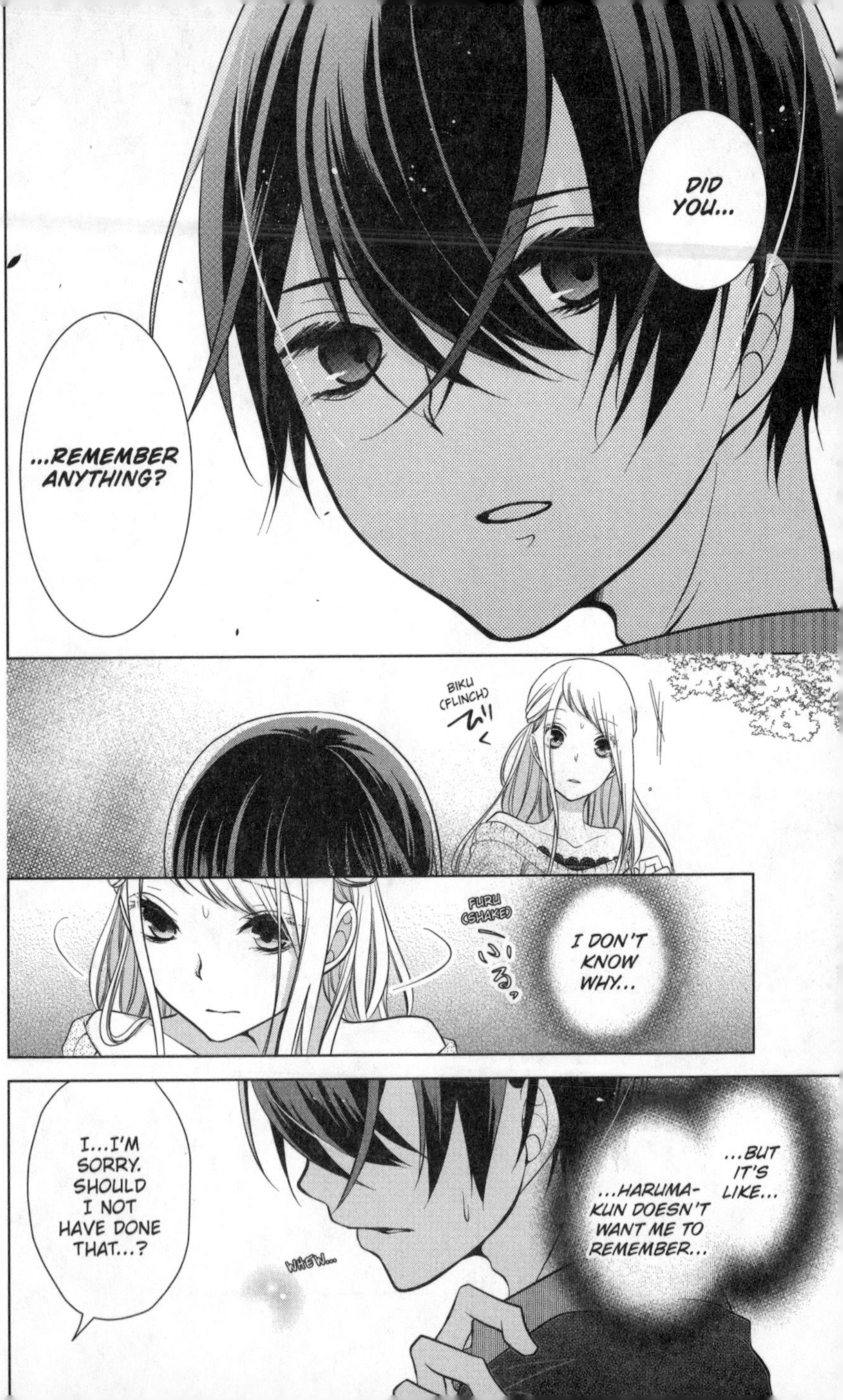
DID YOU...
...REMEMBER ANYTHING?
BIKU (FLINCH)
FURU (SHAKE)
I DON'T KNOW WHY...
...BUT IT'S LIKE...
...HARUMA-KUN DOESN'T WANT ME TO REMEMBER...
I...I'M SORRY. SHOULD I NOT HAVE DONE THAT...?
WHEW...

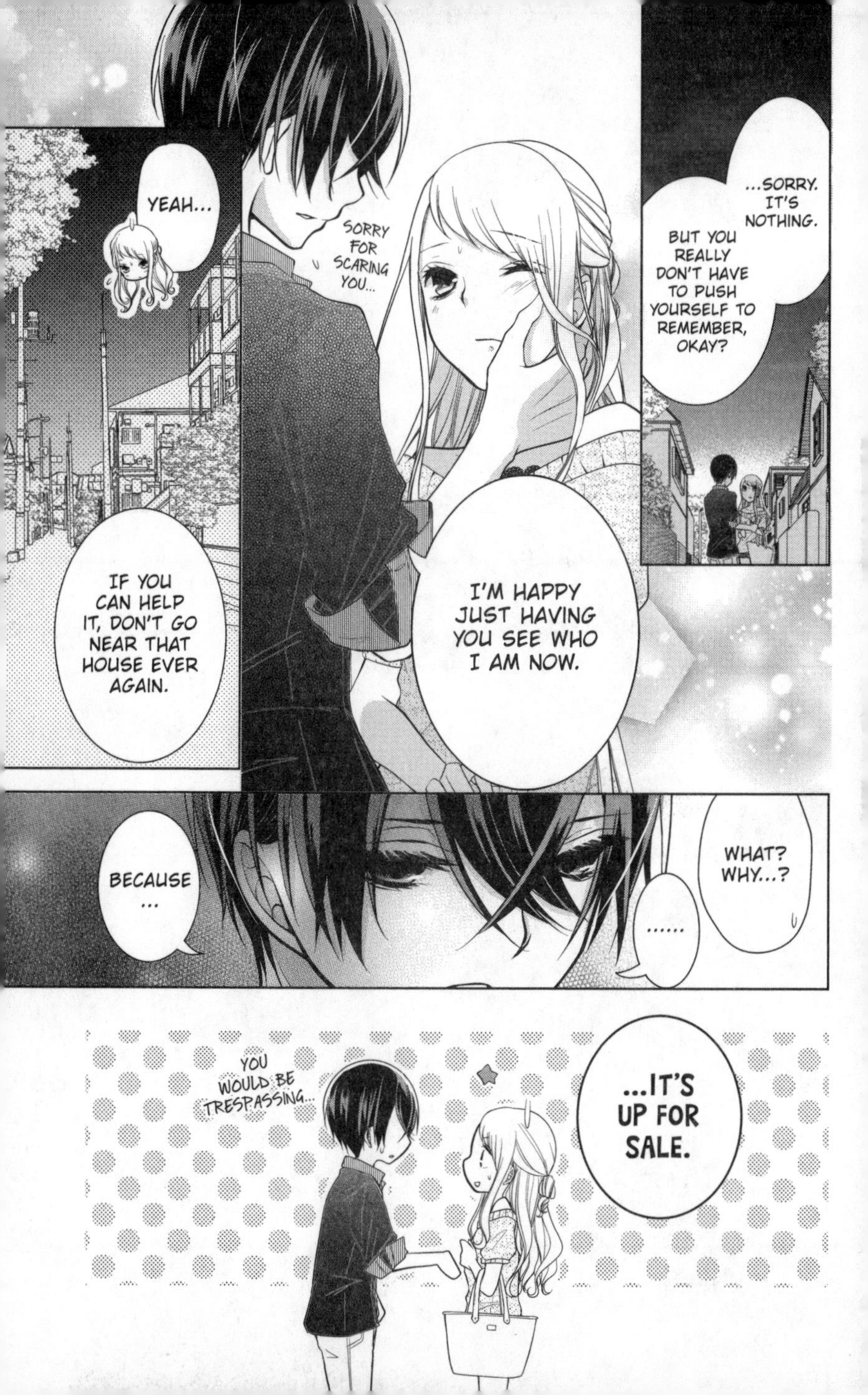
...SORRY. IT'S NOTHING.
BUT YOU REALLY DON'T HAVE TO PUSH YOURSELF TO REMEMBER, OKAY?
SORRY FOR SCARING YOU...
I'M HAPPY JUST HAVING YOU SEE WHO I AM NOW.
YEAH...
IF YOU CAN HELP IT, DON'T GO NEAR THAT HOUSE EVER AGAIN.
WHAT? WHY...?
......
BECAUSE ...
...IT'S UP FOR SALE.
YOU WOULD BE TRESPASSING...

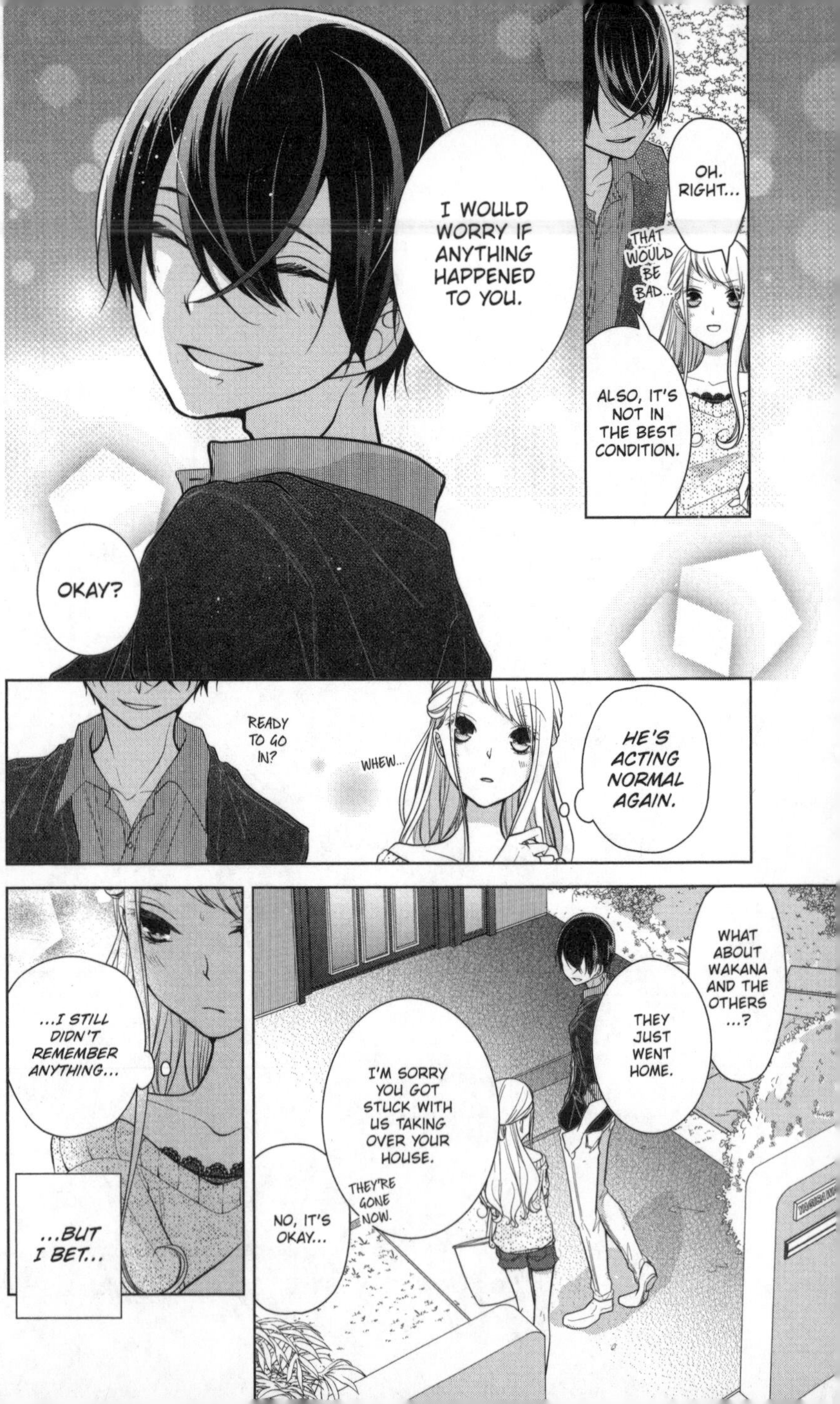
OH. RIGHT...
THAT WOULD BE BAD...
ALSO, IT'S NOT IN THE BEST CONDITION.
I WOULD WORRY IF ANYTHING HAPPENED TO YOU.
OKAY?
HE'S ACTING NORMAL AGAIN.
WHEW...
READY TO GO IN?
WHAT ABOUT WAKANA AND THE OTHERS ...?
THEY JUST WENT HOME.
I'M SORRY YOU GOT STUCK WITH US TAKING OVER YOUR HOUSE.
THEY'RE GONE NOW.
NO, IT'S OKAY...
...I STILL DIDN'T REMEMBER ANYTHING...
...BUT I BET...

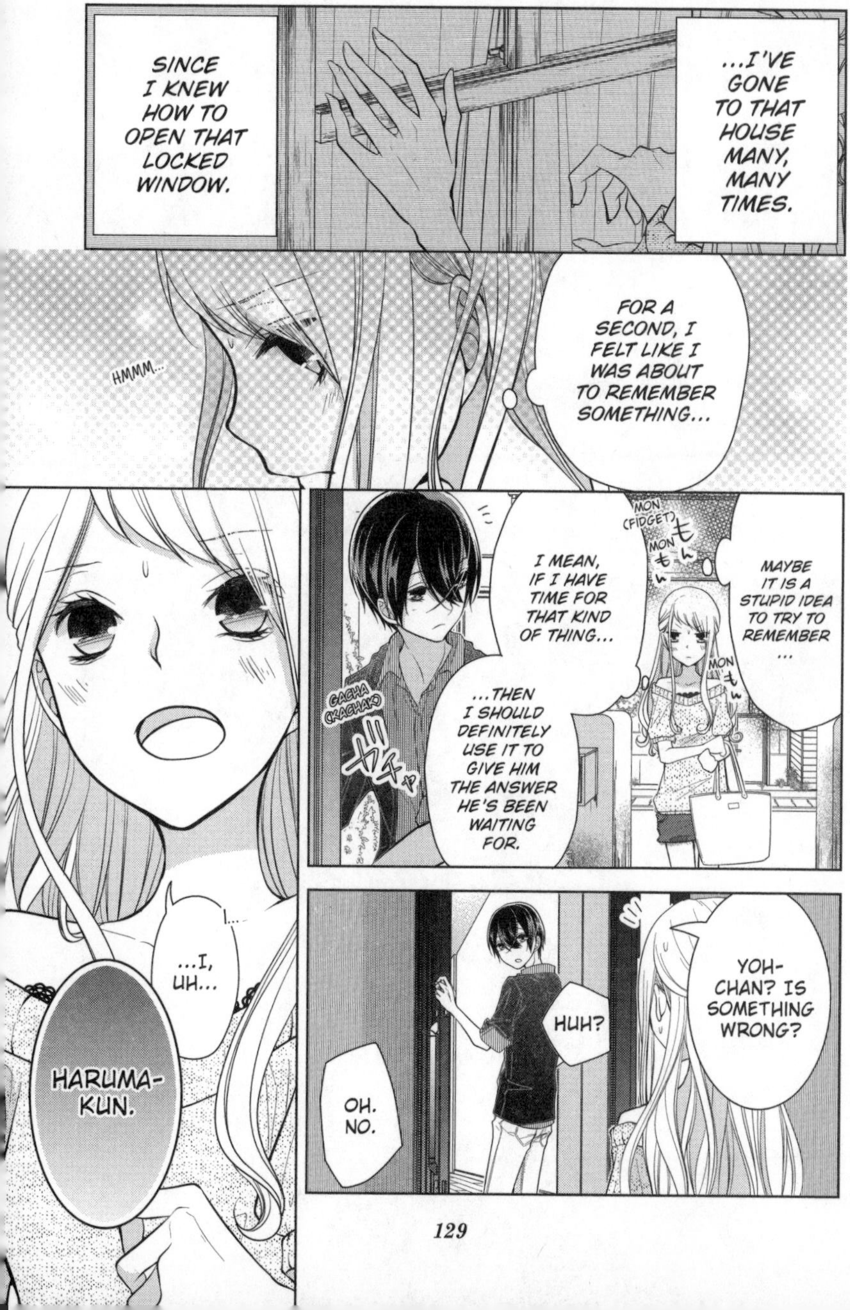
...I'VE GONE TO THAT HOUSE MANY, MANY TIMES.
SINCE I KNEW HOW TO OPEN THAT LOCKED WINDOW.
FOR A SECOND, I FELT LIKE I WAS ABOUT TO REMEMBER SOMETHING...
HMMM...
MAYBE IT IS A STUPID IDEA TO TRY TO REMEMBER ...
MON (FIDGET) MON MON
I MEAN, IF I HAVE TIME FOR THAT KIND OF THING...
...THEN I SHOULD DEFINITELY USE IT TO GIVE HIM THE ANSWER HE'S BEEN WAITING FOR.
GACHA (KACHAK)
YOH-CHAN? IS SOMETHING WRONG?
HUH?
OH. NO.
I...
...I, UH...
HARUMA-KUN.

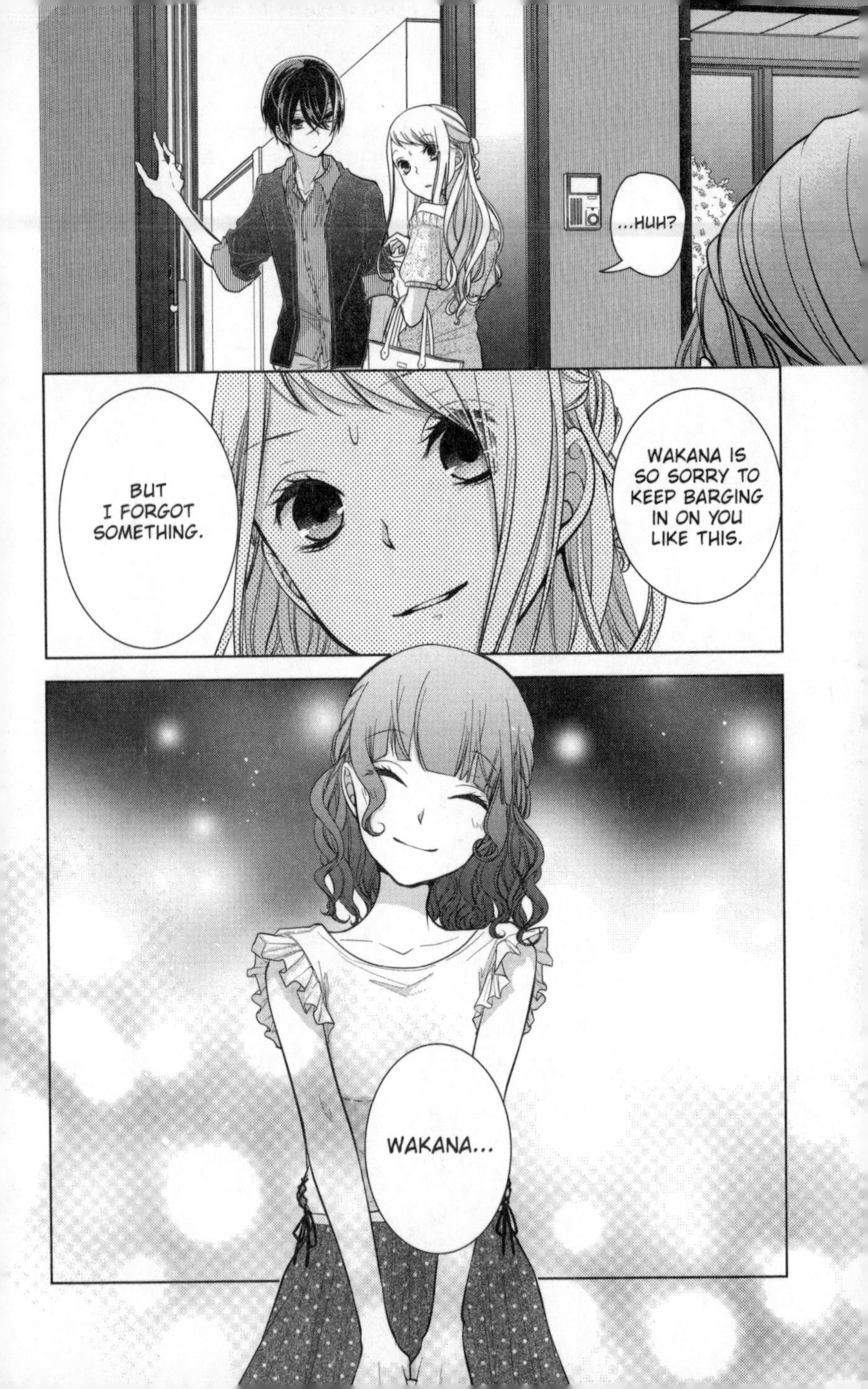
...HUH?
WAKANA IS SO SORRY TO KEEP BARGING IN ON YOU LIKE THIS.
BUT I FORGOT SOMETHING.
WAKANA...

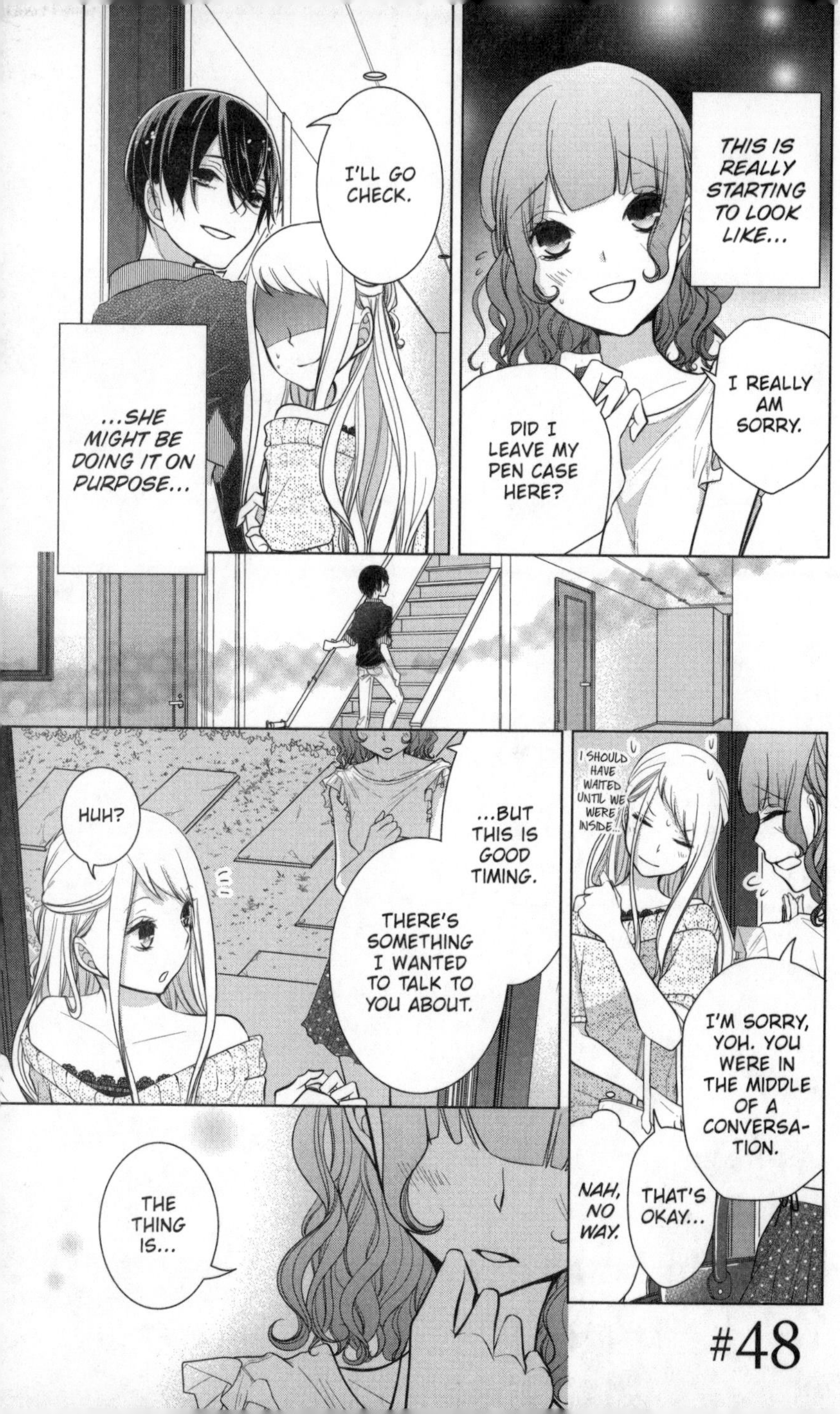
THIS IS REALLY STARTING TO LOOK LIKE...
I REALLY AM SORRY.
DID I LEAVE MY PEN CASE HERE?
I'LL GO CHECK.
...SHE MIGHT BE DOING IT ON PURPOSE...
I SHOULD HAVE WAITED UNTIL WE WERE INSIDE...
I'M SORRY, YOH. YOU WERE IN THE MIDDLE OF A CONVERSATION.
THAT'S OKAY...
NAH, NO WAY.
...BUT THIS IS GOOD TIMING.
THERE'S SOMETHING I WANTED TO TALK TO YOU ABOUT.
HUH?
THE THING IS...

#48

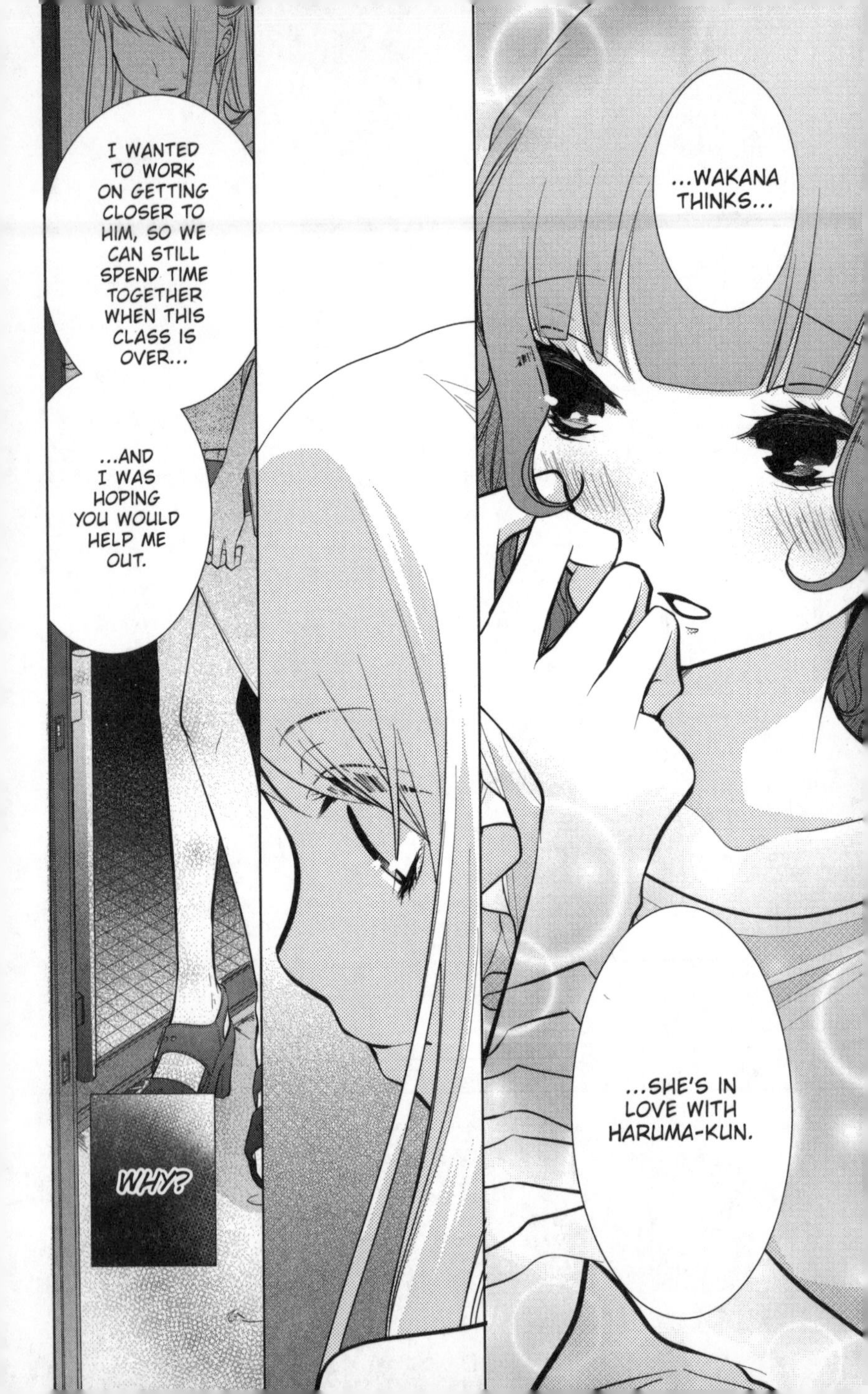
...WAKANA THINKS...
...SHE'S IN LOVE WITH HARUMA-KUN.
I WANTED TO WORK ON GETTING CLOSER TO HIM, SO WE CAN STILL SPEND TIME TOGETHER WHEN THIS CLASS IS OVER...
...AND I WAS HOPING YOU WOULD HELP ME OUT.
WHY?

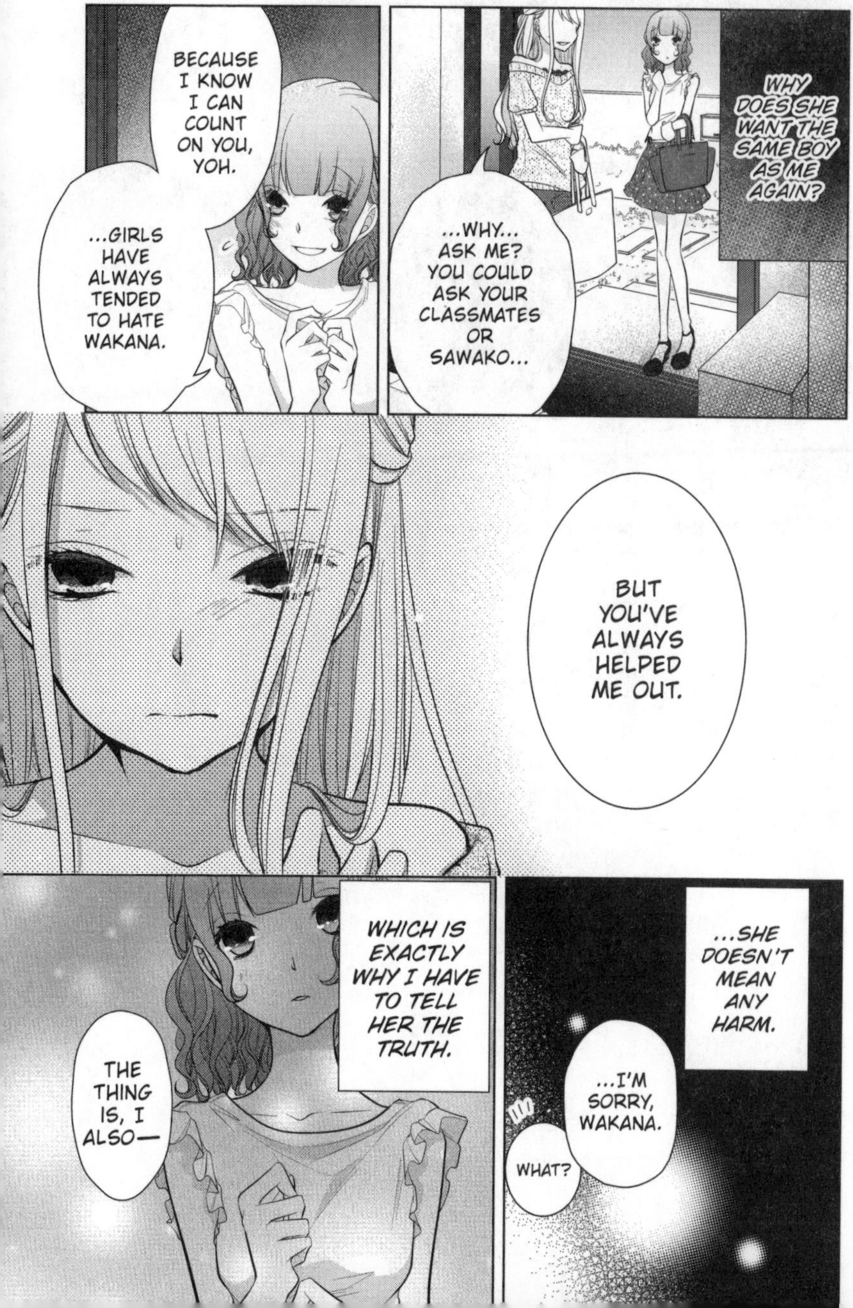
WHY DOES SHE WANT THE SAME BOY AS ME AGAIN?
...WHY... ASK ME? YOU COULD ASK YOUR CLASSMATES OR SAWAKO...
BECAUSE I KNOW I CAN COUNT ON YOU, YOH.
...GIRLS HAVE ALWAYS TENDED TO HATE WAKANA.
BUT YOU'VE ALWAYS HELPED ME OUT.
...SHE DOESN'T MEAN ANY HARM.
...I'M SORRY, WAKANA.
WHAT?
WHICH IS EXACTLY WHY I HAVE TO TELL HER THE TRUTH.
THE THING IS, I ALSO—

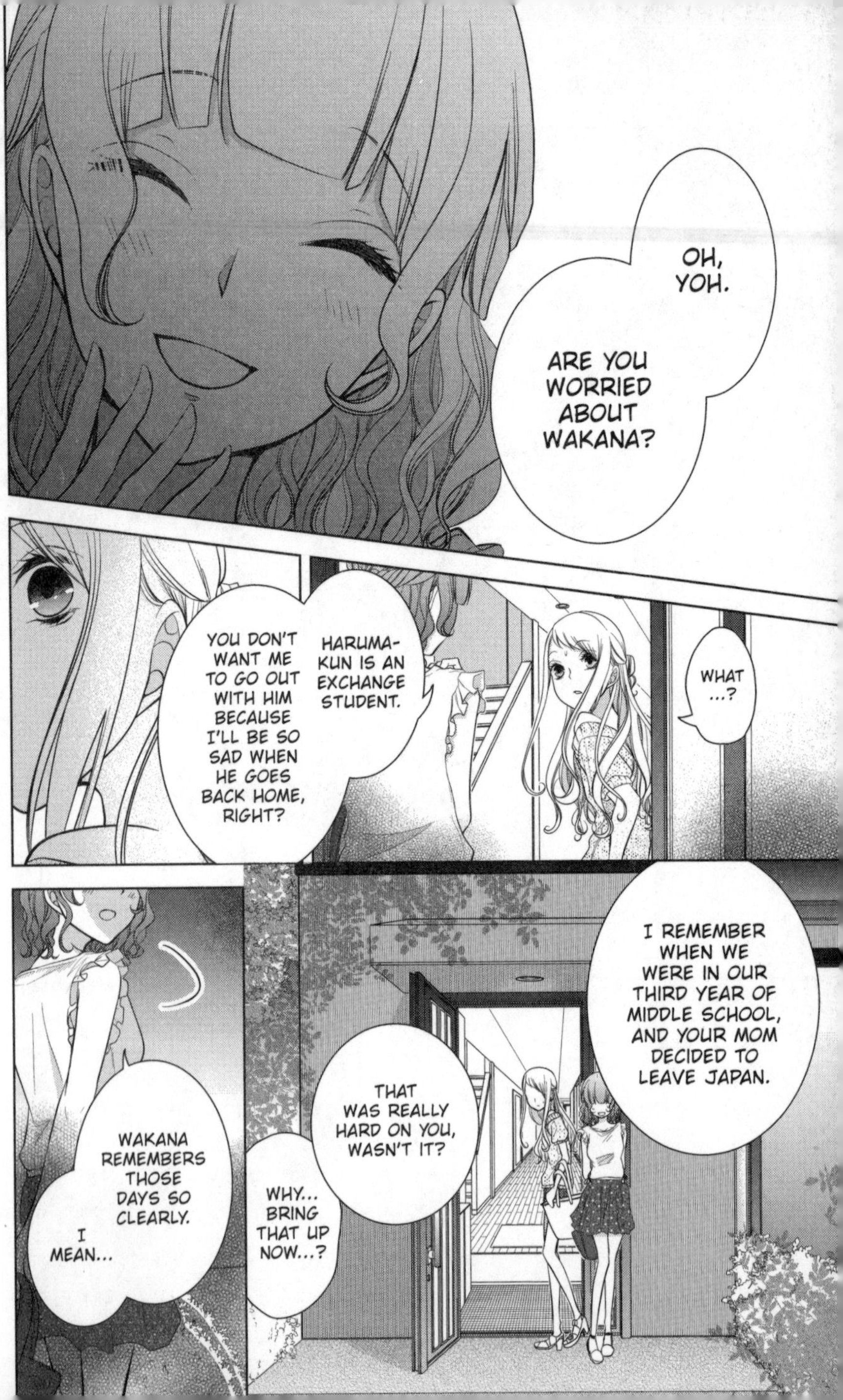
OH, YOH.
ARE YOU WORRIED ABOUT WAKANA?
WHAT ...?
HARUMA-KUN IS AN EXCHANGE STUDENT.
YOU DON'T WANT ME TO GO OUT WITH HIM BECAUSE I'LL BE SO SAD WHEN HE GOES BACK HOME, RIGHT?
I REMEMBER WHEN WE WERE IN OUR THIRD YEAR OF MIDDLE SCHOOL, AND YOUR MOM DECIDED TO LEAVE JAPAN.
THAT WAS REALLY HARD ON YOU, WASN'T IT?
WHY... BRING THAT UP NOW...?
WAKANA REMEMBERS THOSE DAYS SO CLEARLY.
I MEAN...

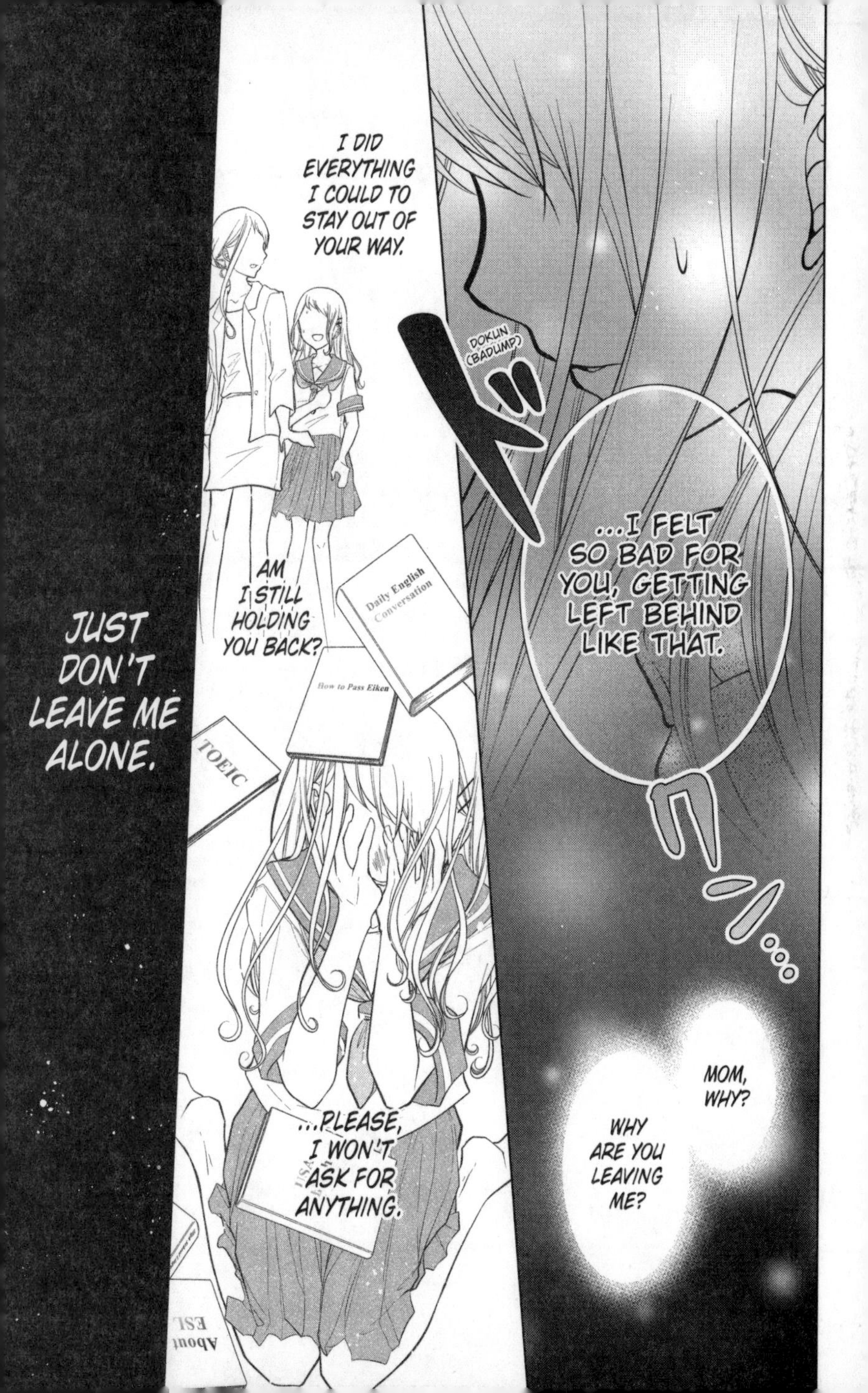
DOKUN (BADUMP)
...I FELT SO BAD FOR YOU, GETTING LEFT BEHIND LIKE THAT.
MOM, WHY?
WHY ARE YOU LEAVING ME?
I DID EVERYTHING I COULD TO STAY OUT OF YOUR WAY.
AM I STILL HOLDING YOU BACK?
Daily English Conversation
How to Pass Eiken
TOEIC
...PLEASE, I WON'T ASK FOR ANYTHING.
About ESL
JUST DON'T LEAVE ME ALONE.

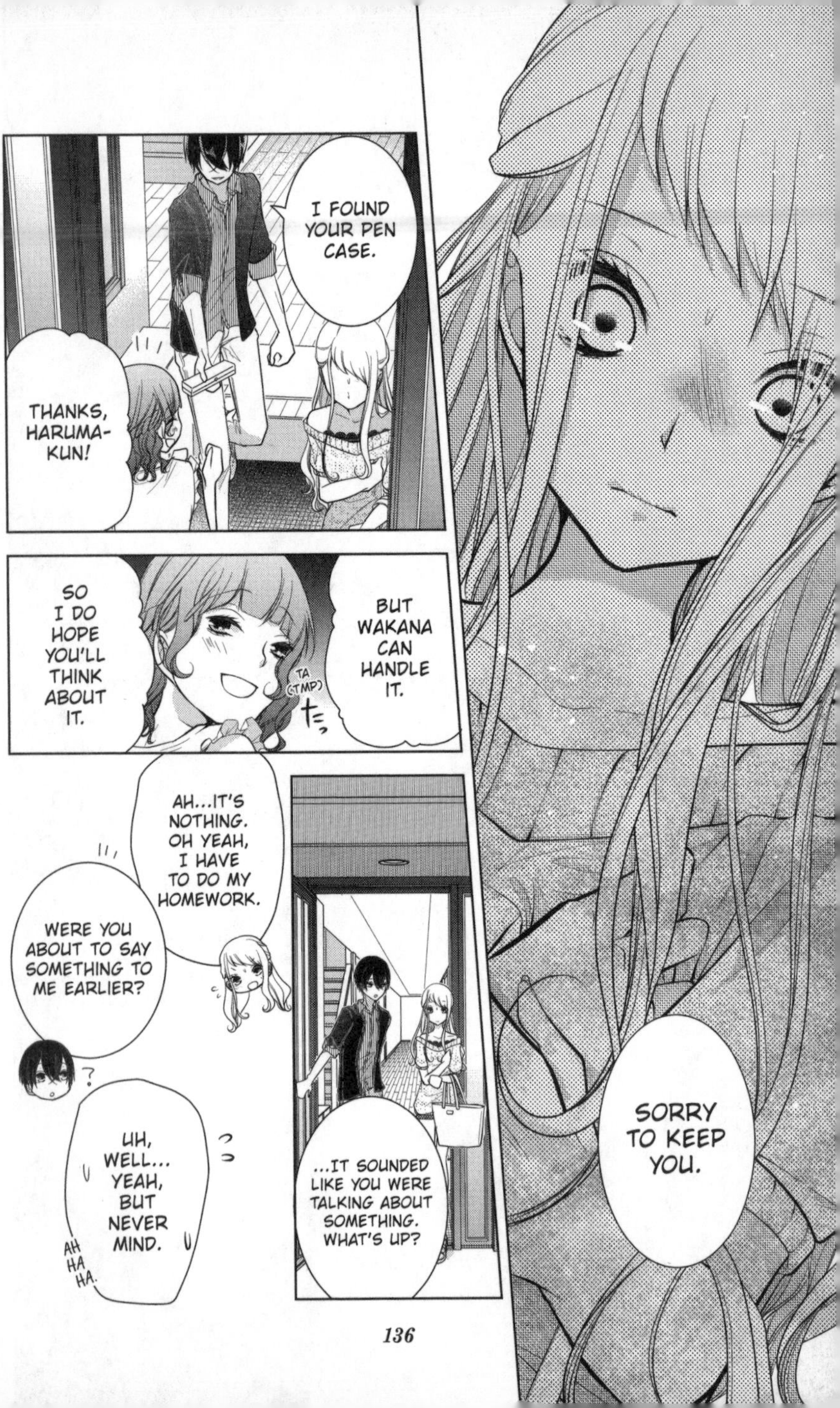
SORRY TO KEEP YOU.
I FOUND YOUR PEN CASE.
THANKS, HARUMA-KUN!
BUT WAKANA CAN HANDLE IT.
TA (TMP)
SO I DO HOPE YOU'LL THINK ABOUT IT.
...IT SOUNDED LIKE YOU WERE TALKING ABOUT SOMETHING. WHAT'S UP?
AH...IT'S NOTHING. OH YEAH, I HAVE TO DO MY HOMEWORK.
WERE YOU ABOUT TO SAY SOMETHING TO ME EARLIER?
UH, WELL... YEAH, BUT NEVER MIND.
AH HA HA.

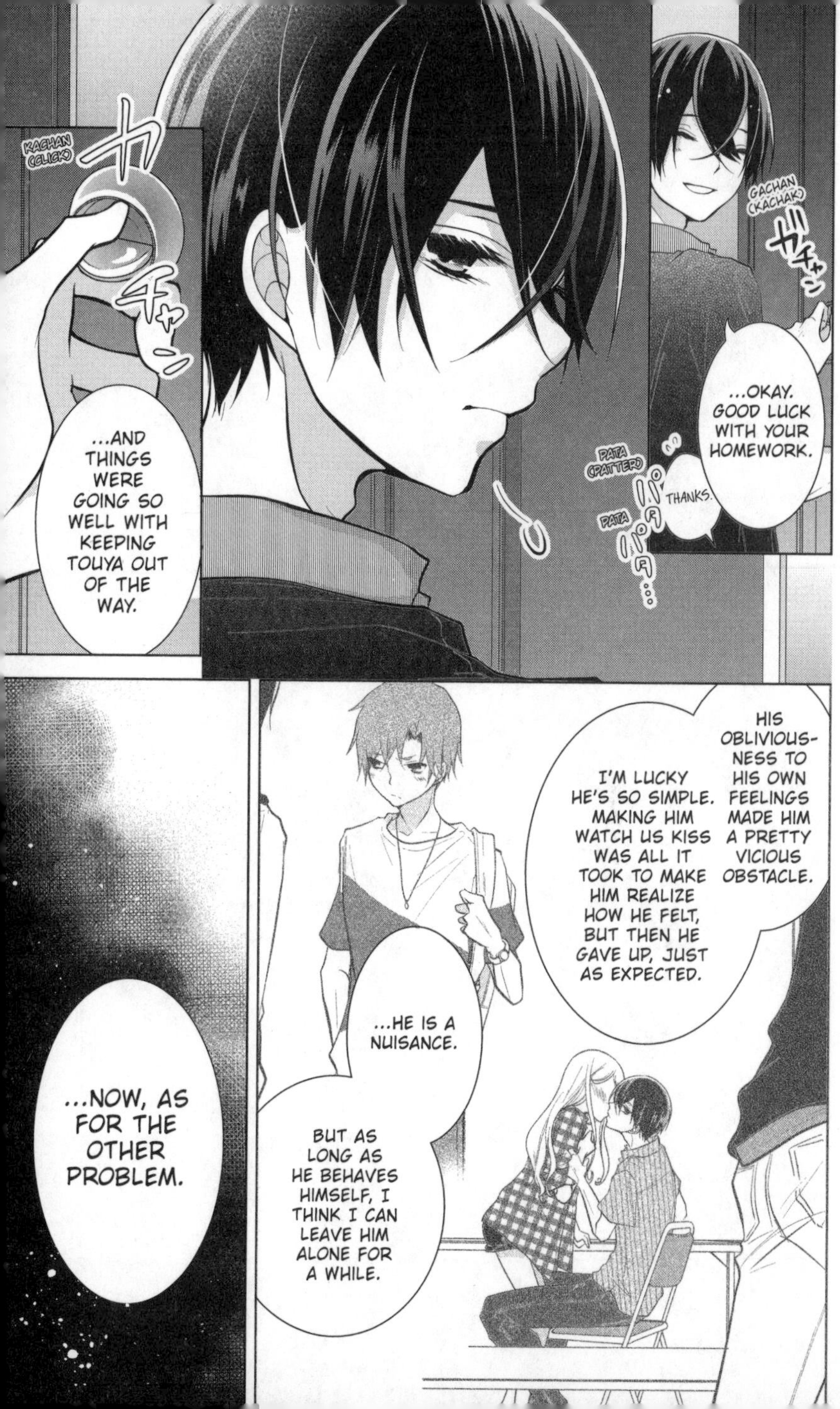
GACHAN (KACHAK)
...OKAY. GOOD LUCK WITH YOUR HOMEWORK.
PATA (PATTER)
PATA
THANKS.
KACHAN (CLICK)
...AND THINGS WERE GOING SO WELL WITH KEEPING TOUYA OUT OF THE WAY.
HIS OBLIVIOUS-NESS TO HIS OWN FEELINGS MADE HIM A PRETTY VICIOUS OBSTACLE.
I'M LUCKY HE'S SO SIMPLE. MAKING HIM WATCH US KISS WAS ALL IT TOOK TO MAKE HIM REALIZE HOW HE FELT, BUT THEN HE GAVE UP, JUST AS EXPECTED.
...HE IS A NUISANCE.
BUT AS LONG AS HE BEHAVES HIMSELF, I THINK I CAN LEAVE HIM ALONE FOR A WHILE.
...NOW, AS FOR THE OTHER PROBLEM.

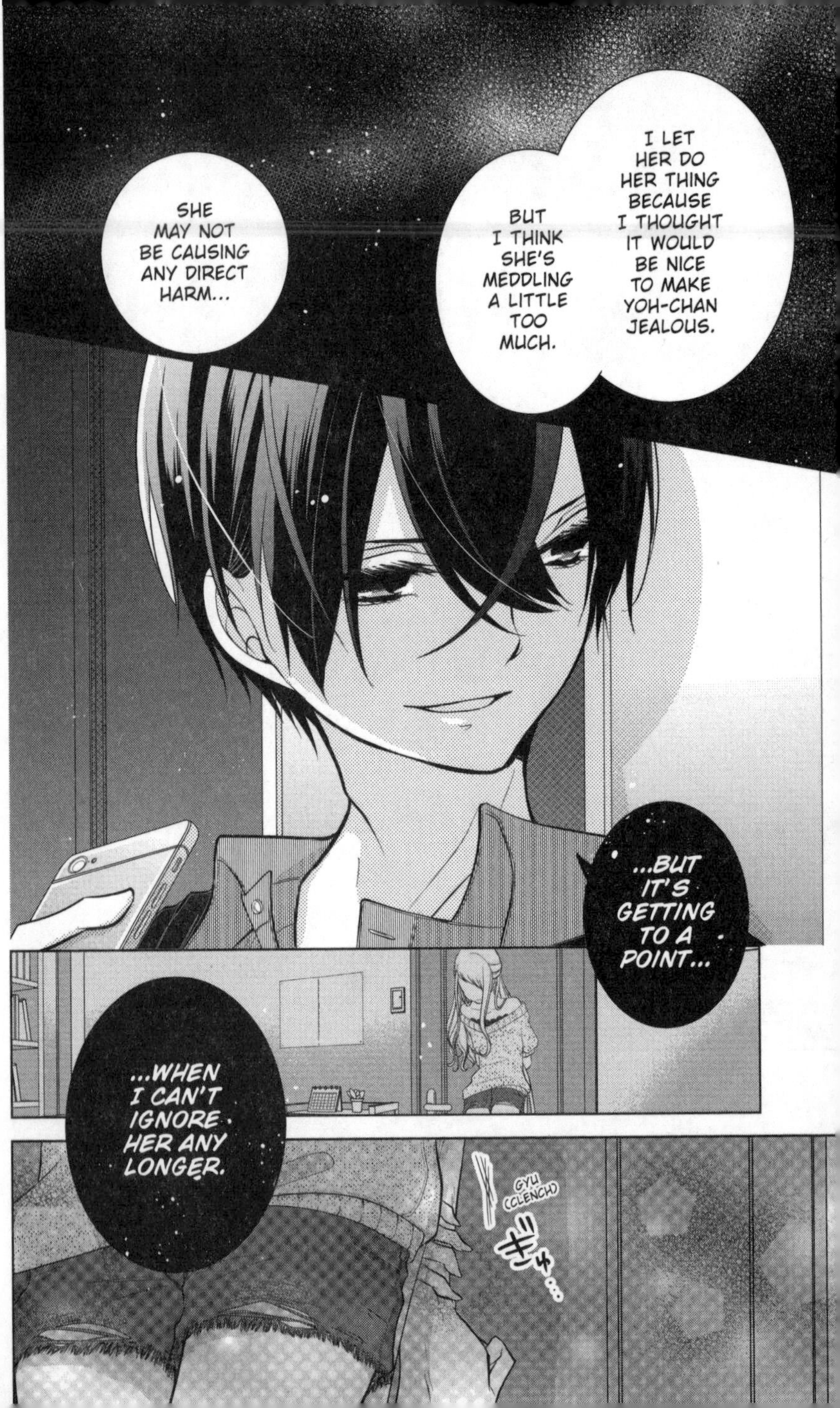
I LET HER DO HER THING BECAUSE I THOUGHT IT WOULD BE NICE TO MAKE YOH-CHAN JEALOUS.
BUT I THINK SHE'S MEDDLING A LITTLE TOO MUCH.
SHE MAY NOT BE CAUSING ANY DIRECT HARM...
...BUT IT'S GETTING TO A POINT...
...WHEN I CAN'T IGNORE HER ANY LONGER.
GYU (CLENCH)

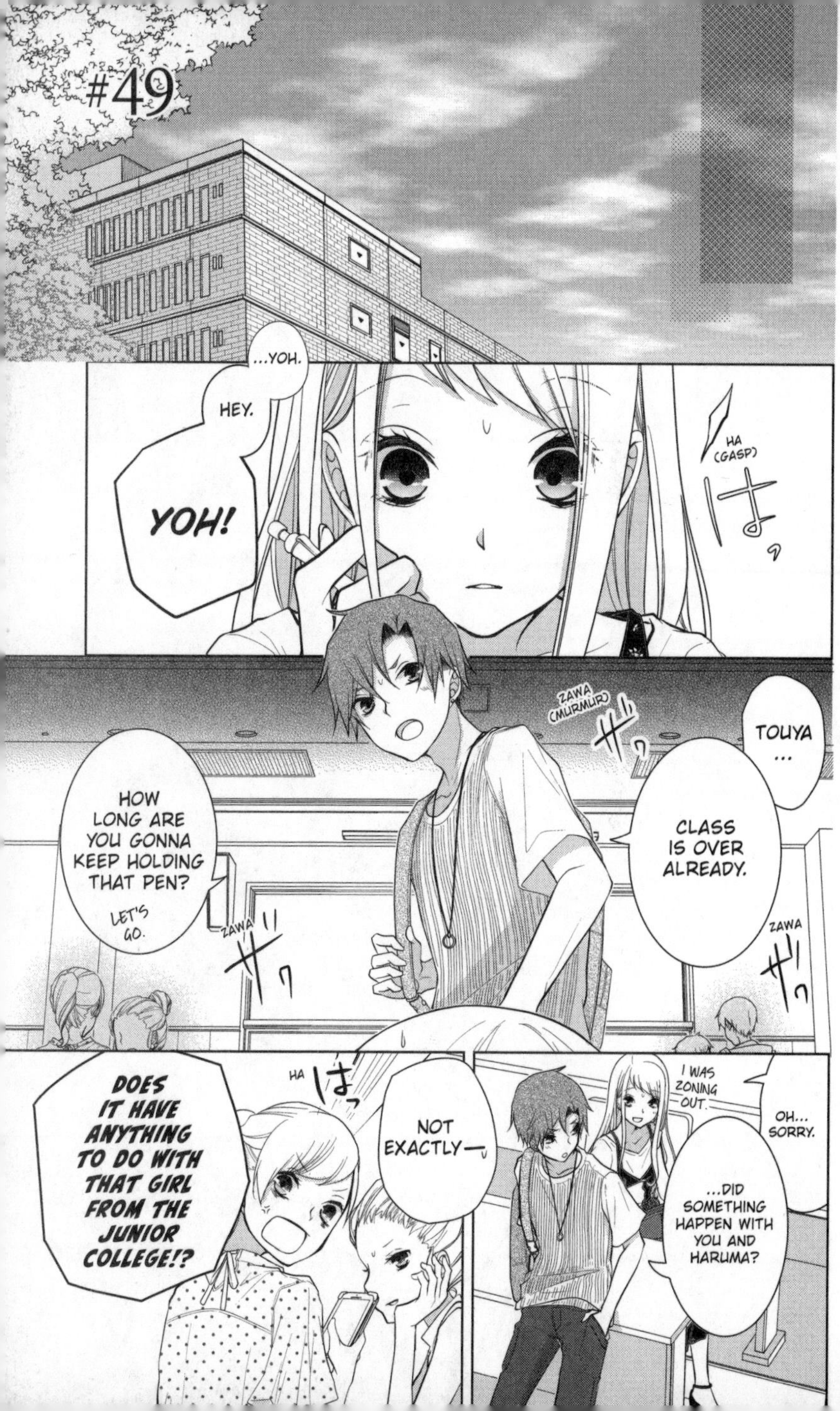
#49
HA (GASP) はっ
...YOH.
HEY.
YOH!
TOUYA ...
ZAWA (MURMUR) ザワッ
CLASS IS OVER ALREADY.
HOW LONG ARE YOU GONNA KEEP HOLDING THAT PEN?
LET'S GO.
ZAWA ザワッ
ZAWA ザワッ
OH... SORRY.
I WAS ZONING OUT.
...DID SOMETHING HAPPEN WITH YOU AND HARUMA?
HA はっ
NOT EXACTLY—
DOES IT HAVE ANYTHING TO DO WITH THAT GIRL FROM THE JUNIOR COLLEGE!?

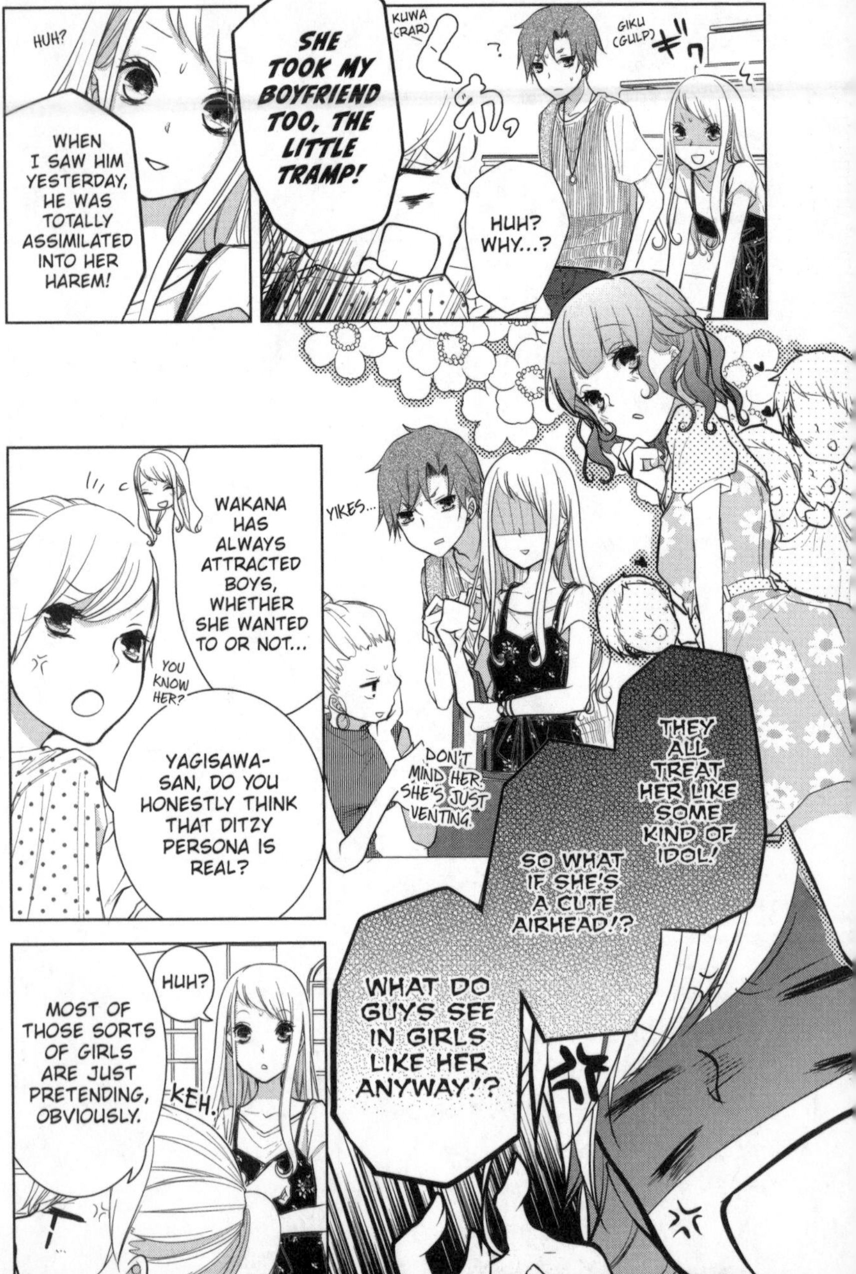
GIKU (GULP)
?
KUWA (RAR)
SHE TOOK MY BOYFRIEND TOO, THE LITTLE TRAMP!
HUH? WHY...?
HUH?
WHEN I SAW HIM YESTERDAY, HE WAS TOTALLY ASSIMILATED INTO HER HAREM!
THEY ALL TREAT HER LIKE SOME KIND OF IDOL!
YIKES...
SO WHAT IF SHE'S A CUTE AIRHEAD!?
DON'T MIND HER. SHE'S JUST VENTING.
WHAT DO GUYS SEE IN GIRLS LIKE HER ANYWAY!?
WAKANA HAS ALWAYS ATTRACTED BOYS, WHETHER SHE WANTED TO OR NOT...
YOU KNOW HER?
YAGISAWA-SAN, DO YOU HONESTLY THINK THAT DITZY PERSONA IS REAL?
HUH?
MOST OF THOSE SORTS OF GIRLS ARE JUST PRETENDING, OBVIOUSLY.
KEH.

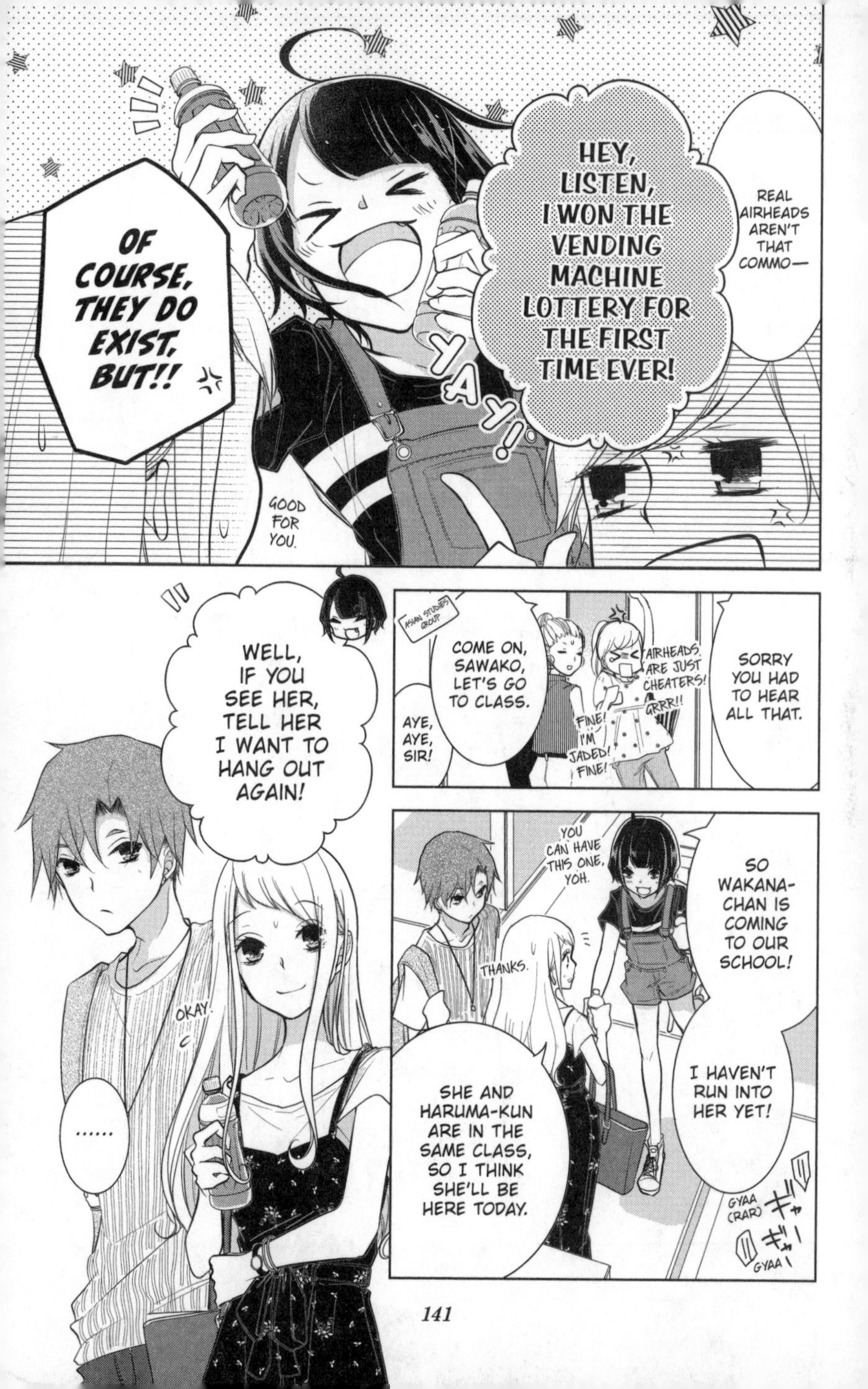
REAL AIRHEADS AREN'T THAT COMMO—
HEY, LISTEN, I WON THE VENDING MACHINE LOTTERY FOR THE FIRST TIME EVER!
YAY!
OF COURSE, THEY DO EXIST, BUT!!
GOOD FOR YOU.
SORRY YOU HAD TO HEAR ALL THAT.
AIRHEADS ARE JUST CHEATERS! GRRR!!
FINE! I'M JADED! FINE!
ASIAN STUDIES GROUP
COME ON, SAWAKO, LET'S GO TO CLASS.
AYE, AYE, SIR!
SO WAKANA-CHAN IS COMING TO OUR SCHOOL!
YOU CAN HAVE THIS ONE, YOH.
THANKS.
I HAVEN'T RUN INTO HER YET!
SHE AND HARUMA-KUN ARE IN THE SAME CLASS, SO I THINK SHE'LL BE HERE TODAY.
GYAA (RAR)
GYAA
WELL, IF YOU SEE HER, TELL HER I WANT TO HANG OUT AGAIN!
OKAY.
......

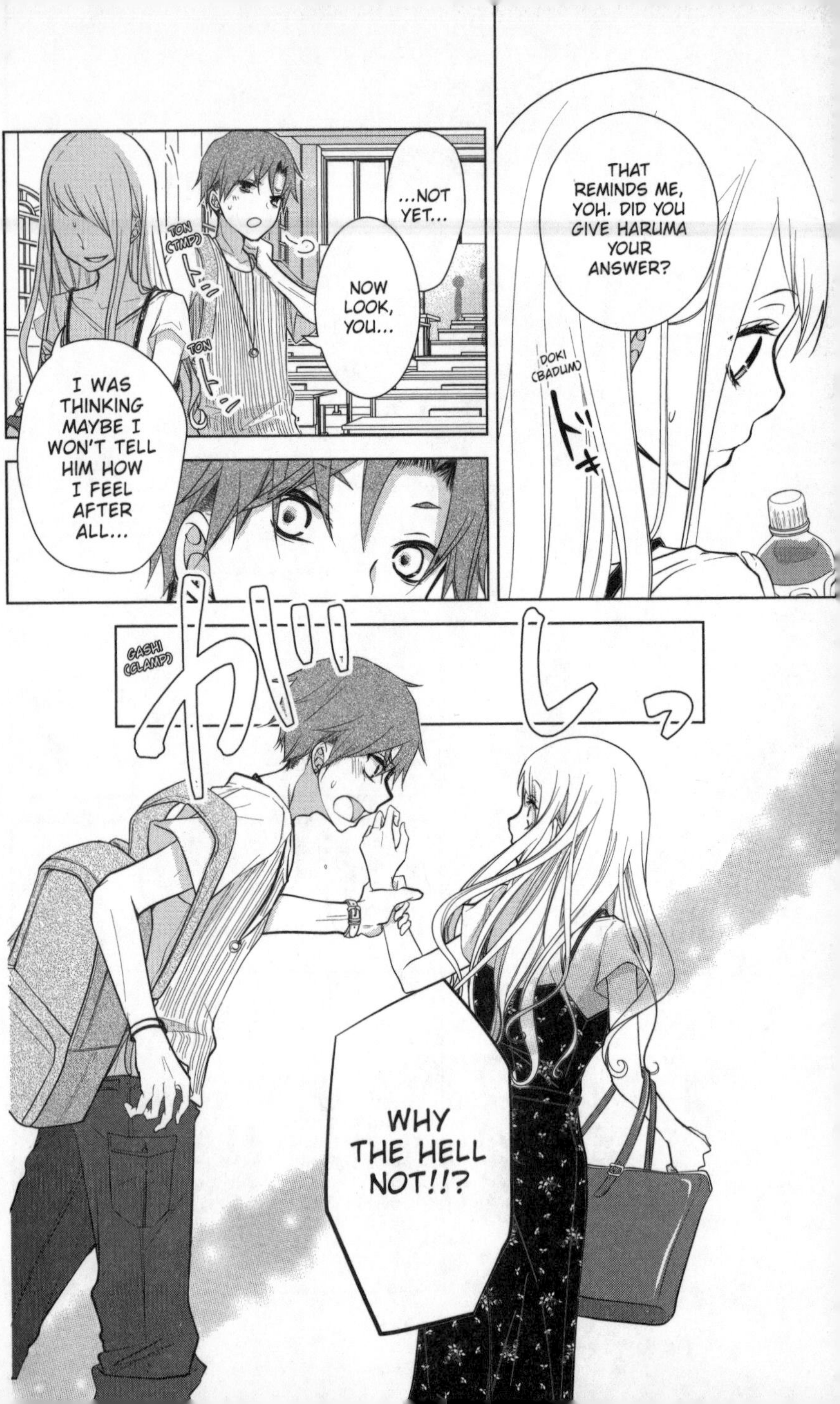
THAT REMINDS ME, YOH. DID YOU GIVE HARUMA YOUR ANSWER?
DOKI (BADUM)
...NOT YET...
NOW LOOK, YOU...
TON (TMP)
TON
I WAS THINKING MAYBE I WON'T TELL HIM HOW I FEEL AFTER ALL...
GASHI (CLAMP)
WHY THE HELL NOT!!?

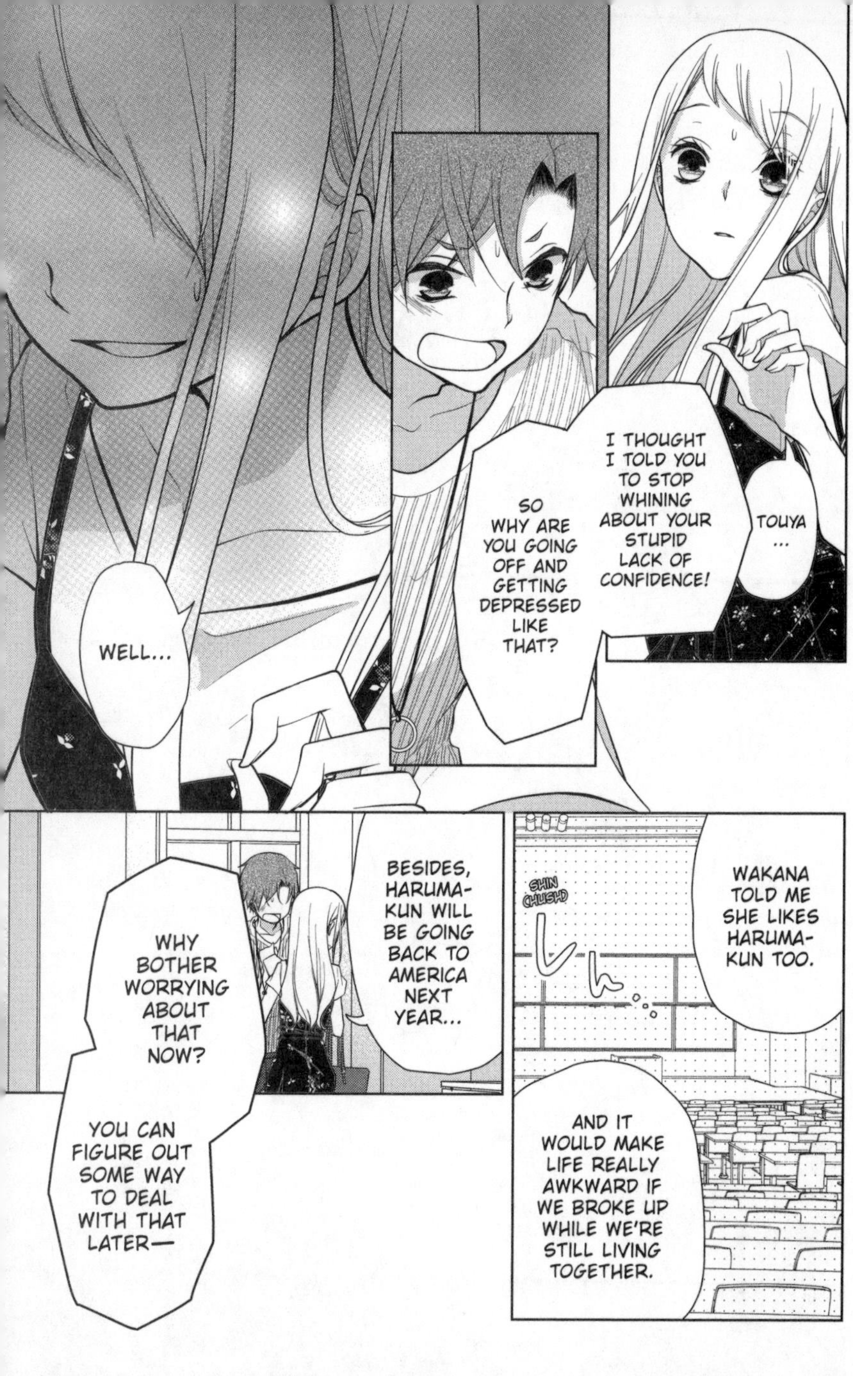
TOUYA...
I THOUGHT I TOLD YOU TO STOP WHINING ABOUT YOUR STUPID LACK OF CONFIDENCE!
SO WHY ARE YOU GOING OFF AND GETTING DEPRESSED LIKE THAT?
WELL...
WAKANA TOLD ME SHE LIKES HARUMA-KUN TOO.
SHIN (HUSH)
AND IT WOULD MAKE LIFE REALLY AWKWARD IF WE BROKE UP WHILE WE'RE STILL LIVING TOGETHER.
BESIDES, HARUMA-KUN WILL BE GOING BACK TO AMERICA NEXT YEAR...
WHY BOTHER WORRYING ABOUT THAT NOW?
YOU CAN FIGURE OUT SOME WAY TO DEAL WITH THAT LATER—

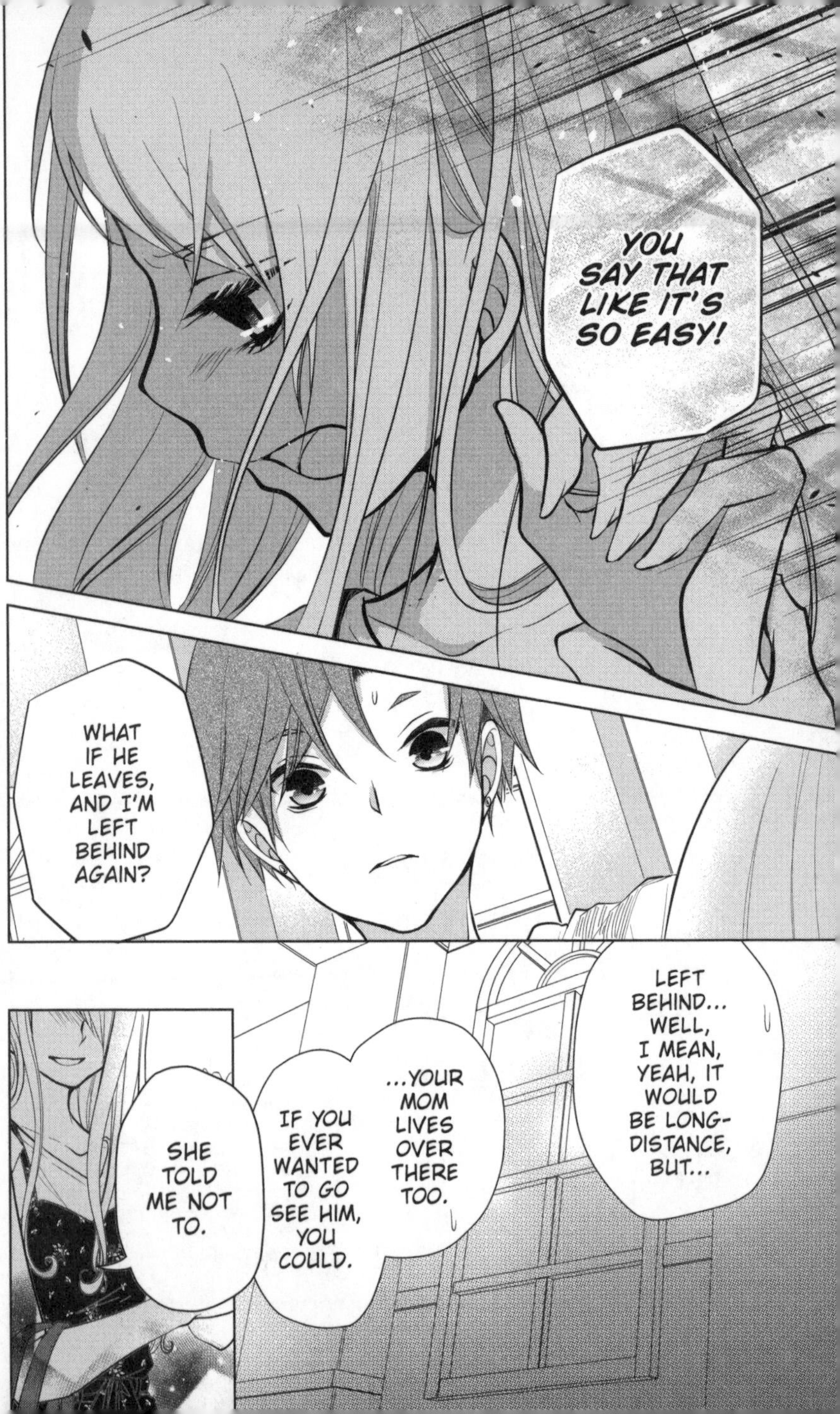
YOU SAY THAT LIKE IT'S SO EASY!
WHAT IF HE LEAVES, AND I'M LEFT BEHIND AGAIN?
LEFT BEHIND... WELL, I MEAN, YEAH, IT WOULD BE LONG-DISTANCE, BUT...
...YOUR MOM LIVES OVER THERE TOO.
IF YOU EVER WANTED TO GO SEE HIM, YOU COULD.
SHE TOLD ME NOT TO.

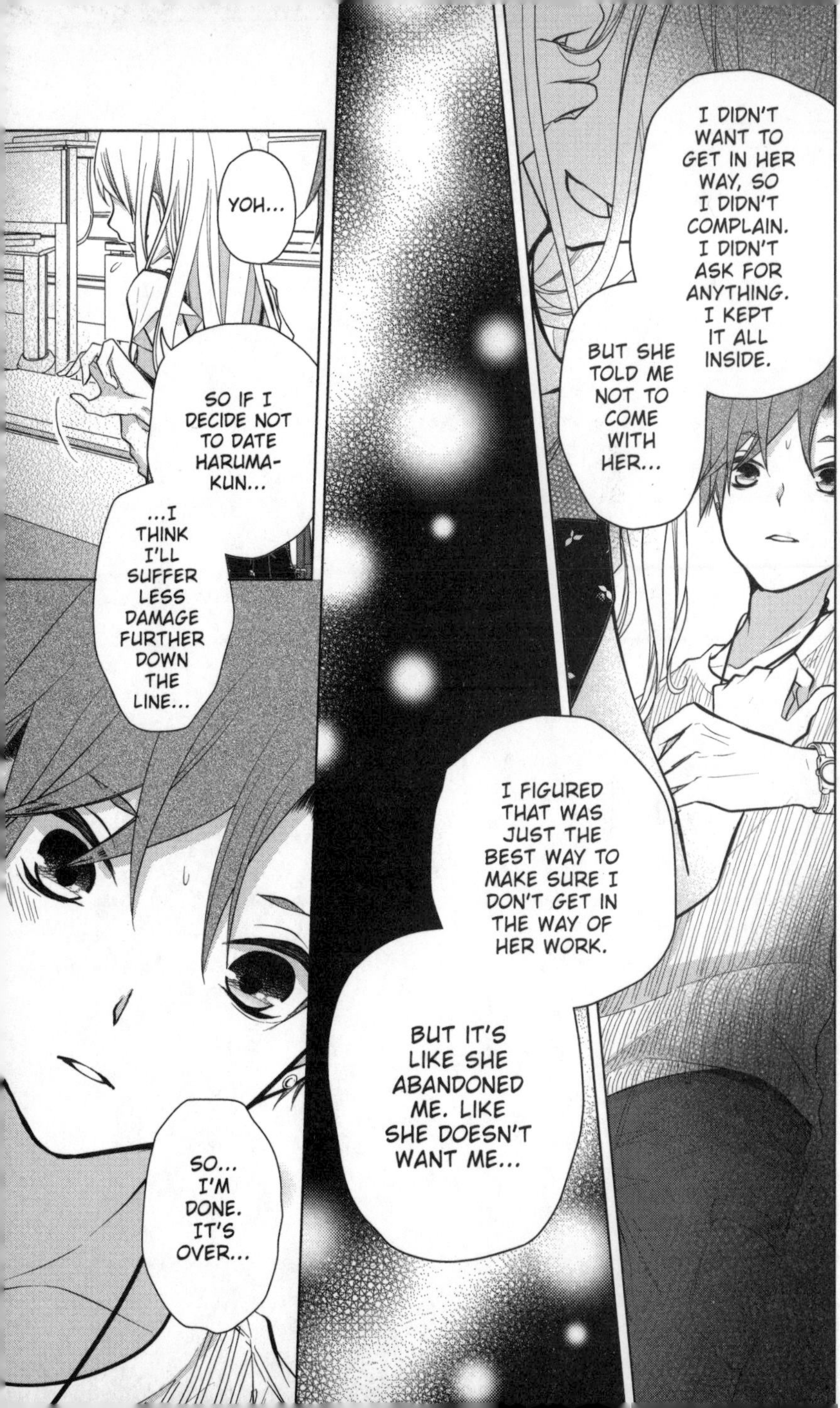
I DIDN'T WANT TO GET IN HER WAY, SO I DIDN'T COMPLAIN. I DIDN'T ASK FOR ANYTHING. I KEPT IT ALL INSIDE.
BUT SHE TOLD ME NOT TO COME WITH HER...
I FIGURED THAT WAS JUST THE BEST WAY TO MAKE SURE I DON'T GET IN THE WAY OF HER WORK.
BUT IT'S LIKE SHE ABANDONED ME. LIKE SHE DOESN'T WANT ME...
YOH...
SO IF I DECIDE NOT TO DATE HARUMA-KUN...
...I THINK I'LL SUFFER LESS DAMAGE FURTHER DOWN THE LINE...
SO... I'M DONE. IT'S OVER...

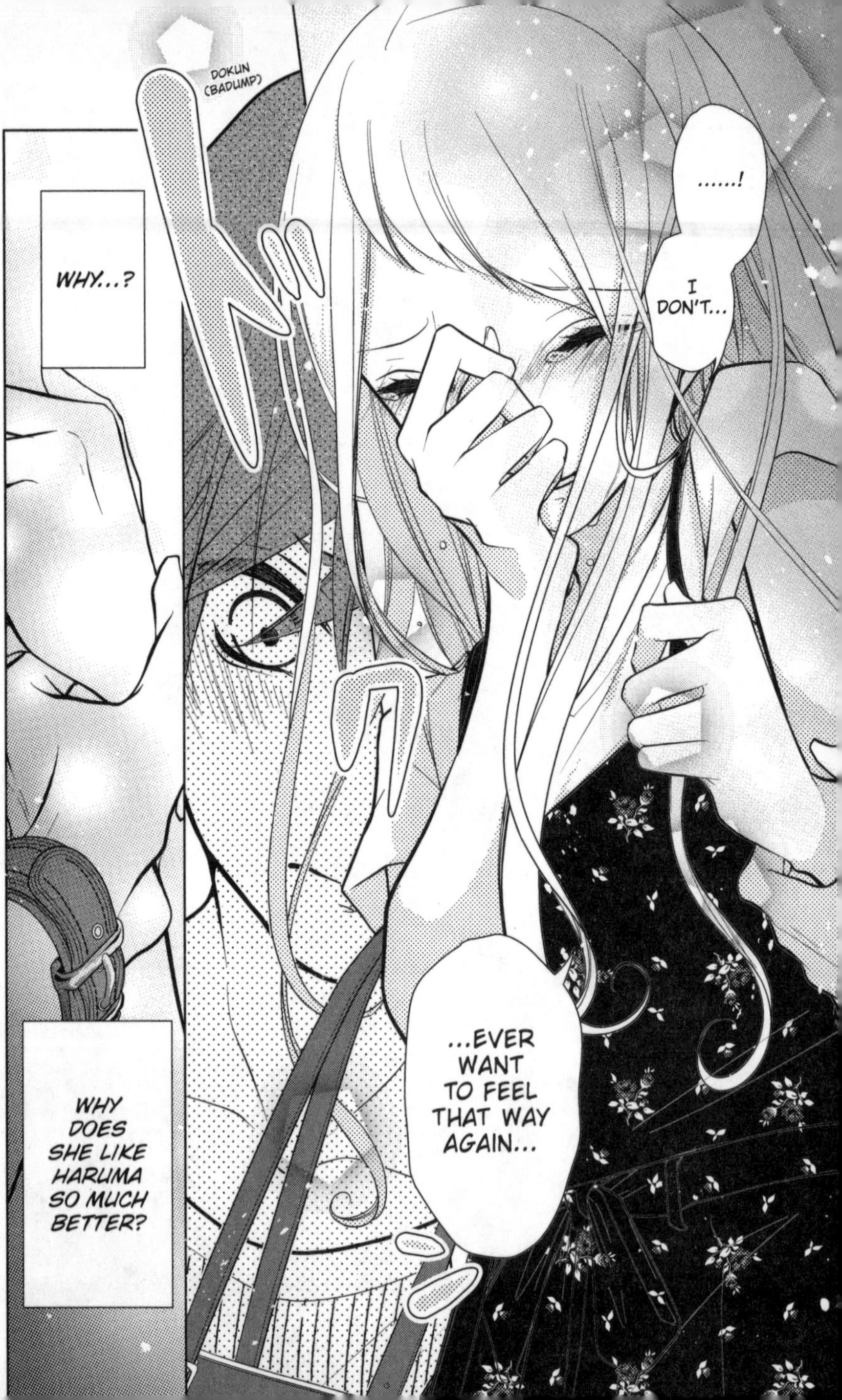
DOKUN (BADUMP)
......!
I DON'T...
...EVER WANT TO FEEL THAT WAY AGAIN...
WHY...?
WHY DOES SHE LIKE HARUMA SO MUCH BETTER?

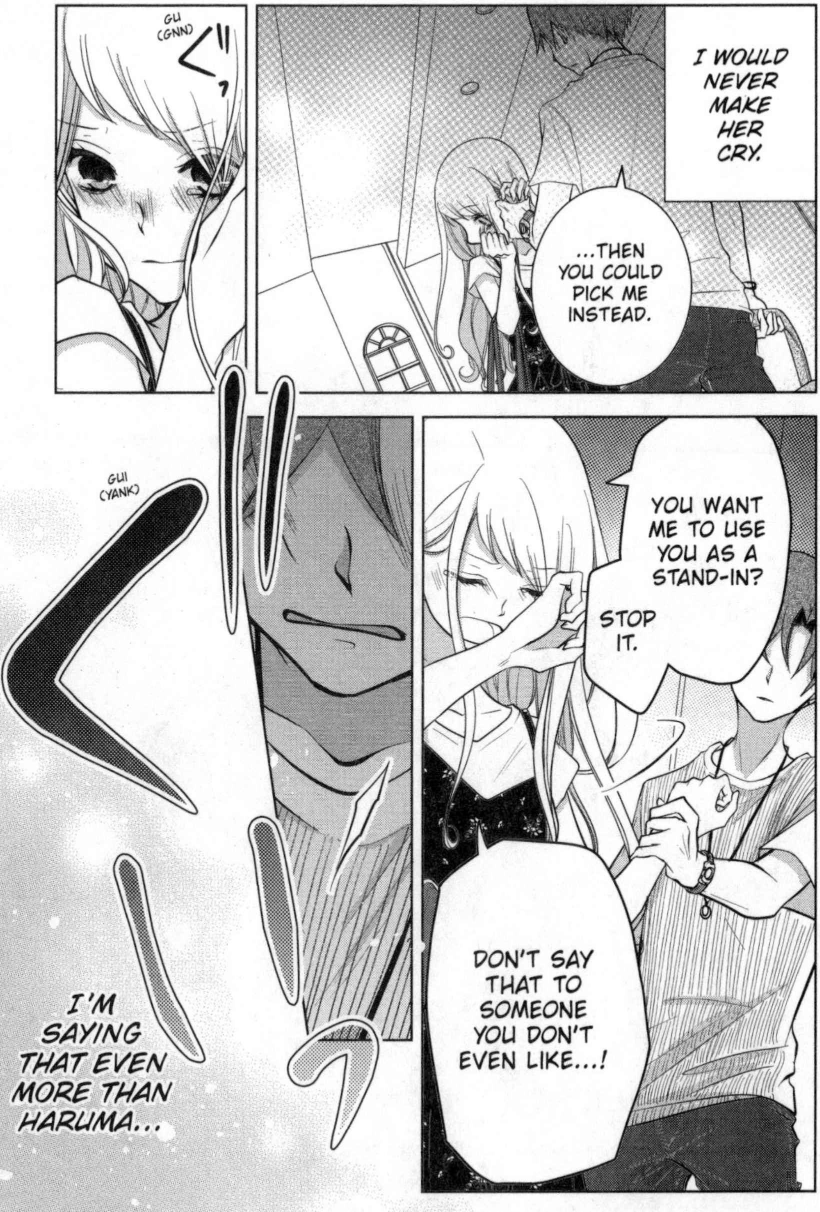
I WOULD NEVER MAKE HER CRY.
...THEN YOU COULD PICK ME INSTEAD.
GU (GNN)
YOU WANT ME TO USE YOU AS A STAND-IN?
STOP IT.
DON'T SAY THAT TO SOMEONE YOU DON'T EVEN LIKE...!
GUI (YANK)
I'M SAYING THAT EVEN MORE THAN HARUMA...

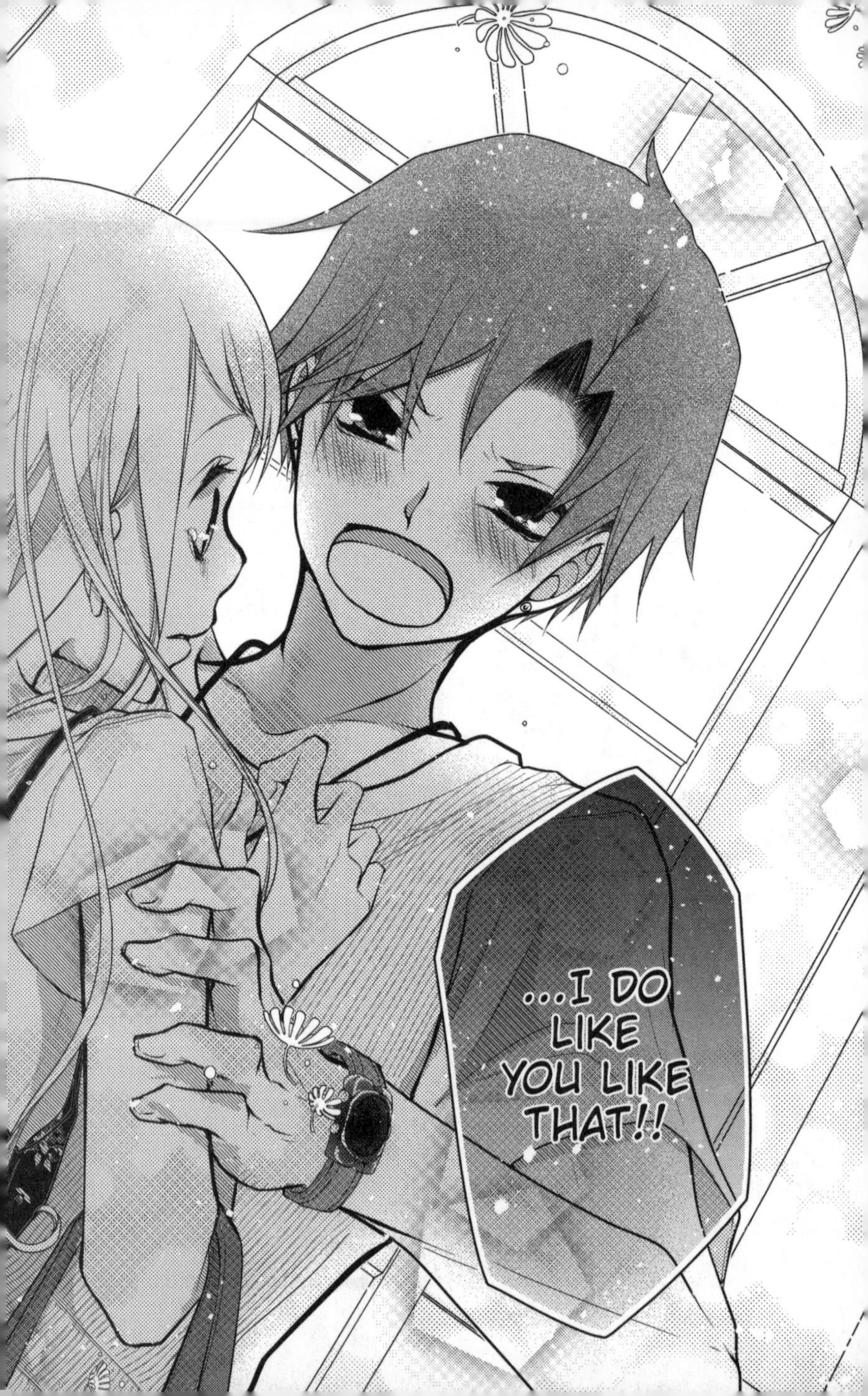
...I DO LIKE YOU LIKE THAT!!

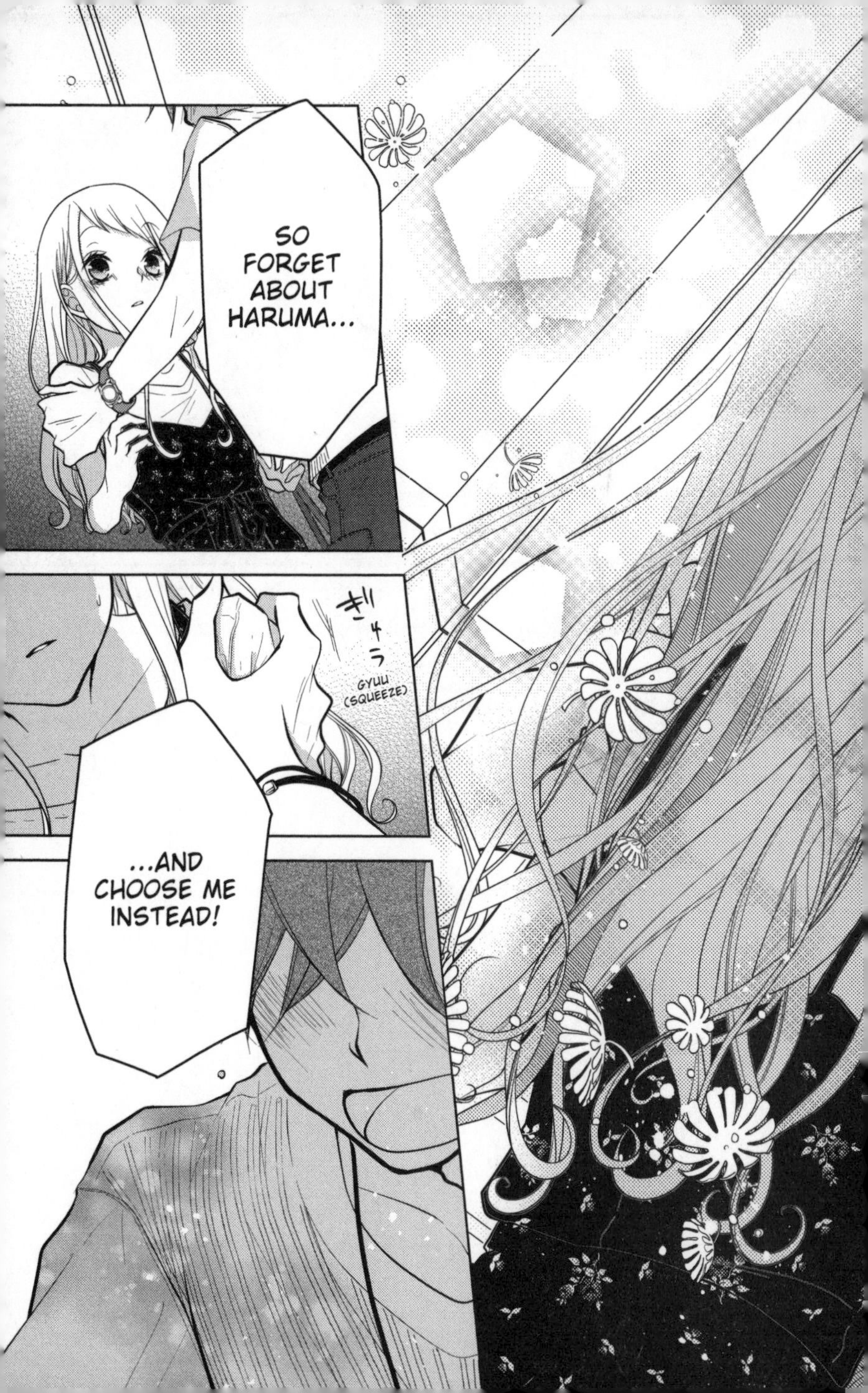
SO FORGET ABOUT HARUMA...
ぎゅう
GYUU (SQUEEZE)
...AND CHOOSE ME INSTEAD!

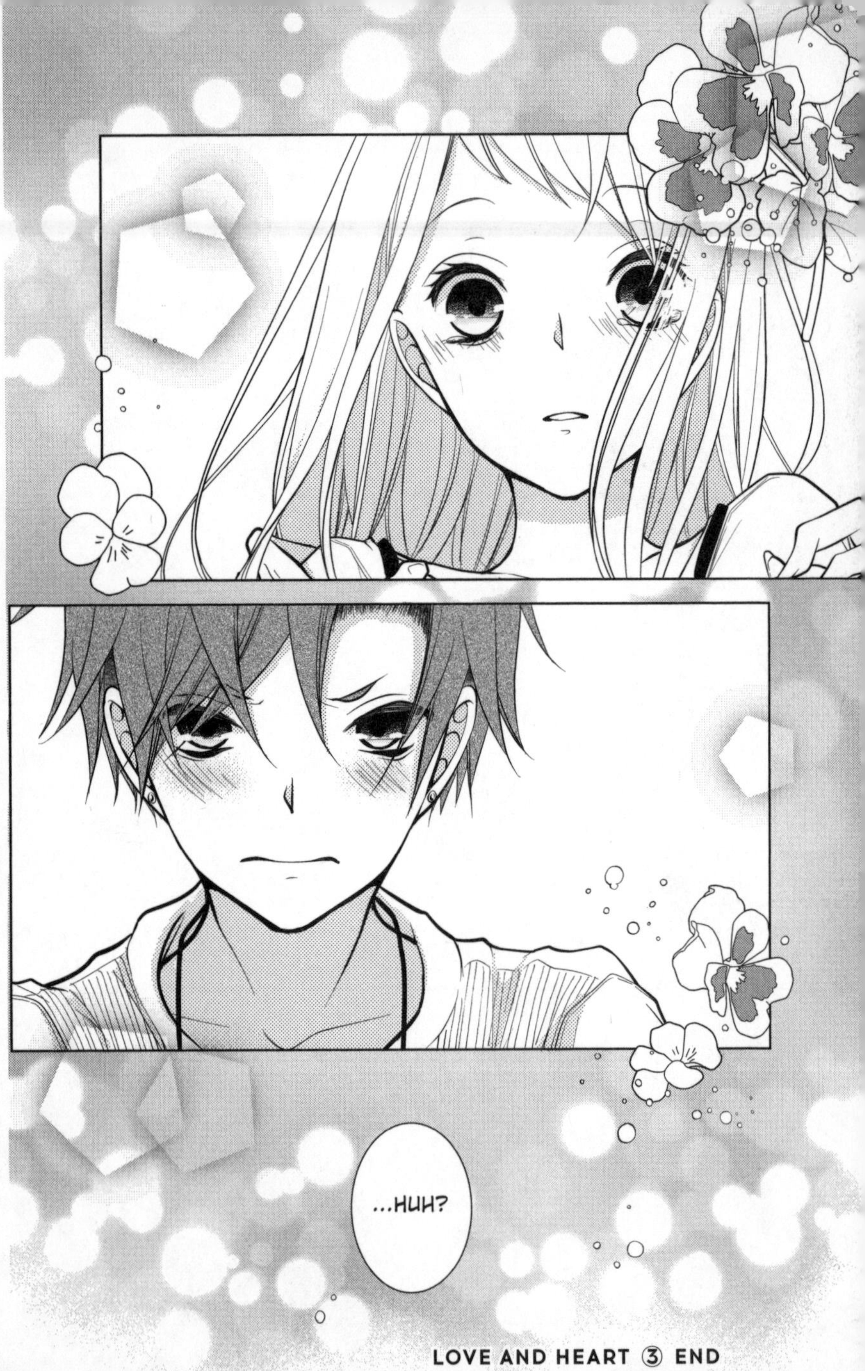
...HUH?

LOVE AND HEART ③ END

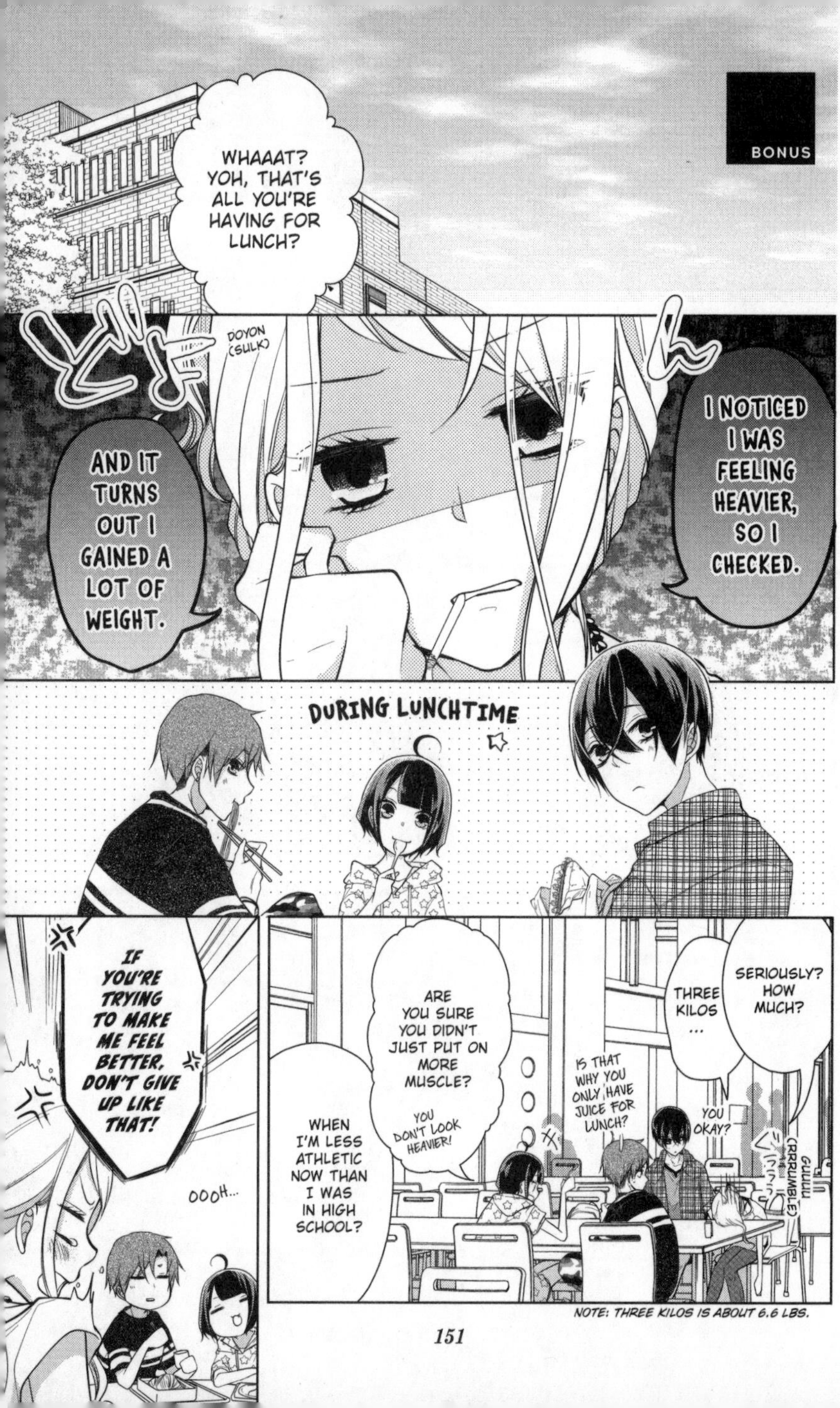
BONUS
WHAAAT? YOH, THAT'S ALL YOU'RE HAVING FOR LUNCH?
I NOTICED I WAS FEELING HEAVIER, SO I CHECKED.
DOYON (SULK)
AND IT TURNS OUT I GAINED A LOT OF WEIGHT.
DURING LUNCHTIME
SERIOUSLY? HOW MUCH?
THREE KILOS...
YOU OKAY?
GUUUU (RRRUMBLE)
IS THAT WHY YOU ONLY HAVE JUICE FOR LUNCH?
ARE YOU SURE YOU DIDN'T JUST PUT ON MORE MUSCLE?
YOU DON'T LOOK HEAVIER!
WHEN I'M LESS ATHLETIC NOW THAN I WAS IN HIGH SCHOOL?
IF YOU'RE TRYING TO MAKE ME FEEL BETTER, DON'T GIVE UP LIKE THAT!
OOOH...

NOTE: THREE KILOS IS ABOUT 6.6 LBS.

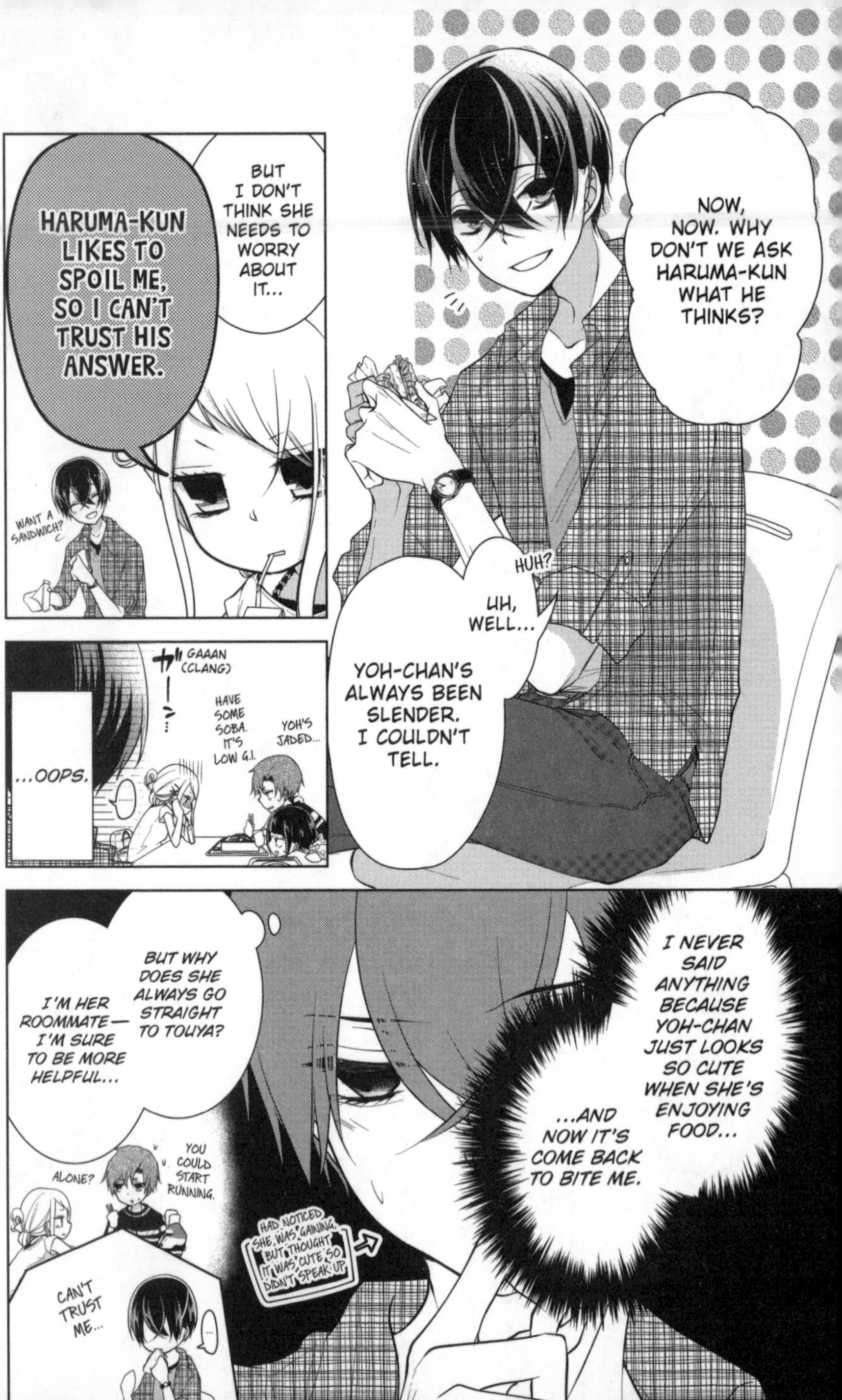
NOW, NOW. WHY DON'T WE ASK HARUMA-KUN WHAT HE THINKS?
HUH?
UH, WELL...
YOH-CHAN'S ALWAYS BEEN SLENDER. I COULDN'T TELL.
BUT I DON'T THINK SHE NEEDS TO WORRY ABOUT IT...
HARUMA-KUN LIKES TO SPOIL ME, SO I CAN'T TRUST HIS ANSWER.
WANT A SANDWICH?
GAAAN (CLANG)
HAVE SOME SOBA. IT'S LOW G.I.
YOH'S JADED...
......
...OOPS.
I NEVER SAID ANYTHING BECAUSE YOH-CHAN JUST LOOKS SO CUTE WHEN SHE'S ENJOYING FOOD...
...AND NOW IT'S COME BACK TO BITE ME.
HAD NOTICED SHE WAS GAINING, BUT THOUGHT IT WAS CUTE SO DIDN'T SPEAK UP
BUT WHY DOES SHE ALWAYS GO STRAIGHT TO TOUYA?
I'M HER ROOMMATE— I'M SURE TO BE MORE HELPFUL...
YOU COULD START RUNNING.
ALONE?
CAN'T TRUST ME...
...

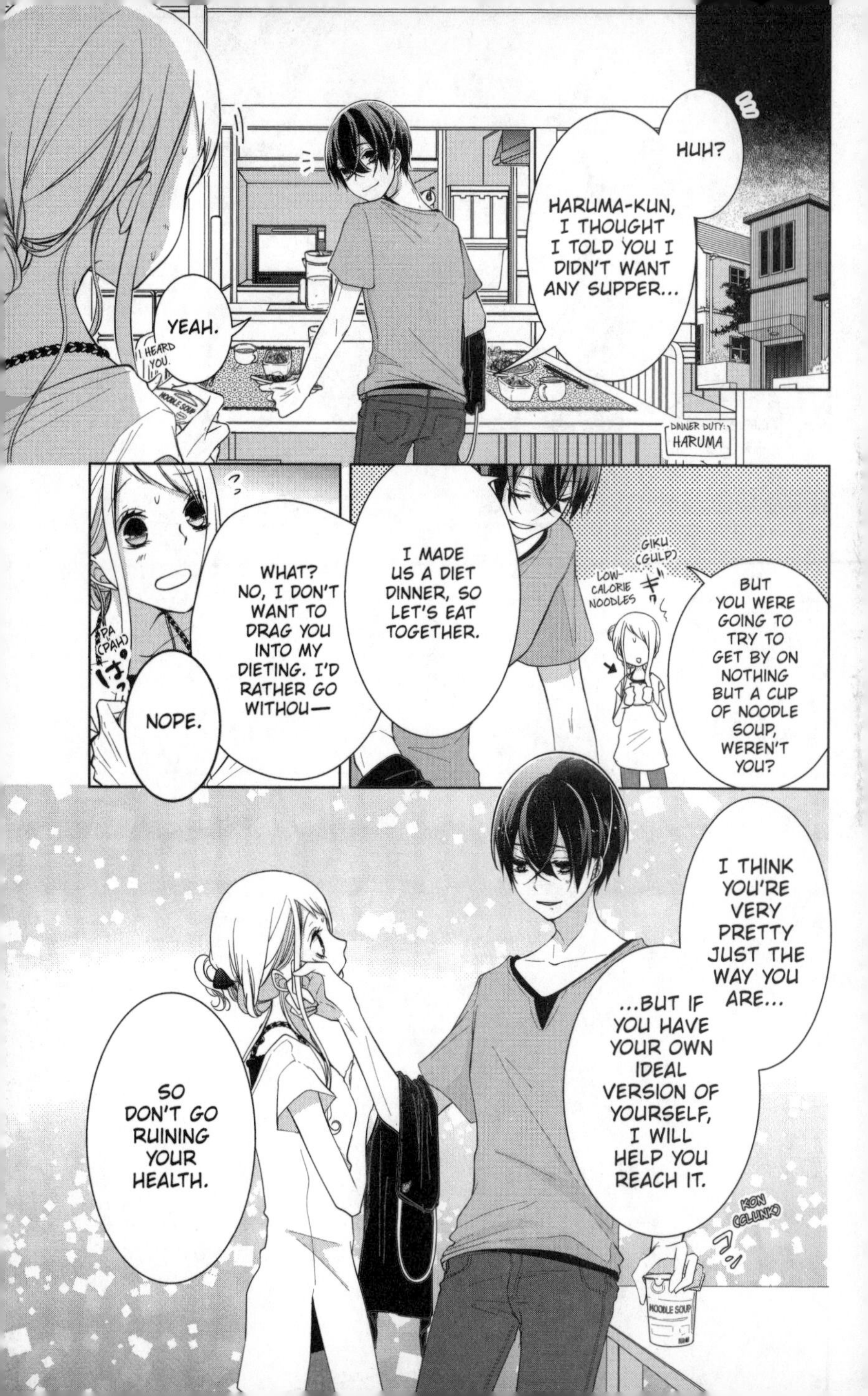
HUH?
HARUMA-KUN, I THOUGHT I TOLD YOU I DIDN'T WANT ANY SUPPER...
YEAH.
I HEARD YOU.
NOODLE SOUP
DINNER DUTY: HARUMA
GIKU (GULP)
LOW-CALORIE NOODLES
BUT YOU WERE GOING TO TRY TO GET BY ON NOTHING BUT A CUP OF NOODLE SOUP, WEREN'T YOU?
I MADE US A DIET DINNER, SO LET'S EAT TOGETHER.
WHAT? NO, I DON'T WANT TO DRAG YOU INTO MY DIETING. I'D RATHER GO WITHOU—
PA (PAH)
NOPE.
I THINK YOU'RE VERY PRETTY JUST THE WAY YOU ARE...
...BUT IF YOU HAVE YOUR OWN IDEAL VERSION OF YOURSELF, I WILL HELP YOU REACH IT.
KON (CLUNK)
SO DON'T GO RUINING YOUR HEALTH.
NOODLE SOUP

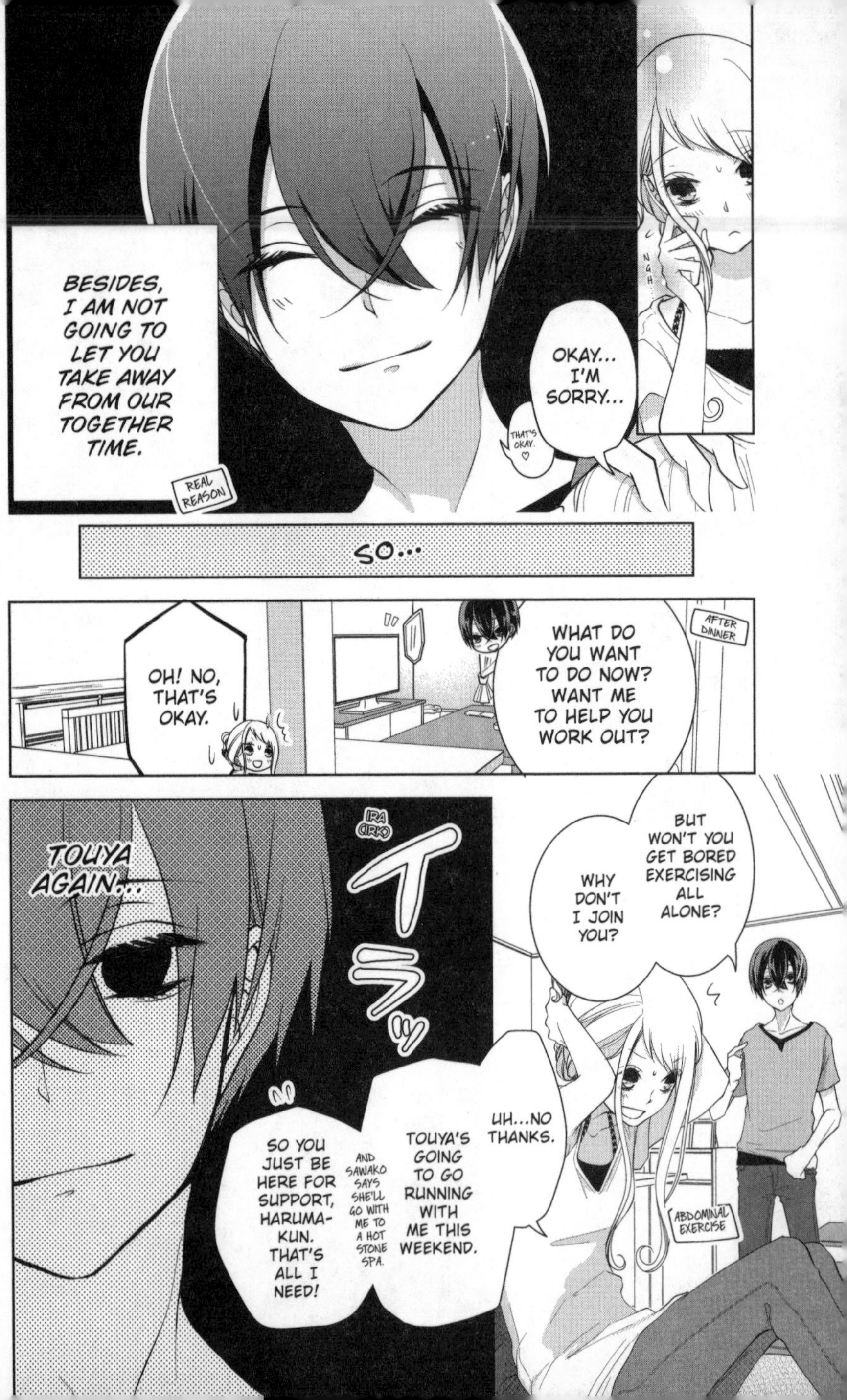
NGH...
OKAY... I'M SORRY...
THAT'S OKAY. ♡
BESIDES, I AM NOT GOING TO LET YOU TAKE AWAY FROM OUR TOGETHER TIME.
REAL REASON
SO...
AFTER DINNER
WHAT DO YOU WANT TO DO NOW? WANT ME TO HELP YOU WORK OUT?
OH! NO, THAT'S OKAY.
BUT WON'T YOU GET BORED EXERCISING ALL ALONE?
WHY DON'T I JOIN YOU?
UH...NO THANKS.
ABDOMINAL EXERCISE
TOUYA'S GOING TO GO RUNNING WITH ME THIS WEEKEND.
AND SAWAKO SAYS SHE'LL GO WITH ME TO A HOT STONE SPA.
SO YOU JUST BE HERE FOR SUPPORT, HARUMA-KUN. THAT'S ALL I NEED!
IRA (IRK)
TOUYA AGAIN...

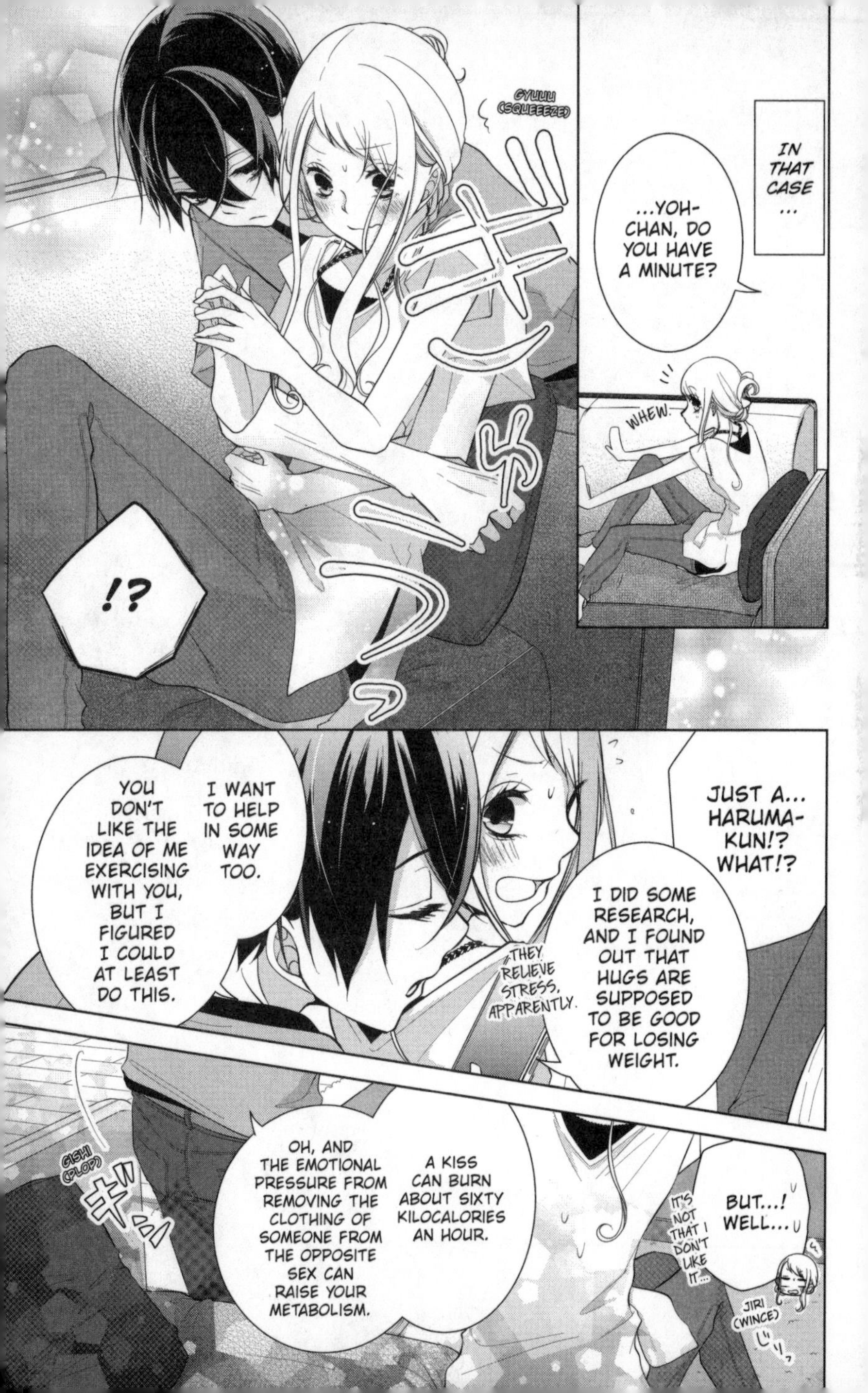
IN THAT CASE...
...YOH-CHAN, DO YOU HAVE A MINUTE?
WHEW.
GYUUU (SQUEEEZE)
!?
JUST A... HARUMA-KUN!? WHAT!?
I DID SOME RESEARCH, AND I FOUND OUT THAT HUGS ARE SUPPOSED TO BE GOOD FOR LOSING WEIGHT.
THEY RELIEVE STRESS, APPARENTLY.
I WANT TO HELP IN SOME WAY TOO.
YOU DON'T LIKE THE IDEA OF ME EXERCISING WITH YOU, BUT I FIGURED I COULD AT LEAST DO THIS.
BUT...! WELL...
IT'S NOT THAT I DON'T LIKE IT...
JIRI (WINCE)
A KISS CAN BURN ABOUT SIXTY KILOCALORIES AN HOUR.
OH, AND THE EMOTIONAL PRESSURE FROM REMOVING THE CLOTHING OF SOMEONE FROM THE OPPOSITE SEX CAN RAISE YOUR METABOLISM.
GISHI (PLOP)

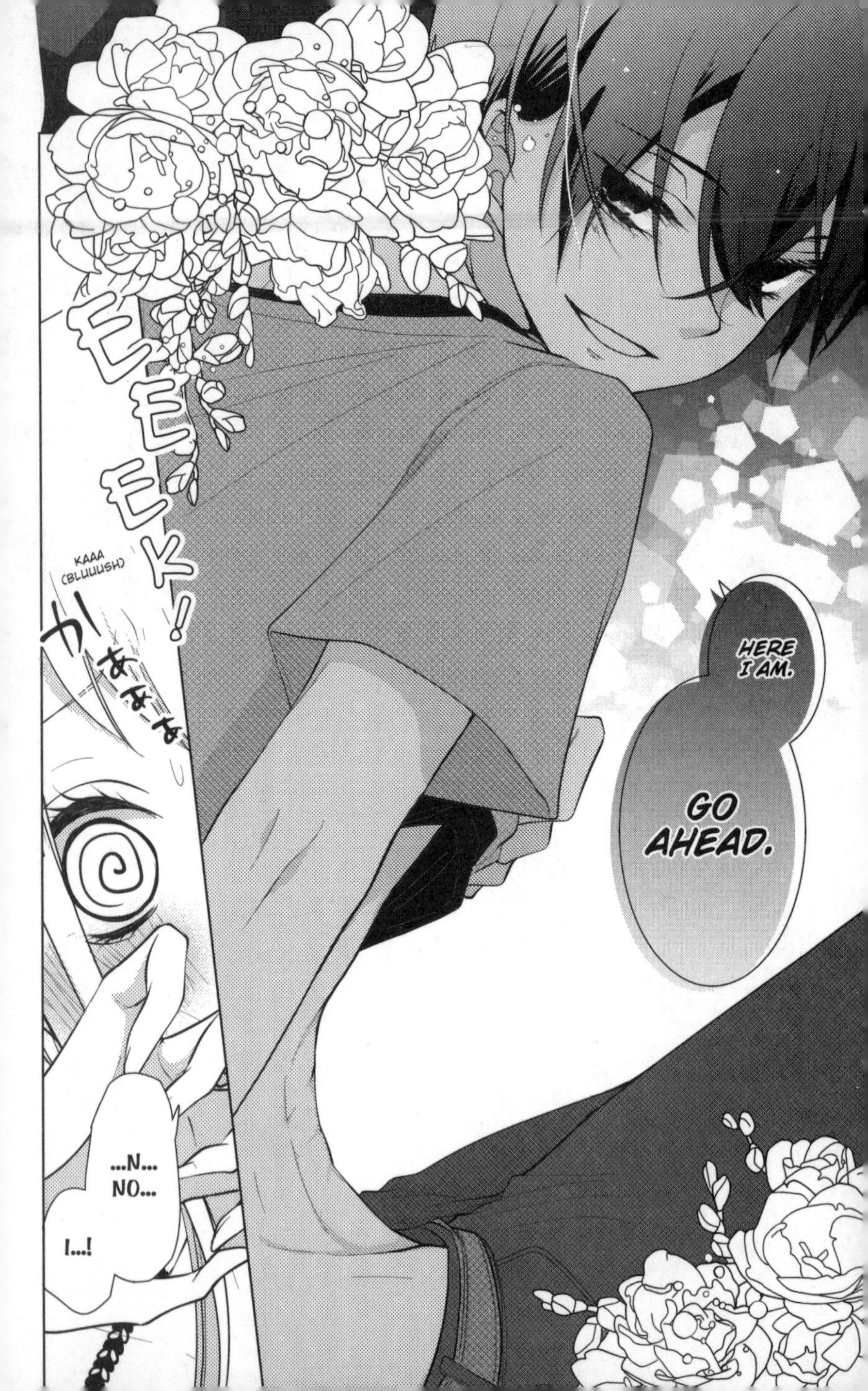
HERE I AM.
GO AHEAD.
EEEEK!
KAAA (BLUUUSH)
...N... NO...
I...!

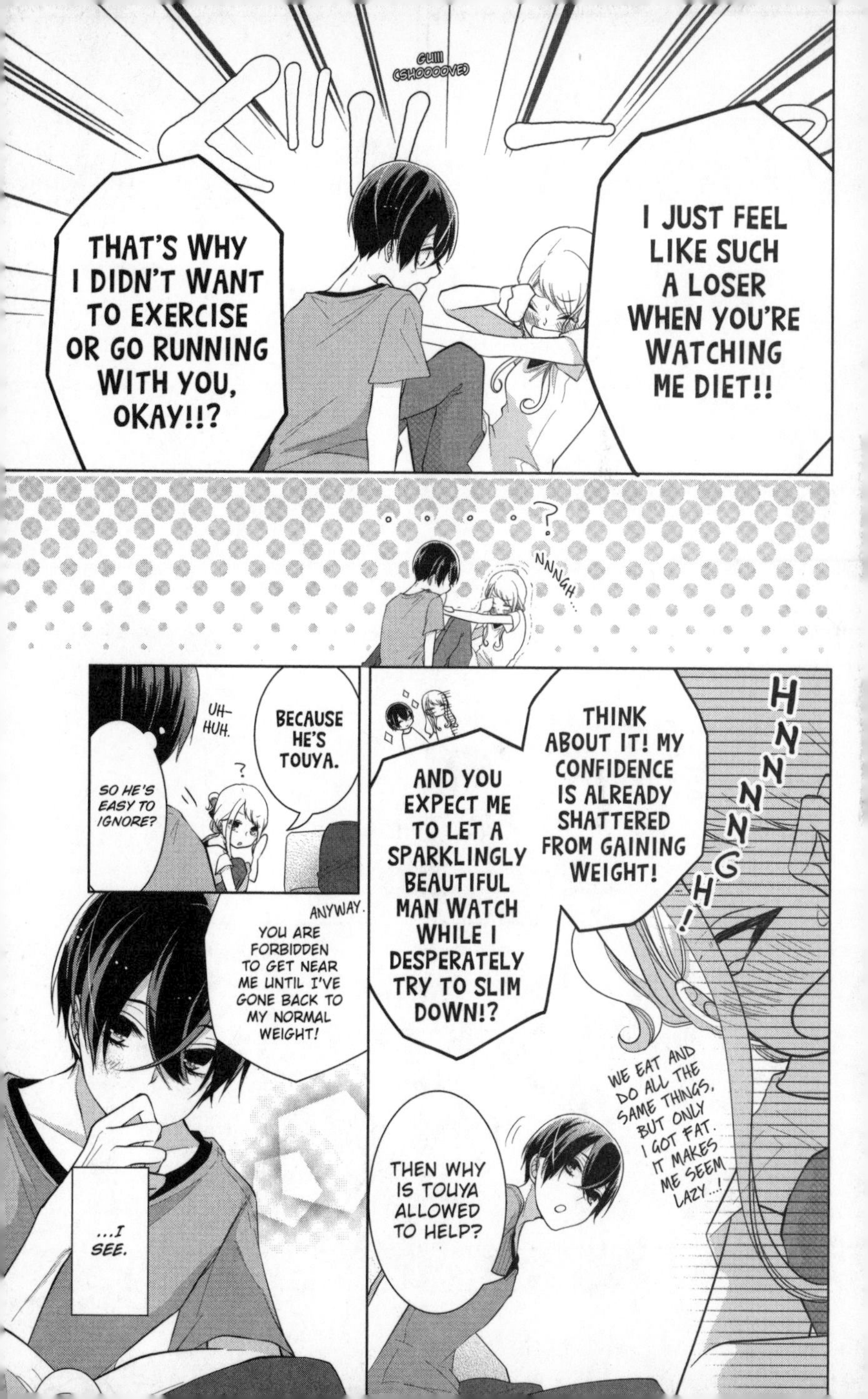
GUIII (SHOOOOVE)
I JUST FEEL LIKE SUCH A LOSER WHEN YOU'RE WATCHING ME DIET!!
THAT'S WHY I DIDN'T WANT TO EXERCISE OR GO RUNNING WITH YOU, OKAY!!?
...?
NNNGH...
HNNNNGH!
THINK ABOUT IT! MY CONFIDENCE IS ALREADY SHATTERED FROM GAINING WEIGHT!
AND YOU EXPECT ME TO LET A SPARKLINGLY BEAUTIFUL MAN WATCH WHILE I DESPERATELY TRY TO SLIM DOWN!?
WE EAT AND DO ALL THE SAME THINGS, BUT ONLY I GOT FAT. IT MAKES ME SEEM LAZY...!
THEN WHY IS TOUYA ALLOWED TO HELP?
BECAUSE HE'S TOUYA.
UH-HUH.
?
SO HE'S EASY TO IGNORE?
ANYWAY.
YOU ARE FORBIDDEN TO GET NEAR ME UNTIL I'VE GONE BACK TO MY NORMAL WEIGHT!
...I SEE.

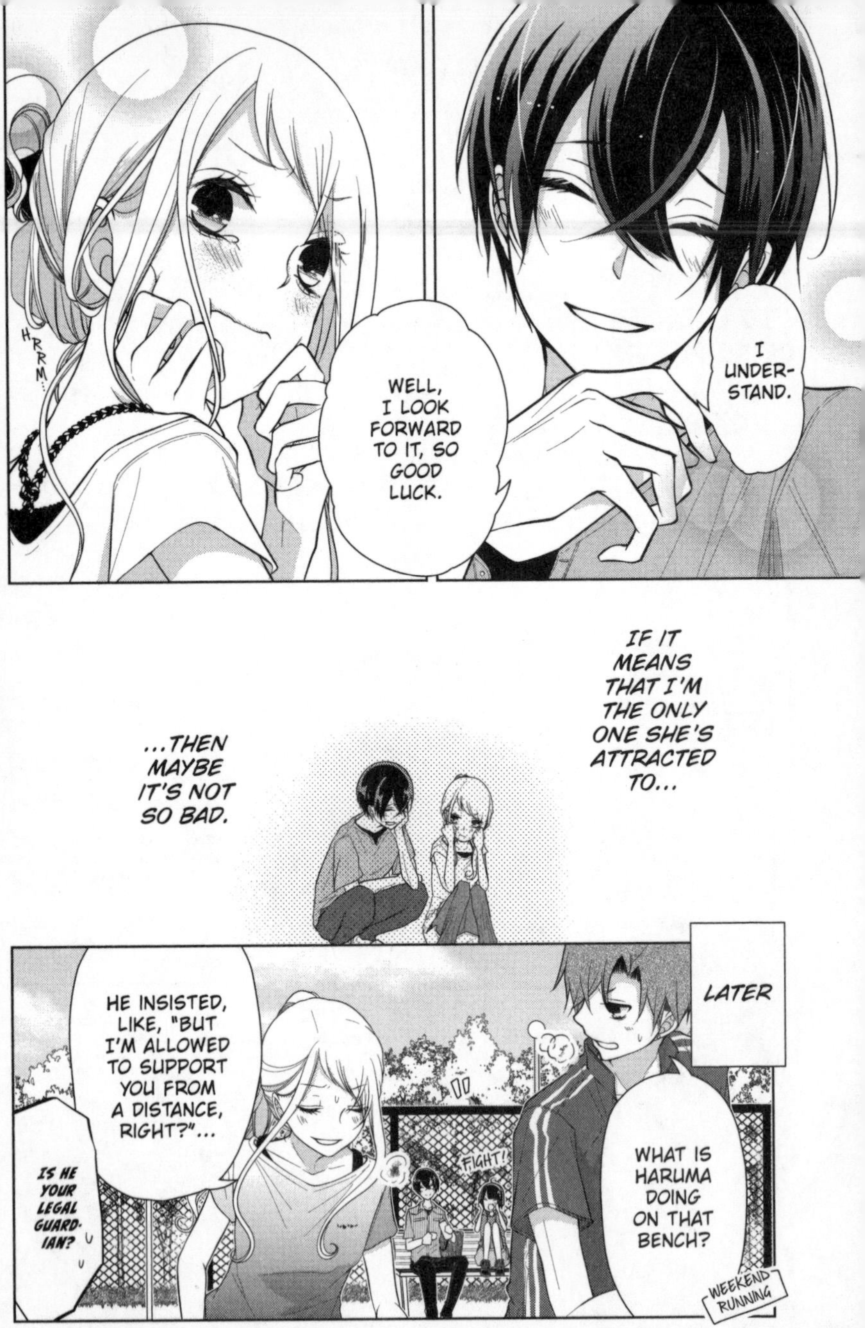
I UNDER-STAND.
WELL, I LOOK FORWARD TO IT, SO GOOD LUCK.
HRRM...
IF IT MEANS THAT I'M THE ONLY ONE SHE'S ATTRACTED TO...
...THEN MAYBE IT'S NOT SO BAD.
LATER
WHAT IS HARUMA DOING ON THAT BENCH?
WEEKEND RUNNING
FIGHT!
HE INSISTED, LIKE, "BUT I'M ALLOWED TO SUPPORT YOU FROM A DISTANCE, RIGHT?"...
IS HE YOUR LEGAL GUARD-IAN?

BONUS / END

TRANSLATION NOTES

Common Honorifics

no honorific: Indicates familiarity or closeness; if used without permission or reason, addressing someone in this manner would constitute an insult.

-san: The Japanese equivalent of Mr./Mrs./Miss. If a situation calls for politeness, this is the fail-safe honorific.

-sama: Conveys great respect; may also indicate that the social status of the speaker is lower than that of the addressee.

-kun: Used most often when referring to boys, this indicates affection or familiarity. Occasionally used by older men among their peers, but it may also be used by anyone referring to a person of lower standing.

-chan: An affectionate honorific indicating familiarity used mostly in reference to girls; also used in reference to cute persons or animals of either gender.

-senpai: A term commonly used to respectfully refer to upperclassmen in school or seniors at work. Its antonym, used for underclassmen, is *kouhai*.

Page 57

A *monaka* is a Japanese confection consisting of sweet *azuki* bean paste sandwiched between two wafers of *mochi* rice cake. In this case, Sawako is referring to the chocolate variety of *monaka*, called *choco monaka*, which is a frozen treat that can be purchased from vending machines. Instead of *azuki* paste, the outer shell is filled with vanilla ice cream and a chocolate center.

Page 73

Normally, takoyaki consists of an outer layer made from batter with octopus (*tako*) as the main filling, but when holding a **takoyaki party**, the octopus can be replaced with tuna, shrimp, wieners, or whatever other ingredients are available. Some flavor combinations are extremely intense and possibly inedible, but since the filling is hidden, it makes for an exciting game of chance akin to Russian roulette.

Page 87

Wakana frequently refers to herself in the third person, which in Japanese is sometimes done by girls who are (or wish to be perceived as) childish or cutesy.

Page 135

TOEIC and **Eiken** are two of the more common English proficiency tests for non-native speakers in Japan. TOEIC is an international standard for working professionals, while Eiken is a domestically produced test that is targeted more at students.

Page 141

Some of Japan's many **vending machines** have a **lottery** feature, where there is a chance following a purchase to win an extra drink. The odds can be manipulated by the owner, but generally do not rise above 2 percent.

3

CHITOSE KAIDO

Translation: **ALETHEA AND ATHENA NIBLEY**

Lettering: **CHIHO CHRISTIE**

KOI TO SHINZO by Chitose Kaido
© Chitose Kaido 2019
All rights reserved.
First published in Japan in 2019 by HAKUSENSHA, INC., Tokyo.
English translation rights in U.S.A., Canada and U.K. arranged with HAKUSENSHA, INC., Tokyo through TUTTLE-MORI AGENCY, INC., Tokyo.

English translation © 2021 by Yen Press, LLC

Yen Press
150 West 30th Street, 19th Floor
New York, NY 10001

Visit us at yenpress.com
facebook.com/yenpress † twitter.com/yenpress
yenpress.tumblr.com † instagram.com/yenpress

First Yen Press Edition: September 2021

Yen Press is an imprint of Yen Press, LLC.
The Yen Press name and logo are trademarks of Yen Press, LLC.

The publisher is not responsible for websites (or their content) that are not owned by the publisher.

Library of Congress Control Number: 2020950226

ISBNs: 978-1-9753-2046-1 (paperback)
978-1-9753-2047-8 (ebook)

10 9 8 7 6 5 4 3 2 1

WOR

Printed in the United States of America